Redeeming the Republic

In the original of this print from a contemporary Boston almanac, the Constitution and national redemption are linked by the words "Federal Chariot" and "For the Year of our Redemption, 1788." Driving the federal chariot are Washington and Franklin, while thirteen freemen, representing the states, pull the vehicle toward ratification. Washington holds in hand the Constitution, and Franklin a staff and liberty cap; overhead a bright sun has emerged from behind dark clouds, and the goddess of fame proclaims the happy news of the Constitution's arrival. From *Bickerstaff's Boston Almanack; or, The Federal Calendar*, pamphlet, 4th ed. (Boston: E. Russell, 1788). Photograph courtesy of the American Antiquarian Society, Worcester, Mass.

Redeeming the Republic

FEDERALISTS, TAXATION,
AND THE ORIGINS OF
THE CONSTITUTION

★

Roger H. Brown

THE JOHNS HOPKINS UNIVERSITY PRESS

BALTIMORE & LONDON

© 1993 The Johns Hopkins University Press
All rights reserved
Printed in the United States of America on acid-free paper

The Johns Hopkins University Press
2715 North Charles Street
Baltimore, Maryland 21218-4319
The Johns Hopkins Press Ltd., London

Library of Congress Cataloging-in-Publication Data
Brown, Roger H.
Redeeming the Republic : Federalists, taxation, and the origins
of the Constitution / Roger H. Brown.
p.   cm.
Includes bibliographical references (p.   ) and index.
ISBN 0-8018-4497-5 (H : alk. paper)
1. Taxation—United States—History—18th century.
2. Taxation—United States—States—History—18th
century.   3. United States. Constitutional Convention
(1787)   4. United States—Constitutional history.
5. United States—Politics and government—1783–1789.
I. Title.
HJ2368.B76   1993
336.2'00973'09033—dc20   92-28958

A catalog record for this book is available
from the British Library.

FOR NANCY

CONTENTS

PART IV

AN EMERGING FEDERALIST AGENDA
AND ITS OPPONENTS

PART V

BEYOND RATIFICATION

LIST OF TABLES

PREFACE AND ACKNOWLEDGMENTS

M Y TITLE, *Redeeming the Republic*, echoes James Madison's words, written shortly before the 1787 Constitutional Convention, that "the real friends to the Revolution" must move to frame a new system of centralized republican government that "will perpetuate the Union, and redeem the honor of the Republican name."[1] These words capture key ideas that have guided the writing of this book. Madison at the time feared that a bankrupt Congress would disband and that the Union would devolve into regional republics. He also was worried that the perceived instability of the state governments would turn the propertied classes against republican government and toward monarchy. Concerned about the drift toward monarchy and regional republics, Madison wanted the Convention to preclude these possibilities by reconstituting the central government into a single national republic, both more powerful and more independent of the people. The Framers' belief that they must rebuild the Republic in order to save the Republic is thus my first reading of *redeeming*.

The phrase *redeeming the republic* also connotes civic as well as fiscal restoration. By reconstituting the Republic, the Framers would reform unvirtuous members of the unpropertied lower classes into industrious, frugal, and orderly citizens. Reconstitution would assure the federal and state creditors that their interest would be reliably paid in sound money. Similar ideas had guided the Framers earlier in the Confederation era. Immediately after the Revolution, these men had led the states to enact hard money taxes for Congress's support, the common people's reformation, and payment of the public creditors. But cash-poor farmers had blocked tax officials by physical force, and state legislatures had bowed to rural demands for relief measures. These events, in turn, had produced Congress's financial insolvency and consequent diplomatic and military weakness. At this point the Federalists launched their movement to engineer a stronger, more efficient central government that would perpetuate the Union and redeem republican government.

Recurring cycles of state tax crackdowns and destabilizing popular resistance propelled upper-class property-owning state elites toward the constitutional revolution of 1787. In this interpretation, the Constitution resulted not so much from threats of disunion and anarchy as from upperclass disillusion with the state governments' perceived inability to stand up to rural counterpressures that left Congress crippled, hurt business, and shackled economic investment and growth. By contrast with the decen-

tralized Confederation, the Framers believed, a centralized national government more powerful and more independent of the people could tax with
greater energy and force. By the same token, a strong central government
could manage the armed forces, foreign relations, the money supply, and
foreign and domestic commerce more effectively than could the confederation. Besides national security, the Framers wanted a more hospitable
environment for capitalist development both for that development's own
sake and because it would restore the confidence of the propertied classes
in republican government. In this sense, the Constitution captured both
the capitalist goals of its upper-class Framers and the revolutionary generation's desire to build a republic that would lead the world to a better
future.

Over the years required to write this book, I have benefited from the
generous help of many individuals. The librarians and professional staffs
of the following depositories kindly granted me access to their collections:
the Maine Historical Society, the Massachusetts Historical Society, the
Massachusetts State Archives, the Boston Public Library, the Rhode Island Historical Society, the Rhode Island State Archives, the John Carter
Brown Library, the Connecticut Historical Society, the Connecticut State
Archives, the Wadsworth Athenaeum, the New-York Historical Society,
Columbia University Library, the Pierpont Morgan Library, the Historical Society of Pennsylvania, the American Philosophical Society Library, the Pennsylvania Historical and Museum Commission, the Delaware Historical Society, the Delaware State Archives, the Maryland
Historical Society, the Maryland State Archives, the Virginia Historical
Society, the Virginia State Archives, the University of North Carolina Library, Duke University Library, the North Carolina Department of Archives and History, the South Carolina State Archives, the University of
South Carolina Library, the Charleston Library Society, the Georgia Historical Society, the Georgia State Archives, and the National Archives.

I also wish to thank the librarians and staffs of Baker Library, Dartmouth College, the Henry Huntington Library, the William L. Clements
Library, and the Library of Congress (Microform Reading Room, Newspaper Reading Room, and Manuscript Division) for many courtesies, including providing me with office space, arranging interlibrary loans, and
filling many requests for material.

During the early stages of this project Gaspar Saladino and Kenneth R.
Bowling, editors of the Documentary History of the Ratification of the
Constitution series, kindly permitted me access to the collected materials
in their possession. This opportunity not only saved me precious research
time but produced helpful information about the location of sources.

Early in this project the Harvard University Center for the Study of
the History of Liberty in America and the John Simon Guggenheim

Foundation awarded me generous fellowships for which I am grateful. My own home institution, the American University, Washington, D.C., granted me course reductions, sabbatical leaves, and other supports, which I acknowledge with special thanks.

I wish also with thanks to acknowledge permission from the following institutions for permission to quote, within the limits of their rights, from manuscript sources in their possession. These are the Boston Public Library; the William L. Clements Library; the Rare Book and Manuscript Library of Columbia University; the Huntington Library; the Massachusetts Historical Society; the Pierpont Morgan Library; the New-York Historical Society; the Swem Library, College of William and Mary; and the Yale University Library.

Friends, students, colleagues, and family members have also helped in the creation of this book by conducting research, reading critically, and making valuable contributions. They are Angela Blake, Christine Brown, Matthew Brown, Jennifer Brown, Sally Brown, Ruth Herndon, Peter J. Kuznick, Patricia MacDonald, William G. Miller, Jeffrey Reiman, Joseph Walwick, and Karin Wulf. I also acknowledge with thanks James Banner, James Henretta, and the members of the Washington, D.C., seminar in American history and culture for helpful criticism.

All my colleagues in the Department of History at the American University have contributed to this project by their interest, the example of their own scholarship, and their critical responses to my ideas. I am especially grateful to Richard Breitman and Allan Lichtman, who gave me invaluable encouragement, criticism, and suggestions at a crucial stage.

I also wish to express thanks to Robert J. Brugger, editor, the Johns Hopkins University Press, and Van Beck Hall, professor of history, University of Pittsburgh, for extremely valuable suggestions. I also thank Martha Murphy for efficiently typing the manuscript, Roberta Hughey for exemplary copyediting, and Penny Moudrianakis for skillfully presiding over the final phase of publication.

Two persons have played indispensable roles in the writing of this book. My brother, Edward R. Brown, believed in the project from its earliest beginnings and has been unstinting with his encouragement and constructive criticism. My wife, Nancy Barrow Brown, has helped me in countless ways. Not only has she read numerous drafts, but her insight, knowledge, suggestions, and critical judgment have been indispensable from the moment she first heard my ideas.

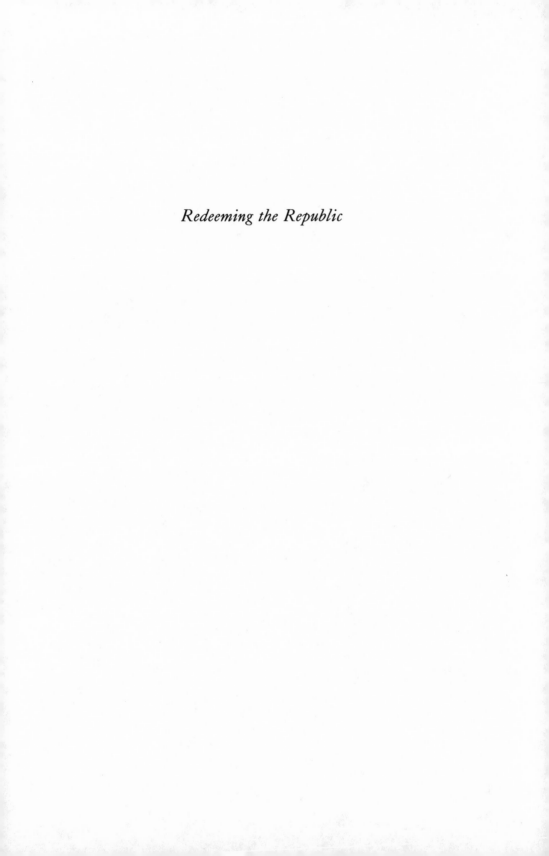

Redeeming the Republic

INTRODUCTION

Two months after the federal Constitution was published but before any of the states had ratified, a member of the Connecticut clergy described the document's fundamental reconstitution of the structure and powers of the American Confederation. "We are upon the Eve of another Revolution in the System of Government," the Reverend Ebenezer Dibblee informed an English correspondent. Delegates are elected to meet in Hartford next January "to adopt or reject the new form of Government appointed by the Commissioners, which leaves but the shadow of power in the States, utterly destroys the Old Ship, and [provides] a new one built, in which we must embark or sink." Dibblee's formulation introduces the historical problem I address in this book: why did the Framers replace the "Old Ship" Confederation with a new-modeled federal Constitution?[1]

I confront this question by investigating the Framers' failed attempts to have the state governments enforce taxation on their own people. Acknowledging Congress's diplomatic, military, and fiscal failures, I argue that the key to the constitutional Revolution of 1787 is to be found in the Framers' experience with taxation by the state governments and in the Framers' perceptions of why their plans for taxation failed. Facing heavy state and federal financial obligations, state legislatures levied specie taxes on cash-poor farmers who could not pay. When the states attempted to force collection, they met protest and resistance. Backing off, legislatures voted paper money and other reliefs for rural majorities. These episodes created an impression that the state governments did not have the requisite force and firmness to compel an unvirtuous people to pay taxes in sound money.

The Constitution proposed a central government that could do more than levy and collect taxes. It also empowered the central government to regulate commerce, issue money, and raise military and naval forces. The experience of the states' inability to collect taxes implied the Republic's ineffectiveness in these fields of endeavor also. Seeing tax collection as a fundamental test of the strength of the government, the Framers determined on fundamental reconstitution.

The experience with the breakdown of taxation thus drove the constitutional Revolution of 1787. A recent study of finance and taxation in eighteenth-century Britain argues that the ability to levy and collect taxes was the most important determinant in the rise of the British "fiscal-military" state. The English government's increased ability to collect money

by taxation provided the essential "sinews of power" that enabled the eighteenth-century British state to become a world power.[2] The Framers of the
Constitution did not have such ambitions for the United States for the immediate future, but they knew that the ability to collect taxes was essential
if the Republic was to be effective in diplomacy, war, and finance. Antifederalists argued that the simple addition of a 5 percent federal impost
tax would enable the existing Congress to raise an army and navy and service the national debt without basic structural change. Without stronger
enforcement power at the center, however, the Framers believed, the central government would be no more effective collecting taxes than the state
governments had been. From their perspective, the central government
needed not merely the constitutional power to tax, but greater energy, tenacity, and penetration of execution—"efficient" power, as the Federalists
put it.[3] This meant restructuring the central government into executive
and judicial branches and investing the government with the requisite
power to compel obedience. Other schemes for improving enforcement
discussed at the time included monarchy, military government, and regional republics—all having a greater power of execution than the individual state governments. Prompted by their commitment to union and
republican government, however, the Framers designed a strong national
or continental republic that combined greater power, structural reorga-
nization, and direct jurisdiction over the territory and people of the United
States.

Because the state governments play such a crucial role in this story, I
concentrate in this book on four major state governments of the Confederation system—Pennsylvania, South Carolina, Rhode Island, and Massachusetts. No other study investigates the subject of taxation by the states
for the period immediately preceding the Constitution's framing or links
it to the genesis of the Constitution. A study of taxation in Confederation
New York by Thomas Cochran and a study of taxation in the states during
the Revolution by Robert Becker anticipate some of my conclusions, but
neither investigates the common pattern of coercion-cum-resistance that
stymied tax collection throughout the Confederation in 1786–87.[4] The
four case studies present variations on a common theme in the thirteen
states during the Confederation era: the on-again-off-again attempts to
force tax collection for federal and state purposes. Other published studies
tell part of this story, but none describes, as does this one, how forced
collection produced backlash and paralysis.[5] In a summary chapter I ex-
plore the Confederation history of the remaining nine states.

I both build on and modify major interpretations of the politics of the
Confederation and Constitution eras. Most historians accept a continuity
between the political divisions over state fiscal and money policy during
the Confederation era and the divisions for and against the Constitution.

According to one view, the protagonists in these battles were persons whose position on the Constitution was determined by differentials in wealth, geographical location, occupation, and world view. Residing in less commercial, rural parts of their states, agrarian localists were persons of moderate wealth, narrow horizon, and parochial outlook; favoring local autonomy, they opposed the Constitution. Commercial cosmopolitans, on the other hand, who lived in or near urban, commercial areas, were wealthier, better educated, more traveled, and more in touch with the outside world; they had a broad outlook that prompted them to favor a centralized government. Yet during the 1780s, localists and cosmopolitans sometimes switched sides on crucial support for Congress and other central government-related issues; thus the dichotomy of agrarian localists and commercial cosmopolitans does not explain their behavior.[6] A more consistent interpretation identifies the major contestants over the Constitution as state-centered coalitions of wealthy versus moderately well-to-do political notables whose class-specific views of the common people's ability to cope with taxes shaped their positions on the Constitution. From different premises about the common farmer's ability to pay heavy taxes, each group derived different policy positions; and from different experiences in translating these policy positions into law at the level of the state governments, they evolved into Federalists and Antifederalists. Joining the wealthier Federalist core group were merchant, professional, artisan-mechanic, and better-off rural communities, who backed the Constitution because it promised stronger government, sound money, and better times. Except in New Jersey, Delaware, and Georgia—where special circumstances dictated uniformly popular support for the Constitution—most middle- and lower-class agrarian communities opposed the Constitution because they saw no good reason to abandon the Confederation system, having previously benefited from the majoritarian flexibility of the state governments.

I account for reconstitution in terms of the Framers' disenchantment with the state governments' ability to carry out their tax programs. This motive, rather than a strategy of recapturing power (as suggested by some historians), explains why the Federalists took the much harder road of reconstituting the central government root and branch instead of the easier one of limited amendment. The most recent major study to tackle the question of reconstitution is Gordon Wood's *Creation of the American Republic*. Wood argues that the Federalists undertook reconstitution because it enabled them to engineer a central government that would promote rule by upper-class leaders. By creating a central government founded on large election districts (relative to the smaller election districts of the state governments), the Federalists created conditions that favored election of notables whose property, experience, education, and standing would give them an advantage in elections over local politicians, whom the upper-class

Federalists held responsible for the vices of the state governments.[7] But Wood's argument about enlarged election districts overlooks the more important Federalist purpose of building a government that could govern with "energy" and "efficiency" (frequently used Federalist terms). Furthermore, it ignores the fact that at least one Framer, John Dickinson, wanted a centralized restructured government that would be chosen by state legislatures—again evidence that the central purpose was "energy" through centralized power and tripartite structure, not an enlarged, extended Republic that would tip elections in favor of the upper class.[8]

In this book I also advance a modified chronology of the timing of the process by which Federalists were converted from support for the state-centered Confederation system to support for a reconstituted centralized government able to enforce law. Some historians hold that Nationalists were present early in the Revolution; others that conversion to a stronger, reconstituted central government occurred late in the 1780s at the time of Shays's Rebellion.[9] I take a middle ground, arguing that the Federalists first tried to make the Confederation system work for Congress's benefit through the levying and collection of taxes by the state governments, but that they became disillusioned with the state governments when these initiatives failed. This pre-1786 conversion chronology explains why, within one short week of convening at Philadelphia, the Framers could agree to the basic format of the Virginia Plan for a reconstituted central government.[10]

I also build on a revisionist interpretation, recently argued by Daniel Walker Howe, that holds that the Framers had a positive view of human nature. Often portrayed as Hobbesian Calvinists who believed that sinful humanity needed the stern and constant control of strong government, the Framers, Howe argues, as students of the new social science of faculty psychology, believed that behavior could be improved by the exercise of reasoning and moral faculties.[11] Belief in the improvability of behavior explains why the Framers espoused a republic built on the premise of popular sovereignty and voluntary consent yet capable of mobilizing a coercive force when necessary instead of a leviathan government that would direct its citizens' every move and not be accountable to them. Although skeptical that Americans were virtuous enough to be governed by the weak, unstable state governments, the Federalists hoped that stronger, more stable government at the center would guide Americans into improved behavior by both deterrence and encouragement.

On this note, I conclude that the Framers reconstituted the Republic in order to redeem it. In addition to stabilizing the currency, financing the public debt, encouraging commerce, and protecting national security, an energetic, steady central government, the Framers believed, would make Americans into the hardworking, honest, lawful citizens a successful republic required. I thus join the ranks of those historians who hold that the Framers were as much if not more preoccupied with fulfilling the republican promise of the Revolution as they were with protecting property or class interests.[12]

My introduction to the scholarly controversies over the Constitution's origins began in the late 1950s when I was working on the origins of the Anglo-American War of 1812. Investigation of the Jeffersonian Republicans' motivation behind the 1812 war declaration against Great Britain uncovered a concern for the operational effectiveness of the Republic that the Framers had created in 1787–88. The Republicans declared the second war against Great Britain partly out of concern for the Republic's ability to stand its ground and carry out its purposes.[13] Could the same motivation have guided those who had framed the Republic in 1787 in Philadelphia? Before I could begin this project, however, Gordon Wood and others had developed the concern-for-the-republic theme so well that to build a new study around it seemed unpromising.[14]

Yet neither Wood's nor other recent studies have satisfactorily addressed why the Framers departed so radically from the Confederation system. The Framers might have followed a more conservative approach of strengthening the existing Confederation by limited amendment. Had they done so they could have avoided the arduous difficulties of framing a reconstituted government acceptable both to their own constituency and to the Antifederalist opposition, not to mention to a large proportion of the U.S. electorate. Despite these obstacles, the Framers made no secret of the fact that anything less than the central government's fundamental reconstitution would be unsatisfactory. "An entire new government," a "good Govt. on new principles," as Federalists put it, was their deliberate, all-important objective.[15]

Early in my research I was struck by the Framers' frequent comparison between the "stable, efficient" central government contemplated by the Constitution and the "inefficient" Confederation. They invoked adjectives such as "energetic," "stable," "powerful," and "independent" to contrast the Constitution with the "weak," "lax," "inefficient" Confederation system. That *Congress* under the Confederation lacked the constitutional power to enforce its will on the state governments and the people of the states is well known. But the attribution of weakness and instability to the *state governments*—the only entities in the Confederation with substantive constitutional powers to act directly on individuals—has not been adequately investigated. In explaining why the Framers pursued the central government's radical reconstitution, I have taken the story back to the state governments, where the attributions of weakness and instability originated in the Framers' diagnosis of the requisition system's breakdown—a diagnosis that was grounded in the collapse of specie taxing for federal purposes by the states. This was the process that educated the Framers to the structural inadequacies of the state governments and disposed them toward reconstitution at the center ("an entire new government").

The widespread recognition among the Framers at the time of the Constitution's framing of "the weakness & inefficacy of the State Governments" was the original impetus for my decision to concentrate on the Confederation state governments.[16] What specifically did the Framers have in mind when they made such statements? Although other manifestations of weakness such as the breakdown of debt collection played some role in educating Federalists to the inadequacy of the state governments, my investigation into the states' Confederation history has indicated taxation as the central factor. First, there is the contemporary evidence from legislative journals, newspapers, and private correspondence that indicates the salience of the tax problem.[17] Second, there is the pivotal role played by Congress's insolvency in the constitutional movement (a result of the failure of the states to collect taxes for federal requisitions). Third, there is the sense among Federalists in 1786–87 of the collapse of state authority ("lax government") and of the need to recast radically the central government in order to make government work. These Federalist statements point to the breakdown of taxation (as reflected in Congress's bankruptcy) as the explicit or implicit referent. The prominence of the tax issue in the Confederation politics of the states, an issue that in most previous accounts is marginal, places taxation at the center of the movement that produced the Constitution.

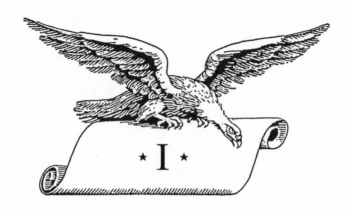

The
Confederation Congress and
the Requisition System

AN INSOLVENT CONGRESS

BECAUSE Congress's insolvency precipitated the movement that led to the federal Constitution, the logical place to begin the analysis of Congress's financial troubles is with the federal requisition system, which was the Confederation Congress's main source of revenue. Under the Confederation, Congress had no independent taxing power but had to obtain money from the states to finance its operations. When the states did not furnish Congress with the money it asked for, Congress could not raise and maintain requisite military and naval forces, conduct a strong diplomacy, or meet its foreign and domestic debt obligations. Congress's inability to deal with these matters does not per se explain why the Framers reconstituted the central government, but it does provide the necessary first step toward understanding why they did so.

The Articles of Confederation (drafted in 1777, adopted in 1781) formally vested Congress with the constitutional responsibility for managing defense, foreign affairs, war and peace, treaties, relations with the Indians, disputes among the states over land, the postal service, a federal currency, and federal military and naval forces. Implicitly and explicitly the Articles also indicated what powers the thirteen member-state governments of the Confederation would exercise. The state governments had exclusive power to levy taxes for themselves and the federal treasury. The state governments had exclusive power to draft men for the federal armed forces, regulate commerce within state borders and with foreign nations, and enforce federal treaties and the federal government's directives on Indian affairs. Thus the central government under the Articles had no constitutional jurisdiction over taxes, troop levies, or domestic and foreign commerce. It also lacked the constitutional authority to require any state or individual to obey its directives in those matters over which it did have jurisdiction.[1]

The Requisition System

Because Congress could not constitutionally levy and collect taxes through direct taxes on polls and property or indirect duties on foreign imports or excises on domestic sales or other transactions, it had to rely on the state governments for financial support. During the Revolution's early stages, Congress financed the war effort by fiat paper money (Continental currency), by foreign and domestic loans, and by the impressment of specific supplies. Fearing that the support of neutrals and waverers would be lost if the state governments taxed their citizens for war purposes, Congress deliberately avoided making heavy financial requests of the state governments, financing its war operations by these other means. But when federal credit and the Continental currency collapsed, Congress had to ask the state governments for money that would both fund the federal treasury and bolster the value of its Continental currency. As the Revolution wound down, Congress drew ever more heavily on the states for money to supply and pay the Continental army and navy and to meet its debt obligations to foreign and domestic creditors. With the onset of peace, more money was required to pay federal creditors (including army veterans' back pay), the peacetime military establishment, and the wages of members of Congress and of Congress's small civil staff. Congress turned to the states, levying federal requisitions, that is, quotaed federal levies on the state governments.[2]

The process by which Congress quotaed and levied financial requisitions on the Confederation's member-state governments was cumbersome. But the real problem was the states' incomplete response. Because Congress had no constitutional or practical power to compel payment, whether or not the state governments honored Congress's monetary requisitions obviously depended on their own willingness and ability to comply. The money they supplied the federal treasury never came close to the amount Congress requested.[3]

Yet the requisition system did not completely fail. Congress's six federal requisitions between October 1781 and August 1786 show an overall rate of compliance by the state governments of 37 percent. Moreover, the payment rate of requisitions in hard-to-get specie (solid coin) shows a higher rate of compliance (48 percent specie) than does the payment rate in indents, the de facto federal paper money that Congress ordered printed and paid out as annual interest on federal debt obligations (27 percent indents; see table 1).[4] During the period 1781–87, monetary contributions by the member-state governments to the federal treasury totaled $5,071,237. Requisitions were most productive during the years 1781–84 when Robert Morris was federal superintendent of finance. Following Morris's departure from the federal government's Office of Finance, however, requisition payments by the state governments into the federal treasury diminished, until by early 1787 they had almost completely ceased. Yet they never stopped altogether, and by March 1788 payments by the state governments had picked up modestly.[5]

In fact, the state governments met a greater proportion of their quotas than is often recognized. Thus the often repeated generalization that the Confederation state governments were too preoccupied with state and local concerns or too parochial in outlook to comply with federal requisitions seems overstated. The fact that several of them made substantial payments suggests that they did not cavalierly ignore the central government's monetary requisitions. As the case studies in the next section show, several state governments did try to comply with federal requisitions by levying and collecting taxes.

The Central Government Presses the States for Money

Under the requisition system, Congress elicited participation by the Confederation system's member-state governments by legislative resolution or some other formal directive. Congress would recommend a specific policy or course of action that would then be conveyed to state government officials either by the federal post office, federal messenger, or some federal officer on duty in the states. But having neither the legal power nor the legal machinery to compel any state government to comply, Congress could only verbally exhort state governments that delayed or refused compliance. Presuming that the states lagged more from inaction than from necessity, members of Congress and federal officials tried persuasion through personal contacts, lobbying by federal officials and interest groups, and organized pressure.

In December 1780 Charles Thomson, Congress's semipermanent secretary and an important member of Congress's nascent administration, followed up on a conversation with congressional member and Delaware legislative leader John Dickinson on how to make the Confederation operate more effectively by sending Dickinson a detailed plan for restoring the Confederation system's deranged finances and enabling Congress to finish out the Revolution through better taxation by the states. Hinting that the legislatures had been too much guided by considerations of popularity, Thomson wrote, "It appears to me that during the present controversy, the people have been always readier to pay than the legislatures to lay or call for taxes." And even if money were scarce and taxes burdensome, Thomson asserted, taxes would be "a stimulus to excite in the people a desire of procuring the new money and consequently induce them freely to part with their produce and the fruits of their labour to obtain it and will operate in giving it a credit and circulation better than [a] thousand compulsory acts or *tender laws*." Thomson recommended not just the levying of new taxes by the individual state governments but their prompt and

TABLE 1.
CONGRESSIONAL REQUISITIONS:
STATE QUOTAS AND PAYMENTS, 31 MARCH 1788

State	Quota	Payment Total (% in parentheses)	In Specie	In Indents
N.H.	$ 532,618	$ 106,295 (20)	$ 19,821	$ 86,474
Mass.	2,114,147	816,459 (39)	363,413	453,046
R.I.	319,712	75,711 (24)	75,711	0
Conn.	1,253,564	251,579 (20)	180,981	70,598
N.Y.	965,788	648,528 (67)	249,170	399,358
N.J.	779,823	151,636 (19)	151,636	0
Penn.	1,900,062	1,077,884 (57)	643,619	434,265
Del.	199,744	78,497 (39)	32,233	46,264
Md.	1,398,724	400,664 (29)	400,664	0
Va.	2,277,382	992,297 (44)	601,166	391,131
N.C.	1,016,079	28,486 (3)	28,486	0
S.C.	802,192	443,244 (55)	443,244	0
Ga.	117,561	0	0	0
Total	$13,677,466	$5,071,287 (37)	$3,190,149	$1,881,138

Sources: "Schedule of Requisitions on the Several States by the United States in Congress Assembled," 31 March 1788, Papers of the Continental Congress, 1774–89, microfilm M247, roll 154. Estimates of the Board of Treasury 1780–89 (item 141, vol. 1, no. 75), National Archives. This printed schedule tabulates quotas and payments on Congress's requisitions of 30 October 1781, 10 September 1782, 27 and 28 April 1784, 27 September 1785, 2 August 1786, and 11 October 1787. Similar printed schedules, available on the same M247, roll 154, item 141, but intermingled with other Board of Treasury financial papers, tabulate quotas and returns for 30 September 1786 (vol. 2, no. 433), 1 January 1787 (vol. 1, no. 153), 31 March 1787 (vol. 2, no. 123), and 31 December 1787 (vol. 2, no. 484).

effective collection. "As the whole success of the foregoing plan depends upon the punctual collection of the taxes, I find upon farther inquiry, that the Connecticut law pays a particular attention to that matter." Thomson then described in detail Connecticut's collection system, which employed the state treasurer's execution warrant to coerce local town collectors into performing their assigned duty.[6]

Federal Superintendent of Finance (1781–84) Robert Morris not only pressured the state governments but urged economic and fiscal measures to stimulate the states' economic recovery by encouraging greater capital investment on the part of merchants and greater industriousness on the part of farmers and artisans. Although Morris is best remembered for enhancing the central government through having engineered such measures as the Bank of North America and for urging direct tax powers for Congress, he also made an invigorated state-centered requisition system a central part of his policy.[7]

Within a few days after he took the oath of office as superintendent of finance, Morris turned his attention to state requisitions. Although state governments had fallen far short of meeting their quotas on Congress's previous requisitions, Morris was cautiously hopeful the state governments could be prodded into compliance. The first of several printed circulars was dispatched to the thirteen state executives pointedly urging them to make good on their state's large outstanding and overdue requisition payments; in addition Morris recommended that each state enact new "generous grants of solid Revenue" for Congress's benefit and take "energetic measures to collect that Revenue," for "it is by being just to Individuals, to each other, to the Union, to all, . . . and not by complainings, vauntings, or recriminations that these States must expect to establish their Independence and rise into Power, Consequence, and Grandeur."[8]

Morris also asked the state executives to supply him information about how their governments levied and collected taxes; about the condition of their states' paper currency; and about when state legislatures were scheduled to meet so that "any proposals to be made to them may arrive in season for their attentive deliberation." Morris then began the task of balancing and settling Revolutionary accounts between the federal government and the state governments—a proceeding, he felt, that would encourage the state governments to step up their compliance with federal requisitions by showing them exactly what they owed. Throughout the rest of 1781 and well into 1782 Morris continued to urge, coax, and prod the state governors to have their governments put requisition money into the federal treasury.[9]

Morris was clear in his own mind how the state governments could levy taxes and meet their requisition quotas. If they legislated fiscal monetary measures that stimulated investment, productivity, and exports, taxes would not be hard for the people to pay. The states should fund their public debts, stabilize their currencies, repeal their tender laws, and levy and appropriate permanent taxes earmarked for interest payments on the state and federal public debts. Like Thomson, Morris would have the state governments collect taxes promptly either by applying existing methods of collection more energetically or by adopting better collection methods.[10]

Morris often worked by indirection. When Congress was in session in Philadelphia, Morris met with congressional state delegations and urged them to get their state governments to comply with federal requisitions. Sometimes he tried more blunt tactics. To pressure the North Carolina,

South Carolina, and Georgia legislatures to levy taxes, Morris delivered a stern message to their congressional delegations and governors. He would not, he said, allow federal tax receivers to issue special paper notes in payment for army supplies and payable as taxes until those states actually enacted tax laws that showed they meant to comply with federal requisitions.[11] Morris also encouraged federal receivers of taxes—new officers Congress had authorized to receive and handle state requisition payments—to lobby state legislatures and state executives to meet their requisition quotas.[12]

To mobilize public pressure in the cause of state compliance, Morris instructed federal tax receivers to publish the amounts of each state's deficiencies in local newspapers:

> I wish that these publications may promote enquiries where the fault lies, that if the public treasure when collected has been misapplied, or if necessary laws for collecting it or the collection have been delayed by faction, disaffection, or other improper causes, the whole may be known, and the guilty punished. . . . The taxes necessary for this war can by no means be very burthensome, if they are equally and punctually collected, and justly and oeconomically applied.[13]

To mobilize unpaid lobbyists to his cause, in May 1782 Morris stopped the payment of interest on federal loan office certificates held by the federal government's domestic creditors. When prominent Pennsylvania public creditors called on Morris to urge that the central government renew payment, Morris told them that money was not available and to "unite and use their Influence to turn out [state legislative] Members" who "opposed every kind of Taxation from local and Popular Views." He gave other federal creditors with claims on Congress the same message: "I must candidly declare to every public Creditor, that while the Wealth of the People is in the Hands of the several Legislatures, Redress must come from them and from them only."[14] Morris also withheld the monthly pay for the Continental army, until the state governments complied with their unpaid federal quotas—a tactic intended to turn the pressure of the unpaid officers and men onto the state governments.[15]

Thus for more than two years as federal superintendent of finance, Robert Morris struggled to get the states to comply with federal requisitions. He had modest success. During his three years in office the states contributed $2,190,734 in specie to the federal treasury. These figures help explain why Alexander Hamilton could regret Morris's pending resignation in 1784 thus: "I believe no man in this country but himself could have kept the money-making machine a going during the period he has been in office."[16] By 1787, however, Morris favored reconstituting the central government root and branch.

debt by making payments in bills of exchange and Continental cur-[25] Increasingly lacking the wherewithal to make interest payments ... of the incompleteness of state requisition payments, in 1781 Con-... unsuccessfully sought an independent revenue source by asking the ... to grant it a 5 percent federal duty on imports (5 percent impost) ... ould be appropriated to the payment of annual interest on the public ... In 1783 Congress asked the states to approve a modified Continental ... —the funding requisition of 1783—but again the unanimous ap-... of the states could not be obtained. Pursuing another approach, ... ress in its 1784 requisition plan instructed federal loan officers in ... the states to issue special indents (certificates of interest) as interest ... nts to holders of federal loan office and final settlement certificates. ... paper indents were then to be collected as taxes by the states and paid ... gress as part of each state's requisition quota.[26]

... ause their interchangeability with hard specie at par was not assured, ... rket value of indents quickly fell below their stated value in specie. ... rly because creditors lacked confidence in Congress's ability both to ... interest payments at full specie value and to pay the full specie ... t on the federal debt, the market value of federal securities declined ... itously as well. Depending on the time period, market values of fed-... rtificates dropped to as low as two shillings in the pound and rarely ... ed above five shillings in the pound.[27] Although many security hold-... lieved that full payment would be possible once Congress acquired ... percent federal impost, others looked to the state governments for ... Some state governments took over the temporary payment of the ... st on this federal "public debt," just as they had previously done with ... portions of the federal debt.[28]

... ne of these diplomatic, military, and financial episodes posed an im-... te threat to the vital interests, territory, security, or integrity of the ... d States. Yet each highlighted the adverse consequences of the central ... nment's inability to command money through the state requisition ... . In the eyes of many, the failure of the state governments to put ... h money into Congress's treasury translated into the larger question ... ether the central government could protect the nation's territory, for-... commerce, or other vital interests without more adequate financial ... rces.

... ese episodes are often cited as the primary cause of the movement that ... ced the federal Constitution. Indeed, some historians hold that these ... olved diplomatic, border, and financial problems posed such a se-... threat to the United States that merely to cite Congress's inability to ... ith them is to explain the federal Constitution.[29] But while exposing ... ntral government's financial impotence, they should be distinguished ... the deeper problem of the requisition system's breakdown. They

Others in the central government who would become Framers in 1787 tried to make the system of state requisitions work in the early 1780s. James Madison, a Virginia member of Congress from 1780 to 1783, urged that steps be taken that built on this system rather than departed from it. Madison's proposals included an amendment to the Articles of Confederation that would empower Congress to coerce any state that did not meet its requisition quota and that would formally lay legal responsibility for financing the federal debt on the states through state funding (permanent state taxes). Neither Morris nor Madison was ready at this juncture to "challenge the purposes or structure of the federal government as defined by the Articles of Confederation."[17]

The Fruits of Insolvency

Without sufficient money, Congress could not forcefully respond to the British government's refusal to evacuate nine military posts on U.S. soil along the U.S.–British Canada border. These posts, on the shores of the Great Lakes and in northern New York state, commanded important strategic sites. The Anglo-American 1783 peace treaty required their cession by their British occupants to the United States, but the British government, claiming prior violation of the treaty by the United States, would not order the transfer. U.S. diplomatic protests delivered in London and a special mission sent to Canada proved fruitless. More money in the federal treasury would have enabled Congress to increase its minuscule army (625 officers and men) and put military pressure on the British. Military weakness "resulting from a lack of funds" was, a leading student of the subject judges, the major cause of Congress's inability to force the transfer.[18]

Congress temporized when the Spanish government closed the Mississippi River and port of New Orleans to U.S. riverboat traffic (1784–88). The Mississippi–New Orleans outlet was crucial to the riverborne exports of growing U.S. settlements in Tennessee and Kentucky. Although the 1783 Anglo-American peace treaty guaranteed free access of the Mississippi to Americans, Spain was not a party to the treaty. In 1784 the Spanish government closed the Mississippi to all traffic except that conducted by its own subjects, and in 1787 Spanish authorities at Natchez arrested a U.S. riverboat captain and confiscated his goods. At the same time and over U.S. protests, Spanish troops continued to occupy military posts in the area between the thirty-first and thirty-second degrees (central and northern Mississippi and Alabama), an area claimed by both the United States and Spain.

In 1785 Spain's Don Diego de Gardoqui arrived in New York to negotiate with the U.S. secretary for foreign affairs, John Jay. Without military or naval power, however, Jay felt too weak to offer a strong challenge. Hence he agreed to a treaty formula that postponed resolution of the Mississippi–New Orleans issue in return for other Spanish commercial and territorial concessions. But southern members of Congress protested so strongly that the draft Jay-Gardoqui treaty was shelved. Had Congress been able to finance a military or naval buildup, these issues could have been pushed more forcefully.[19]

An insolvent Congress could also do little about hostage-taking and demands for payments by the Barbary states on the Mediterranean's North African coast (Algiers, Tunis, Tripoli, and Morocco). During the 1780s, private armed ships from the Barbary states seized and held hostage dozens of ships and thousands of sailors belonging to the European maritime powers. European governments paid tribute to the Barbary states as protection money, preferring cash payments to the greater expense of armed force. U.S. merchant ships in the Mediterranean were also seized and their crews held hostage (1 in 1783; 2 in 1785). When Congress-appointed envoys Thomas Barclay and John Lamb tried to purchase protection, Algiers, Tunis, and Tripoli demanded more than Congress could pay and the negotiations failed. Simultaneously, the U.S. minister to France, Thomas Jefferson, and the secretary for foreign affairs, John Jay, developed plans for contributing U.S. naval vessels to a joint U.S.–Europe naval force that would protect shipping in the region. But Congress, because it could not finance a contribution, refused approval. The hostages were not released, and U.S. ships avoided the Mediterranean. U.S. diplomats worked resourcefully, but as one authority writes, "Without money treaties could not be obtained either amicably or by force from the piratical states."[20]

Without sufficient funds, Congress could neither prevent nor terminate hostilities between white settlers and Indians in western Georgia, Virginia, and Pennsylvania in 1786–87. Most of Congress's regular army (625 men) was stationed in western Pennsylvania, but the force was too small, too poorly equipped, and too scattered to prevent white squatters and Indians from coming to blows. Commanded by Lt. Colonel Josiah Harmar, the U.S. troops in western Pennsylvania built and garrisoned posts, went on patrol, accompanied U.S commissioners in treaty negotiations with Indian tribes, protected the geographer of the United States in the Seven Ranges survey, and established a garrison at the French frontier settlement of Vincennes in 1787. Realizing that peace was not possible unless white trespassers were removed from Indian lands, Harmar ordered his troops to eject squatters but without success. After failing to obtain more troops and supplies from an impecunious Congress, Harmar concluded in 1788 that "the Government is so feeble as not to afford three or four Regiments

of national troops properly organized, who woul[d] with these perfidious Villains upon the Wabash[ ] subject explains: "With his small force spread th[ ] Harmar was not able to halt the drift toward [ ] Much the same process of uncontrolled white intr[ ] apparently was occurring along the Virginia and [ ] no regular troops on those frontiers, things were [ ] clashes between whites and Indians mounted.[22]

Short of funds, Congress could not make requ[ ] foreign creditors. Congress had borrowed money [ ] ernment ($6,376,832), the Spanish government, a[ ] bankers ($3,600,000) to help finance the Revolut[ ] paid annually, and principal payments were sched[ ] Although for a time Congress sent specie and othe[ ] the French and Dutch (the Spanish received no pay[ ] ways fell short, and further loans for the purpose [ ] higher interest rates from Dutch bankers (March [ ] 1787, $400,000; and March 1788, $400,000). [ ] ments to the French government were in default, and[ ] attaching merchandise purchased by Congress awa[ ] United States. When the date came due for the first [ ] the French government (September 1787), Congres[ ] able to make the payment. Responding to French p[ ] Foreign Affairs Jay could only promise that Congr[ ] engagement as soon as possible. Congress's Dutch c[ ] for payment, but by now Congress's financial insol[ ] mittances from the United States impossible.[23]

An insolvent Congress also could not make promis[ ] on money owed creditors within the United States. T[ ] debt, which totaled about $26,200,000, was a lega[ ] Revolution and represented money that Congress ha[ ] rowing and the value of army pay and military supplie[ ] interest-bearing loan office certificates and federal ce[ ] tional equivalent of interest-bearing war bonds). By [ ] central government's Revolutionary debt was held by i[ ] north of Maryland, especially Pennsylvania, New Y[ ] and Massachusetts. Pared down by write-offs and d[ ] cumulated domestic federal debt included federal [ ] tificates ($11,500,000), final settlement certificates ([ ] five years' pay to Continental army officers ($11,00[ ] the $26,200,000 debt carried annual 6 percent in[ ] $1,572,000 or more.[24]

During the Revolution's first years Congress paid in[ ]

were results, not causes, of the central government's inability to raise money through state requisitions.

Moreover, if these finance-based diplomatic, military, and debt problems had been a central cause of the federal Constitution, why was not vesting Congress with an independent federal taxing power a sufficient solution? The Constitutional Convention framed structural revisions and centralization in the central government that went far beyond the simple addition of a tax power. Conceivably, as is sometimes argued, Congress's diplomatic and military weakness required the creation of a restructured central government having a strong executive armed with diplomatic and military powers. But the Framers regarded Congress as the proper repository for the management of foreign and military policy and until the last weeks of the Convention were ready to vest basic if not exclusive control of these matters in Congress.[30] Congress's foreign policy, military, and financial failures thus do not adequately explain the Framers' decision to carry out the central government's radical overhaul.

★ 2 ★

THE FAILED QUEST
FOR A FEDERAL TAX POWER

Twice between the end of the Revolution and the Constitutional Convention, Congress almost broke free from dependency on state requisitions by acquiring a federal power to tax through state approval of a federal amendment. In a third instance, Congress's decision to pursue a different strategy eventually resulted in a radical revision of the central government.

Congress's 1781 Impost Plan

Congress first requested the states to vest it with the power to tax for federal purposes in February 1781 when it sought a 5 percent impost exclusively for payment of the interest and principal on the federal debt, to cease when the debt was extinguished. This was a narrower version of a proposal that Congress had previously rejected, which would have invested Congress with an exclusive power to tax imports brought into the United States for whatever purposes it might determine. Various considerations account for why the narrower version was preferred, including members' belief that the requisition system could still be made to work, their unwillingness to set a precedent by vesting Congress with the power to levy and expend general funds at will, and their belief that the state governments would not approve any broader grant of federal taxing power.[1]

By mid-1782 all the state governments except Rhode Island had approved Congress's limited 5 percent federal impost proposal. In November 1782 Rhode Island's legislature rejected the proposal by a vote of 53–0. Many popular arguments were mounted against the five percent, but taxes were the crux of the matter. Concerned at reports of popular resistance against heavy direct taxes in Massachusetts and Virginia,[2] Rhode Island leaders were preparing a state funding system that depended on income from a state impost on foreign imports. Establishment of the federal impost would require additional direct taxes and thus increase the tax burden on the state's artisans and farmers, who formed a majority of the state's qualified voters.[3]

Congress's 1783 Impost-Funding Requisition Plan

In March 1783—two years later—Congress made a second attempt to get the states to invest it with a federal power to tax. Again the state governments were asked to empower Congress to raise revenue that would be specifically earmarked for payment of the federal debt. The new plan met previously stated objections by vesting collection in the hands of state-appointed officers, mandating that the impost would cease to operate at the end of twenty-five years, and urging that the landed states cede all their land claims to Congress. Because the impost's anticipated income would not meet the estimated annual sum required to finance the accumulated federal debt, the states were also asked to establish permanent supplementary tax funds for this purpose with the receipts appropriated to payment of the debt's remaining annual interest.[4] While Rhode Island's decisive rejection of the 5 percent impost in late 1782 in part explains the timing of this new plan, the pressure of Continental army officers encamped at Newburgh, New York, who wanted Congress to assume and pay their accumulated claims for unpaid back pay, also accounts for this second congressional proposal.[5]

Despite its more limited scope compared to other tax-granting proposals (the plan that Robert Morris and Alexander Hamilton proposed would have invested Congress with direct taxes on improved lands and houses), Congress's bid for federal taxes again foundered on the holdout opposition of a single state. This time not Rhode Island, which approved the 1783 measure (February 1785), but New York was the culprit. Like Rhode Island, New York was a commercial state with a heavy volume of imports and exports, and like Rhode Island, New York had a lucrative state impost that supported its fiscal-monetary system. Having recently enacted a paper money relief-recovery program that made £200,000 in state bills of credit available for loan to tax-burdened farmers, New York advocates of this paper money system were anxious to bolster the paper's value by making the paper acceptable for any federal impost payment on a par with specie. Accordingly, they made it a condition of the enabling legislation that New York's paper money be acceptable tender under the federal 5 percent impost plan. Because Congress's plan required that the 5 percent impost be paid in gold and silver coin only (to pay the interest and principal on the foreign debt), the two provisions were incompatible.[6]

Still, by July 1786 every state except New York had approved the 5 percent federal impost without qualification, and at least some members of Congress were optimistic that New York could be brought around. Indeed, agreement seemed so near that Congress that July set up a committee to draft the requisite legislation that would make the federal impost operative once New York made the necessary concessions. After accepting a committee report that listed the points at which New York's enabling legislation and Congress's original request were at odds, Congress ordered that a special committee be established, that this committee draft a federal ordinance that would put the 5 percent impost into effect once New York met Congress's conditions, and that Governor George Clinton of New York be asked to call a special legislative session to bring New York's enabling ordinance into compliance with Congress's requirements. But Clinton would not call a special session, and the following February New York's legislature repeated its de facto rejection of the 5 percent by again voting its previously stated conditions. On this de facto rejection, this second effort to provide Congress with financial independence foundered.[7]

Yet, by 1786, all the Confederation's member-state governments had approved, in principle if not in technical detail, investiture of the central government with a federal power to tax. Nevertheless, because the Articles of Confederation required that the plan not take effect until the state governments had reached an exact agreement among themselves and Congress on the terms by which the federal impost would operate, Congress never gained a taxing power. Given Congress's acute financial necessity and given that Congress's need for an impost was widely accepted, it is possible that one more effort to get the states to approve a limited federal taxing power would have succeeded. Noting just how much wide support for the Articles' amendment actually had developed by 1786, E. James Ferguson judges that, although the formal grants of the holdout states did not accord with those of the rest, by 1786 there did exist grounds for the Articles' amendment: "For such general agreement existed as to the need for a moderate increase in federal powers that by 1786 all the states approved the impost in principle."[8] In fact, when the Framers in late 1786–early 1787 organized for the federal convention at Philadelphia—an event that required the state legislatures to select and instruct convention delegates—they shrewdly capitalized on this sentiment by drafting resolutions of instructions that endorsed the idea of strengthening Congress's financial powers by limited amendment. But by this time, Federalist leaders were girding for an expanded, far more radical agenda.

Breakdown of the Requisition System (1786–1787)

The stalled 5 percent federal impost was only the tip of the iceberg. By late 1786, the yield from state requisitions had dwindled drastically.

Without money from the states, a nearly bankrupt Congress had no other resource but further borrowing. Yet when Congress tried to borrow, no one subscribed.

Even though the sums were never all that Congress asked for, until late 1786 the state governments had contributed just enough money to keep Congress afloat. During Robert Morris's three years as superintendent of finance (1781–84), the states paid over two million dollars into the federal treasury enabling Congress to make interest payments on its foreign debt and to pay its own housekeeping and operating expenses. During the ensuing three years (1784–86) when the Board of Treasury presided over federal finances, requisition payments by the states declined substantially. Although no exact figures have been found, the fact that earlier requisitions achieved higher payment percentages than later requisitions is indicative. By 31 March 1787, the states had paid 66 percent of the federal requisitions of 30 October 1781 and 27 and 28 April 1784, 35 percent of the federal requisition of 10 September 1782, 20 percent of the federal requisition of 27 September 1785, but only 2 percent of the federal requisition of 2 August 1786.[9]

In fact, the more recent the requisition, the smaller the payments made. On 2 August 1786, Congress voted a requisition on the states of $3,777,062 to pay current interest and principal on the French, Dutch, and Spanish loans, interest on the domestic debt, and current operating expenses including the pay and supply of the military and civil departments.[10] Between 30 September 1786 and 31 March 1787 payments on five earlier requisitions of 1781, 1782, 1784, and 1785 totaled $203,529. Yet during the same six-month period, the August 1786 requisition elicited no payments at all from twelve of the thirteen states and only $663 from Pennsylvania (see table 2). Furthermore, since the $203,529 received on earlier requisitions was committed to payment of the interest on the federal foreign and domestic debt and other expenses for previous years, it could not legally be used for current needs. By the end of 1786, Congress literally was receiving no money from the states for current federal needs and expenses.

Late in 1786 a second attempt by Congress to raise money through the states proved equally unsuccessful. In October 1786 Congress voted to borrow $500,000 by selling 6 percent bonds to private subscribers and asked the states to pledge money for repayment by voting tax funds. These measures were to finance an emergency increase in the federal army. The money from the loan was to pay and equip 1,340 new troops requisitioned by Congress on the states to help put down rural disturbances in Massachusetts (Shays's Rebellion) and to guard the federal arsenal at Springfield from possible seizure by the rebelling farmers.[11] But the loan and the requests for taxes proved a total failure. Twelve of the thirteen state gov-

TABLE 2.
CONGRESSIONAL REQUISITIONS: COMBINED STATE PAYMENTS,
30 SEPTEMBER 1786–31 MARCH 1787

Requisition Title and Amount	Amount Paid	Amount Paid Previously	In Arrears (% in parentheses)
30 Oct. 1781 and April 1784 $4,000,000	$63,531	$2,627,938	$1,372,064 (34)
10 Sept. 1782 $1,200,000	63,541	372,000	764,459 (64)
27 Sept. 1785 $3,000,000	76,457	529,871	2,393,667 (80)
2 Aug. 1786 $3,777,062	663	64,079 (S.C. offset)[a]	3,712,320 (98)

Source: "Schedules of the Requisition Payments on the Several States," 30 September 1786 (vol. 2, no. 433), 1 January 1787 (vol. 1, no. 153), 31 March 1787 (vol. 2, no. 123), Papers of the Continental Congress, 1774–1789, microfilm M247, roll 154, Estimates of the Board of Treasury, 1780–89 (item 141, vol. 1, no. 75), National Archives.

[a]The $64,079 was credited to South Carolina's quota as an offset on a previous claim against the central government. Thus, in terms of actual money received, Congress got only $663 for the 2 August 1786 requisition.

ernments took no action to provide tax funds, and only the Virginia legislature levied a special tax to finance its quota. Asked by Congress to contribute $90,630, Virginia's legislature enacted a state tax on tobacco exports, but the proceeds were estimated at only $40,000 per annum. With the prospect for repayment thus highly remote, the $500,000 loan attracted not one subscriber.[12]

With nothing except $663 specie available for current expenses, the Board of Treasury could not make any further monthly payments for the pay and support of federal troops on the western Pennsylvania frontier. By 31 December 1787, the arrearages due for the pay and subsistence of the federal troops in Congress's service totaled more than $50,000.[13] The salaries of federal employees were not paid; for example, during the last six months of 1786 the Continental loan officers who handled Congress's financial dealings in the states received neither salary nor compensation for expenses.[14] Nor could the federal government make even a slight dent in the $1,721,229 of principal and interest due in 1787 on French, Dutch, and Spanish debts.[15]

Members of Congress had long known of the precarious state of the central government's finances. Nevertheless, if state requisitions had always fallen short of the amounts Congress asked, some cash had usually been available for current expenses. Now the central government was so destitute of funds and credit that it could neither pay its own civil officers nor borrow one penny from its own citizens.

Deploring the failure of the states to respond to the 1786 requisitions, members of Congress wondered whether Congress could carry on as a government. Could a central authority that could not pay its own civil officers, its own army, its own employees, and its debts last much longer? Having no funds to finance the domestic and foreign debt was bad enough, but the nonpayment of its own members, officers, and staff would ultimately force the government to disband and its members to go home. If Congress dissolved, how would the states coordinate their common interests and resolve disputes? If a foreign government seized the moment to attack the United States, how could the several state governments respond effectively without a Congress? With no common forum in which state delegates could meet, discuss, resolve differences, and coordinate action, sooner or later the Confederation too would dissolve and the union of the states come to an end. The letters of members of Congress at this time sound more pessimistic than usual.

Stephen M. Mitchell, Congress member from Connecticut, found "the situation of Congress . . . truely deplorable, no one seems willing to contribute a Mite to extricate us from the mire into which we are fallen. . . . I cannot see there remains any necessity for keeping up a Representation in Congress, in our present situation, all we can possibly do, is to recommend, which is an old, stale device & no better than the wish of a few Individuals relative to public Concerns."[16] Roger Alden, also a member from Connecticut, wrote a constituent, "I cannot flatter you with any hopes, for the final success of your application to Congress—matters of justice or generosity are not the subjects of deliberation—the question now is—can the Government any longer exist? where are the supplies by which it is to be supported—in this melancholy dilemma—in so critical a situation, we have more reason to fear worse, than hope for better times."[17] James Madison, member from Virginia, saw around him "men of reflection much less sanguine as to a new than despondent as to the present System. Indeed the present System neither has nor deserves advocates; and if some very strong props are not applied will quickly tumble to the ground. No money is paid into the public Treasury; no respect is paid to the federal authority. Not a single State complies with the requisitions, several pass them over in silence, and some positively reject them. The payments ever since the peace have been decreasing, and of late fall short even of the pittance necessary for the Civil list of the Confederacy. It is not possible that a Government can last long under these circumstances. If the appro[a]ching Convention should not agree on some remedy, I am persuaded that some very different arrangement will ensue."[18]

Thus, by the time the federal convention gathered at Philadelphia in May 1787, Congress's financial crisis had already generated a series of gloomy prognostications about Congress's and the Union's future. More than ever, the convention seemed the best, perhaps the only opportunity to clothe Congress with an independent financial power (5 percent impost) that would rescue it from possible disbandment with unpredictable consequences for the Union. Coinciding as it did with the Annapolis Convention's call for the states to send delegations to a second federal convention at Philadelphia, the financial crisis in the federal government during the months between the two conventions helped propel twelve of the thirteen state legislatures that authorized delegates to attend the Constitutional Convention into this decision.

From Annapolis to Philadelphia

Yet the chain of events that led to the Constitutional Convention at Philadelphia was not the direct outcome of Congress's empty treasury. Rather, the triggering event was the happenstance gathering of an interstate trade convention at Annapolis in September 1786—the Annapolis Convention.

In August 1786 Congress had debated whether the states should be asked to approve not one but several amendments to the Articles of Confederation that went much further than any previous Congress-initiated proposal. The proposed amendments would empower Congress to legislate a federal impost, regulate commerce, compel the collection of federal requisitions by direct enforcement action against individual citizens, enact further revenues with the consent of only eleven state governments rather than all thirteen, and establish a federal court for trying federal issues related to the regulation of commerce or collection of revenues. However ambitious, this scheme still required that the Confederation's thirteen member-state governments approve each amendment unanimously. Because this quite radical approach stood little or no chance of success, Congress had shelved the plan.[19] Some members had wondered whether an interstate convention might be a more successful vehicle than Congress for the central government's reform. In addition to a practical concern for its own impost-supported paper money program, the New York legislature had refused to ratify the 5 percent federal impost according to Congress's specifications because members suspected that this congressional request for the 5 percent federal impost might have some hidden, even sinister design behind it. By its very nature—ad hoc, temporary, and representing the individual states—an interstate convention would blunt the argument, which Congress's advocacy of the 5 percent invariably generated, that the federal impost was intended to equip Congress with powers that would then be used for Congress's own self-aggrandizement.[20]

By coincidence, an opportunity for this more indirect approach presented itself in the guise of the Annapolis Convention, the trade convention that was scheduled to meet in the Maryland capital in September 1786. In March 1785 delegates from Maryland and Virginia had met at George Washington's Mount Vernon home to conclude an agreement over the jurisdiction and joint use of the shared waterways of Chesapeake Bay and the Potomac and Pocomoke rivers. Transmitted to the Maryland and Virginia legislatures for approval, the Mount Vernon accords became the occasion for Virginia legislator James Madison to propose that the Virginia legislature approve not only the accords themselves but a pending proposal to invest Congress with powers over foreign commerce. In 1784 Congress had requested the state governments to approve a limited federal power that would allow Congress to retaliate against the ships and merchandise of Great Britain, which had closed its own West Indies to U.S.-owned merchant vessels after the Revolution. This first plan, much narrower than others simultaneously bruited about, would allow Congress to impose only discriminatory duties against the trade of any nation not in commercial treaty with the United States (Great Britain). Submitted to the state governments for approval, the proposal had stalled; Congress, undaunted, in 1785 had again asked the state governments to approve this power. When the Mount Vernon accords reached the Virginia legislature, Madison tried to couple the two. But after approving the accords, the Virginia legislature voted down Madison's broader proposal. He countered by proposing that a trade convention be held with all thirteen states invited to send delegates to discuss commercial subjects and make recommendations. Madison's more modest proposal carried, delegates were selected, a date and site were decided upon, and invitations to the other state legislatures were dispatched.[21]

Held in the Maryland state capitol building in September 1786, the Annapolis Convention afforded an opportunity not just for outmaneuvering the opposition to Congress's plan for a 5 percent impost but for setting the stage for a possible radical recasting of the central government itself. Although slim attendance foreclosed the Annapolis Convention from making any substantive recommendations (only twelve delegates from five states actually were present), those few delegates who did attend drafted and sent to Congress and the state governments an elliptically worded recommendation for a second convention that would address the central government's various defects. As the convention's final recommendation stated, a second interstate convention should be held in Philadelphia the second Monday in May 1787 to "devise such further provisions as shall appear to them necessary to render the constitution of the Federal Government adequate to the exigencies of the Union."[22] This proposed second convention was the body that produced the federal Constitution.

Historians disagree over whether the Annapolis Convention, when it called for a second convention at Philadelphia, had in mind the radical recasting that became the federal Constitution, or whether its views were confined to Congress's limited amendment.[23] Both positions have validity. Convinced by Congress's increasingly desperate financial predicament that Congress must be empowered with independent financial powers by limited amendment, some of the Annapolis delegates also entertained the hope that a second convention might tackle the central government's radical reconstitution. Radical reconstitution was by no means the unfamiliar idea in September 1786 that some historians have portrayed. Nor was it without strong backing at the time the Annapolis Convention met. Proposals for such reconstitution had been aired even before the Annapolis Convention gathered (see chapter 12). Many of the several states' top echelon of elite political leaders were already so thoroughly disenchanted with the state governments' ability to legislate and enforce temporarily unpopular and inconvenient laws, notably taxes, that they were by this time friends if not advocates of the central government's radical reform. By February 1787, enough of these advocates existed to enable member of Congress William Irvine to write a trusted political confidante that the projected convention at Philadelphia would attempt to engineer *either* Congress's ad hoc reform or "frame an entire new Government"—strong proof that radical reconstitution had substantial backing well before the Philadelphia convention, enough at least to make an attempt at the convention a distinct possibility.[24] The Constitutional Convention's agreement that the central government should be radically reconstituted, reached in principle in the very first week of sessions, is further proof that a majority of the delegates came to Philadelphia with a pretty clear idea that this was the direction they wanted to go.[25]

Yet given existing political realities, to have publicly avowed the purpose of radical reconstitution at this time would have killed the convention before it could meet. No convention could succeed without representation from most of the Confederation's thirteen member-states. Yet in late 1786 and early 1787 the advocates of the central government's substantial reform were still a small minority. Supporters of Congress's limited amendment by the 5 percent impost were numerous, but supporters for root-and-branch reconstitution were few. Hence when they drafted the enabling resolutions to be passed by their legislatures, the Federalists concentrated on limited amendment and carefully avoided (without closing the door entirely) any public reference to the central government's radical revision.[26]

An Entirely New Government

By the time the Framers gathered at Philadelphia, state and national government leaders around the country of various political hues believed that Congress must have greater financial power of its own. Even Antifederalists who opposed the federal Constitution's adoption supported the modest, least drastic plan of investing Congress with an independent revenue-raising power of some kind—the five percent impost being the most widely favored. Antifederalists believed that the Confederation's diplomatic, military, and financial problems could be effectively addressed if Congress were vested with a federal impost power. Armed with the 5 percent impost, Congress could then finance a larger army, start a navy, and, with its hand thus strengthened, begin to solve the diplomatic and security problems of the Confederation era—the Barbary pirates, squatters and Indians, the disputes with the British and Spanish. Together with the sale of public lands, the impost might even enable Congress to pay the interest and principal on the domestic and foreign debt.

Yet when the Framers designed the federal Constitution, they first engineered a different structure of tripartite legislative, executive, and judicial central government, then added a broad array of new powers to the central government, including not only the power to tax but many other substantive powers as well. In short, as their own spokespersons put it, they built an "entire new Government" on "new principles."[27]

★ 3 ★

HEAVY STATE TAXATION

E XPLAINING the failure of the requisition system, historians often de-
pict the state governments as preoccupied with state interests, parochial in outlook, or fearful of an overmighty Congress, so that state legislatures neglected the financial requests of the only authority capable of
thinking and acting "continentally" on behalf of the nation as a whole.[1]
Yet such descriptions fail to capture how contemporaries familiar with
Confederation finances explained the states' failure to support Congress
more effectively.

The Requisition System's Failure

Shortly before the Constitutional Convention, Virginia's Edmund Pendleton wrote James Madison of what "every man must be convinced
of," namely, the central government's "Imbecility on the subject of
finan[ces]." Pendleton hoped that the convention would vest the central
government with "independent, coercive powers" to levy and collect
money to pay the public debt and its own expenses. "To depend upon requisitions for adjusted Quotas annually, & those upon the various Senti-
ments & whims of 13 different Assemblies, has proved as unproductive
in practice, as it is futile in reason."[2] Pendleton's language suggests that
he saw the problem as the legislatures' proneness to changeability rather
than simple indifference. Late in 1786, Virginia's Governor Edmund
Randolph explained to George Washington why Virginia had no money
to send Congress: "The nerves of government seem unstrung, both in energy and moneys, and the fashion of the day is to calumniate the best ser-
vices, if unsuccessful." A subsequent Randolph letter was a bit more explicit: "To you I need not press our present dangers. The inefficiency of
Congress you have often felt in your official character: the increasing languor of our associated republics you hourly see; and a dissolution would
be I know to you a source of the deepest mortification."[3]

John Jay, federal secretary for foreign affairs, took the analysis slightly
further. Regretting Congress's depleted finances, Jay pointed to "relaxa-

tion in Govermt." and "Extravagance in Individuals" as the cause. The remedy, he indicated in another letter, was a "Mode of Govt. that can easily & irrisistably [*sic*] open [citizens'] Purses."[4] In March 1787, another framer, William Samuel Johnson, focused on Massachusetts and Maryland, recently disrupted by taxpayers' revolts (Shays's Rebellion). Shortly before he departed for the Philadelphia convention as a member of the Connecticut delegation, Johnson, then a member of Congress, tersely linked these states with the treasury crisis. Did Johnson mean to say that these disturbances had caused the Massachusetts and Maryland governments to cease collecting money for Congress? "Our Affairs are daily growing worse & worse," he wrote, dividing the blame between the two states. "I will not despair but I own I do not foresee what will become of us." If the convention failed, "at best I fear we shall soon be in a deplorable situation."[5]

Still another tantalizing glimpse was offered by the federal Board of Treasury in a letter to Dutch bankers in February 1788 explaining why interest currently due from Congress could not be paid. "It becomes our duty to inform you that such is the stagnation in the receipt of Taxes at present throughout every State in the Union, that it is impossible to devise any mode of making you a Remittance in season for this Purpose."[6]

Unfortunately, none of these statements is as explicit as we would wish. Yet indifference, jealousy, and parochialism in the state governments do not seem the ideas they were meant to convey. Rather than shed fresh light on the problem of the requisition system's failure, they raise further questions. Did the state governments try to raise money for Congress? If so, what happened to their attempts? What was meant by "relaxation in Govermt.," "the nerves of government seem unstrung, both in energy and moneys," and "the stagnation in the receipt of taxes"?

The Burden of Taxation

By contrast with figures from the colonial period, my estimates of taxation during the early years of the Confederation show that the average per capita tax burden in four key states during the early 1780s increased severalfold over the prewar load (Pennsylvania, South Carolina, Rhode Island, and Massachusetts, representing the Confederation's three geographic sections). This increase was the more painful because of the economic downturn of the mid-1780s that caused agricultural prices to fall, siphoned money from circulation, and forced a sharp contraction of private credit.

Taxation throughout the colonial period, recent studies argue, had been "extremely light." Especially during peacetime, but also during wartime, colonial taxpayers are held to have paid the lightest taxes of any people in the Anglo-European world.[7] Most of the cost of several eighteenth-century Anglo-colonial wars against France was borne by English taxpayers, and sizable cash reimbursements for colonial war expenditures by the English government had helped the colonies defray such war expenditures as they did incur. Beginning in the late 1740s and continuing up to the Revolution, English military and naval forces expended large amounts of money in the colonies which helped cushion colonial taxes further.[8]

According to this scholarship, the annual per capita tax burden in the colonies in the decade before the Revolution ranged from 2 to 4 shillings per capita and averaged about 3 shillings (colonial currencies).[9] By contrast, during the Confederation era the annual per capita tax in direct specie and paper taxes (state currencies) for the four key states ranged from 10 shillings in South Carolina to £1/5 in Pennsylvania—a severalfold per capita increase for each state. The average annual per household (5.8–9.5 persons to a household) direct tax in the four states ranged from £3 in Rhode Island to £7/10 in Pennsylvania. Converted to their contemporary dollar unit equivalents (the standard common unit among the states) and averaged for the four states, the annual per capita tax in specie and paper was $2.27 and per household $15.35. Equally significant, the average per capita tax in specie for these states was $1.34, and the average tax per household was $8.36 (see table 3).

To compare these figures with modern taxes overlooks the crucial point that the task of finding cash sufficient to pay taxes was a far greater challenge for rural folk in Confederation America than for Americans today.[10] Like the colonial economy, the economy of rural Confederation America was a "world of scarcity," to use Robert Gross's term.[11] Eighteenth-century farm families might possess land, stock, tools, and other capital assets, but except for the well-to-do, cash assets were small or nil. Even when farm commodity prices were high, farmers had to work and save diligently to raise specie coin enough to pay eight dollars. The Revolution left little specie coin circulating—a fact that did not escape the notice of specie tax advocates. Robert Morris, Alexander Hamilton, and others held that specie taxes would spur farmers, artisans, and the rest of the laboring population to greater productivity. More goods at lower prices would then become available for export, and specie would flow back into the economy from overseas sales. This would enable men to pay their taxes. Contrary to prediction, the expected prosperity did not materialize, and the payment of taxes became increasingly hard.[12] My limited investigation of the other nine Confederation states indicates that similar conditions in those states made payment of taxes difficult there as well.

The severalfold increase in the post-Revolution tax load was the direct result of the war and of the realities of independence. To finance the war, the state governments had issued paper money, borrowed specie, and paid

TABLE 3.
AVERAGE ANNUAL TAXES PER CAPITA AND
PER HOUSEHOLD (IN DOLLARS OF THE PERIOD)

State and Tax	Per Capita[a]	Per Household[b]
Massachusetts (1781–86)		
Specie and paper	$2.00 [£0/12 Mass.][c]	$11.60 [£3/10 Mass.]
Specie	1.00 [0/6 Mass.]	5.80 [1/15 Mass.]
Rhode Island (1781–85)		
Specie and paper	1.60 [£0.10 R.I.]	9.60 [£3 R.I.]
Specie	1.53 [0/9 R.I.]	9.18 [2/14 R.I.]
Pennsylvania (1781–83)		
Specie and paper	3.36 [£1/5 Pa.]	20.16 [£7/10 Pa.]
Specie	2.35 [0.18 Pa.]	14.10 [5/8 Pa.]
South Carolina (1783–85)		
Specie and paper	2.11 [£0/10 S.C.]	20.05 [£4/15 S.C.]
Specie[d]	.46 [0/2 S.C.]	4.37 [0/19 S.C.]

Sources: Population Figures for 1783: The Report on Restoring Public Credit, 6 March 1783, *Journals of the Continental Congress* (Washington, D.C.: U.S. Government Printing Office, 1922), xxv, 953; Philip J. Greven, Jr., "The Average Size of Families and Households in the Province of Massachusetts in 1764 and in the United States in 1790: An Overview," in *Household and Family in Past Time,* ed. Peter Laslett and Richard Wall (Cambridge: Cambridge University Press, 1972), 552; Francis White, *The Philadelphia Directory* (Philadelphia: Young, Stewart & McCulloch, 1785), 99, Evans #19385, Early Amerian Imprints Collection.

[a] For average annual per capita tax: divide sum of all taxes for indicated years by state's population. State statutes indicate total amount of tax (see appendix 1).

[b] For total per household tax: use multiplier for the average number of persons in a household: Massachusetts, 5.8; Rhode Island and Pennsylvania, 6; South Carolina, 9.5.

[c] For conversion: tax amounts in brackets are dollar equivalents in state money of account (pounds and shillings). Massachusetts and Rhode Island = 6 shillings per dollar; Pennsylvania = 7/6 per dollar; South Carolina = 4/8 per dollar.

[d] These figures represent the annual average tax per capita and per household for 1783, 1784, and 1785. For 1783 alone, the only year the state levied a specie tax, the per capita tax in specie was $1.38 [£0/6] and per household, $13.11 [£2/17].

for military service, provisions, and equipment by interest-bearing certificates that promised future payment in cash. By consolidating these debts after the war, the state governments took responsibility for large sums of yearly interest and eventual principal payments. Because independence also meant the end of the English subsidies, the state governments for the first time shouldered their entire war debt. For the first time also, U.S. taxpayers were to pay taxes to support a central authority, Congress. Before the Revolution, London had considered making requisitions on the colonies but decided to raise money by new taxes on colonial imports instead. Especially during the early 1780s, federal requisitions bulked large in state budgets. Not only did the state governments enact heavy direct specie taxes to finance federal requisitions, but when Congress's finances worsened, crackdowns were ordered. Overlooked by historians, the efforts by the state governments to raise and collect specie taxes for Congress produced more destabilizing protest and turmoil than did any of the states' debt financing policies. State debt policy forms an important part of the story of Confederation state finance and state politics, but not in the same way and with the same importance as do the attempts by the states to collect specie for Congress (see table 4).[13]

Because the Revolution had destroyed farms, crops, and urban property, especially in the South, New Jersey, and New York, and because the states needed time for commerce to become productive, state legislatures faced the difficult problem of raising money by taxes that cash-poor citizens could pay. In the colonial period, the least painful mode of taxation had been indirect impost and excise taxes levied on imported foreign goods and domestic sales. These revenues taxed consumers and raised revenue from persons able and willing to pay higher prices voluntarily. Following colonial precedents, all the Confederation legislatures established impost and excise taxes. Those states with large foreign imports (New York and Pennsylvania) raised substantial yearly sums from state imposts, while those states with fewer direct imports (New Jersey and Delaware) raised little. The lighter direct tax burden that a lucrative state impost made possible explains the unwillingness of Rhode Island and New York leaders to approve the federal impost unless off-setting compensations were agreed to by the other states.

State legislators' political sensitivity over direct taxes also promoted efforts to find ways to reduce the state debt. By accepting debt certificates for payment of confiscated Loyalist properties, the government reduced the state's public debt substantially. States with unsold public lands (Virginia, New York, Pennsylvania, South Carolina, and others) reduced their debts by exchanging land for debt certificates.[14] Nevertheless, the combined total of federal requisitions, public debt payments, and operating expenses was far greater than the impost, excise, and these other sources could finance. Direct taxes thus had to be levied in order to meet both federal and state obligations.[15]

Direct taxes levied by the states during the 1780s consisted of a mixture of progressive and regressive taxes on persons and property. Most states levied head or poll taxes on each free adult male that made no differentiation according to the ability to pay. On the other hand, property taxes on personal and real estate property, established at values set by local assessors, were calibrated according to ability to pay, and in some cases taxes

TABLE 4.
STATES' TAX AND BUDGET ALLOCATIONS TO CONGRESS
(IN DOLLARS OF THE PERIOD)
(PERCENTAGES IN PARENTHESES)

State	Amount of State's Direct Taxes Allocated to Congress	Amount of State's Budget Allocated to Congress
Massachusetts		
1781–86	$2,480,850 (59)[a] [£745,000 Mass.][b]	
Rhode Island		
1781–85	225,731 (56)[a] [67,787 R.I.]	
Pennsylvania		
1781–83	3,006,999 (93)[a] [1,126,217 Pa.]	
South Carolina		
1783		$191,976 (52)[c] [£45,600 S.C.]
1784		149,206 (27) [35,441 S.C.]
1785		0

Source: For conversion rates to dollars, see Francis White, *The Philadelphia Directory* (Philadelphia: Young, Stewart & McCulloch, 1785), 99, Evans #19385.

[a] Figures for Massachusetts, Rhode Island and Pennsylvania are the total direct taxes allocated for Congress. Percentages represent the money earmarked for Congress as a portion of the total taxes for both federal and state purposes as described in the statutes summarized in appendix 1.

[b] For conversion: tax amounts in brackets are dollar equivalents in state money of account. Massachusetts and Rhode Island = 6 shillings per dollar; Pennsylvania = 7/6 per dollar; South Carolina = 4/8 per dollar.

[c] South Carolina tax statutes do not specify amounts. The sums allocated Congress by South Carolina must be derived from the state's total annual budget (see appendix 1 for method).

on business and professional income presaged the modern income tax. Despite their progressive features, however, direct taxes in specie were the most painful mode of taxation of the 1780s because they did not allow choice, because taxpayers were not accustomed to heavy payments, because specie was scarce, and because the taxes formed a heavier burden for certain strata of the population than for others. During the 1780s much of the country's rural middle and lower classes could not command credit, had less ready access to marketing facilities, and realized minimal income because of depressed commodity prices. These groups found direct taxes difficult to pay, and large arrearages accumulated.

Between 1781 and 1787 the state legislatures levied direct taxes to finance federal requisitions, public debts, and civil establishments. But because payment of both interest and principal on large state debts would have required increasing the already heavy load of direct taxes well beyond the capacity of householders to manage, the states enacted funding systems. Funding involved a statutory commitment of current tax revenues to annual interest payments on public debts and a pledge of future revenues to repay the principal. Developed first in England during the late seventeenth century, funding enabled a government to sustain its credit by future pledges of payment to its creditors through effective taxes.[16] By funding, the state governments could keep their faith to creditors and simultaneously stretch out the time when the principal had to be paid. Typically, the states carried out funding hand in hand with a "consolidation" of all public debts, a process by which debts were revalued in terms of specie equivalents. In funding public debts, some states committed revenue from their state imposts to pay the annual interest (for example, Massachusetts and Rhode Island); others committed portions of direct taxes or proceeds from the sale of confiscated estates (Maryland). Because the state debts became increasingly concentrated in the hands of the well-to-do investors and monied men who purchased state debt securities at depreciated value, the fairness of these arrangements became a political issue. Most states funded their debts, but probably because funding seemed potentially damaging to the party fortunes of the ascendent Republicans, the Pennsylvania assembly initially avoided a funding system and paid creditors out of the state's common treasury.

Virginia's Richard Henry Lee explained funding as a means of holding taxes down in 1784. Discussing how to pay Virginia's war debt when "our taxes are extremely heavy," Lee wanted the state government to pay interest on the state debt but not pay the principal until such time as the economy had recovered and money became plentiful. To attempt to pay the principal too quickly, he said, would be ruinous. "The only mode appears to be, a funding of the whole debt, so as certainly to pay the interest, and slowly the principal. Cannot a sinking fund be brought to bear upon the latter, by throwing all overflowings of taxes into a reservoir for gathering interest upon interest."[17] Funding became the method by which the government honored its pledges to public creditors but tried to avoid unbearably heavy direct taxes on taxpayers.

Nevertheless, the federally quotaed financial requisitions had to be provided for. Committed by the Articles of Confederation to support Congress with money, at first the states exerted themselves to meet Congress's demands. Sometimes legislatures met federal requisitions by explicitly committing the returns of a specific direct tax for this purpose. Sometimes the legislatures ordered that money be appropriated out of the common treasury from receipts of direct taxes and the state impost. Because Congress required that a high proportion of quotas be paid in specie and because the small quantity of specie in circulation diminished rapidly, the money for Congress's requisitions became more and more difficult to collect. With direct taxation the principal means by which the states raised money for Congress, requisition payments to Congress varied in proportion to what the states could collect from their own populations.

During the early 1780s, as we have seen, the amount of specie the states paid the federal government was greater than it was later in the decade. The decline in requisitions is best explained by shortages of circulating specie, not by localism. The stock of specie, in turn, depended on such factors as the international balance of payments, the willingness of monied men in the United States to loan, and foreign investment. The depression that began in 1784 saw farm prices decline, circulating specie disappear, and credit shrink. Although the causes of this depression are debated, certain factors seem clear. Initially, the high price of U.S. farm products relative to prices in Europe diminished foreign purchases of exports which, in turn, widened the trade gap and depleted the stock of available specie. The adverse trade gap was further increased by pent-up U.S. buying of English manufactured imports immediately after the war. Moreover, with the war over, the British government closed its West Indian ports to U.S. vessels and imposed prohibitions and restrictions on U.S. fish, rum, salt meat, whale oil, and other products that further cut into exports and tipped the trade balance further against the United States.[18] The termination of British military expenditures and reimbursements in the colony-states struck a lethal blow to another vital source of specie.[19] Compounding these unfavorable conditions was the nervousness of monied men in the United States over the prospect of possible state tax and debt relief legislation; at the very slightest rumor of paper money, hoarding of specie began, and the capital flow abroad increased.[20] By the same token, British merchants, also mistrustful of paper money, reduced credit and investment in the United States. All these factors explain the downward slide in prices that began in 1784.[21]

Specie taxes for Congress put heavy pressure on those classes most severely handicapped by slumping prices, marketing difficulties, the specie shortage, and poor credit. Most studies of the period agree that the hardest hit were the small farmers, rural artisans, and farm laborers of the northern and middle states and the small farmers, rural artisans, and middling planters of the South. A study of Confederation New Hampshire indicates the severe nature of the specie shortage. Only 3.8 percent of sampled wills in New Hampshire counties had any cash listed among the deceased's assets. Many probated wills show sizable property in land, stock, and buildings, but little or no hard cash.[22] The makers of these wills had probably expended what little cash they had in tax payments to the state.

Rural dwellers throughout the Confederation experienced much the same acute shortage of cash. Until some of the states printed paper money and made it available on loan for taxes, the direct specie levied by the states during the Confederation era constituted a painfully heavy burden; often farmers simply could not pay. And if a man did not pay his taxes, he was subject to harsh penalties. Although state legislatures frequently extended due dates and enacted other forms of tax relief, the law required that local tax collectors seize and sell at auction the movable property of tax delinquents within a short time after the expired date. Until state legislatures forced seizure-and-sale proceedings, however, local collectors often indulged cashless taxables by allowing them further time to pay. The crackdowns on delinquent taxes, not simply the existence of heavy taxes as such, detonated the rural violence that rocked the Confederation state governments and forced them to suspend collection and vote relief.

★4★

TAXERS AND RELIEFERS

T HE PATRONS of hard money taxes were recognized elites of wealthy and accomplished merchants, bankers, lawyers, and planters who held office in the postwar state governments as legislators, executives, and judges. These "Taxers" believed that taxes could be paid if the common people were frugal and industrious. Descriptives such as the "first gentlemen of Boston," "the great people" and "the aristocracy" of Charleston bespeak a recognition by contemporaries of their wealth, social rank, and political influence.[1] Until the Revolution, the colonial assemblies had been a relatively safe position for such gentleman-politicians. But with the Revolution, the departure of Loyalist gentry created positions for newcomers to fill, and the growth in the political consciousness and confidence of the middle and lower classes meant their greater participation.[2] Popular politicians, often with middle- and lower-class followings, then confronted the power and policies of established elites. Presenting themselves as friends of the common people, "Reliefers" sponsored special benefit legislation, including paper money, legal tender, and other fiscal-monetary measures to lighten the burden of the lower classes.[3] Taxes in hard money were a natural issue for them to seize upon.

Patrons of Hard Money Taxes

In 1781 Robert Morris, the wealthy merchant-financier and federal superintendent of finance (1781–84), persuaded the Pennsylvania assembly, with its recently acquired Republican majority, to enact hard money taxes into law.[4] Supporting Morris in this endeavor were wealthy Philadelphia lawyers George Clymer and James Wilson, and merchant-banker Thomas Fitzsimons. Morris, Clymer, Fitzsimons, and Wilson were chieftains of the recently organized Republican party, which was contesting the Constitutionalists, a popular party of artisans, small professionals, and farmers who had organized in 1776 to uphold the new majoritarian state constitution. In the fall 1780 state legislative elections, candidates backed by the Morris-headed Republican party won a majority of legislative seats, and the party's leadership took control of the state assembly. But their position was not secure, and in October 1784 they lost control of the assembly to the Constitutionalists.[5]

After the turmoil of the Revolution, power in South Carolina's first postwar legislature came to rest in the survivors of the upper-class oligarchy that had dominated the legislature before the Revolution. Principals included the Rutledge brothers (John, Hugh, and Edward), the Pinckneys (Thomas, Charles, and Charles Cotesworth), John Mathews, Thomas Bee, Thomas Heyward, Christopher Gadsden, and Dr. David Ramsay. When their hard-money taxes threatened rural constituents with bankruptcy, Reliefers became active and the elite eased the pressure.[6] A different set of events occurred in Confederation Rhode Island, where a coalition of the state's wealthiest, most prominent lawyers, merchants, and bankers from Providence and Newport and other seaport towns controlled the state government. Included in this group were Governor William Greene, Jabez Bowen, William Bradford, William Channing, James Mitchell Varnum, Welcome Arnold, and Nicholas and John Brown. In April 1786, amidst much rural distress over taxes, the voters returned a Reliefer majority to power, and the coalition became the minority.[7]

In Massachusetts an urban merchant-lawyer-professional establishment controlled the senate, but the house of representatives was changeable, and the popular John Hancock, a political maverick, was in the governor's chair (1780–85). Such notables as John Lowell, Caleb Davis, William and Samuel Phillips, Nathaniel Gorham, David Sewall, Theophilus Parsons, and James Bowdoin were either members of the state government or influential behind the scenes. In the 1785 elections, the elite strengthened their power when Bowdoin was chosen governor, but in March 1787 the voters turned Bowdoin out of office and returned a sizable number of Reliefers to both the house and senate.[8]

Philadelphia's urban-commercial political elite has recently been described as obsessed with wealth and social status.[9] A closer look shows more complex motivation. The desire for wealth, status, and recognition animated some. But the values of an upper-class patrician code required men of wealth and talent to serve their communities and the lower classes. The Enlightenment improvement societies of the Confederation era are the best proof of this generalization. Nearly every important member of the elite just named was an officer or member of one or more of the Enlightenment improvement societies that blossomed during the 1780s decade.

The roster of six Philadelphia improvement societies demonstrates this point (see appendix 2). Except for the American Philosophical Society (a joint Republican-Constitutionalist organization), each of these societies—

the Library Company of Philadelphia, the Philadelphia Society for the Promotion of Agriculture, the Philadelphia Dispensary, the Society for Political Inquiries, and the Pennsylvania Society for the Encouragement of Manufactures and Useful Arts—was an organization in which members of this upper-class elite alone were active. Republican party chieftain George Clymer played a role in five of these societies; Robert Morris and James Wilson, also Republican party chieftains, played roles in four; Henry Hill, Charles Thomson, William Bingham, Samuel Powell, and John Dickinson in two; and Thomas Fitzsimons, Thomas Willing, and other Philadelphia notables, in one each.

South Carolina's lawyer-planter elite were also much involved with improvement societies and projects. During the 1780s Rutledges, Pinckneys, Thomas Heyward, John Mathews, and Thomas Bee revitalized the Charleston Library Society (a pre-Revolution library and scientific society), restored the Mount Sion Society (an education society), and founded the South Carolina Society for Promoting and Improving Agriculture and other Rural Concerns.[10]

In Rhode Island, Providence and Newport merchants, lawyers, and bankers Governor William Greene, Jabez Bowen, William Bradford, William Channing, James Mitchell Varnum, Welcome Arnold, and Nicholas, John, Moses, and Joseph Brown were, to use James Branch Hedges's term, "men of civic responsibility" who financed and revitalized the College of Rhode Island, restored library companies, and founded and improved schools.[11]

The Massachusetts gentry founded the American Academy of Arts and Sciences (1780), the Massachusetts Humane Society, the Massachusetts Historical Society, the Massachusetts Society for Promoting Agriculture, and The Phillips Andover (1778) and Phillips Exeter (1781) academies. The roster of gentlemen involved in these improvement undertakings represents a *Who's Who* of the Massachusetts political establishment. Thus the mainstay of the American Academy of Arts and Sciences was James Bowdoin, the wealthy Boston merchant and governor at the time of Shays's Rebellion; also prominent in the Academy were John Lowell, Theodore Sedgwick, Robert Treat Paine, Francis Dana, Jonathan Jackson, Caleb Strong, Samuel Phillips, and David Sewall. The Humane Society had among its members Bowdoin, Lowell, Dana, Jackson, Paine, and Sewall, plus Rev. Jeremy Belknap, Samuel Breck, Caleb Davis, Stephen Higginson, and Benjamin Lincoln. Samuel Phillips, founder of Andover Academy, was the longtime president of the state senate. The principal force behind the Massachusetts Society for Promoting Agriculture was the Boston lawyer-politician, John Lowell, and behind the Massachusetts Historical Society, Rev. Jeremy Belknap.[12]

Popular Politicians

The popular politicians of Pennsylvania, South Carolina, Rhode Island, and Massachusetts came from different backgrounds and had different motives for objecting to the hard money taxes of the postwar era. The easiest to understand are those from rural areas with firsthand knowledge of the difficulty of earning hard coin in the cash-depleted rural economy of the 1780s. Sympathy for their poorer neighbors and a concern that the lower classes would rebel guided their relief activism. Reliefers from urban areas are more difficult to decipher but were motivated mainly by politics. Doubting the loyalty to the Republic of the wealthy elite class, they courted rural votes in order to check their adversaries' political power. Relief measures would also increase the support of the middle and lower classes for their state governments—what Edward Countryman has identified for the New York Clinton party as a strategy of legitimating the new government by "popular measures."[13] More firmly and accurately than upper-class leaders, these rural and urban Reliefers grasped the reality of how heavy taxation could threaten the livelihoods of rural dwellers. Rather than be stripped of their property by tax auction sales, farmers, rural artisans, and laborers would take the law into their own hands and resist the new state governments of the Confederation by physical force.

In Pennsylvania during the 1780s the Constitutionalist party carried the relief banner. The party had been organized to secure the state's new majoritarian assembly-centered government from replacement by a more balanced tripartite form preferred by the elite (the Republicans criticized the 1776 state constitution as excessively dependent on popular opinion). Party leadership then had gravitated from the radical artisans who founded the party into the hands of middle-class Philadelphia professionals and merchants, including state supreme court justice George Bryan, College of Philadelphia president Rev. John Ewing, Dr. James Hutchinson, Dr. William Shippen, and merchant Charles Pettit. The party's high command also included country leaders from central and western Pennsylvania—William Findley of Westmoreland County, John Smiley of Fayette County, and Robert Whitehill of Cumberland County. The western wing's ability to communicate with eastern urban Constitutionalist leaders explains the party's support for rural tax relief.[14]

Philadelphia's urban Constitutionalist party leaders seem unlikely friends of the farmer and rural artisan. But their support for relief is to be explained by larger Constitutionalist party objectives. From the beginning of the Revolution, party leaders had courted middle- and lower-class support for Pennsylvania's annually elected assembly-centered state government. Relief for distressed farmers would demonstrate the new government's responsiveness and thus further this objective.

Constitutionalist leaders also distrusted the great wealth, elegance and sophistication, and haughty demeanor of Morris, Clymer, and their political allies. Upper-class Republican chieftains seemed out of touch with the common people and politically unreliable. Some Constitutionalists even suspected Morris and Wilson of plotting to discredit republican government by deliberately driving the common people into riot and rebellion.[15] Constitutionalists thus bent much effort toward controlling the all-important assembly by building a statewide party and agitating a variety of issues. The political attacks on "the present Aristocratical Faction," on Robert Morris's Bank of North America as the source of "fatal effects upon the community" (1784–85), and on Republican proposals to reinstate "Tory" Quaker nonjurors to full voting status (1783–86) were part and parcel of this vote-getting strategy. Lighter taxes, tax postponements, paper money loans, and other relief proposals were part of it also. ("If some of our gentlemen knew how hard it is for their constituents to pay taxes, they would be more frugal of the treasury.")[16]

South Carolina had urban and rural popular politicians who championed relief, but they were not organized or united. By contrast with Pennsylvania's Constitutionalists, Carolina Reliefers were a mixed assortment of middle-class politicians who operated independently of each other. Commodore Alexander Gillon, a Dutch immigrant ship captain, self-made merchant, and owner of extensive property in Charleston and the country, made a career of attacking the "nabob," "Aristocratical gentry" headed by the Rutledges, Pinckneys, Governor John Mathews, and Thomas Bee. Nursing personal grievances against these "haughty lordlings," Gillon doubted their commitment to popular government and believed them too high-toned to be trusted with the common person's everyday struggles. Part of his strategy was to promote formation of marine societies composed of Charleston maritime artisans and seamen in order to pressure the assembly. Gillon was also at the ready to fault upper-class tax policy and on the alert for rural votes to bolster his position in the assembly. Other Reliefers in the Palmetto State included Aedanus Burke, an Ireland-born lawyer and state superior court justice; Thomas Sumter, the former Revolutionary guerilla general and up-country planter; and Rawlins Lowndes, a former Loyalist who was first elected to the assembly in 1786. Quite independently of each other, Gillon, Burke, Sumter, Lowndes, and others championed tax reliefs for rural Carolina.[17]

Reliefer forces in Rhode Island constituted a different cast of characters. They were small-town politicians with roots in the state's country towns. Watching neighbors struggle with heavy taxes, in March 1786 they organized a "country party," formed an election ticket, campaigned on a program of "relief for the distressed," and captured control of both legislative houses and the governorship. Although information about them is scanty, their major leaders included Jonathan J. Hazard, George Irish, Elijah Cobb, John Gardner, James Arnold, and the Newport merchant-farmer and former Patriot leader, John Collins. After turning the upper-class leadership out of office in the April 1786 state election, they legislated a relief program that suspended tax collection and issued £100,000 in legal tender paper money for farmers to borrow.[18]

In Massachusetts, Reliefers were also small-town country politicians who spoke for the state's poorer, more isolated rural areas against the government's tax policies. Examples who served in the house and senate are Sutton's Amos Singletary, Leicester's Colonel Seth Washburn, Rutland's John Fessenden, and Danvers's Colonel Israel Hutchinson. Men of some property themselves, they worked their own farms, probably with the help of hired hands. By the very fact of their residence in these poorer towns, they knew the hardships of rural life in a way the urban elite did not. Seeing how the state's property and poll taxes were grinding down their poorer neighbors, they introduced relief measures to postpone tax deadlines, abate taxes for individual towns, reduce the salaries of government officials, reduce the value of the consolidated state debt from its stated value to its market value in order to tap revenue from a state excise-impost fund, and issue government paper money payable for taxes. But without a party organization, they could not build consensus or maintain discipline; hence the dozens of Reliefers who passed through the Massachusetts house never united around a common program, much less voted one into law. When Shays's Rebellion rocked the state government, however, they built organizations at the county level and challenged upper-class leadership more effectively.[19]

Reliefer politicians also operated individually, through political clubs, or through nascent parties in the other states of Confederation America. In New York, George Clinton's semiorganized country party of rural politicians enacted relief policies that relied heavily on the state's lucrative impost, a paper money issue, and tax reductions for middle and small landholders. In Maryland, Samuel Chase pursued tax reliefs; in Virginia, Patrick Henry; in North Carolina, Timothy Bloodworth; in Georgia, George Walton; in New Jersey, Abraham Clark; and in Connecticut, General James Wadsworth.[20]

Some historians label these men "agrarian-localists" and explain their politics by citing the narrow isolation of their rural lives and their alleged indifference to national affairs. In this view, their opposition to federal taxes, the proposed 5 percent federal impost, and the federal Constitution is explained as the natural outgrowth of a rural lifestyle and their circumscribed experience. But these Reliefers were not indifferent to Congress's financial requirements. Some cobbled relief for their rural constituents with requisitions for Congress. Thus Governor Clinton's administration in New York lightened land and poll taxes but made substantial contributions from the state impost to the federal treasury.[21] The Constitutionalist assembly leader Charles Pettit eased the currency shortage in Pennsylvania by crafting a bill that temporarily assumed the federal debt owed Pennsylvania creditors, paid interest to these creditors in newly printed state paper money, and loaned the new state paper money to farmers for taxes. But Pettit's legislation would devolve the assumed federal debt back to Congress once the economy had recovered and taxation had resumed.[22]

Battles over tax policy polarized the politics of the Confederation era, in part because the stakes seemed so high. Reliefers deeply mistrusted the commitment of their adversaries to the Republic, some even believing that taxes were designed to provoke the people to violence, thus discrediting republican government. Upper-class notables believed that Reliefers were playing politics with the tax issue; taxes were too important, too indispensable to the security and future of the Republic to be thus politicized. ("Your Excellency well knows that it is common for representatives to aim at popularity by lessening or procrastinating the Taxes of their Constituents.")[23] As the political combat continued, party-building and party agitation further nourished suspicion and mistrust.[24] Partly because tax relief seemed to encourage popular indolence and profusion ("corruption of morals"), partly because they had so little experience with party-forming behavior and agitation, upper-class notables perceived their Reliefer adversaries as "factious" and "turbulent" politicians who made careers by destabilizing the government's operations and weakening its authority. ("Yet a serious & determined Opposition [to the federal Constitution] may be expected, from a Class of people in each state—whose Political existance depends upon Anearchy & Confusion.")[25] Such mistrust, such misperception of sordid, even sinister purpose, echoes the mistrust and suspicion that fed the Federalist-Republican party conflict of the 1790s and early 1800s. Exactly as in the 1790s, the roots of this mistrust are to be found partly in clashes over one issue (that is, tax policy), but partly also in clashes over a whole range of issues. Exactly as in the 1790s the party building and popular agitation resorted to by each side further fueled and fed this partisanship.

Persistence of Elites' Support for Taxes

Despite the risks of handing their political enemies a winning issue, the elites pursued hard money taxes when they saw an opportunity. This persistence requires some further explanation. In part, it followed from a clear-eyed recognition that the hard money from state requisitions was the only way Congress could make interest and principal payments to its Dutch and French creditors overseas. Because paper money finance had failed ("not worth a Continental"), hard money from the states also seemed the best way for Congress to finance its small army and pay its domestic creditors as well. And although state imposts and excises bore the main brunt of interest payments on funded state debts, hard money from direct taxes was needed as supplementary interest payments to state creditors. These important policy goals help explain why hard money taxes were pursued despite the political dangers they posed.

Some historians hold that the states' postwar fiscal programs were primarily designed to put scarce hard money into the pockets of well-to-do investors who had purchased large quantities of the state and federal debt. Undeniably some of the advocates of hard money taxes owned state and federal debt certificates that would appreciate in value by regular interest payments in specie. But interest payments to state and federal creditors represented only a relatively small proportion of what these direct specie taxes were earmarked for; other requirements bulked larger. While Congress needed money to pay the annual interest owed domestic creditors, the largest part of the specie in the federal budget was earmarked to pay Congress's French, Dutch, and Spanish creditors, the federal army, Indian tribes, and the salaries of federal officials.[26] And when these taxes were first enacted, state debt holdings were too small and widely dispersed to be credible as a source of motivation; only later did state debts become concentrated in fewer hands. Furthermore, the state debt does not explain the motivation of Pennsylvania's hard money taxes, which were almost entirely earmarked for Congress.[27]

The persistence of the patrons of hard money taxes also resulted from their conviction that such taxes would spur the economy and thus make taxes easier to pay. By paying the annual interest on state debts in specie and enabling Congress to pay domestic creditors in the same medium, the state governments would signal a mistrustful commercial community that property rights under the new popular assemblies would be protected and that the inflated money of the Revolution would be stabilized. Thus reassured, cautious merchants would extend credit and invest in commercial and manufacturing enterprises, and the entire economy including the farming sector would prosper—the trickle-down effect.[28]

In fact, members of this elite regarded taxes as a prosperity-producing stimulant to lower-class industriousness and saving. Alexander Hamilton justified an early proposal for creating a permanent federal debt to be funded by permanent *state* revenues by arguing that taxes would "be a spur to industry" and thus instill a healthy "habit of labour in the people." Robert Morris also believed that taxes would counter the natural human disposition to "indolence and profusion" and stimulate the economy's re covery. Hard money taxes, Morris believed, would force individual productivity and saving, increase the total volume of exports and decrease imports, and thus bring specie into the economy from trade abroad. Whether through renewed commercial confidence or the common people's increased productivity and saving, taxes would thus produce prosperity and contentment for all classes.[29]

The prevalent upper-class view held that payment of taxes was a matter of personal discipline and effort and that failure to pay was entirely an individual's own fault. When sums of unpaid taxes accumulated, upper-class leaders blamed not depressed agricultural prices, frozen credit, or unprofitable markets, but the indolence and extravagance of individuals. Because tax relief by the state governments would merely encourage further indolence and extravagance, firm collection of hard money taxes seemed a logical cure. (By a similar doctrine of individual responsibility, U.S. and British upper classes in the eighteenth century explained poverty as a function of individual moral failure.)[30] The antidote for the mounting arrearages of unpaid taxes was not tax relief, but firmer collection by the government.

Taxation for some of the elite also became a practical test of the workability of the Confederation system of state republics, which were regarded as "experiments." Europeans depicted republican government as unsuitable for the modern state and cited the failed republics of ancient and recent history as proof that such a system had fatal flaws. Republican government might be appropriate for the tiny, homogeneous Swiss city-republics and for Venice, the Netherlands, and a few other small states. Limited constitutional monarchy was better suited for larger, more populous countries. Because republican governments were chosen by election rather than by hereditary descent, because the voters were volatile and changeable, republics seemed less stable, less energetic, less able to mobilize national power and resources than the nonrepublican systems of Europe.[31]

Taxation thus became a test of whether a continental confederation of state republics could effectively secure the independence and vital interests of the new United States. In 1783 Matthew Ridley, a Baltimore merchant and manufacturer, declared in a letter from Paris that the people of his country must begin to pay taxes, or "the business is yet but very imperfectly done." He appeared certain that France would "give no more Money. They have refused some time since.—Peace is in a manner made; of course France concludes now we must help ourselves—the Grand cause for which the War began is settled—Hopes and Fears are no longer to be worked upon; & unless the Citizens of America begin to see the necessity of providing Funds themselves & will do it, they have fought to little purpose & confusion worse than any they have yet experienced must ensue."[32]

But to describe the major players, their assumptions, their policy measures, and their perceptions of each other is prologue. The real drama would begin when pressure from the center produced popular resistance. Shaken by taxpayer violence, each of the governments in question would do an about-face and relax its collection operations. This retreat from vigorous enforcement, not indifference to federal requisitions, explains the requisition system's breakdown.

THE STATES

★ 5 ★

PENNSYLVANIA

THE HISTORY of taxation in Confederation Pennsylvania demonstrates how the pressure-resistance-retreat process spelled the failure of the requisition system. Historians of Confederation Pennsylvania have not focused on the role of taxes in the Republican-Constitutionalist party struggle. Standard accounts describe such issues as the Constitutionalists' repeal of the charters of Robert Morris's Bank of North America (1784–85) and of the College of Philadelphia (1779); the fight over the Republicans' repeal of Constitutionalist test laws that had disfranchised many potential Republican voters (1784–87); and the Republican attempts to replace the 1776 assembly-centered state constitution with a balanced three-branch system.[1] Yet the records of the assembly, of the Supreme Executive Council, and of local tax and judicial officers and the centrality of fiscal-monetary policy revealed in a recent study of Constitutionalist fiscal-monetary measures during the Revolution (1776–83) indicate that taxation was *the* most important issue.[2]

When the Republicans gained a majority in the state assembly elections in October 1780, they enacted the state's first specie taxes since the colonial era. (The taxes levied by the Constitutionalist majority during its term of power, 1776–80, were payable in Continental and state paper money, not gold and silver specie.)[3] Guided by Robert Morris, who delayed taking office as federal superintendent of finances until legislation for "effective Taxes in hard money" had been enacted, the Republican-controlled assembly first repealed an existing state tender law and a state embargo and then legislated the first of three tax levies in specie coin, each of which committed revenues for Congress's treasury. Together, the specie taxes of 1781, 1782, and 1783 totaled £745,297.[4]

While acknowledging that specie was scarce, Morris insisted that any able-bodied householder who was industrious and thrifty could pay. Hard money taxes, Morris argued, would spur the people into greater productivity and translate into specie-producing exports to the West Indies and Europe. Morris even predicted that specie taxes would prove so beneficial and bring so much coin and other "advantages flowing from these foundations" to Pennsylvania that the state would become a model for her sister states.[5] Whether the Pennsylvania government had the political will to collect such taxes was yet to be tested.[6]

Pennsylvania's tax system had ingenious mechanisms for collection that put enforcement in the hands of local collection officers elected by the voters. Management of collection at the local level was vested in county boards of popularly elected commissioners (three-year terms); in turn, these elected officials directed township assessors and collectors, who performed the actual work of assessment and collection. Thus, when the assembly voted taxes, it assigned each of Pennsylvania's twelve counties an apportioned quota based on population and assessed property. The county board of commissioners would then order township assessors to assess each taxable person's real and personal property and order collectors to carry out collection. County commissioners also appointed and discharged collectors and assessors, heard complaints about assessments, and granted exemptions.

The law also provided a method for forcing payment from a defaulting taxable. Much as happens today in debt foreclosure actions, the town collector was required to seize a defaulter's personal property, real estate, or both by legal attachment and put them up for sale at public auction. To ensure that collectors did their duty, the law made them personally liable. If they failed to collect the required amount, *their* property was to be attached by the county sheriff acting on orders of the county commissioners. If this still did not bring payment, the collectors' property was to be sold at auction, and the proceeds applied to make up the deficiency.

Centralized oversight of this county-centered system was vested in the top level of the Pennsylvania executive—the elected twelve-person Supreme Executive Council. Because county commissioners were locally elected every three years and could not be removed from office except at election time, they could remain in office as long as their conduct satisfied the voters. But the Supreme Executive Council was required to levy a fine of up to £500 on an indulgent or negligent commissioner, and to order the county sheriff to attach the property of any commissioner up to that amount. If, in turn, the Supreme Executive Council dragged its feet, the all-powerful assembly could order the council to perform its duty. But the law had loopholes. Reporting and accounting were not effectively provided for, so the legal responsibility for uncollected taxes could be evaded. Without complete financial data, the only way the Supreme Executive Council could discipline local commissioners was to order the state's attorney general to sue them for neglect of duty. Because local juries determined the final judgment in such cases, and because juries often favored indulgent commissioners, this system was not as reliable (or draconian) as the more centralized systems of Rhode Island and Massachusetts.[7]

The manuscript minute books kept by these county boards and available on microfilm in the Pennsylvania Historical and Museum Commission at Harrisburg afford fascinating glimpses into how this system worked at the local level. A few generalizations may be made. First, during the early part of the Confederation era, tax collectors faced many obstacles when they dunned the farmers, laborers, and artisans of rural Pennsylvania for money.

> Josiah Ferguson Collectr of Plumsted appeared—and made Complaint against Matthew Hughes who refused to deliver the Goods sold for his Taxes that he had Locked up the Bars Gates Doors &c—Commrs Granted him a Special Warrant, ordering and Empowering him in the Day time to break Open any Gate Door Lock and &c that might be in his way. To Deliver the Good sold. (Bucks County Commissioners)

> The Collectors of the aforesd Townships appd and made complaint of their Delinquency in payg off the amot of their Taxes &c. that the Money could not be procured of the Inhabitants, without greatly Distressing of them &c but the Collectors of this Tax had cheafly paid, and would settle off at December Court &c. (Bucks County Commissioners)

> The collectors of the Townships aforesd appeared and made Complaint the Tax was not to be had—in so short a time as was limited by Law or their Warrants but they was a doing every thing that Lay in their Power to procure the Tax &c. The people were willing to pay but not able—this was their General complaint—The commrs agreed and allowed them untill 10th December next &c &c. (Bucks County Commissioners)[8]

Second, tax collectors seized and sold at auction the property of many rural folk who did not pay.

> Phillips Smith Collector of Richland and Adam Shib of Rockhill appeared before the Board of Commissioners—and Laid their Accounts of their Seizures and Sales made by them of Sundry Persons who refused to pay their Taxes. (Bucks County Commissioners)

> Thomas Wright Collector of Plumstead Township laid before the Board of Commissioners an account of all the Seizures & Sales made on sundry Persons in sd. Township who refused to pay their Tax. (Bucks County Commissioners)

> The Collectors of Hilltown, Beeminster, and New brittain appeared likewise [before the Board] and produced their Bills of Seizure & Sales—but not their Receipts of their full payment. (Bucks County Commissioners)[9]

Third, when township collectors failed to deliver their money quotas, county boards summoned them for questioning and issued execution warrants that directed county sheriffs to attach their property. The boards then used the threat of sale as a club to force the collector to seize and sell the property of taxables.

Issued a Venditioni Exponas Against Phillips Smith a late Collector of Richland Township for Deficiency of Taxes—1781 Lev'd; And sd Execution was handed to Alexander Hughes to hand to the Sheriff unless the Tax was Dischargd in a short time &c. (Bucks County Commissioners)

Having thus met, the Comrs inquired into the Arrearages of Taxes, due by the Collectors, Orders were given to the Clerk, to make out Writs against the Delinquents which being done, and the Writs signed by the Commrs and delivd. into the hands of the Sheff, who was ordered to make return to the Commrs. on the 24th day of March inst. (York County Commissioners)

Employed in Settling with the Collectors. The Clk is ordered to issue writs immediately against every Delinquent Collr for all Taxes deficient. Except the last County Tax. (Chester County Commissioners)

[The Board] proceeded to Examine the Treasurers Books of Delinquent Collectors of Classes & other Taxes wherein they found several Delinquents. Orders were given to the Clerk, to make out Writs against those Delinquents, the Writs being wrote, signed by the Comms & delivered to the Sheriff, directing him to notify the Commis of his Proceedings against the Eight or ninth day of October next following. (York County Commissioners)[10]

Fourth, despite allegations that tax delinquency resulted from poor work habits and extravagance, too many taxables appeared in person before the boards of commissioners to plead for relief to be characterized en masse as shirkers and spendthrifts.

Several Persons appeared here this Day on account of their class Tax, and made complaint before the board of commrs. that their stock of Cattle &c were much Diminished on acct of being sold by the Collectors for the Last State Taxes &c which they thought a hardship to pay the Tax for them— when being sold for the sd. Taxes &c &c. The Comms made such Releif as they thought proper &c. (Bucks County Commissioners)

Negroe Bill in Middletown Township made Complaint that all his goods & chattles were seized and sold for former Taxes and that he was not abal to pay any more without Distressing his family &c—Comms agreed to consider the same complaint and make what Relief they could with doing Justice to the publick &c. (Bucks County Commissioners)

Some Persons from Lowr Makefield Township appeard and made Complaint they was not at Present Abble to pay the Taxes, and Desird that the Commis would not permit the Collector to strain from them &c. (Bucks County Commissioners)[11]

Measured by the percentages of returns during the Republicans' as-
cendency (1781–84), however, this system generated uneven results.
Comparison of monies received at the central treasury up to 1784 show
that Constitutionalist taxes in paper money had a much higher collection
rate than did Republican-legislated specie taxes. Of the total payments
made in Continental and state paper money taxes since 1778 (including
several Constitutionalist-levied taxes), the counties paid 85 percent. By
contrast, Republican specie taxes yielded a comparatively low 36 percent,
leaving 64 percent of the total due in specie still to be collected (see
table 5).

County by county, the collection percentages show significant sectional
disparities also. While all the county governments had substantial deficits,
the deficits of the central and western counties (York, Cumberland, Bedford, Northumberland, Westmoreland, and Washington) were proportionately greater than those of the eastern counties (Philadelphia city and
county, Bucks, Chester, Lancaster, Berks, and Northampton) (see table
6). Difficult transportation, inaccessible markets, and especially the inability of farmers and artisans in the rural central and western parts of the
state to obtain specie either by marketing their produce or by borrowing
caused these deficit differentials. In addition, the postwar trade deficit with
Great Britain and Europe drained cash out of the economy, which in turn
resulted in lower agricultural prices.

While acknowledging that these structural factors made paying taxes
more difficult, Republicans held that good work habits, initiative, per-

TABLE 5.
PENNSYLVANIA TAXES COLLECTED AND IN ARREARS,
1778 TO MARCH 1783 (AS OF 1 AUGUST 1784)
(PERCENTAGES IN PARENTHESES)

Taxes	Specie	Continental Paper	State Paper
Total Levied	$1,988,943 [£747,297][a]	$56,061,997 [£20,996,995]	$980,640 [£367,281]
Collected	718,385 (36) [269,058]	47,619,712 (85) [17,835,098]	615,702 (62) [230,600]
In Arrears	1,271,558 (64) [476,239]	8,442,265 (15) [3,161,897]	364,938 (38) [136,681]

Source: Report of Assembly Committee on Tax Collection Arrears, introduced 1 December 1784, Pennsylvania Assembly Minutes, 1784–85, 1st sess., 49–52, 72–74.
[a] Indicates Pennsylvania money of account.

TABLE 6.
PENNSYLVANIA TAXES IN ARREARS BY COUNTY
(AS OF 1 AUGUST 1784)
(IN PERCENTAGES)

County	Specie Due	Continental Paper Due	State Paper Due	Total Taxes Due
EASTERN COUNTIES				
Philadelphia (city and co.)	44	0	7	1
Bucks	44	6	17	8
Chester	49	7	33	9
Lancaster	75	0	51	3
Berks	77	14	25	17
Northampton	67	6	28	9
CENTRAL AND WESTERN COUNTIES				
York	79	27	66	30
Cumberland	95	23	86	26
Bedford	95	94	89	92
Northumberland	98	99	93	99
Westmoreland	100	100	100	100
Washington	99	na	na	99

Source: Report of Assembly Committee on Tax Collection Arrears, introduced 1 December 1784, *Pennsylvania Assembly Minutes*, 1784–85, 1st sess., 49–52, 72–74.

sonal thrift and saving, and honest, frugal living—were more important. Like poverty, tax delinquency was viewed by Pennsylvania's wealthy class as a failure more of the individual than of the system or of society.[12] So convinced was the Republican elite of the validity of its position that in 1784 its members went on record that "the blessings of a general peace and a free commerce puts it in the power of every county to make good former [tax] deficiencies."[13]

This background makes the Republican attempt to squeeze hard money from the people of rural Pennsylvania by forced collection understandable.

Pressure

As early as January 1781, the assembly expressed concern that "many of the public officers" had not submitted their tax collection accounts. Yet, the assembly resolved the following November, "solid revenues" must be provided for. In February 1782 the assembly urged "the several county commissioners, to expedite the collection of the arrearages of the eighteen-penny taxes in specie, according to the laws now in force." In August 1782 the assembly asked "all the executive officers of this state, to urge, and to all the good citizens thereof, to contribute to the punctual, effectual, and speedy collection of public taxes." By September 1782 the assembly was ready to adopt a more forceful approach. When the Ways and Means Committee tersely deplored "the delay and neglect which often take place in laying and collecting the public taxes" and recommended that this tendency be "radically cured and prevented," the assembly accepted the committee's recommendation that "the executive, in every branch, should faithfully and punctually comply with the directions of the laws." By formal resolution, the assembly then directed the Supreme Executive Council to "inquire into the conduct of the executive officers of government, especially such as are officers of revenue; and without delay or favor cause the laws to be put in force against all delinquents."[14]

Thus directed, the council could have ordered the state attorney general to begin legal suits against boards of deficient counties. But because the twelve-person council was closely divided between Republican and Constitutionalist members, the threat of prosecution after several months' delay was the most that could be carried. The year before (December 1781), the council had circularized the county boards "to use the utmost possible exertions to cause the several taxes now due and the fines on the delinquent classes to be collected as soon as possible."[15] Now, slowed by partisan infighting, the council delayed until May 1783 before ordering its secretary, John Armstrong, to warn the boards. Unless "every possible exertion be made in the collection of public taxes," Armstrong wrote, and "should not the arrears due upon the class & Effective Supply Taxes be immediately discharged, [the SEC] will feel themselves constrained to adopt a more decisive line of conduct & exert those powers, with which they are invested by law."[16] A similar circular, described by a recipient as "very feeling and threatening," was sent the following July.[17] Thus, in August 1783, the president of the Supreme Executive Council, John Dickinson, could report to the assembly that "since your recess, we have diligently endeavoured to forward the collection of public taxes, of which we hope your honorable house will be convinced by the enclosed papers.— The deficiencies in several parts of the state are still considerable."[18]

Intending to lay the legal groundwork for yet stronger action, the Republican assembly at its fall session instructed the Ways and Means Committee to "form an estimate of the deficiencies, throughout the state, of taxes directed to be laid for continental and state purposes, since the revolution." More to the point, the committee was to report new legislation "for the effectual and speedy collection of such actual arrearages as may appear indispensable to this House."[19] Simultaneously, the Republican high command hatched a scheme for building public support for stronger legislation through that constitutional oddity provided for by Pennsylvania's 1776 state constitution—the Council of Censors.

Under the terms of the 1776 constitution, the Council of Censors, a temporary twenty-four person body, was to be elected every seven years to investigate and report the conduct of all legislative, executive, and judicial officials. In preparation for their contemplated tax enforcement legislation, the Republicans decided on a strategy of exposing the misdoings of Constitutionalist tax officials through a Council of Censors' investigation. Presumably, such exposure would outrage thrifty, diligent taxpayers who had paid their taxes promptly and also further justify the enactment of a stronger tax enforcement law.

Republican chieftains Thomas Fitzsimons, Samuel Miles, and Anthony Wayne tried, when they controlled the Council of Censors by one vote during the first session, to get reports published that called for a state constitutional convention and that condemned alleged misdoings and neglect of duty by county boards of commissioners and other tax collection officials, including Constitutionalist members of the Supreme Executive Council. When unforeseen events—a death and a resignation—changed the partisan lineup of the Council of Censors and gave the Constitutionalists a slim majority, this strategy failed.[20] Instead, the new Constitutionalist majority killed the two pending Republican reports that recommended both a constitutional convention and stronger legal powers for tax officials, replacing them with reports lauding the 1776 state constitution and indicting the existing and three previous Republican assemblies for alleged misdoings and abuse of power. Timing their action to coincide with the annual October 1784 state elections, the Constitutionalist Council of Censors' majority then ordered both their reports printed in English and German "for the purpose of being distributed among the people."[21]

Resistance

Republican hopes for stronger legislative action against delinquent taxables were further dashed when the Constitutionalists carried the October 1784 assembly elections. Instead of voting new coercive measures, the Constitutionalist assembly enacted a program of paper money tax relief that stymied Republican attempts to force collection.

By late 1783 the Supreme Executive Council's written warnings, circulated to all the county boards the previous May and July, had increased the pressure on taxpayers. With suits by the Supreme Executive Council now a possibility, commissioners pressured collectors more closely, and they in turn pressured their constituents. How much was squeezed from the people of rural Pennsylvania as a result cannot be determined, but the evidence indicates that auctions were held and some specie was produced. Once again the familiar tactic of having sheriffs attach collectors' property proved a handy club to force collectors into action.

In Bucks County, for example, the receipt of the council's July 1783 letter immediately prompted the board of commissioners to order "the Clerk to write Immediately to the Difft. Collectors, Ordering them to discharge the Taxes without Delay or Executions will be issued against them."[22] In the ensuing weeks, Bucks collectors held auction sales and squeezed enough additional specie from the county to enable the county treasurer to settle with the state treasurer, David Rittenhouse (August 1784), for the total sum of £8,393 specie.[23] Nevertheless, as the Bucks County board explained, although "the Collectors have been notified often, threatened, and summoned to answer for Delinquency," the board would not direct that collectors' property under execution be sold because it is "hard and impolitic to execute the Rigours of the Law upon the Collectors."[24]

In York County, where the tax deficits were very large, the county board put such heavy pressure on collectors that collectors removed "Goods to town, upward of twenty miles, on which they have distrained for the discharge of the Taxes." As in Bucks County, however, the York commissioners would not order collectors' property already under execution to be sold because it would force collectors to seize and sell massive amounts of property belonging to the county's farmers and rural mechanics. As the York board informed the council, the directive of 24 July was "very feeling and threatning, and if closely pursued ruinous to our County, few Individuals could escape the Gaol, money has no Circulation with our Inhabitants, as it can have in other more Populous Places."[25] At the same time other boards sent written pleas to the Supreme Executive Council for "indulgence from the Honorable Council, untill the people have time to carry what they can spare of their produce to Market and in the mean time we will not fail to use our Influence in raising the taxes of our County."[26]

Combined with the news from Philadelphia that new enforcement legislation was being planned, the action to force collection alarmed many rural folk and prompted them to look for ways to protect their farms and property. Petitions urging tax relief were drafted and sent to the government in Philadelphia in 1784.

> The prayer of your petitioners is that in your wisdom and justice (which they are certain you possess) such measures may be adopted as shall secure as much of their property as possible and alleviate their present burthen of taxes. (Sixty-two York farmers, May 1784)

> The Petition of divers inhabitants of the County of Westmoreland, Sheweth,

that we have for a considerable length of time Alarmingly seen and felt the dificulties which the Inhabitants of this County (amongst others) hath laboured under by the Privation, and want of Speacie. . . . Do therefore most earnestly Sollicit and intreat your Honourable house (as the alone means that Can Save this State from inevitable ruin) that you will be pleasd, as soon as possiable, to institute and open a loan office, for the accomadation of the Citizens and Inhabitants of this State upon the antient Safe and Suseseful plan. (Fifty-three Westmoreland farmers, August 1784)

That your Petitioners have for some Considerable time with Grief beheld and personally experienced the sad and awful effects occasioned to themselves and others by a General Scarcity of hard Money, so that public Trade and Private Transactions of Human Life is nearly reduced to a total stagnation, nor are our fears likely to subside, for at a Period not far Distant we have just reason to Dread a Complication of still more fatal Calamities. (Sixty Lancaster farmers, May 1784)[27]

Others tried more forceful tactics. Rather than have their stock, produce, and lands sold for much-reduced prices, some farmers simply refused to pay; some resorted to that classic tactic of rural neighbors faced with a farm auction—the no-bid covenant. This, as much as the shortage of cash, explains why the Cumberland County Board of Commissioners reported to President Dickinson that: "Collectors have Distrained and Could not sell any property for want of Buyers, some persons indeed who have demands on the Public think it very hard to pay taxes while large sums are due them." In York County, the collectors recorded: "Some class and other Collectors also attended who were sued, prayed longer time, that such Goods they had Distrained upon, could not be sold for want of Buyers and the Want of Cash." In Fayette County, a commissioner reported, "Some attempts have been made to raise the money by the sale of goods taken by the collectors for the taxes, but no one would bid for them. Thus the laws are eluded without being openly opposed."[28]

Physical obstruction was another weapon. In rural Westmoreland, a tax official trying to do his duty was confronted by a crowd; weapons at the ready, some fired over his head and forced him to flee. Thus obstructed, the Westmoreland board reported, "We could not proceed to Quota the County." Presumably intimidation explained why "many of the Assessors [are] not making any Returns" and why the board asked the council to "overlook the failures that we cannot possibly perform." In Fayette County, an official reported, "The County Commissioners are so much counteracted by the rabble of this country, that it appears hardly probable the Taxes will ever be collected on the present mode." Threats and intimidation had, he reported, been the tactic of the people of one town: "The terror of undertaking the duty of Collector, has determined several to refuse it under the high penalty annexed." Two men did take the job, "and these have both been robbed by some ruffians unknown, and in the night, of their Duplicates. The inhabitants of the other townships have not gone to such lengths, but complain so much of the hardship and the want of money that I fear very little is to be hoped from them."[29] Similarly in Washington County, obstruction hampered if not paralyzed the collection process. Assuring the council of its desire to carry out its duty "with the Greatest punctuality," the board reported that "the Distressed situation of our frontier County together with a Disspostion in a number of people for some time past to oppose taxation makes our Business very Difficult."[30]

The exact extent of this rural stonewalling and obstructionism is hard to gauge. Judging by the reports quoted, it was probably scattered, isolated, and unorganized. Yet its very occurrence shocked tax officials, who had no stomach for provoking further violence by forcing collection. Accordingly, if the report is accurate, by the spring of 1784 tax collection had virtually ceased throughout most of the state. Addressing the Pennsylvania president and council in April 1784, state treasurer David Rittenhouse declared: "Permit me, Sir, likewise to inform Council that there seems to be almost a total stop in the Collecting of Taxes."[31]

Retreat

Historians of the Pennsylvania party struggle rightly emphasize the decisive nature of the Republican defeat in the October 1784 elections. From an assembly majority of 38 to 29, the Republicans were reduced to a small minority of 19 to 57—a net increase of 28 Constitutionalist assembly seats. Several of the Constitutionalist gains came in rural counties (Lancaster, Chester, and York), but the party also swept the Philadelphia city and county elections.[32] The victory is best explained by the impact of the tax issue.

For two years before the election, Constitutionalist newspaper propagandists had been faulting the Republicans for rapaciously taxing the people. By 1784 the Republicans had become identified in the public mind as the party of heavy taxes and stern collection.[33]

Constitutionalist charges that Republican tax measures had stripped specie from the countryside combined with Constitutionalist promises of a paper money relief-recovery program that would fund debts hit home with rural and urban voters at the very period that auction sales threatened ruinous losses. The assembly's proceedings during its spring-summer 1784 session indicate that by then taxes had become a consuming issue. Committees reported on the rural obstruction of collection, petitions for tax relief were received and read, and the assembly devoted days to various loan office proposals before finally tabling a bill that would print and loan £100,000.[34] Other issues became prominent later in the summer, such as the college charter, repeal of the test laws, and a constitutional convention to replace the 1776 assembly-centered constitution. The Constitutionalists launched their first attacks on Morris's Bank of North America at this time as well. No doubt these issues contributed significantly to Constitutionalist election success.[35] But because they did not become prominent until late in the summer, they do not explain the first Republican election loss in Philadelphia that spring.[36] By then not only were rural voters worried over losing their stock and farms, but Philadelphia city and county voters were anxious at the reports of rural clamor and resistance to law. The breakdown of taxation throughout rural Pennsylvania conveyed a sense that the party of heavy taxes and stern enforcement had failed entirely to manage the state's finances. With Charles Pettit, reputedly Morris's equal in public finance, assuming Constitutionalist leadership in the assembly, the Constitutionalists offered an appealing agenda of public debt interest payments and tax relief that promised to get the economy and taxation moving again. Urban and rural voters alike would have found this Constitutionalist program attractive even if the test law, state constitution, and college charter had not become issues.

The Constitutionalists' new assembly majority converted the party's election promise of relief for farmers and interest payments to state creditors into law as soon as the new house convened in the fall. The foundations of their relief program were quickly laid—a combined debt-funding–paper money–tax relief bill. Becoming law at the second March 1785 session (the 1776 constitution mandated that no bill could become law until the session subsequent to its enactment), the measure provided for the printing and emission of £150,000 in paper bills to be paid as interest to state and federal public creditors who were Pennsylvania citizens and also to be offered as tax relief loans to farmers. This legislation *temporarily* assumed the federal debt owed to Pennsylvania citizens; combined this obligation with the existing state debt in a new consolidated state debt; and ordered that £100,000 of the newly struck paper money be paid by the state as interest to both sets of creditors. Further, it ordered that £50,000 more be loaned through special county loan office commissioners to farmers on the basis of land mortgages. In addition, it established a new tax of £76,945 to be annually levied and payable in these bills. The money was to be equivalent in value to gold and silver and made legally receivable for all taxes owed the state, past and present (including the arrearages), as well as for state impost and excise duties and payments for state lands. Finally, the legislation established new collection procedures that made tax collection more flexible and responsive to local conditions. Before a tax collector could seize the property of any delinquent for auction, he had to submit the delinquent's name to an elected county justice of the peace who would then decide whether the case was justified and issue a special warrant. Since county magistrates were popularly elected officials, this meant another protective barrier for any hard-pressed taxpayer against a too-zealous tax collector.[37]

At the same time, the Constitutionalist majority quashed another Republican move to force the payment of unpaid taxes. In December 1784 Republican floor leader Anthony Wayne proposed a series of resolutions that would have the assembly make the Supreme Executive Council renew the pressure on local collectors. These resolutions, introduced more to establish a record for the future than with any hope of current enactment, repeated the Republican contention that current commercial conditions made the payment of taxes in specie both possible and reasonable. Wayne, a former censor and longtime member of the Chester County legislative delegation, would have the assembly: (1) bar any new tax levies until the large outstanding arrearages had been fully collected; (2) direct the Supreme Executive Council "to cause the proper officers in the respective counties of this state, forthwith to collect the arrearages of taxes due by the individuals in their several respective counties and districts"; and (3) commit the assembly to "strengthen the hands of Council by a law adequate to the purpose" if that body "should be of opinion, that the laws now in force are insufficient to compel the payment of the taxes now due." Countering with their own softer language, the Constitutionalists suggested that the Supreme Executive Council "be earnestly desired to take the most speedy and effectual measures to cause the proper officers in the respective counties to collect and forward to the state treasury the arrearages of taxes now due" and to prepare a "just report of such other causes as may impede the final collection and payment into the treasury of any of the said arrearages." As soon as these resolutions were brought to the floor, Wayne again proposed that the assembly affirm the Republicans' position that "the blessings of a general peace and free commerce" enabled the counties to "make good former real deficiencies" and reiterated that new taxes ought not to be levied "without taking effectual measures at the same time to compel the speedy payment of such arrearages of taxes as remain justly due, from such members of the community as have hitherto made default." By a vote of 17 to 39, Wayne's substitute resolutions were voted down, and the original Constitutionalist resolutions passed.[38]

Even then the Republican leadership would not let go. Having gained just enough seats in the twelve-member Supreme Executive Council to elect their man John Dickinson as president in 1783, the Republicans tried to turn this slim majority in that body to advantage. Seizing the excuse presented by a partisan Constitutionalist assembly resolution that criticized the Republican-headed Supreme Executive Council for allegedly neglecting enforcement of the collection of taxes, the council prodded the county boards of commissioners again. That January (1785) a new circular was sent to county boards with instructions "that you proceed in the most effectual way to the Collection of taxes in your County" and warning that "to obviate all objection on this score hereafter, Council feel themselves called upon by this declaration of the Legislature to execute the Laws instantly, and without discrimination."[39]

The following July (1785) the council took the last step up the legal ladder by ordering the state attorney general to commence suits against the county commissioners for neglect of duty, resolving "that the Attorney General be and he is hereby instructed forthwith to commence such prosecutions as by the laws of this State he is authorized to institute, in order to compel the levying and raising of the said taxes."[40] Later that year and the following spring, Attorney General William Bradford, carrying out the council's orders, began several legal prosecutions. Suits for neglect of duty were entered before the state supreme court, sitting as a court of oyer and terminer, against the boards of commissioners of Philadelphia, Chester, York, and Cumberland. Apprised of these proceedings, the boards, in turn, summoned tax collectors and warned they would be dealt with "in the most strenuous terms" if they did not collect. But when a grand jury in Constitutionalist-controlled Cumberland County delivered a finding of "ignoramus," and the case was dismissed, the attorney general dropped the proceedings.[41] With the legal threat removed, the boards of commissioners could relax.[42]

Meanwhile, in the October (1785) elections, the Republicans recovered part of their former ground by gaining fourteen assembly seats, which gave them parity with the Constitutionalists.[43] Both Philadelphia city and county returned to the Republican column, and Robert Morris, George Clymer, and Thomas Fitzsimons were among the city's assembly delegates. This early reversal of fortune is best explained by the city's disenchantment with the Constitutionalists' handling of the state's ailing economy. Although the Constitutionalist paper money program was helping farmers, the well-to-do urban class deeply distrusted paper money, viewing it as a threat to property rights. After enactment of the funding–paper money relief program, credit in the city shrank,[44] and the Constitutionalist assembly's repeal of the charter of the Bank of North America (September 1785) made monied men even warier. Thus specie was hoarded or invested abroad, and even the artisans of Philadelphia, longtime Constitutionalist supporters, became concerned about credit and prices and began to back the Republicans.[45]

Yet rank-and-file Republican assembly members were not enthusiastic about any new attempt to squeeze more hard money from rural Pennsylvania if it meant risking another political backlash. This reluctance —and the assembly's evenly balanced numbers—explain the curiously cobbled and ambiguous law passed in March 1786, apparently with full Constitutionalist support. "An act to enforce the due collection and payment of Taxes within this Commonwealth" ostensibly provided Philadelphia officials with strong new powers to sue commissioners who allowed collectors to indulge taxables. The act began by condemning state officials who indulged people who had not paid their taxes. Such indulgence not only compromised "public measures," not only burdened those who paid their taxes, but operated "to the great distress of many persons who are liable for such arrears, and who could have discharged the same with less difficulty, if such illegal and false indulgences had not been practiced." But a key provision vested the power to settle the accounts of county treasurers in the hands of the state comptroller general, who was to report to the Supreme Executive Council "in order that such delinquent [commissioners] may be proceeded against according to law." Because no specific deadline stated when the state comptroller general had to settle these accounts, and because the Constitutionalist party leader, John Nicholson, currently held that office, the decision about which commissioners should be sued and when was his alone to make.[46]

But beyond this the Republican rank and file would not go. In April 1786 Republican assembly member George Logan, a Philadelphia patrician, proposed that any voting Pennsylvania citizen must, before he could vote in any state or local election, submit proof of having paid all his taxes due the previous year. Seconded by Robert Morris, Republican chair of the House Ways and Means Committee, and supported by member George Clymer, the measure was too extreme (and politically dangerous) for two-thirds of the Republican members, who joined with their Constitutionalist opponents to vote it down, 60 to 10.[47]

Indeed, most Republicans preferred to temporize rather than to risk another election turnover by renewing the taxation battle. In the October 1786 elections, the Republicans added to their numbers and regained control of the assembly. Yet still they did not press the collection issue. Nor did they reintroduce the fiscal-monetary budget proposal designed by Robert Morris for revamping the state's existing finances which the assembly had narrowly defeated in December 1785. Morris's proposal would have replaced the Constitutionalists' paper money funding system with a loan of Bank of North America money to federal creditors on the government's account, called in and destroyed the 1785 paper money, levied new specie taxes for Congress, invited payment of back taxes in Continental paper up to a certain date, and created an impost-excise sinking fund to support the combined federal-state debt.[48]

Yet the Republicans did help keep Congress afloat with small payments of specie. By allowing unpaid specie taxes previously committed for Congress's several requisitions to be paid in state paper money (1785 Paper Money Loan-Relief Act), the Constitutionalists had killed any prospect of collecting the specie that Congress required for requisitions. But the state impost on imports at the port of Philadelphia produced some specie. As these revenues had not been specifically committed to pay the interest on the funded state debt but were pooled with other revenues in the state's treasury, they could be appropriated as needed. While hardly more than a small fraction of the state's outstanding quota of unpaid requisitions, some state monies were transferred to Congress's account by order of the assembly (Republican assembly leader and Framer Thomas Fitzsimons played a major role in these transactions).[49] Thus, while most other state governments (except New York and Maryland) paid little or nothing into the federal treasury during the six-month period from 30 September 1786 to 1 April 1787, Pennsylvania paid $31,271 in specie. Yet taking the total figure of $643,619 in specie paid by the state to Congress's account over the six years between 1782 and 1788, this payment was substantially less than the state's six-month average of $53,634. The bulk of Republican legislators would not press for hard money for Congress either by enforcing collection of unpaid taxes in specie or by levying new taxes.

Far from demonstrating that indifference to Congress caused the requisition system to fail, the case of Pennsylvania indicates another explanation. Believing that firmly enforced tax collection could be translated into money for the federal treasury, the Republicans raised the pressure on the tax system until a rural backlash blocked collection and cost them control of the assembly. Then, when the Constitutionalists' paper money tax relief program took effect, the possibility that specie could be collected for Congress evaporated. Taken together, these events demonstrated to the Republican leadership the Pennsylvania government's structural weakness and instability. Even Robert Morris's less draconian financial reform proposal of 1785–86 (backed by Clymer and Fitzsimons, Federalist delegates to the Constitutional Convention all) failed to persuade timid Republican assembly members to make another try. Rather than force the issue, they preferred small contributions to Congress from the politically uncontroversial state impost. Direct specie taxes for federal requisitions could not be collected without measures that were far too risky.

★ 6 ★

SOUTH CAROLINA

D ESPITE differences between the states in economy, culture, and location, Confederation South Carolina has a history that closely par-
allels Pennsylvania's. Carolina's wealthy lawyer-planter elite, for example,
also imposed heavy postwar taxes in hard money that rural taxpayers could
not pay and that Reliefers made a political issue. By passing their own relief
program, however, the Carolina elite preempted the relief issue and clung
to power.

Early in the Confederation era, the South Carolina assembly levied the
first heavy property tax in hard money.[1] In a message to the general assembly (January 1783), the wealthy lawyer-planter Governor John Mathews recommended that provision be made for raising money to meet
both federal and state requirements. Submitting requests from the federal
superintendent of finance, Robert Morris, for requisitions totaling
$192,000, Mathews asked the legislature to consider a new tax act for "the
regular and substantial support of this Government, and [for] satisfying
the demands of the United States." The means by which this revenue was
to be raised, Mathews continued, was "a subject that ought to be treated
with the greatest tenderness, at the same time it requires firmness & decision."[2] Following the governor's cue, Carolina's assembly legislated a
direct tax, payable in specie, on property and slaves and a state impost,
also payable in specie, on imported foreign goods. The general assembly
funded the state's revolutionary war debt, allocated money from the state
impost for federal requisitions, and earmarked a total of $192,000 in its
budget for federal purposes.[3]

In March 1784 and again in March 1785 the general assembly levied
two more direct property taxes but lightened the burden by providing for
partial payment in special paper interest indents, a form of paper money
paid by the government as the annual interest on the state's funded debt.
Because the collection of specie under the 1783 act was lagging, and because the value of the paper indents would be supported by taxation, the
government authorized the 1784 and 1785 taxes to be paid in this paper.
The taxes levied by the 1784 and 1785 laws were also payable in specie,
but with specie at a high premium, paper indents were obviously the pre-

ferred mode of payment, and no specie was collected under the 1784 and 1785 acts.[4] Furthermore, for the first time in Carolina's history, provision was made for the assessment of lands for taxes according to quality and value rather than at a standard rate per acre. Both the 1784 and 1785 laws eased taxes on the middling and poorer classes, whose lands were less valuable than those of the wealthy rice-growing planter class. The elite's political adversaries claimed that these changes had been forced on the assembly by the backcountry membership, but the politically adroit elite assembly leadership were their active sponsors.[5]

When specie tax payments did not materialize, Carolina's patrician leadership also scaled down the state's specie contribution to Congress. In 1783 the assembly allocated the total sum of $192,000 (52 percent of its budget), as Superintendent Morris and Governor Mathews had recommended. But when the requisite amounts in direct hard money taxes could not be collected, the assembly reallocated the priorities of its 1784 and 1785 budgets for other state purposes. The 1784 budget reduced the proportion of revenue allocated for Congress from 52 percent to 28 percent. The 1785 budget made no provision for Congress at all; the income from the state impost was reassigned to pay the state's civil list, the interest of the state's foreign debt, and the interest of the state's domestic debt. None of the subsequent budgets (1786, 1787) made provision for any federal payments either.[6] The specie shortfall occurred despite a tax system that was more centralized, less susceptible to popular influence, and presumably more efficient than Pennsylvania's.

In Pennsylvania local tax collectors were appointed and directed by locally elected county boards of commissioners; in Carolina, the general assembly each year assigned a roster of tax collectors to each parish and district of the state. These collectors were required to post personal bonds that pledged the full, faithful performance of their duty and accepted legal liability for any deficiency. When notified by the two treasury commissioners headquartered at the capital at Charleston, collectors were to assess taxpayers' property, collect the tax, and return the sums to the central treasury by a certain date. If a taxable person did not pay his tax, the collector, after due warning, was to issue an attachment writ against the delinquent's land or other property; the writ would then be served by the parish or district constable or sheriff, who would seize and sell the property at auction or confine the delinquent to jail.[7]

But although smaller in per capita amounts than the taxes levied by Pennsylvania, Rhode Island, and Massachusetts, this first postwar tax in specie was a heavy personal burden for many planters and farmers in mid- and up-country rural Carolina. Even more than Pennsylvania, much of Carolina had suffered from war devastation and British occupation; an estimated 25,000 slaves had either fled or been carried off; and countless fences, barns, and fields had been destroyed. The money required for new materials, equipment, and slaves siphoned much specie out of the state.[8] Moreover, after an initial high level relative to English imports, agricultural prices declined, which made the trade deficit even more unfavorable. As a result of these factors, specie became extremely scarce, and much of the 1783 specie tax could not be collected. By August 1785 some £33,431 in specie had been paid into the central treasury—at most some 62% of the 1783 specie tax. In fact, the treasury records indicate that in some parts of Carolina no taxes were collected at all. By February 1787 thirteen of the state's thirty-seven tax districts had made no returns to the central treasury even under the less onerous 1784 and 1785 acts. Because no exact figures are available for the state's thirty-seven collection districts, a comparative district-by-district analysis has not been possible. Yet these records suggest that taxpayers in the low-country districts near Charleston, where the market was closer, credit accessible, and paper indents available, paid higher proportions of their quotas than did those in the up-country and backcountry districts (see table 7).[9]

Even so, in districts where specie was more plentiful, collection by forced sales was not uncommon. In St. Bartholomew parish, for example, a partly low-country, partly up-country district within a day or two's ride from Charleston, the forced collection of taxes by distress-and-sale action generated 7 percent of one collector's receipts. Two other St. Bartholomew collectors reported sums raised "by Execution" that totaled 15 percent of the final tally; that this forced collection came from fourteen out of fifty-two taxables meant that 27 percent of the taxpaying population in the district had their property seized and sold at auction.[10]

According to W. Patrick Higgins, once paper interest indents were issued to holders of the public debt, this paper was the only form of money that was paid into the system in taxes. But under the 1783 tax law, which authorized only specie, payments in specie continued, albeit in small amounts. The treasury commissioners' accounts show that specie taxes reached them every month until August 1785, when the obstruction that swept the countryside ended specie collection. The small sums in specie collected before August 1785 and their total cessation after August 1785 explain why the state government paid Congress only small proportions of its quotaed requisitions in specie up to 1785 and did not do so after that date.[11]

While acknowledging that unforeseen misfortune could cause individuals to default on their taxes, Carolina's well-to-do gentlemen-politicians still shared the assumption of their class that when taxes went unpaid, the individuals, not the system, must be at fault. Moreover, Carolina's gentry believed that the minimal taxation of the Revolution had accustomed Carolinians to a free and easy life-style that meant paying no taxes. As Edward

TABLE 7.

SOUTH CAROLINA TAXES COLLECTED AND IN ARREARS, 1783–1787
(PERCENTAGES IN PARENTHESES)

Tax	Collected	In Arrears	Collected	In Arrears
	as of August 1785		as of February 1787	
1783[a]				
$228,409	$140,745	$87,664 (38)	$140,589	$87,820(38)
[£54,254][b]	[£33,431]	[£20,823]	[£33,394]	[£20,860]
1784				
$333,032	143,763	189,269 (57)	231,318	101,714 (30)
[£79,105]	[34,148]	[44,957]	[54,945]	[24,160]
1785				
$299,436			122,722	176,714 (59)
[£71,125]			[29,150]	[41,975]
Totals				
1783, 1784				
$561,441	284,508	276,933 (49)	371,907	189,534 (33)
[£133,359]	[67,579]	[65,780]	[88,339]	[45,020]
1783, 1784, 1785				
$860,877			494,629	366,248 (43)
[£204,484]			[117,489]	[86,995]

Sources: For receipts, see Report on the Treasury, S.C. House Journal, January–March 1786 sess., 275–79; A State of General Tax Received into the Public Treasury for the years 1783, 1784, and 1785, Ways and Means Committee Report, 20 February 1787, Committee Reports, General Assembly Papers, 1787, #105, S.C. Department of Archives and History, Columbia. The figures for the total amount of direct taxes for each year are estimates and depend upon the assumption that 62% of the annual budget was to come from direct taxes and 38% from the state impost and other sources; see Second Report of the Committee of Ways and Means, 15 February 1786, where estimated returns from the impost, slave duty, vendue duty, and other sources total £45,610 ($192,018), and the estimated total income from the direct tax totals £75,600 ($318,276) (Evans #19253, Early American Imprints Collection). For annual budget estimates, see figures in the tax acts for the desired year in *Acts and Ordinances of the General Assembly of South Carolina*, Early American Imprints Collection, and the Early State Records Collection, Library of Congress.

[a]The 1783 tax was payable in specie only, but after April 1786 it was payable in state loan office bills. The 1784 and 1785 taxes were payable in either specie or state paper indents, but after April 1786 they too could be paid in state loan office bills.

[b]£ indicates South Carolina money of account.

Rutledge warned, many years would be required "before our people will be convinced of the Necessity of paying Taxes which may be seen." Dr. David Ramsay believed the Revolution had accustomed the common people to defy any authority. "This revolution has introduced so much anarchy that it will take half a century to eradicate the licentiousness of the people." In 1786 Chief Justice Henry Pendleton of the state circuit court system explained the collapse of tax and debt collection throughout rural Carolina as the result of the people's "folly and extravagance."[12] This wealthy elite was more politically flexible than other state postwar establishments. But it believed that to make the people pay their taxes, the government had to be ready to apply force.

Pressure

South Carolina's patrician leaders thus wrote tough enforcement penalties into the tax acts previously described. Each law vested strong sanctions in the two treasury commissioners, who had offices in Charleston. If a district collector failed to complete his account with the treasury, the commissioners could order him jailed without bail until he did so, issue execution writs on his property to be served by a sheriff, and, finally, prosecute him for "neglect of duty" in any local court. The treasury commissioners also were empowered to issue execution writs against any delinquent taxable person, again to be served by county sheriffs, who were to post advance notice of an impending distress sale at the door of the county courthouse.[13]

Much as in Pennsylvania, the treasury commissioner's execution writ was an effective means of exerting pressure on collectors. In Charleston in early 1784, treasury commissioners Edward Blake and Peter Bocquet published preliminary notices in the newspapers that warned all 1783 tax collectors that they must finish collection or face action. The following August the treasurers published "this Last Notice to all Tax Collectors, that unless those for Charleston close their returns by the 22 instant, and all those for the Country by the 15th day of September next, they will positively be proceeded against as the law directs."[14] But because a too-literal interpretation of the assembly's order would push matters too far, the treasury commissioners sometimes extended deadlines beyond the assigned date. Moreover, they issued execution writs but did not require sheriffs actually to put the property up for sale. Though the commissioners did not force collectors to the wall, the increased flow of receipts at the central treasury shows that the use of execution writs squeezed additional specie from the countryside.[15]

Eventually, because the large deficit on the 1783 specie tax continued, the patrician leaders of the assembly tried to force the system into even tougher action. Early in the January–March 1785 session, the House appointed a special blue ribbon committee to investigate "what taxes were collected for the Year 1783, and what progress has been made in the Collection of the Taxes for the Year 1784." Comprised of one member from each district and parish, the committee was chaired by Dr. David Ramsay, the gentleman from Charleston who believed, as his correspondence makes clear, that strong government operations were needed to force men into habits of discipline and honesty. Reporting a month later, Ramsay's committee took a hard line. In order to force tax collectors to foreclose on delinquent taxpayers, the committee recommended that, if by 2 May 1785 the treasury commissioners had not "executed the Law against such of the Collectors and Assessors of the Tax for the Year 1783, as shall not have finally closed their accounts for that year before that date," the state attorney general was to prosecute the said treasury commissioners "for neglect of Duty."[16]

Initially approved by the house, Ramsay's proposed resolution was postponed by the senate. Rather than compel the treasury commissioners to enforce the 1783 tax law, which required payment in specie, by legal prosecution, the two houses instead incorporated standardized phrasing taken from the two previous tax acts, that the treasury commissioners "be hereby empowered and required to grant executions against all former constables and collectors" whose accounts were still unsettled.[17] Nevertheless, Ramsay's postponed resolutions implied possible prosecution in the future if the treasury commissioners did not do their duty. Aware of this possibility, the commissioners put new pressure on local collectors. Specie payments into the treasury at Charleston accordingly increased (see table 8).[18]

Moreover, in September 1785 the treasurers formally requested that the governor grant them permission to postpone issuing executions against all collectors in default until a pending emergency session of the assembly, further evidence that the treasurers used execution writs to pressure collectors as the law prescribed. Hearing reports that tax collectors and constables in up-country and backcountry districts were being obstructed and physically prevented from collecting, the commissioners requested Governor William Moultrie for permission to extend the time for issuing writs until the general assembly convened. As the record tersely states, the commissioners asked the governor "whether they should be permitted to postpone issuing writs against the collectors in the country who have not made their return of taxes until the next meeting of the Legislature." Consulting with the Privy Council, Governor Moultrie turned down the request on the grounds that he and the council "cannot interfere, the law being positive and which must be [the commissioners'] guide."[19]

TABLE 8.

MONTHLY SPECIE RECEIVED AT SOUTH CAROLINA TREASURY
FROM 1783 TAX, 1783–1785 (AS OF AUGUST 1785)

Year	Month	Amount	Action
1783	July	£3,860[a]	1st tax installment due
	December	5,448	2nd tax installment due
1784	January	581	
	February	4,105	3rd tax installment due; treasurers issue 1st warning[b]
	March	2,741	
	April	311	Tax collectors issue warnings
	May	1,551	
	June	5,652	
	July	763	Tax collectors issue warnings
	August	829	Treasurers issue final warnings
	September	649	
	October	593	
	November	267	
	December	239	
1785	January	153	
	February	366	House votes to sue treasury commissioners, but senate votes to postpone; treasurers issue new warning
	March	696	
	April	886	Tax collectors issue warnings
	May	1,768	
	June	1,717	
	July	525	Tax collectors issue warnings
	August	352	
	September		Treasurers seek postponement of deadline for issue of execution writs.

Source: General Tax Receipts, General Account with Treasurer, Report of Committee to Audit the Accounts of the Treasury Commissioners, S.C. Assembly Journal, January–March 1786 sess., 275–79.

[a]£ indicates South Carolina money of account.

[b]Each year the commissioners of the treasury published preliminary warnings in January–February and final warnings in July–August; tax collectors published warnings in April–May and again in July–August. See the published treasury commissioners' and tax collectors' notices in *South Carolina Gazette and General Advertiser*, 27 May 1783, 10–12 August 1784, 16–20 April 1785; *State Gazette of South Carolina*, 16 February 1786, 10 April 1786; *Charleston Morning Post and Daily Advertiser*, 7 February 1787.

Resistance

Because specie had almost vanished from the countryside, because loans were not available, and because farm prices were low, the tax coercion that began in spring 1785 fell heavily on rural Carolina. First, as the increased amount of specie received at Charleston indicates, the pressure on taxpayers in arrears for the 1783 specie tax increased. By the 1783 law, final payments were supposed to have been made in early 1784; now the pressures from Charleston extracted additional cash from the countryside (see table 8).[20] Second, the pressure for tax payments in specie prompted taxpayers who had loaned money to turn on their own debtors and press them for cash. Third, rumors of a paper money relief act prompted Charleston merchants to go to law to recover what they could before their debts depreciated.[21] Finally, in many country districts, the threat of ruinous tax and debt foreclosure sales triggered protest, petitioning, and outright resistance.

By sheer coincidence, early that same spring (March 1785) the general assembly legislated a system of new county common pleas courts for Carolina's thirty-three counties. Intended in part to coax hard money into circulation by enabling foreign and domestic lenders to sue for debts more easily, the plan boomeranged by opening new paths to debt recovery actions by creditors under pressure by tax collectors or fearing the depreciation of their debts.[22] Pressure from the center on the local tax system together with resort to law by persons wanting money generated a flurry of foreclosure actions against both delinquent taxpayers and private debtors. These actions explain the double-pronged attempts by taxpayers and debtors to ward off disastrous property losses by peaceful petition and physical violence during that 1785 spring, summer, and fall.

Promising they would pay their taxes and debts once cash became available, taxpayers from the up-country Camden district urged the government in Charleston to extend relief. Speaking for the taxpayers under his jurisdiction, Camden collector John Milling asked the Privy Council "whether the inhabitants in Camden District shall be allowed to pay their taxes for the year one thousand seven hundred and eighty-three in special indents instead of specie," a request the council denied.[23] Other up-country Camden petitioners cited "an absolute necessity, for emitting a circulating medium, appropriated to the exigencies of the state, which may enable the citizen to discharge his debts, both public and private." They pointed to "the example of other states in the union, who with fewer resources, have adopted the measure with the desired success."[24] Still other petitioners emphasized the impossibility of paying either their public or private dues. As 189 petitioners from the backcountry districts of Little River and

Ninety-Six explained, they had not yet recovered from the war's destruction, much less been able to earn what the tax collector wanted from them: "The ravages of the Enemy [in the] late war having greatly reduced the Inhabitants of this District so that payment of a Tax in money for the year 1785 [is] impossible; [we] therefore pray that said Tax may be payable in produce or Indents."[25]

The physical obstruction of the law was the other method by which up-country and backcountry people acted to prevent ruin by distress sales. Appealing to the men of the Ninety-Six District to "despise those little petty actions of rising into dishonorable mobs, until something is first attempted by petition," a "Backcountry-man" implicitly acknowledged that if petition failed, force would be justified.[26]

After the general assembly rejected several relief proposals during its January–March 1785 session and the new tax and debt pressures were felt,[27] that time must have seemed at hand. That summer, in St. Bartholomew parish, four defiant taxpayers forcibly obstructed collector John Croskey and kept him from carrying out collection. Tersely recording this action as a "positive denial," the Privy Council at Charleston ordered the state attorney general to proceed against the four offenders "agreeable to law."[28] That same summer, in the backcountry district Eastward of the Wateree, when the collector issued a spate of execution writs, the constable, either directly threatened or fearing he would be, would not act. As collector William Murrell swore on oath, he had "issued Executions against all and singular the defaulters"—a total of forty-five persons out of eighty-nine taxables (50 percent) for £177 out of a total quota of £297 (59 percent). But the constable had not served the executions, and he, Murrell, could not, therefore, deliver his own assigned quota.[29] These were not isolated incidents. "In many parts of the State," a North Carolina visitor reported late that summer from Charleston after talking with government leaders, "the Collection of Taxes . . . have been impeded and law proceedings altogether put a stop to, by the disorderly behavior of some of the Citizens."[30]

More visibly, the new county court of common pleas in up-country Camden County became the target of obstruction. Just as the first court session was opening, a crowd surrounded the courthouse. Crowd leaders informed the judge he could try criminal cases "without impediment," but no private debt actions could be tried; the judge "immediately submitted." Because court officers understood that similar actions against their courts were likely if they tried debt cases, outside Charleston proper most of the common pleas courts suspended suits for debts.[31]

Thus, except for the Charleston region, by late summer 1785 the state's tax and debt collection had broken down. This explains why recorded receipts of specie into the central treasury end abruptly with the last entry in August 1785.[32] And why a "Planter" publicly declared in a newspaper essay that if the government wanted tax and debt collection resumed, it must make it possible for the people to obtain money: "But I never believed that men in their senses would submit to have their property sold, either for taxes or debts at one-tenth or one-twentieth of their value. Let a medium be circulated through the state and the backcountry will pay its taxes and debts with as much alacrity as those parts of the state where specie can be had."[33]

Retreat

With tax and debt collection at a standstill outside Charleston, Governor William Moultrie summoned the general assembly into a special emergency session. Moultrie's first message to the legislators late that September described the crisis: "Your Courts being insulted, your Laws set at defiance and civil Process confined to a small part of the State." Moultrie then asked for legislation that "may restore harmony and Good Government again throughout all ranks and in every part of the State."[34]

At this point, events take a turn that differs from the pattern set in Pennsylvania and later to be repeated in Rhode Island and Massachusetts. In those states resurgent Reliefers either gained control of the assembly or came so close to control that the government had to back down. In South Carolina the lawyer-planter elite preempted the relief issue.

Early in 1783 Alexander Gillon and Aedanus Burke began their covert guerilla war against the Carolina lawyer-planter oligarchy. Working independently but using newspapers and pamphlets, seaman's clubs, and street demonstrations, the two politicians and their allies had tried to discredit the "great people" and take control of the assembly. Gillon's journalist supporters scourged assembly leaders as a "nabob gentry" of "ambitious lordlings," singled out "R[utledge], B[ee], and M[athews]" for assault, and urged the voters to replace these "rotten hulks" with independent men not under their direction.[35] Backed by seamen, marine artisans, and laborers and meeting at the City Tavern, the Marine Anti-Britannic Society (by 1786 Gillon was its official president) printed and circulated handbills to up-country leaders urging them to form "Clubs on principles similar to ours" that would check the "aristocracy."[36] Upcountry voters were warned that the "liberty and happiness of the *middling* and the *poor* are at stake," and that only men who will not "sit still and see their country *ruined* and *enslaved*" should be elected to the assembly.[37] Like Gillon, Aedanus Burke tried to conceal his hand, but his anonymous pamphlet attack in 1783 on the Society of the Cincinnati warned that the "gentry below" formed an incipient "aristocracy." By 1785 Gillon and Burke were taking relief policy positions, proposing at various times officials' salary and lawyers' fee reductions (1784–85), a debt installment bill (1786–87), and a paper money bill (1787). Although the absence of formal roll call lists makes voting alignments impossible to determine, Gillon and Burke surely opposed the assembly's attempted tax crackdown.[38]

The Rutledge-Bee-Mathews assembly leadership fought this opposition with various tactics. When the Marine Anti-Britannic Society staged a street parade on 8 July 1784 to protest a recent government amnesty to former Loyalists, Carolina patricians raised a mounted corps of volunteer cavalry that charged the marchers and broke up their demonstration. Henry Peronneau, Anti-Britannic officer and organizer, was arrested and jailed. To counter Anti-Britannic propaganda, editor John Miller, a London printer, was brought in as official state printer to edit the *South Carolina Gazette and General Advertiser*; Miller's assignment was (in the words of one public letter) "to keep the eyes of the people open to the manoevres of that despicable set of speculators, who have made for six months such fruitless attempts to get into power." Gillon loyalists Benjamin Waller and Benjamin Cudworth, auctioneers, were arrested for violation of the city code on private auction sales. And in the fall 1786 assembly elections, an election ticket secretly circulated by Charleston intendant Richard Hutson kept Gillon and Burke off the Charleston assembly delegation. Both Gillon and Burke quickly found up-country districts that returned them to the assembly.[39]

Rather than allow their political opponents to capitalize on the sporadic violence in the countryside, the upper-class political elite put forth a relief program of its own design. When the governor called the assembly into emergency session in Charleston (September–October 1785), special house committees recommended relief legislation for both taxpayers and debtors. With the house and senate quickly falling into line, the Loan Office Act and Sheriff's Sale Valuation Law were adopted.[40]

An emergency relief measure, the Loan Office Act provided that £100,000 in paper money bills be printed and loaned to qualified applicants through a state loan office. No person could borrow more than £250 nor less than £30; any loan had to be secured by a land mortgage worth three times the principal or by a deposit of gold and silver plate worth double the principal. Borrowers were to pay 7 percent interest and repay the entire debt at the end of five years. The new money was not legal tender but was payable for taxes or for any other government obligation due at the treasury after 1 May 1786. The law's basic objective was to provide a medium of circulation for commercial purposes and thus revive trade, but uncollected taxes were also important. By making the bills payable for future taxes and other government obligations and by authorizing the government to use the currency to pay interest on the state's public debt, the civil list, and other government expenses, the government confessed its inability to raise any further specie by taxation.[41]

Legislation for private debt relief was also passed, in the form of the famous Sheriff's Sale Valuation Law. Before creditors could sue debtors, they had to give the debtors due notice; the debtors, then, could offer property at a value set by three neighborhood appraisers. If the creditor refused the property and sued, any property then attached and offered for sale at a sheriff's auction could not be sold for less than three-quarters of its appraised value. This law also specified that all currently jailed debtors be released, and that no debtor whose auctioned property failed to cover an unpaid debt could henceforth be jailed. This measure, as Chief Justice Pendleton later explained, had been "founded in a preference to one of several bad expedients which were proposed, as being the least exceptionable."[42]

This retreat from the stern measures of the previous assembly session represented a tactical maneuver, not a change of conviction about preferred policy. In principle, the Carolina elite still favored pressing its tax and debt collection measures.[43] But to have done so would have required a much stronger dose of government coercion than was practically or politically possible. As Chief Justice Pendleton recalled, the government's alternatives during that September–October 1785 period had been four: quiet the disorder by legislative reliefs, close the courts entirely, do nothing, or raise an armed force to enforce the law.[44] Although Pendleton did not say so, he and his colleagues surely realized that enforcing the law by armed force would have either produced armed clashes or tipped the scales in the assembly in favor of the Gillon-Burke axis. Because Carolina's legislative forces were closely balanced in terms of low-country, up-country, and backcountry representation, it seems likely that a resort to coercion by low-country leaders would have forfeited their up-country and backcountry support, and with it their precarious control of the assembly.[45]

Even as they remained convinced that the people's "folly and extravagance" were the key to the recent disturbances, this upper-class leadership developed an explanation that implicated their assembly adversaries. Capitalizing on the people's susceptibilities, they claimed, certain "adventurers" who had "run deep in debt for dry goods and for slaves" had stirred up this rural opposition to save themselves from their creditors' legal actions. Unable to pay their British creditors, "they openly oppose the Execution of the laws, and clamour against British Merchants and others, their Creditors, as having combined to ruin the State. The common people ever ready for novelty imbibe their doctrine with avidity."[46]

Although the gentry's moderate relief program gave it a temporary political advantage, the assemblies of 1786 and 1787 saw a further erosion in the upper class's power to control events. Early in 1787 wealthy lawyer

Edward Rutledge got the assembly to pass a bill prohibiting further imports of slaves from Africa or the West Indies for a period of three years, which would curtail planters' and farmers' outlays for slave purchases, so that taxes and debts could be paid. When the legislation finally passed as a rider to a debt installment bill sponsored by Alexander Gillon, Rutledge took this success as a small sign of the assembly's returning moral honesty ("a Disposition to be honest").[47] A similar success for the elite, although more symbolic than substantive, was the denial of Lewis Hallam and John Henry's petition for the assembly's permission to establish a theater in Charleston; merchant William Smith's report against the application on the grounds that a new theater would encourage further pleasure seeking and personal extravagance was accepted.[48]

But other measures carried the relief program farther than the Rutledge-Pinckney-Mathews leadership wanted to go. Special emissions of £83,184 (1786) and £64,000 (1787) in special paper interest indents were ordered printed and paid to the state's public creditors as annual interest on the public debt. Despite the recommendation of a committee chaired by Mathews that the indents be payable only for current taxes, these indents were made payable for the taxes of 1784, 1785, and 1786. When house member Alexander Gillon introduced a debt installment bill that made debtors legally liable for private debts in three equal installments beginning 1 January 1788, it carried into law despite David Ramsay's attacks on the bill as a further incentive to "idleness" and "extravagance."[49] The assembly also voted that state loan office paper money, authorized in October 1785 and issued on loan in 1786, could be used to pay any tax, duty, or debt due at the treasury *before* 1 May 1786: any unpaid taxes on the 1783 tax act, heretofore payable only in specie, could now be paid in paper.[50]

In this situation, renewal of the pressure on delinquent taxpayers and debtors was politically and practically impossible. In the January–March 1786 session, a special house committee chaired by patrician Thomas Farr reported the sums of taxes yet outstanding. For the 1783 tax, Farr reported, £33,431 in specie had been collected, but "many of the Collectors for that year have not made any return of Taxes received." For the 1784 tax, £34,148 in specie and indents had been received, "but a great part of the Tax for the said year is not yet collected." Merely noting the fact, Farr's committee made no recommendation for dealing with the situation.[51] Nor did the January–March 1787 assembly take any action. Instead of requiring that delinquent tax collectors be compelled to collect and deliver their uncollected quotas, the assembly merely ordered the treasury commissioners to publish in the public press both the names of all deficient collectors for the 1783, 1784, and 1785 taxes and "of all Defaulters who have neglected or do refuse to pay their Tax."[52]

Like their counterparts in Pennsylvania, Carolina's upper-class legislators lived through and witnessed the failure of their state government to
raise specie taxes for both Congress and their own state budget. When
pressure on the system from Charleston was intensified, farmers and planters resisted tax and debt collection officers and thus staved off ruin. More
flexible politically than their Pennsylvania counterparts, the South Carolina lawyer-planter elite countered by legislating a loan office paper money
act and a property valuation law. These relief measures saved some of their
power, but the enactment of other relief measures over their objection
doomed any hope of raising specie coin for Congress. When the 1783
specie tax act became payable in paper money, the last remaining bastion
of support for Congress crumbled. Unable to collect specie because of
rural resistance and because paper money was now the state's official legal
medium, by 1786–87 the South Carolina government was unable to pay
a financially crippled Congress a single farthing.

★ 7 ★

RHODE ISLAND

B Y PROVIDING moderate relief, South Carolina's embattled political
elite preserved a semblance of power. Their Rhode Island counterparts, while initially more successful in collecting taxes, proved less politically adroit. In the early 1780s Rhode Island's well-to-do political elite
enacted debt funding, currency retirement, and federal requisition measures, financed by eight direct property poll taxes payable partly in specie,
partly in paper (1781–86). State impost and excise taxes added further
revenue. Three of these direct taxes passed in the postwar era (1783,
1784, 1785), amounting to £20,000 each, and payable in specie and federal indents, specifically earmarked funds for Congress.[1] By collecting
these taxes the Rhode Island government was able to pay Congress
$75,111 in hard money (1781–86).

Some Rhode Island leaders worried whether the people of Rhode Island
would pay these taxes. Hearing of rural riots against taxes in Virginia and
Massachusetts, in June 1782 Dr. Jonathan Arnold reported that in Rhode
Island "the people yet continue to exert themselves, and altho' Money is
extremely scarce—Taxation continues—and they act as though they intended to fulfil their duty."[2] Later that same year resistance against taxes
flared in the country town of Glocester, but the arrest of leaders ended the
episode.[3] Because a maximum yield from indirect taxes would ease the direct tax burden, the assembly guarded the state's impost-excise system jeal-
ously. State imposts and excises, a legislative committee pointedly announced, should tax "those Articles which are generally consumed by the
Rich and Affluent . . . as high as they will conveniently bear, that the Industrious Farmer and Mechanic may be relieved." To protect the revenue
raised by the state impost, the Rhode Island assembly in 1782 unanimously rejected the proposed federal 5 percent impost that would have
vested Congress with an independent source of revenue.[4]

Rhode Island's changeful structure of "democratic" government, with
its annually elected upper house and governor and semiannually elected
lower house, increased the political risks of levying direct taxes. A car-
ryover from the colonial period, the Rhode Island government was susceptible to takeovers by local oppositions. Bitter colonywide election battles

between the factions headed by Stephen Hopkins (centered in Providence) and Samuel Ward (centered in Newport) during the late colonial era had produced frequent changes. Thus one Rhode Island politician described the state as "long . . . noted for one of the most fluctuating Governments in the Union."[5] Yet the administration of the well-to-do Warwick merchant Governor William Greene (1778–86) maintained a solid political front, with the two sets of former adversaries as key allies. Shortly before the Revolution, these regional factions had buried the hatchet, and they cooperated with each other closely during the 1770s and 1780s.

Nevertheless, the taxes enacted during the Confederation era burdened rural Rhode Islanders. Rhode Island taxes were levied partly as a flat per capita tax per poll and partly as property tax based on assessed evaluations. The estimated annual per household levy of nine dollars in specie seems fairly light, but the specie shortage that settled on rural Rhode Island during the Confederation era meant that these taxes weighed heavily on the state's small farmer majority. Robert Becker reports rural discontent over taxes during the Revolution and early Confederation eras, but the rejection of the proposed 5 percent federal impost, the government's willingness to postpone due dates, and other concessions to taxpayers seem to have kept this discontent manageable until early 1786.[6]

The Rhode Island tax collection system had an enforcement mechanism that permitted the assembly to bring pressure on taxpayers from the center. When the general assembly voted a direct tax, the general treasurer assigned quotas to each of the state's thirty towns and ordered locally elected town treasurers and collectors to begin collection. At the town treasurer's order, the town collector collected local taxes and delivered the proceeds to that officer to be accounted for and transmitted to the state's central treasury. If, however, a town collector failed to deliver the full amount, the town treasurer was to sue the delinquent collector in a local court for the amount outstanding. If judgment was obtained, the county sheriff attached and sold at auction enough of the collector's property to cover the deficient sums. In order to guarantee that town treasurers carried out their duty of supervising and disciplining town collectors, the general treasurer at the capitol issued an execution writ against any town treasurer whose accounts were unsettled. Addressed to the county sheriff, the general treasurer's execution writ, printed on a standardized form, ordered the sheriff to begin distress-and-sale proceedings against the treasurer's property and to sell it to make up the deficit. Alternatively, the sheriff could commit the town treasurer to jail until either the latter came up with the required amount or satisfied the sheriff that he would shortly do so.[7] The general treasurer's execution writ thus gave the general assembly leverage over the entire tax collection system.

Between the end of the Revolution and the election turnover of 1786, the general assembly managed this process of centrally directed tax collection operations with no little ingenuity. In 1782 the assembly combined coaxing, concessions, threats, pressure, and general treasurer's execution writs in various combinations. First, the assembly called on taxpayers to pay their taxes by publicly declaring that it was the sacred duty of "every Citizen chearfully to exert themselves to pay their Taxes punctually, as well as of the several Collectors to use their greatest Diligence in collecting and paying the same." Next, the assembly warned that serious consequences would befall any delinquent collector. "Several Collectors of Taxes, regardless of the public Good, have been very Negligent, and in many Instances used great partiality" in making collection. Henceforth, the assembly resolved, any collector who, "through Indolence in Duty, or any Neglect whatever on his or their part," caused any town treasurer to be jailed, such collector was henceforth disqualified from further collection and would be prosecuted. That August the assembly eased the pressure by granting an extension of two months on a £12,000 Continental tax earmarked for a federal requisition quota, at the same time declaring that it had received "the strongest Assurances that the utmost Vigilance will be immediately used for collecting and paying the said Taxes." When October arrived, the assembly turned up the pressure, ordering that the collectors "use their utmost Exertions, in order to collect the deficient Taxes, with the Interest, and pay the same into the General-Treasury," and that if by November's end, "any of the Towns shall be delinquent . . . the sheriffs be and they hereby are directed to re-commit them to Gaol, there to remain until the same shall be paid." Finally, going all out that November, the assembly ordered the general treasurer "to issue his Executions against the delinquent Towns within this State, for the Sums due from them respectively of Taxes assessed in this Year."[8]

Because taxes were heavy and specie in the country districts was scarce, rural taxpayers found the payment of taxes burdensome. Taxes levied in the early 1780s were easier to pay than those levied later. The general treasurer's accounts show that by the end of 1780 the entire amount on seven individual taxes levied that year and payable in paper money or specific supplies was collected; similarly, two state taxes in 1781 and the Continental tax in 1782 were fully paid by the due dates.[9] But collection lagged for the 1783, 1784, and 1785 taxes, all payable in specie. Six months after the due date of 20 December 1783, £7,471 of the £20,000 specie tax had not been paid—a proportion of 37 percent.[10] Five months after the due date of 1 January 1785, £9,606 on the £20,000 1784 specie-paper indent tax of 1784 had not been collected—a proportion of 48 percent.[11]

Yet Rhode Island's governing elite (the oligarchy headed by Governor William Greene, Deputy Governor Jabez Bowen, and upper house assistants Welcome Arnold and Nicholas Brown) shared the general assumption of their class that unpaid taxes resulted from deficiency of character and behavior. This was the unspoken premise behind Jabez Bowen's indignant rejection in 1786 of the allegation that Rhode Island taxes were too heavy for the poor farmer to pay: "I cannot believe that any Citizen, who wishes well to the State, can be unwilling to part with a small Proportion of his Property, to satisfy the Public Creditors, and Defray the Expences of Civil Government.— This is required of all civilized Governments in the World; and I know of no State in the Union, in which Citizens pay less than in this."[12]

Pressure

Through the power it exerted in the postwar assemblies, Rhode Island's governing class alternately eased, coaxed, threatened, and pressured taxpayers by methods that balanced short-term leniency with ultimate coercion. Postponements were often voted—in May 1783, one month; February 1784, three months; May 1784, one month; June 1784, two months; August 1784, one month; May 1785, two months; June 1785, two months; and August 1785, two months.

The assembly also made special provision for the poor by empowering town clerks "to consider the Circumstances of the Poor, in their respective Towns, and exempt such from the Poll-Tax, as they shall think unable to pay the same."[13] Because specie was scarce, the assembly granted taxpayers the option of paying part of their taxes in special state paper indents that the general treasurer issued as interest payments to Rhode Island holders of the federal debt.[14] Towns where the proportion of the poor was especially high got special concessions: thus South Kingston, because of "the great scarcity of circulating Cash, and the Poverty of the said town," was repeatedly granted extensions, suspensions, and concessions until at last, in October 1785, the general treasurer was to issue his executions "to collect the deficiency in Gold or Silver."[15]

Ultimately, however, the assembly took a hard line. When town treasurers complained about the slow pace and high cost of suits in the local courts against delinquent town collectors, the assembly at its February 1783 session established special local tax courts that would try treasurers' suits against tax collectors and issue execution writs.[16] When farmers' boycotts of collectors' seizure-and-sale auctions stalled collection, the assembly authorized town collectors "to remove Stock or other Property, by them distrained from any of the Inhabitants of this State that are delinquent in the Payment of their Taxes, to any part of the State where the same may be sold to the best Advantage."[17] On at least five occasions after general treasurer execution writs had gone out to sheriffs, the assembly suspended them by ordering that distress-and-sale action against town treasurers cease or that a jailed town treasurer be released from jail. But in the same order, the assembly set a final deadline for resuming the suspended action.[18]

Invariably, when all the concessions, coaxing, and threats had been exhausted, the assembly would order the general treasurer to issue his execution writs to sheriffs and set a final deadline for them to be carried out.[19] Town treasurers would then have to sue town collectors, and town collectors, facing the loss of their property, would have to seize the property of the delinquent taxpayers or go to jail. Either the taxpayer then came up with the required amount, or the collector sold the taxpayer's horses, cows, other animals, corn, hay, or other farm products at auction. When the town collector could not squeeze out the required amount by these methods, the collector's property would be seized and sold.

The small but not insignificant amount of money raised from the sale of town collectors' property suggests that the forced sales of taxpayers' property must have been quite extensive. Although town collectors postponed the unpleasant task of seizing and selling their neighbors' property at low prevailing prices, it seems unlikely that collectors would temporize when their own property was taken and sold. Sale of collectors' property occurred only after previous seizure-and-sale proceedings against delinquent taxpayers had so depleted taxpayers' holdings that not enough property was left over to pay the overdue sums. According to one general treasurer's account compiled in February 1785, the amount collected by sheriffs from seizure-and-sale proceedings against town collectors ("pd by the Shereff") on the £20,000 tax of 1783 amounted to £1,988—10 percent of the total.

Indeed, town tax collectors were not to be envied. Whether taxpayers in their assigned jurisdictions could or could not pay, the collectors were, in the final analysis, accountable. Town collectors' pleas to the assembly for temporary postponements and easements speak volumes. Collector Fleet Brown of Foster petitioned the assembly: would their honors delay a sheriff's execution sale against his property for the uncollected sum of £150? The assembly granted Brown a forty-day extension but ordered the sheriff if the sum was not collected by then "to settle the same in the usual way."[20] When Caleb Arnold, a Glocester tax collector, died with his accounts in arrears, his son petitioned the assembly to stop the sheriff from selling "the Real Estate left by his s[a]id hon[ore]d father decesased." The assembly ordered a two-month stay but mandated that "if the aforesaid taxes shall not be collected within said time in such case the Sheriff is directed to proceed to sell ye Estates as tho no such Resolve had passed."[21] In February 1786 collector Reynolds Knowles of North Kingston asked to be allowed to pay his town tax quota in federal loan office certificates because he was "now in danger of having his stock taken" for sale to cover the uncollected amount.[22] Collector Abel Barnes, petitioning the assembly for more time, pled not his own lack of zeal, but rather an excess of compassion. He had done everything possible to get his taxpayer neighbors to pay their taxes short of driving their cattle out of town to some other town where buyers could be found. Now, with the town treasurer committed to jail by virtue of a treasurer's execution warrant, Barnes confessed to giving "too much Indulgence to many People in Pitying them when they complained of the hardness of the times and that they could not pay their Taxes. And now the Town Treasurer hath called a Special Court against your Petitioner and his Bondsmen and your Petitioners Real Estate and Personal is now attached and to be sold at Public Vendue on the fifteenth day of November next to satisfie said Tax which if sold in this scarce time of money will be likely to Ruin your Petitioner."[23]

In South Kingston, where the tax arrearages were enormous, collector Richard Gardner estimated that even if he took "all the Stock in the town belonging to the Persons who are deficient with their taxes if it was exposed to the public Ven[d]ue within a few days it would not amount to a sufficiency to discharge their Taxes." When Gardner finally defaulted rather than thus strip his neighbors of their means of livelihood, his own farm was seized and put up for sale at auction; when no one stepped forth with an acceptable offer, the state itself assumed title.[24]

By contrast with Pennsylvania and South Carolina, where large tax arrearages remained extant, the collection system under the Rhode Island assembly's direction ultimately prevailed. As the 1780s wore on, Rhode Island taxes were collected less promptly than earlier, but in the end they *were* collected in their entirety. Of five state and continental taxes levied by the Rhode Island government between 1782 and 1785, by February 1785 the first four had been almost entirely discharged. The fifth and last, due 1 January 1785, was still unpaid by a proportion of 71 percent (see table 9). Yet by May 1786, the deficiency on the 1784 tax had been reduced to a mere 8 percent (see table 9). Month by month during the intervening period, the Rhode Island tax collection system had ground relentlessly onwards.[25]

Resistance

Only occasionally between 1782 and 1786 did Rhode Island farmers, rural artisans, and country laborers try to fend off the government's dunning. Voicing distress, the Glocester town meeting in January 1783 "prayed" the general assembly "not to lay on taxes so fast & hard as they have done." The previous December, Glocester town collector Caleb Ar-

TABLE 9.
RHODE ISLAND TAXES COLLECTED AND IN ARREARS,
FEBRUARY 1785–MAY 1786
(PERCENTAGES IN PARENTHESES)

Tax and Date Due	Collected	In Arrears	Collected	In Arrears
	as of February 1785		as of 5 May 1786	
Jan. 1782, State				
$39,960	$38,142 (95)	$1,818 (5)	$39,477 (99)	$483 (1)
[£12,000]ᵃ	[£11,454]	[£546]	[£11,855]	[£145]
1 Aug. 1782				
Feb. 1782, Continental				
$19,980	19,284 (97)	696 (3)	19,880 (99+)	100 (1−)
[£6,000]	[5,791]	[209]	[5,970]	[30]
1 Sept. 1782				
June 1782, Continental				
$39,960	36,537 (91)	3,423 (9)	37,472 (94)	2,487 (6)
[£12,000]	[10,972]	[1,028]	[11,253]	[747]
1 Sept. 1782				
June, 1783, State				
$66,600	58,005 (87)	8,598 (13)	63,873 (96)	2,727 (4)
[£20,000]	[17,419]	[2,582]	[19,181]	[819]
20 Dec. 1783				
June 1784, State				
$66,600	19,433 (29)	47,166 (71)	60,942 (92)	5,658 (8)
[£20,000]	[5,836]	[14,164]	[18,301]	[1,699]
1 Jan. 1785				
Total				
$233,100	171,402 (74)	61,702 (26)	221,645 (95)	11,455 (5)
[£70,000]	[51,472]	[18,529]	[66,560]	[3,440]

Sources: "Account of the Several Towns Deficient in their Taxes," 26 February 1785, in *Taxes Ft.-1 1779–1787*; "Present State of the Taxes," Newport, 7 May 1785, and "Present State of the Taxes," 5 May 1786, *Papers Relating to the Adoption of the Constitution of the United States*, 105, 102, Rhode Island State Archives, Providence.

ᵃ£ indicates amount in Rhode Island money of account.

nold reported being "assaulted by a number of Persons who rescued some
Cattle and sheep" out of his possession that he had earlier seized from persons who "had Refused to pay their Taxes under pretence of a Tender Conscience." But once several of the "mob" had been arrested, jailed, and required to post bond for good behavior, he had been able to resume
collection.[26] Protests such as these help explain why the general assembly
in late 1782 and early 1783 lightened the rural tax burden by enacting
higher state impost-excise taxes and by rejecting the proposed 5 percent
congressional impost.

Nevertheless, with the government's tax collection system extracting
money from the countryside, country towns protested and urged relief
with increasing frequency. By early 1786 these pleas had become a
groundswell. At a series of special meetings held throughout the state that
February, country towns called on the general assembly to legislate bud-
get-cutting economies, a paper money land bank, and a temporary postponement of taxes. Glocester's town meeting instructed its deputies "to get
a bank of paper currency made" and to find "a more easy & Equitable way
of Paying Taxes." Middletown's town meeting, after positing that the gold
and silver coin now in circulation was "inadequate for a Medium of Trade
and to answer the Requisitions of Government," called for "a moderate
sum of paper Money to be emitted and let out on Land Security." Coventry, Cranston, Warwick, and Foster town meetings also urged, in Coventry's words, "a paper Currency made on the best and surest footing that
may be made In order to Relieve the present Distresses of the Inhabitants
of this State." Smithfield's town meeting petitioned the assembly to postpone the due date of the 1785 tax for £20,000, for "Although [a] great
part of that Tax may be paid with Interest Certificates It is no advantage,
to much the Greatest part of this State For it Takes money to Purchase
them and But few men have it to pay."[27]

But the substantial relief the country towns were asking for was not to
be. By a majority of 43 to 18, the general assembly that March (1786)
rejected the rural deputies' bill for a state paper money land bank. At the
same time, the assembly relaxed its harshest pressure by voting limited
concessions. The due date of the 1785 £20,000 tax was postponed by four
months from 1 January to 1 May 1786; special certificate bounties, payable as taxes, were ordered to be printed and issued to growers of hemp
and raisers of sheep. A tender-stay law that freed jailed debtors who paid
their creditors in real or personal property at a value set by three impartial
neighborhood referees was voted; real estate auction sales of debtors' property were postponed for nine months.[28] Intended to quiet rural discontent,
the assembly's concessions were too few and too limited to do so.

Indeed, even before the March 1786 assembly session, the state's country districts were in an uproar. Between 1 January and the 19 April 1786

state election, local tax collection operations throughout Rhode Island collapsed as farmers, rural artisans, and laborers refused to pay collectors and threatened them with physical resistance if they tried to seize their property. During this period Rhode Island collectors could collect only the tiny sum of £118 for the 1785 £20,000 tax—a proportion of 0.5 percent. By contrast, during a comparable period just one year earlier, collectors had collected £11,194 on the £20,000 1784 tax, or 56 percent.[29]

Two weeks before the 19 April election day, some twenty small-town leaders gathered in East Greenwich to plan strategy for ousting the current Rhode Island government. They agreed upon an election slate and ordered tickets printed ("proxes") that bore the names of candidates offering to replace Governor Greene, Deputy Governor Bowen, and their upper-house supporters. At the same time candidates were recruited for the lower house. For governor, the convention nominated John Collins, a Newport merchant-farmer and former Patriot leader whose sympathy for farmers was well known. Runners then distributed the printed election "proxes" to freemen to be cast as ballots in town meeting on election day, transmitting these names to qualified voters throughout the state. As its masthead the ticket bore the caption "To Relieve the Distressed."[30]

During this same preelection period, country politicians bitterly attacked the Greene government, promising tax relief for the country and fanning rural suspicion that linked heavy taxes to the current government's waste and profusion. The shortage of circulating cash was blamed on importing merchants who allegedly sent "Every dollar to Europe thay Could git" "to make a private forten to them Selves at the destruction of the Country."[31] Across the tiny state in taverns, in town meetings, and on village greens, Reliefer candidates and operatives carried these messages to voters. Only by voting the relief ticket and choosing a new government pledged to postponing taxes and legislating a government paper money relief bank could the countryside be saved.

The result was a wave of rural votes that drove Governor Greene, Deputy Governor Bowen, and their legislative supporters from power. Drawing votes from the middle and lower classes of rural Rhode Island and from lower classes in the towns also, the entire Reliefer slate for governor, deputy governor, and assistants was elected, and the lower house had a Reliefer majority as well.[32]

As the full extent of the sweep became known, supporters of the defeated administration reacted with dismay. Peregrine Foster wrote his older brother, the staunch Greene loyalist and Providence lawyer Dwight Foster: "We are now experiencing one of the greatest Revolutions ever known in this State which has long been noted for one of the most fluctuating Governments in the Union—A Paper Currency is thot. to be inevitable which if made will be frought with a thousand Evils."[33] John Brown and

George Benson, Providence merchants, reacted to the election with similar
feeling. In their eyes, it epitomized both Rhode Island's unstable government and the inability of this government to enforce laws necessary for
creditor and commercial confidence. "The revolution now introducing in
Gover[n]ment & the expectation of a Paper Currency is fatal to Credit
and of course Embarrasses Trade which we apprehend will Languish &
Decline 'till a restoration of Good Government [takes place] & till our
Laws acquire stability & energy."[34]

By contrast, rural folk celebrated. A homespun poet compared the event
with a previous 19 April when farmers had resisted the British at Lexington and Concord.

> 19th of April as they say,
> freedom's sons Began the way
> The day we ever observe with admiration
> Resembling almost a newe Creation
> Of numerous Gentle Men to prevent
> the total wast[e] of estates that is almost spent
> By Spendthrifts who heretofore have Ruled the Ro[o]st
> and of freedom much they made their Boast
> But now alas the[y] do appear
> Like Breathless Corps[es] that none do fear.[35]

Rhode Island's 1786 political revolution was under way.

Retreat

Preparing to leave office, Governor Greene charged that the opposition
had carried the election by privately circulating "entirely groundless" attacks against his administration, which had produced "this surprising and
very extraordinary Majority"; indeed, "until very lately I have not known
that there was any Dissatisfaction."[36] But Greene must have known, for
the battle had been joined well before the election. In Cranston, as Nicholas Brown's political agent Joseph Shaw reported, the contest had
sharply divided the town's leaders. Through an informer, Brown had also
kept close tabs on the convention at East Greenwich where the Collins
ticket had originated.[37]

Shortly before the election, Greene loyalists in the country towns had
tried, without success, to neutralize the opposition's growing strength.
Two days before the poll, Deputy Governor Jabez Bowen had published
a pamphlet that coldly attacked the "present Opposition" for propagating
misinformation about the present government, at the same time calling on
the electorate to vote for the present government—and pay their taxes.[38]

But such efforts had not stemmed the tide. Describing the battle in Scituate the day before the election, Rufus Hopkins reported he was certain that a "Large majority of the Town in Principle [were] against [paper money], but as the other side have taken unwearied pains and Propegated every Kind of falshood, and but little said on the other side the Question has I make no Doubt Lead many out of the way, which might have been easily Kept right."[39]

The new Reliefer assembly quickly acted to save the property of their rural supporters. First, the new majority legislated the paper money relief program that its candidates had promised the voters during the campaign. Administered through a government paper money land bank that colonial Rhode Island legislatures had frequently used to deal with a money shortage, the assembly enacted the most famous paper money bill in U.S. history. By the assembly's order at its May 1786 session, £100,000 in legal tender paper money bills were to be printed and loaned to farmers through special government-appointed town trustees. Both to relieve farmers' financial burdens and to support the money's acceptability at par, the assembly ordered that the paper be receivable for all taxes; that it be legal tender for all debts past, present, and future; that borrowers secure their loans by mortgaging land worth double the sum borrowed; and that borrowers pay 4 percent annual interest and begin repayment of the principal in seven years.[40]

The legislation had one basic objective—to relieve the threat of ruin hanging over the farmers, rural laborers, and rural artisans of Rhode Island. The Providence *Chronicle* reported that, according to Reliefer legislators, "there was no Money in the Country—That the Lands and Stock of the Farmer were daily sold at the post, by the Collectors of Taxes, and Sheriffs, for one-Quarter Part of their real Value—That Silver Money could not be hired by Persons who were possessed of good Estates at any Premium whatever—That the Distresses of the People in the Country was such as demanded Relief—and that no other Mode could be devised but by a Paper Emission."[41]

Newspaper articles sympathetic to the plight of rural citizens also urged the necessity of a paper money emission. The charge that the only persons needing relief were poor debtors was angrily rebutted. "Many irreproachable characters, who are perfectly clear of debt likewise . . . are persuaded that without any increase of medium the middling and lower class of mankind must be ruined by gaols and sheriffs' vendues."[42]

Humanitarian sympathy was part of their motivation, but the new Reliefer legislative majority also grasped that if the government did not enact rural relief farmers would turn to violence. In the months before the 19 April election, anger against the government's tax policies had intensified. Providence merchant Moses Brown had been informed by an anonymous correspondent that the country people inflame each other with heated talk of the current government's fiscal abuses and that popular agitators "are taking the lead in this dispute with the Rable at their heals and Expect to be very popelar and have been so with the same Rable after them . . . These men Live away and when thay want money thay think of subduing Kings and States."[43]

From this perspective, the country party's paper money law had the double purpose of offering humanitarian aid to farmers and countering the threat of rural violence against the government itself. The law's written text itself conveys this double motivation. Paper money loans, the preamble stated, "will have the greatest Tendency of any Thing within the Wisdom of this Legislature to quiet the Minds, and to alleviate the distressed Situation and Circumstances of the good Citizens of this State."[44] As the nineteenth-century Rhode Island historian Wilkins Updike put it, Rhode Island's 1786 paper money land bank was, in the view of its sponsors, "the only measure of State policy to prevent civil commotion."[45]

Yet because they did not grasp the farmers' plight, Greene loyalists viewed the new paper money as a cynical ploy to corrupt the voters. Thus it became for them the task of honest men to expose its true character and discredit its value. Welcome Arnold and Samuel Ward launched what became a strategy of sabotage by the Providence and Newport commercial communities.[46] When farmers and country artisans came to Providence and Newport to purchase supplies, the paper money they offered was rejected. When lower-class Providence and Newport townspeople tried to buy food from local shopkeepers with the new paper, they were told to take their business elsewhere. Attempts to pay interest or principal on their private debts were also rejected. Righteously indignant at the prospect of personal financial losses because of the government's presumed political corruption of the voters, men who had formerly insisted on obedience to the law now defied it.[47]

Thus rebuffed by the Newport and Providence business communities, the paper money collapsed. By early June 1786 a dollar in the new paper was one-quarter the value of a dollar in specie.[48] In the country districts, farmers promised tar and feathers to compel country storekeepers to accept the paper money. In Providence, a crowd tried to force the paper on one refusing merchant who would not take the paper for flour. Action thus begat reaction in a polarizing cycle of confrontation and retaliation that threatened armed combat between the new money's advocates and its opponents.[49]

The Reliefer government retreated another stride from previous administration policy when in June 1786 the assembly voted heavy legal penalties to compel the public to accept its paper money. Any action that depreciated the money's real value, whether by refusal, verbal disparagement, or acceptance of it at discount, was to be considered "subversive of those Laws and Principles upon which the Happiness, Welfare and Safety of the People depend." The penalty for a first offense was a fine of £100; for a second, disfranchisement and disablement from holding any public office.[50]

Once again, the Providence-Newport merchant community met law with defiance. In order to foreclose the government from prosecution, merchants and shopkeepers in concert shut their shops and stores and suspended business; with nothing for sale, there could be no violation of the law. To head off possible mobs from breaking and plundering their stores, merchants shipped their goods to nearby Massachusetts and Connecticut or hid them in homes and warehouses. In response to this new tactic, paper money men called country town meetings and county conventions and passed resolutions urging farmers and artisans to boycott merchants by withholding their products from sale. Passions flared hotly when, in search of bread, a Newport crowd broke into a shop where grain was stored. But as Newport merchant William Ellery described, they were "resisted, checked, and forced to retire": "If they had succeeded, no one can say where they would have stopped."[51] In Providence angry pro–paper money men hinted a grisly penalty for those who defied the £100 penal law. As a frightened Greene loyalist reported: "The carrying the Heads of those who will not render an implicit Obedience to the [Penal] Law aforesaid on Polls through the Streets has been publicly talked of—How unhappy the People where the Laws are so unstable as Ours or rather where there is none at all."[52]

Meanwhile, as the paper money became available, the payment of taxes revived. Paralyzed during the four months before the April 1786 election, by midsummer tax collection in the countryside had begun again. Between 1 January and 1 June 1786 only £118—a minuscule 0.5 percent—had been collected on the 1785 £20,000 tax. Once the paper money was printed and became available, however, Rhode Islanders paid to tax collectors £19,929, or 99 percent of the total. Eight months after the £100,000 paper money loan bank was enacted, the entire tax of £20,000 for 1785 had reached the general treasurer's office.[53]

With paper money to pay taxes now plentiful in the countryside, the general assembly moved up the final due date on the 1785 state and federal tax from 1 January 1787 to 1 November 1786. The assembly also addressed the question of payment of the state's most recent federal quota, now long overdue. As prescribed by Congress, the 1785 requisition required payment partly in specie, partly in federal interest indents. But because Rhode Island taxpayers were paying taxes only in paper money and since no specie was being received by the state's treasury, any payment to Congress in that latter medium was out of the question. Accordingly, the

assembly voted that same August to authorize local collectors to accept the
new paper money in payment for all taxes previously enacted by the Rhode
Island government and earmarked for Congress. Not only the most recent
such tax passed the previous August 1785, but any tax owed for any previous federal requisition could now be paid "in the Paper Currency, lately
emitted by this State."[54] With Rhode Island specifically in mind, however,
Congress in September 1786 rejected any idea of requisition payments in
state paper money. Congress's insistence that all requisition quotas be paid
in specie or federal indents was transmitted by the federal Board of Treasury to Rhode Island federal receiver-of-taxes William Ellery with instructions to refuse any Rhode Island paper. Ellery, staunchly antipaper
himself, bitterly expressed his feelings thus: "This State, under such an
administration as the present will never, I believe, order a specie tax upon
the inhabs. —Nothing but compulsion will induce an efficacious compliance with the requisitions of Congress."[55]

In December 1786 the Reliefer assembly dealt another blow to the fiscal-monetary arrangements of the previous Greene administration. Directing that the state's public creditors be paid by outlays from the central
treasury's accumulating paper money fund (which the cascade of country
district tax payments in paper money was filling), the assembly called for
the first of several scheduled installments on the principal of the state-
funded debt to be paid.[56] As Green loyalists saw it, instead of taxing Rhode
Island taxpayers in sound money and using it to pay the public creditors
their full value, Rhode Island's charlatan government not only was about
to pay Rhode Island creditors money worth only twenty-five cents on the
dollar but also, by thus writing off the state's heavy debt and saving its
taxpayer constituents from future taxes, was going to increase its popularity, and consolidate its power.[57] With these directives to pay the state's
Continental requisition quotas and its own public debt in Rhode Island
paper money, the Rhode Island Reliefers pushed their relief program into
even more radical territory.

In the smallest state in the Union, the same pattern of on-again, off-
again tax collection for federal purposes by a Confederation-era state government was thus dramatically played out. Congress and the Rhode Island
state government remained at an impasse; not a penny in hard money was
paid Congress by Rhode Island during the rest of the Confederation era.
Hence the state, as one observer put it, hung as "a dead Weight in the
Federal Government."[58]

⋆ 8 ⋆

MASSACHUSETTS

C ONFEDERATION Massachusetts was a fourth case of a state government that yielded to rural protest and resistance and whose attempts to raise specie for Congress by taxation broke down.[1] Abandoning the paper currency finance methods of the early Revolution, in 1780 the Massachusetts general court (the legislature) began legislating direct taxes in order to comply with Congress's federal requisitions and to finance the state's war effort. These taxes, levied between 1780 and 1782, were to be paid in specie, beef, and Continental paper currency. They were the 1780 Continental paper money tax; the 1780 Gold and Silver Tax; the May and October 1781 specie taxes; and Continental Taxes Numbers 1 and 2 (1782). In the four years of peace that followed, the government legislated three more taxes on polls, property, and income (Tax Numbers 3, 4, and 5). Both sets of direct war and peace taxes included a fixed poll tax on all adult males, a tax on assessed real and personal property, and a tax on personal income. They were to be paid variously in specie, paper money, farm products, or combinations of these (see appendix 1).

Substantial amounts of these direct taxes were earmarked for Congress. Most productive was the October 1781 specie tax for £303,634, £200,000 of which the government collected in response to Congress's October 1781 federal requisition. So effective was the collection of this tax that by June 1782 the general court ordered that £200,000 in specie be immediately paid James Lovell, the receiver of the Continental taxes in Massachusetts and Congress's official agent for receiving requisition payments.[2] Continental Taxes Numbers 1 and 2, each for £200,000, were also earmarked for federal purposes but were payable in beef, Robert Morris's notes and Bank of North America bills. In March 1786 the general court responded to a federal requisition (1785) by voting Tax Number 5, which included provision for a levy of £145,000 payable one-third in specie and two-thirds in federal paper indents. On the other hand, income from Taxes 3, 4, and 5 levied between 1783 and 1786 was earmarked for state purposes, such as payment of part of the annual interest on the state's consolidated debt, government salaries, militia expenses, sundry other operating costs, and back pay owed to soldiers and officers of the

Massachusetts Line. Direct taxes were also intended to stabilize the currency by retiring piecemeal the large quantities of depreciated Continental
and state currency in circulation (see appendix 1).

In addition the government levied substantial indirect taxes including
an impost on designated foreign imports, an excise tax on certain items
sold domestically such as wines and spirits, an excise on certain domestic
manufactures such as cider and clocks, and a tax on horse-drawn pleasure
vehicles. First legislated in November 1781 "for the purpose of paying
the interest on government securities," these indirect taxes earmarked income for annual interest payments to holders of the funded state debt (the
state's public war debt funded by consolidation and refinancing operations). The income from the impost-excise fund paid about 66 percent of
the annual interest on the consolidated state debt, the balance being paid
by direct taxes on polls and property.[3]

The apportionment and collection of state poll, property, and income
taxes was at the direction of the Massachusetts legislature, whose designated executive agent was the state treasurer. In levying a direct tax, the
general court would first prepare budget estimates of the amount required
and then apportion the sum to each of more than two hundred towns. This
done, local town assessors would apportion the town's quota among its inhabitants. When a new tax was legislated and apportioned, the state treasurer would order each town's locally elected tax collector (or constable) to
proceed with collection and to transmit the town's entire quota to the central treasury by a specified date. The collector was also required to use
coercion on any citizens who failed to pay their entire tax. After a preliminary warning, the collector was required by law to seize and sell at public
auction the taxable goods of any delinquents taxable up to the amount required to cover the unpaid balance. If their property thus auctioned did
not cover the full amount, they were to be jailed for forty days. In their
turn, town collectors were personally liable for the town's full quotaed
amount. If any collector did not transmit the entire quota to Boston by the
designated date, the state treasurer, at the general court's explicit direction,
was to issue a treasurer's execution warrant against the defaulting collector.
Printed on a standardized form, this warrant, sent to the county high sheriff for service, ordered that officer to seize and sell at auction such part of
a deficient collector's property as would make up the deficit. If, after such
proceedings, a deficit still existed, the collector was to be jailed.[4]

If at first glance this system seems extremely harsh, there were certain
mitigating features. Ostensibly, the treasurer's execution warrant enabled
the general court to coerce town collectors into carrying out collections
merely by ordering the state treasurer to issue execution warrants against
those collectors who had not met their quotas. But with only his oath of
office to compel him to duty, the county sheriff, whose responsibility it

was to serve the treasurer's execution warrant, could soften the system's worst rigors by perfunctory compliance. Mindful of the cash and credit difficulties that disabled many small farmers of rural Massachusetts from paying their taxes, the sheriffs of the central and western counties of Massachusetts, as well as those of the poorer outlying counties in Maine, Cape Cod, and the islands, often overlooked the legal letter of these warrants and returned them to the state treasurer's office in Boston totally or partially unsatisfied.

Furthermore, the various tax laws themselves had certain progressive features. Granted that all adult males over sixteen were taxed at a standardized rate (variously 11s, 16s 8p, and 25s)—the system's most regressive characteristic—the law also showed special concern for artisans and farmers as well as for householders and purchasers of state government securities by exempting artisans' and farmers' tools and implements, household furnishings, wearing apparel, and government securities from the property tax. The law also empowered elected town tax assessors to exempt any persons "who, through age, infirmity, or poverty, are unable to pay" and also to exempt "any widows or orphans" whom the assessors judged unable to pay. Moreover, the law taxed at a standardized percentage both the annual income from any profession, craft, trade, or employment and the assessed value of property such as real estate, merchandise, shipping, cattle, plate, and "all other property whatsoever" (usually 6 percent).[5] Besides the poll tax, the only other fixed tax the government levied was a flat £5 annual fee on four-wheeled coaches and chariots, and lesser fixed fees on smaller horse-drawn pleasure vehicles—a tax that obviously centered on the well-to-do. (Significantly, no such taxes were levied on farm or work vehicles.) In addition, indirect impost-excise taxes were levied on all imports into the state not destined for reexport, and on domestically manufactured clocks, cider, and other designated nonessential articles of consumption; these too tapped the pockets of the well-to-do more than they did those of the middling and the poor.[6]

Moreover, just as in Rhode Island, the Massachusetts government granted frequent exemptions, suspensions, stays, and abatements in response to specific cases of local hardship. In 1784 the general court thus extended the deadline date for taxes on all Massachusetts towns; suspended treasurer's execution warrants issued against collectors of towns in Cape Cod, in Nantucket, and in Duke's, Lincoln, and York counties; abated the quotas apportioned on the towns of Sherburne (Nantucket) and Belchertown; and recalled execution warrants issued against Sturbridge and Ashfield. In 1785 the general court abated the quotas of Duke's County, of several towns on Cape Cod, and of the towns of Tisbury, Georgetown, and Massabeseck; suspended execution warrants against towns on Cape Cod and in Cumberland County and the towns of Sherburne, Ward, and

Washington; and recalled execution warrants against Leicester and Stock-bridge.[7]

In the four years of peace before Shays's Rebellion (1782–86), this system yielded substantial but diminishing returns. On the one hand, tax collectors did collect large sums and either sent them to the state treasurer's office in Boston or answered treasurer's drafts by direct payments to individuals. In June 1782 the general court was able to order that £200,000 in specie be paid Congress's Continental receiver of taxes, James Lovell. By 1786 the statewide collection rate of taxes levied in 1782, 1783, and 1784 was 75 percent, representing a total of £556,398 collected out of total levies of £740,000. On the other hand, because collectors and sheriffs exercised discretion and did not seize and sell the property of delinquents at auction, substantial sums were not collected. Of the several taxes levied in 1780–81, by 11 November 1785 nearly half, £140,167, had still not been paid into the state treasury (see table 10). Of the five taxes levied between 1781 and 1786 (officially designated State Taxes Numbers 1, 2, 3, 4, 5), varying proportions were in arrears. If the arrearages on the first four taxes levied was comparatively low (12–35 percent), the arrearages of the March 1786 tax remained much higher, 84 percent as late as October 1787 (see table 11).

Analysis of the October 1781 tax and of various other 1780–82 taxes shows that the state's central, western, and northern counties—Hampshire, Worcester, Berkshire and York—where cash, credit, and salable property were shorter than elsewhere, had the largest percentages of unpaid taxes (see table 10). In wealthier eastern Massachusetts, however, where cash and credit were more available, tax collection did much better. In Boston, within a space of only fifteen months, collector Francis Shaw, on a total apportionment of £4,386 on the October 1781 tax, had collected every penny. "For want of goods or estate I have arrested the body of the within same Holden [a Dorchester collector] & committed him to gaol & gave him the Liberty of Gaol," Suffolk County Sheriff Joseph Henderson noted; freed from jail, but facing possible recommitment, Holden collected and transmitted to the state treasurer the full amount within a year.[8] Near Boston, Middlesex County Sheriff Loammi Baldwin by February 1786 had served and successfully discharged treasurer's execution writs totaling £11,770 on the 1781 specie tax and £16,942 on the first half of the Continental tax; taxpayers and collectors who suffered sale of property through such actions must have been numerous. By February 1786 Baldwin's pressure had brought such a high return of war taxes (1780–82) that State Treasurer Ivers could report to the general court that all but relatively small amounts of the taxes under Baldwin's charge had been discharged.[9]

Just as in Pennsylvania, South Carolina, and Rhode Island, the scarcity

TABLE 10.
EIGHT MASSACHUSETTS TAXES COLLECTED AND IN ARREARS,
1780–1782
(AS OF 11 NOVEMBER 1785)

County	Amount of Executions	Collected under Executions	In Arrears (% in parentheses)
Middlesex	$132,151[a] [£39,685][b]	$98,911 [£29,703]	$ 33,240 (25) [£9,982]
Cumberland	17,153 [5,151]	12,338 [3,705]	4,815 (28) [1,446]
Suffolk	91,382 [27,442]	61,109 [18,351]	30,263 (33) [9,088]
Plymouth	58,824 [17,665]	37,929 [11,390]	20,899 (36) [6,276]
Bristol	91,548 [27,492]	54,033 [16,226]	37,512 (41) [11,265]
Lincoln	11,508 [3,456]	6,623 [1,989]	4,885 (42) [1,467]
Essex	111,825 [33,581]	62,015 [18,623]	49,813 (45) [14,959]
York	56,640 [17,009]	26,923 [8,085]	29,717 (52) [8,924]
Hampshire	148,621 [44,631]	70,499 [21,171]	77,119 (52) [23,159]
Worcester	192,271 [57,739]	57,452 [17,253]	134,815 (70) [40,485]
Berkshire	58,745 [17,641]	14,965 [4,494]	43,676 (74) [13,116]
Total	$970,668 [£291,492]	$502,796 [£150,990]	$466,754 (48) [£140,167]

Source: Ms book labeled "Sheriff's Accounts, 1782–1785," in ms box labeled "Sheriffs' Account Books," Massachusetts Archives, Boston.

[a]The figures represent totals on eight Massachusetts taxes levied from 1780–82 as shown in treasurer's execution warrants issued to sheriffs.

[b]£ indicates Massachusetts money of account.

TABLE II.

FIVE MASSACHUSETTS TAXES COLLECTED AND IN ARREARS,
1782–1786

Tax and Date Due	Purpose	Amount Levied	Amount Collected	In Arrears (% in parentheses)
Tax No. 1 (Jan. 1782)	Federal requisition	$ 666,000 [£200,000]ᵃ	$586,500 [£176,126]	$ 79,500 (12) [£23,874]
Tax No. 2 (1782)	Federal requisition	666,000 [200,000]	445,035 [133,644]	220,965 (33) [66,356]
Tax No. 3 (Mar. 1783)	State gov't expenses; state debt interest	666,000 [200,000]	517,902 [155,526]	148,098 (22) [44,474]
Tax No. 4 (July 1784)	Redemption of army notes	466,200 [140,000]	303,370 [91,102]	162,830 (35) [48,898]
Tax No. 5 (Mar. 1786)	Federal requisition; state gov't. expenses; state debt interest	1,000,462 [300,439]	158,095 [47,476]	842,367 (84) [252,963]
Total		$3,464,662 [£1,040,439]	$2,010,902 [£603,874]	$1,453,760 (42) [£436,965]

Sources: State Treasurer Alexander Hodgdon's March 1788 report, "General State of Balances due from Towns, Collectors & Sheriffs on the Taxes Undermentioned to the 1st October 1787," Massachusetts State Archives Document 2606, Photocopy in Early State Record Collection, microfilm D24, roll 3, Massachusetts, Microform Division, Library of Congress. Taxes 1, 2, 3, 4, and 5 are found in the Early American Imprints Collections: Tax 1 (Evans #44217); Tax 2 (Evans #17597); Tax 3 (Evans #19423); Tax 4 (Evans #18585); Tax 5 (Evans #19782).

ᵃ£ indicates Massachusetts money of account.

of circulating cash, the lack of credit, and the low capital liquidity of most of the inhabitants of central and western Massachusetts often made it impossible for small farmers and rural artisans and laborers to come up with the taxes they owed. Compounding their predicament were low farm prices and low laborers' wages—also the fruits of the cash-credit scarcity during the Confederation's middle years. Yet the upper-class framers of this tax legislation believed that any able-bodied individual could pay these taxes by diligent exertion and frugal housekeeping; if he did not, a strong dose of government coercion would put him right.

Middle-class country Reliefer legislators rejected these assumptions and sought ways to alleviate the tax burden on the western counties. Representing the state's poorer country towns and in closer touch with their realities than were wealthy, upper-class legislators from commercial and coastal areas, rural Reliefer legislators grasped that paying the state's heavy taxes in a depressed economy was beyond what many farmers and rural laborers could manage even with the most strenuous exertion and saving. Hence they urged relief measures such as the postponement of tax deadlines; the abatement of taxes for individual towns; the reduction of government officials' salaries; the reduction of the value of the consolidated debt from its nominal to its market value in order to release revenue from the excise-impost fund; the printing and loaning of paper money payable for taxes to farmers; and other cost-cutting, postponement, and reflation schemes. But with no party organization to coordinate their strategy, maintain discipline, or mobilize outside support, the many Reliefers who passed through the Massachusetts house during the 1780s were repeatedly outmaneuvered or outvoted.[10]

Despite strenuous Reliefer warnings that these taxes could not be paid, in 1781 and again in 1786 the Massachusetts general court launched drives to compel collection of taxes by force. The crackdown resolution that the general court passed in July 1786 declared that unenforced tax collection "discovers want of energy in Government," discourages those who "may exert themselves, for the purpose of paying in due season, their respective proportion of the publick taxes," and "will operate to the real injury of the delinquents."[11]

The First Pressure-Resistance-Retreat Cycle, 1781–1782

In the first of these drives, in May 1781 the general court levied a specie tax on the people of Massachusetts totaling £374,795 to meet a variety of state needs, including pay and supplies for the troops of the Massachusetts Line. The following October 1781 the government levied another specie tax of £303,634, most of which was to meet Congress's October requisition for funds for the war effort and to pay the interest on the federal debt. Each time the general court followed up the levy by ordering that the treasurer issue his execution writs "against Constables & Collectors delinquent in paying in the hard money Tax" if they had not collected their quotas by the given due dates.[12] These enforcement actions set off painful pressures throughout the state, but especially in the central, western, and outlying counties of Massachusetts where circulating cash and credit were scarce.[13]

In March and April 1782 delegates from various country towns in Hampshire, Berkshire, Worcester, and Bristol counties gathered in im-

promptu county conventions and voted petitions to the general court pro-
testing various grievances and asking for tax relief; these were presented
at the general court's May 1782 session. Farmers and rural artisans also
lashed out at town collectors who attempted to collect their quotas. In
Hampshire County, Major Joseph Hawley warned Northampton's general court delegate Ephraim Wright in April 1782 of the consequences
when local collectors tried to collect from ex-Army veterans, whose Continental debt certificates paid no interest: "If Such People once make a
Stand and absolutely refuse to pay their Taxes, as you may be assured, they
are on the point of doing, there is no power Short of the Continental and
French Soldiers, which can compel them to it. . . . It Signifys nothing
to tell these folks, that their interest will be made Principal and all be made
to draw interest, when their Collector is at their doors demanding the hard
cash, they immediately burst out in rage and become desperate."[14]

In Hampshire County that same 1782 spring, resistance flared when
Rev. Samuel Ely harangued Sunderland farmers and laborers against the
excessive salaries of government officials and urged them "to break up the
courts"; Ely was arrested, convicted, fined, and jailed for sedition. On 12
June 100–150 men marched through Northampton to Springfield,
stormed the jail, and set Ely free. Things deteriorated further when Ely
with 600 men marched into Northampton reportedly to burn the town;
he was met by 400 armed men headed by Sheriff Elisha Porter, who eventually got Ely and his forces to withdraw.[15]

At an inn in Lanesborough in Berkshire County, farmers also talked of
using armed force to stop the government's tax collectors, but they were
apparently headed off by James Harris, the local justice of the peace. Although he denounced the government for alleged extravagance, when he
was asked "whether it was best to appear in arms," Harris replied that he
"did not think that would do" but advocated instead "calling a County
Convention to petition the general court for redress of grievances." Shortly
thereafter, Harris was seized bodily by Lanesborough constable Ebenezer
Buck for unpaid taxes; but Harris stood his ground, saying "he would not
go with the officer." Harris urged the town meeting, however, "to interfere for him in particular, & for the future to prevent officers distrain-
ing the property for taxes." Elsewhere in Berkshire, groups of farmers
and rural artisans "covenanted to resist all sheriffs and Collectors in the
levying [of] executions and in collecting taxes." When Pittsfield tax cov-
enanters obstructed the deputy sheriff from seizing and selling off oxen at
auction by recapturing the cattle, the Berkshire high sheriff gathered a
posse, rode out in search of the resisters, and, after a sharp scuffle, captured
twenty of the group and committed them for trial at Great Barrington.[16]

As the county executive officer whose immediate superior was the governor, Sheriff Elisha Porter of Hampshire County sent written reports of

the farmers' mood and of the Ely riot (described in the house journal as "an insurrection") to Governor John Hancock. Hancock in turn transmitted the report to the house of representatives without comment. With the governor either unwilling to take the lead or sitting on the fence, the house suspended habeas corpus for six months so that a county sheriff could seize and hold without trial any suspected troublemaker. But then it ordered Colonel Seth Washburn, a Worcester County member sympathetic to farmers' distress, to "inform the Treasurer that it is the sense of the house that he use his discretion respecting issuing his Executions against Delinquent Towns, for the first moiety of the Tax." The next day the house went further, directing the treasurer "to suspend the sending Executions against delinquent constables & collectors for the New Emission money till the second Wednesday of the next sitting of the Genl court." The house debated "the expediency of issuing a Tax upon the Poles & estates of the Inhabitants of this Commonwealth the present session & after debate determined in the negative"; it also reduced the taxes of several towns; instructed Governor Hancock to write Superintendent Morris "that it would be detrimental to his object to call on the people for taxes the present session of the general court & informing him that it should be the first business of the next sitting"; and approved a bill that provided for the auction sale of attached property at prices set by local appraisers. Lastly, the house appointed a special committee to ride to Hampshire County to talk with the inhabitants. To head this committee, the house named that most trusted veteran of the Revolutionary Patriot leadership, Samuel Adams; other members were the veteran Revolutionary general, Artemas Ward, and the house speaker, Nathaniel Gorham.[17]

With these several concessions, the general court quieted fears in central and western Massachusetts. Mollified and reassured, farmers and rural artisans believed their property and farms were no longer in imminent danger. Samuel Adams and his committee also did much to quiet the Hampshire County countryside. At an impromptu convention at Hatfield early in August with delegates from forty-five Hampshire County towns, Adams, Ward, and Gorham spent four days hearing "Grievances," and "endeavouring to explain public Measures" taken by the general court. At the end of the session, the delegates voted resolutions that balanced stated grievances with pledges of support for the government's policies. On the one hand, the delegates repeated the complaint that their quotaed taxes were disproportionately heavy, given "the distance of the County from market," and that "grants of money by the general court to particular persons & officers in the state are too large." On the other, they pledged their and their constituents' support for "the present Government of this Commonwealth" and the present war effort "by paying all reasonable taxes as fast as they shall be able."[18]

The respite was only temporary, however. During the 1782 house debate over the "insurrection," fifty-four members had voted not for concessions but for a new tax on the people of Massachusetts. Despite the uproar in the countryside, many legislators believed that new taxes could and should be imposed and collected. In 1783 and again in 1784 the general court voted new poll-property levies (Taxes No. 3 and 4). And at the general court's repeated orders, the state treasurer issued execution warrants against collectors and constables whose accounts were in arrears.[19]

Measured by their yield, these new pressures were quite productive. In central and western Massachusetts, taxpayers experienced stern dunning, as the substantial diminishment of arrearages indicates. In Hampshire County, a tabulation of returns indicates that collection of arrearages on selected 1780–82 war taxes over a thirteen-month period (January 1785– February 1786) lowered the arrearages by significant amounts (table 12).

Collection in eastern Massachusetts was even more effective. In Middlesex County, where Sheriff Loammi Baldwin pressured local collectors with stern efficiency, by February 1786 the arrearages on four comparable wartime taxes were almost eliminated (table 13).

Despite the personal hardship these pressures caused, only a few flareups against the system occurred during the next three years (1783–86). The

TABLE 12.
HAMPSHIRE COUNTY TAXES COLLECTED,
JANUARY 1785–FEBRUARY 1786 (1ST MOIETY)

Tax	Amount of Executions	In Arrears (% in parentheses)	
		January 1785	February 1786
Continental Tax No. 1	$67,805 [£20,362]ᵃ	$42,850 (63) [£12,868]	$24,022 (35) [£7,214]
October 1781 Tax	51,658 [15,513]	21,191 (41) [6,364]	12,557 (24) [3,771]
May 1781 Tax	8,318 [2,498]	7,169 (86) [2,153]	4,428 (53) [1,330]
Beef Tax	7,898 [2,372]	6,237 (79) [1,873]	4,366 (55) [1,311]

Source: Hampshire County sheriff's ms account book in ms box labeled "Box 1 Sheriffs' Accounts Barnstable-Plymouth Counties," Massachusetts Archives, Boston.
ᵃ£ indicates Massachusetts money of account.

TABLE 13.
MIDDLESEX COUNTY TAXES COLLECTED,
JANUARY 1785–FEBRUARY 1786 (1ST MOIETY)

Tax	Amount of Executions	In Arrears (% in parentheses)	
		January 1785	February 1786
Continental Tax No. 1	$57,516	$11,152 (19)	$ 552 (1 –)
	[£17,272]ᵃ	[3,349]	[£166]
New Emission Tax	13,936	10,569 (76)	1,329 (10)
	[4,185]	[3,174]	[399]
October 1781 Specie Tax	39,194	?	?
	[11,770]		
Beef Tax	1,928	1,605 (83)	323 (17)
	[579]	[482]	[97]

Source: Middlexsex County sheriff's ms account book in ms box labeled "Box 1 Sheriffs' Accounts Barnstable-Plymouth Counties," Massachusetts Archives, Boston.
ᵃ£ indicates Massachusetts money of account.

pressure from the center was mitigated by stays, exemptions, and concessions granted by the general court to individual towns and counties, and the sheriffs of the central and western counties did not enforce treasurer's execution warrants to the letter. Nevertheless, the flareups testify to continuing pressure. Early in 1783 men from the town of Sutton in Worcester County rode up to Douglas and joined "in a Mob to Resist authority and the Dew oppration of the Law." Not all Sutton taxpayers would go this far, however, for shortly afterward, a Sutton town meeting voted "to divide the house to see what will support good government and will endeavour to pay their taxes and to suppress all mobbs in opposition to the laws of the State."[20] A year later in 1784, a Hampshire County newspaper casually noted the occurrence of "frequent insurrections in this county" that "rather seem to have no head at all" and do "no injury to any man's person or property."[21]

That mass resistance *would* occur if pressure from the top was intensified was the public prediction of an editorial in the Springfield *Hampshire Herald* dated 7 September 1784. "There stands on the Court-house, in this town, an advertisement for the sale of the real estates of seven collectors; and a number of other collectors in the county, are in the same predicament . . . a great part of the taxes committed to them remains uncollected." These collectors had not been negligent, according to the editor; in fact, they had "taken and exposed to sale cattle, and other property, belonging not merely to the poorer people, but to substantial farmers, who would once have disdained to be asked twice for a tax." But because "money has flown away," and because "the farmer and mechanick find no means to procure it," there have been no buyers. With no money to be had even by men "possessed of considerable estates," the editor continued, government must choose whether to "relax" or bring things to a crisis. As yet, "there are no threats of resistance; there is little murmuring; but you may hear the deep sigh of perplexity; you may see the sad face of desperation." Was it therefore "prudent," the editor asked, "to push the matter further at present? Is there not danger, that the powers of Government, stretch'd beyond a certain tone, will burst asunder?"

The Second Pressure-Resistance-Retreat Cycle, 1786–1787: Shays's Rebellion

Despite such warnings, late in 1785 the government in Boston began increasing the pressure once again. With the election of the wealthy Boston merchant–amateur scientist James Bowdoin to the governorship (1785–87), the time seemed favorable for a full application of the government's power. Once in office Bowdoin stated his concern at the lagging payments to Congress and urged the general court to enforce the collection of taxes levied for federal requisitions.[22]

Meeting in Boston, the house and senate leadership moved to require county sheriffs to force deficient town collectors and constables to do their duty. First, a resolution was passed in November 1785 that ordered all county sheriffs to settle their outstanding accounts with the state treasurer within a period of three months; after that time, any sheriff whose accounts remained uncompleted would be called to the house to explain himself. Next, in March 1786, the house leadership summoned sheriffs from Berkshire, Hampshire, Worcester, Essex, Middlesex, Plymouth, and York (the very counties with the largest sums of taxes outstanding) to the house floor and grilled them; whatever interchange took place between legislators and county sheriffs must be imagined. Dismissing the sheriffs with the warning that if they did not soon settle they would be summoned again, the house ordered the treasurer "to renew his demands on the sheriffs of the several counties for the immediate settlement of their accounts & payment of the respective balances in their hands."[23]

Simultaneously, the house leadership streamlined the legal machinery of the tax collection system. House leader John Choate of Ipswich piloted legislation to strengthen existing tax collection procedures. So that no one could plead ignorance of the law, all existing statutory requirements, scattered among several laws, were consolidated into a single statute. The new

act made its purpose abundantly clear in its formal title—"An Act for enforcing the Speedy Payment of Rates and Taxes, and directing the Process
against deficient Constables and Collectors."[24] In addition, the general
court mandated new accounting procedures that simplified and accelerated
the keeping of sheriff's accounts and that required that all town collectors
render their accounts to the state treasurer every two months and that all
town selectmen call on the town collectors for their accounts and transmit
these accounts to the treasurer in Boston.[25]

These initiatives were taken between November 1785 and March
1786, but more was to come. The general court decided to make an example of Berkshire County's Sheriff Hyde whose overdue accounts on unsatisfied treasurer's execution warrants were enormous—on six wartime
taxes his arrears totaled £11,490. The following July, in a measure that
hinted at removal and legal action, the general court formally asked Governor Bowdoin to inquire into Hyde's conduct "relating to the executions
that have been committed to him by the Treasurer of this Commonwealth"
and to "take such measures concerning him, as may be consistent with the
constitution."[26] Then, on 6 July 1786, the general court closed the system's last remaining loophole—the county sheriff's discretionary power to
act on treasurer's execution warrants. Henceforth, the treasurer was to report to the governor and council the name of any sheriff or deputy sheriff
who did not carry out a treasurer's execution warrant to the full amount.
Even harsher, each county sheriff was made personally responsible for
every penny of taxes levied for state or federal purposes *in 1782 and before*.
Thus, if a sheriff, after receiving a treasurer's execution warrant against
a town collector, failed to raise the full amount under any of these taxes
within three months after receiving the warrant, he was to be held personally liable for the entire deficit. Enforcing this draconian measure was
to be another county officer—the county coroner. That no one in Massachusetts might be in doubt about its import, the edict was ordered published in newspapers around the state.[27]

Meanwhile, Treasurer Thomas Ivers dispatched treasurer's execution
warrants to the sheriffs of Worcester, Hampshire, and Berkshire county
requiring that delinquent tax collectors be forced to collect unpaid taxes
levied between 1780 and 1782. Three of these six taxes—the 1780 Gold
and Silver Tax and the May and October 1781 specie taxes—had to be
paid in hard-to-get specie. Two, Continental Tax Numbers 1 and 2, were
payable in federal paper currency—either Morris's notes or Bank of North
America notes. Because the original purpose of the two continental taxes
and of the October 1781 specie tax had been to raise money for Congress,
much of the impulse behind this new initiative was to keep a bankrupt
Congress afloat. Bowdoin himself had indicated this motive when he stated
privately that the states should "exert themselves to pay the arrearage taxes"

(previously voted for Congress), and that unless they did so "the federal government must cease, and the Union with it."[28]

None of these early taxes was intended to pay the interest on the state debt. Because 66 percent of the annual interest on that debt was already being paid out of previously appropriated impost and excise taxes, and because the balance was being paid out of more recent direct taxes, it goes too far to hold that the state's public debt was the policy objective of the state's 1786 tax drive.[29]

The current treasurer, Thomas Ivers, offered little hope of relief. In March 1785 he sent Berkshire County sheriff Caleb Hyde "the Executions against the delinquent collectors Renewed for the Ballances due from them on the several Taxes Committed to them to Collect" and asked him to "Immediately extend the Executions against the Collectors without farther delay, as the many and pressing demands on the Treasury makes it necessary that the money be collected and paid in as soon as possible."[30] In a February 1786 reply to Ivers, Sheriff Hyde returned "all the Executions that I have with what I recd. on them." Of the remainder, he wrote, "I know not how to Collect the Ballances Due as it is almost impossible to Collect Money in this County." Nevertheless, pursuant to the general court's order, on 15 June and again on 5 July 1786 the treasurer dispatched packets of treasurer's execution warrants to the sheriffs of Hampshire, Berkshire, and Worcester requiring that they force the collectors to collect specie for arrearages on the October 1781 specie tax. (Between 1 January 1786 and 1 June 1787, Sheriff Hyde would in fact return at least £567 to the treasury in Boston.)[31]

These actions fell heavily on local tax officials. Even before the 6 July 1786 resolution making sheriffs personally accountable, the Hampshire and Worcester county sheriffs, prodded and threatened by the house and by Ivers's execution warrants, had intensified their pressure on lagging town collectors. Treasurer's execution writs in hand, they and their deputies demanded that town collectors come up with their required specie quotas on the taxes not yet collected; otherwise, collectors would lose their property at auction or go to jail. Just how many auction sales and jailings actually occurred will probably never be known, but the notations by Sheriff Porter of Hampshire County indicate that much property was sold and at least one collector jailed.

Indeed, the pressure on Hampshire County taxpayers was severe. During the winter, spring, and summer of 1786 Sheriff Elijah Porter sent his deputies riding about the county serving treasurer's execution writs on delinquent town collectors and attaching their property. As the notations on these writs indicate, either this property was auctioned, or the threat of auction forced collectors to collect from their neighbors either by actual sale or the threat of sale. These collections yielded at least £1,000; between 1 January 1786 and 1 June 1787, Sheriff Porter transmitted at least £1,152 to the treasury in Boston.[32]

Petitions describe the heavy pressure that the general court's new tax collection offensive put on Hampshire taxpayers. In January 1786 fifty-seven petitioners of Greenwich told the general court that the town collectors "are daily Vandeing our property both Real and Personal." The following June, forty-eight petitioners of Bernardston wrote that their town's uncollected taxes "are to be emediately collected, the Sherrifs have executions upon the Collectors and will levy upon them if the money is not Paid the State . . . the Collectors are indeavouring to gather by seizing and selling but as there is scaresly any money at all in the Town our subsistance must be sold for less than a quarter of its true value . . . we do not Petition for fear of distress at a distance for it is already come upon us . . . some of our Persons are seized for taxes, some children are destitute of milk and other necessaries of life by the driveing of the Collectors."[33]

In Berkshire County, Sheriff Hyde did not pursue the town collectors under his charge with Porter's tenacity. Hyde pressed town collectors whose accounts were overdue, but some of his notations hint that his effort may have been more show than substance: "Berkshire 20 May 1786 by virtue of this writ I have made thorough and diligent search within my precinct and cannot find either the Estate or the Body of the within named Simeon Caulkins [collector of Lee] whereon to levy this Execution therefore I return it wholly unsatisfied. Caleb Hyde Sheriff." Yet on 16 October 1786 Caulkins turned up at Hyde's house in Lenox with £105.9.11 of the £210.5 he owed.[34] Partly for humanitarian reasons and partly because he feared that if town collectors tried to sell their neighbors' property they would be met by force, Hyde returned more than half the writs to State Treasurer Ivers without any payment, each marked with the terse notation, "Returned unsatisfied."

Similarly, as notations on other treasurer's execution warrants indicate, the sheriffs of Worcester, Bristol, Plymouth, and the three Maine counties of York, Cumberland, and Lincoln did not coerce collectors with quite the same severity as did Porter. Nevertheless, with the 6 July 1786 resolution published and known throughout the state, anyone could see that the day was not far off when the sheriffs would have to move forcefully against the collectors, for the coroners would be levying on *their* property as the law now required.[35]

Once again the farmers, laborers, and rural artisans of central and western Massachusetts girded against the loss of stock, produce, and lands. As early as January 1786 Hampshire farmers had petitioned the general court to call off tax collection or otherwise provide them relief: "Unless something takes place more favourable to the people in A Little time att Least one half of our inhabitants in our oppinion will become banckerupt."

The town collectors of Greenwich, they wrote, were "dayly Vandeing our property both Real and Personal our Land after itt is prised by the best judges under oath is sold for about one third of the value of itt our Cattle about one half the Value."[36]

A few months later the picture that farmers in the Worcester County town of Lunenberg drew was equally grim: "The great & insupportable Difficulties arising from the almost total Want of a circulating Medium, whereby the People are disabled from paying their Debts both Public & private, and many have been, and more still are liable to be forced to Gaol to the Great Injury of the Community; many having had all their Cattle taken for Taxes, & are now unable to sell their Lands for the discharge of their remaining Taxes & private Debts; the Town being in Arrear of Taxes about two thousand Pounds."[37]

Similarly, in their petition the farmers of the Hampshire town of Bernardston anticipated either jail or ruin. "There is a few men among us who have the best Estates have Paid their Taxes. . . . The rest of us who have got the Seaven Hundred Pound which is now collecting by distraint to pay." Even if "all the Cattle and Grain that we have was sold at full Price it would Scarce be suficient to Pay but the case with us is that there is not any buyers to Pay money at common market and we are drove to the terrible alternative either to be thrown into Gaol or deliver up what Cattle and Grain we have to be sold at Publick auction if we Prefer the latter which we undoubtedly shall our Cattle and Grain will not at the Best half pay our Taxes in Consequence of which for want of Cattle our lands must be untild our families suffering for the necessaries of life."[38]

Indeed, the petitions warned, rather than go on like this, farmers would leave Massachusetts. Within the past two years, the Greenwich petition declared, "Many have fled others wishing to flee to the State of New york or some other State." Without immediate relief, the Bernardston petition warned, "Many of us must fly to unknown climes or kingdoms for existance."[39]

The protestors tried other strategies. Town meetings, called to deal with the emergency, voted special instructions to the town's general court delegate mandating that he press for various relief measures. While specific remedies varied, the instructions agreed that taxes could not be paid, for the townspeople were "sure, from sad experience, that without a greater quantity of circulating cash" it was "impossible" for them to pay "the sums already assessed." Furthermore, viewing "with grief the heavy taxes, repeatedly laid on the people," they were "almost discouraged from attempting to pay them" when they considered their "complicated difficulties."[40]

Countywide conventions were held and relief resolutions voted. At these improvised gatherings in taverns, courthouses, and private dwellings, delegates pooled ideas into lengthy statements that piled up grievances and remedies. Invariably, they urged various ways to lighten the tax burden. Officials' salaries and interest payments on the funded public debt should be reduced; a paper money land bank should be established to loan farmers money and reflate farm prices. Immediate relief from the current tax collection drive was also pressed.

Considering the calamitous circumstances into which unhappy Debtors are involved, by means of the great scarcity of circulating Cash, by which their property is often taken and sold at one third or one fourth the real value: We do humbly petition, that, for their immediate relief, there may be a suspension of law in all civil cases and collection of Taxes for nine months. (Taunton Convention, Bristol County, 27 June 1786)

The convention from a thorough conviction of great uneasiness, subsisting among the people of the county and commonwealth . . . were of opinion that many grievances and unnecessary burdens now lying upon the people, are the sources of that discontent: The present mode adopted for the payment and speedy collection of the last tax; the present mode of taxation, as it operates unequally between the polls and estates, and between landed and mercantile interests. (Hatfield Convention, Hampshire County, 25 August 1786)

We pray the Honourable Court for a prolongation of the time of the first payment of the present tax. (Paxton Convention, Worcester County, 26 September 1786)[41]

The next increase in counterpressure came through forcible obstruction of the law. Did anyone need to be reminded, a homespun essayist observed, that resistance to the law would occur if money remained unobtainable and "the laws not be discontinued, for enforcing the payment of debts among individuals, and for collecting public taxes"? Farmers had no money to pay either their public or private dues, and now their farms and livelihoods were threatened. "Can the People make bricks without straw? Will they not rather, through *necessity*, (as that is accounted the mother of invention) be reminded of, if not excited to *improve*, the first great law of nature, viz, *self-preservation?*"[42]

Contemporary sources are too fragmentary to show exactly by what methods and how extensively collectors were defied that summer of 1786. By 31 July 1786, as one government sympathizer reported, tax collection in Hampshire County was at a near standstill. He had little or no hope of receiving any money from any tax collector, merchant-contractor Joseph Cranch wrote from Springfield, because of "the Scarcety of Money, added to the disaffected sperit of the People in genl, relative to paying their Taxes in this County." Farmers probably covenanted among themselves not to bid at any public auction for goods or real estate seized for the nonpayment

of taxes, as they had done in 1782. Perhaps anonymous warnings were
scrawled and posted on signposts and trees where collectors on their rounds
could see them, as was done that fall in Maryland. Perhaps collectors were
defied and threatened as they knocked at farmers' doors. They may have
received anonymous warnings, such as the unsigned letter sent to Governor James Bowdoin in Boston "to Lett the gentellmen of Boston [know]
that we Countary men will not pay taxes, as they[y] think. But Lett them
send the Constubel to here and well Nock him Down for ofering to Come
Near us for If you Dont Lower the taxes well pull Down the town house
about yor Ears."[43]

Thus obstructed, further tax collection became impossible. In Berkshire
County, Sheriff Caleb Hyde, fearing to put town collectors and constables
to the risk of life or limb, made no serious attempt to force town collectors
by serving treasurer's execution warrants on their property. Other sheriffs
followed his example. Because auction sales could not be held without provoking violence, sheriffs and town collectors in other middle and western
counties abandoned collection. By late August or early September, the entire tax system was dead in the water.[44]

The final counterpressure move was to block the county courts where
civil and criminal cases were tried. Hampshire farmers led the way; when
the government in Boston forced the issue, farmers in Worcester, Berkshire, and Middlesex followed suit. On the day that a county court was
scheduled to begin quarterly sessions, farmers and rural mechanics would
form ranks in front of the court house, clubs and muskets in hand. They
blocked the justices from reaching the building, handing them petitions
that demanded that the court be adjourned until county conventions could
convey their petitions to the general court ("until the Minds of the People
can be obtained & the resolves of the Convention of the County can have
an opportunity of having their Grievances redressed by the General
Court"). The first such forced adjournment was at Northampton (Hampshire County) on 29 August. Following the governor's hard-line public
proclamation on 2 September, similar actions occurred at Worcester
(Worcester County) on 5–6 September and at Great Barrington (Berkshire County) and Concord (Middlesex County) on 12 September. When
the courts tried to open again in November and December, another cycle
of similar obstruction occurred in Springfield (Hampshire), Pittsfield
(Berkshire), and Worcester (Worcester); only in Concord, where militia
units stood at the ready, did the court open for business.[45]

Because these court closings put an end to legal recovery actions by private creditors against debtors, historians have concluded that creditors'
pressure on private debtors was the principal cause of Shays's Rebellion.
Creditors' foreclosure actions against debtors did require the same painful
seizure-and-sale proceedings that could bankrupt a defaulting taxpayer,

and much complaint about ruinous court actions on the part of debtors was heard at the time. (By adjourning the Hampshire County court, Hampshire militants stated, the justices "will ease in part our heavy Burthens we now labor under at present"). But during this very period when the central government in Boston was accelerating the pressure on delinquent taxpayers (January–August 1786), monthly creditor actions against debtors declined.[46] Moreover, the overall tax burden was both heavier and more widely distributed than the overall debt burden. The McDonalds' researches indicate that the per capita amount of current and overdue taxes in Worcester, Hampshire, and Berkshire counties was five times greater than the per capita amount of unpaid debts—and much more widespread among the population: everyone was taxed; not every one was in debt.[47] Although in 1786 many more delinquent debtors than delinquent taxpayers were in the county jails of central and western Massachusetts, many more people were at greater risk of losing their property from the government's tax crackdown than from debt actions. Thus if the "court-mobbings" (as government leaders' termed them) shielded debtors against creditors, more importantly they signaled the general court in Boston that the people of rural Massachusetts would no longer tolerate the government's tax policies, and that if any law was to operate outside Boston (especially tax collection), these policies must change.[48]

In 1782 militant Hampshire and Berkshire farmers had defied tax collectors and a cautious Governor Hancock had transmitted the sheriff's report to the general court without recommending any action; the general court had voted concessions. But in 1786 with James Bowdoin in the governor's chair, the government in Boston took a different line. Officials were summoned to the governor's office for consultation; hardliner judges Theophilus Parsons (Newburyport) and David Sewall (York) numbered among those at a meeting with the governor on 1 September.[49] Then the governor went on the legal offensive. On 2 September—four days after Hampshire militants forced the Northampton County Court to adjourn— he issued a sternly worded public proclamation that labeled the action at Northampton "treason" and instructed Attorney General Robert Treat Paine "to prosecute and bring to condign punishment the Ringleaders and Abettors of the aforesaid atrocious violation of law and government; and also the Ringleaders and Abettors of any similar violations in future."[50]

When the general court convened in Boston early in October, the governor sought new legislation that would strengthen his hand against any further mob action. At Bowdoin's request, the general court suspended habeas corpus (the executive could now seize and detain without trial) and enacted a revised Riot Act with new streamlined procedures, presumably designed by Judge Theophilus Parsons, for dispersing rioters, and with new penalties for the guilty. Although September and October passed with little action, Bowdoin was biding his time. That November, at word that the court at Concord (Middlesex) would again be blocked, he issued ten arrest warrants against local Middlesex and Hampshire town leaders suspected of inciting the people to obstruction of the county courts. At his order, a sheriff's posse was formed. The posse rode into the Middlesex County town of Groton, arrested three of the men, and returned them to the Boston jail where, at Bowdoin's order again, they were denied bail and not permitted any visitor or written communication with anyone.[51]

Instead of quieting the countryside, however, these actions had the opposite effect. The rural folk of central and western Massachusetts began organizing military units to defend themselves and their farms against arrest and confiscation. Not only farms, property, and livelihoods but life and liberty were at stake. A grimmer, more militant mood can be glimpsed in a crudely written letter sent by self-styled Regulators and citing the request of Captains Daniel Shays and Adam Wheeler to the town of Boylston sometime late that fall of 1786:

> To the good people of boylston as this is perelous times and blood shed and prisoners made by tirants who are a fighting for promotion and to advance their intrest wich will Destory the good people of this Land—we that stile ourselves regelators think it is our Duty to stand for our Lives and for our familys and for our Intrest wich will be taken from us if we Dont Defend them. Therefore we would have you take it into consideration and fly to our assistance and soon as posable in this just and righteous cause as there must be exeration made. This request from Daniel Shays and Adam Wheeler who are Chief Commanders at the army.[52]

Late the following January 1787, Captains Shays and Luke Day, with Hampshire armed units under their command, marched to the Springfield federal arsenal in quest of supplies and barracks. Defending state militia commanded by the sturdy Revolutionary veteran General William Shepherd barred the way, however; after a brief confrontation, cannon fire into the insurgent ranks killed three men and forced the remaining units to withdraw.[53] The decisive blow fell early the following February 1787, when a contingent of government militia commanded by General Benjamin Lincoln, after marching miles through a midnight snowstorm, surprised Shays and his men at Petersham and scattered or captured the entire force. Although localized raiding and intimidation continued to sputter and flare, and government troops in Hampshire and Berkshire counties were harassed during that same winter and spring, after Springfield and Petersham Shays's Rebellion was, for all intents and purposes, over.[54]

Even so, farmers, rural mechanics, and laborers continued to obstruct collectors who seized their property for unpaid taxes. Indeed, it may be doubted that many tax collectors even tried. That April a cavalry man, returning from duty in Berkshire county, noted how grimly determined against taxes he found local inhabitants along the way. According to the trooper, Thompson, "at the public houses where we called, it was very evident that the disaffection to government is by no means removed. They have an idea that all their property will be taken from them to discharge their taxes. There is no reasoning with them: they judge and act by their feelings, and therefore are ready to rebel again upon the first favourable opportunity." Thompson suspected that the country people had "grounds for their bitter complaints. From their representation their taxes were enormous, much larger than they ought to be considering their situation with respect to markets."[55]

Retreat: 1787

As Shays's Rebellion plunged Massachusetts into the worst crisis since the Revolution, the governor and his loyalists bowed to hard reality. The first policy to go was the draconian tax collection established the previous summer. In its fall 1786 session the general court relaxed the order that county coroners seize and sell the property of any county sheriff who did not extract the full quota that each town collector was required to collect on taxes levied in 1782 and before. The government first postponed by four months the date that sheriffs must pay the required sums into the central treasury.[56] The deadline for money due to the government on its most recent tax, No. 5, was postponed from January to April 1787.[57] Most important, the general court adopted Bowdoin's earlier proposal that allowed taxpayers to pay their back taxes, levied before 1784, in various farm products instead of in cash. By the terms of "An Act, providing for the more easy Payment of the Specie Taxes," taxpayers could now pay these taxes in beef, pork, corn, wheat, fish, lumber, and other products of farm, forest, and ocean at preset rates.[58] The general court seemed to take the offensive again the following February 1787 two weeks after Shays's defeat at Petersham, when it ordered town collectors "instantly to exert themselves to collect, and pay into the treasury of the Commonwealth, immediately, that part of the said tax [No. 5], which is to be paid in specie." But no treasurer's execution writs were issued to enforce this order; instead, the general court merely exhorted collectors and sheriffs "forthwith" to collect their quotas—"or so great a part thereof, as they shall be able to obtain."[59]

The general court also took no action on Congress's requests for money that would have required new taxes on the people of Massachusetts. In October 1786 Congress had enacted a requisition levy on the states to finance its emergency $500,000 loan to enlarge the federal army. The general court postponed any action on that part of the request Congress made to Massachusetts for funds. In February 1787, the general court formally postponed the federal requisition a second time, a house committee tersely declaring that, as Massachusetts was "in a state of actual war," a new tax levy at this time was "impracticable."[60]

Shays's Rebellion compromised the government's financial operations in other ways. In addition to its retreat from the forced collection of direct taxes, the general court broke into the impost-excise fund that supported the funded state debt. With tax collection stalled, money to finance the government's military operations against the rebellion had to be found from some other source. Taxes on imports, domestic sales, and pleasure carriages (the impost-excise fund) was the government's only remaining regular income. Yet in its debt-funding operations of 1781–82, the government had pledged the entire income for the support of the state's consolidated funded debt. Because diversion of any part of this revenue would necessarily diminish the government's annual interest payments to its public creditors, thereby undermining confidence in the government's ability to protect property rights, many objected to this plan. Yet despite an initial rejection by the propertied senate, an insistent house majority forced adoption of legislation that would divert one-third of the income from the impost-excise fund from the interest on the funded debt to "the exigencies of government."[61]

In February 1787, after Bowdoin had called on the general court to appropriate £40,000 to finance the government's pending military operations, the general court, with new taxes out of the question, determined to borrow the money from private subscribers. In order to do so, it committed the first receipts from this diverted one-third portion of the impost-excise fund to payment of the interest on such monies as it could raise by borrowing. A previously enacted fund that committed tax monies to comply with the 1785 congressional requisition also was compromised. When Congress requested that the Massachusetts government raise and commit 660 troops to the enlarged federal army Congress was raising to help quell Shays's Rebellion, the general court again decided to raise the money to pay and equip these troops by borrowing. But with new taxes impossible, the general court secured the loan by pledging that it would be repaid out of "the first monies which shall be received into the treasury on account of the tax laid for the specie part of the requisition of Congress, on 27th of September, 1785."[62]

Shaken by Shays's Rebellion, the Massachusetts government retreated on another front. After stormy debates and close roll-call votes, the house forced the senate to accept a Stay-Personal Property Tender law that suspended existing specie requirements for private debt contracts for eight months and allowed debtors to satisfy creditors' suits by paying creditors in articles of personal property appraised by community referees. In addition, the house forced the senate to accept a formal postponement of scheduled sessions of county courts in Berkshire, Hampshire, and Plymouth counties.[63] But all proposals to relieve credit-poor farmers and rural artisans by printing and loaning them paper money through a state bank had little support and were never brought to a vote.[64]

In sum, when farmers blocked tax collectors and courts and when Bowdoin's hard-line response galvanized them into forming military units and preparing to defend their homes against a presumably rapacious Boston government, the general court executed a retreat that was orderly but not precipitous from its previous tax collection drive. This was not the total overturn that had toppled the Rhode Island government the previous April 1786 when the spring elections had seen an opposition Reliefer party sweep into power and vote a paper money program. In Massachusetts the government's retreat was a staged, step-by-step fallback from an advanced outpost position, with administration leaders fighting stubborn rear-guard actions, as it were, along the way.

Shortly before the spring 1787 elections, John Hancock, the former governor, came out of retirement and announced he would again be a candidate for the governorship, much to the alarm of Bowdoin supporters. Handbills distributed to Bowdoin loyalists throughout the state urged men of property to "take an active, decided Part in your respective Towns, to ward off the political Evil and Disgrace that awaits your Country by a Change in the Administration at this difficult Day." Hinting that Hancock was negotiating with a group of paper money advocates, the handbill warned that "if a Paper Currency is introduced, Trade will be destroyed, Men of Property will withdraw from the Government, your Revenue from imposts and Excises will not pay the Expense of Collection, and the same Spirit of Insurrection, which now reigns in some parts of the Country, will be transferred to the Sea-Ports, and universal Anarchy prevail." In short, "the greater Part of the Men of Virtue, Sense and Property in the Capital, and its Vicinity, sensible of the present Governor's great Worth and Abilities," would "willingly avert, by having a proper Influence over those who are removed from Information, the Ruin that must flow from a Change in the Administration at this Time."[65]

For a few anxious weeks, orderly retreat seemed close to a rout. John Hancock swept to victory by nearly 75 percent of the vote cast, and Governor Bowdoin was ousted. That bastion of propertied prudence, the senate, almost fell, as in the counties of Worcester, Middlesex, and Essex, anti-Bowdoin Reliefer foes held county conventions, nominated senate candidates, distributed election tickets, and captured several seats. In the Suffolk County senate election, the tradesman-artisan Benjamin Austin, Jr., author of several popular newspaper articles that attacked and abused lawyers, defeated longtime Bowdoin loyalist Thomas Dawes. Finally, the house of representatives, with a turnover of 71 percent, shifted composition dramatically.[66]

But little new in the way of further substantive relief followed these setbacks. True, several previously voted concessions were continued. The due dates on Tax Numbers 4 and 5 were again extended. The Stay-Personal Property Tender law was renewed. Taxes levied before 1784 could now be paid in produce or various forms of paper—treasurer's orders, army notes, state indents, or state certificates. Hancock's first legislative message touched several bases, promising on the one hand to defend the Massachusetts Constitution and uphold public and private justice, promising on the other "to relieve as much as possible the burdens of the people." Hancock also, in the most dramatic gesture of his administration, returned £300 of his salary to the state treasury (Bowdoin on the eve of the election in March 1787 had vetoed a bill to reduce the governor's salary by this amount). But Hancock did not endorse a paper money relief bank. And when a country town member of the house of representatives proposed that a paper money loan bank be reported on by a committee, the measure was voted down, 47 to 103.[67]

Thus, since no paper money relief bill ever came close to passing in Massachusetts, it may be said that the government did not retreat as far as the Rhode Island government did. Nevertheless, the forced collection of taxes was no more, and given the new house opposition, the chances of another attempt were nil. House leader Theodore Sedgwick, the wealthy gentleman-politician from Stockbridge, described the close balance of house forces. On one side were "men of talents & of integrity" who were "firmly determined to support public justice and private faith." On the other side, supporting paper money and tender laws, were "the dregs and the scum of mankind." The latter were "now attempting the same objects by legislation, which their more manly brethren last winter would have procured by arms." With both senate and house closely balanced, Sedgwick gloomily observed, "All that the friends of Government can reasonably expect is to prevent actual mischief, for they cannot effect any positive good."[68]

This story of the failed attempt to force tax collection in Confederation Massachusetts sounds the same turnabout theme that played out in Pennsylvania, South Carolina, and Rhode Island. Only more belatedly than the other state governments did the Massachusetts government pull back from the high ground of forced tax collection for federal purposes once distressed farmers, rural artisans, and laborers signaled by mass defiance their determination not to be dispossessed of their property. Designed to withstand such shocks by its unified, stable structure and having no well-organized election party opposition to contend with, the Massachusetts government had pressed taxpayers longer and harder than had the other governments until powerful counterpressures forced its retreat. Because it could mobilize greater force and had more structural stability, because no effective means of counterpressure existed except mass obstruction and rebellion, because in short it could exert greater pressure on the system, the reaction was proportionately more extreme. Massachusetts thus became the scene of the Confederation era's most violent mass uprising. But far from being exceptional or isolated in Confederation history, Massachusetts in the Shays's Rebellion era exemplifies only more visibly and dramatically what was occurring or had already occurred elsewhere in the Confederation system.

Rocked by that rebellion, between 30 September 1786 and 31 March 1787 the government of Massachusetts paid exactly $310 in specie to the federal treasury. Governor Bowdoin and his phalanx of supporters had strained to collect the large backlog of unpaid back taxes previously levied for Congress's use. But the shocks and aftershocks of Shays's Rebellion had made further collection of these specie taxes impossible.

★ 9 ★

THE OTHER
NINE STATES

A TTEMPTING to force the common people to pay hard money taxes, the governments of Pennsylvania, South Carolina, Rhode Island, and Massachusetts threatened property sales on a massive scale. Resistance, then retreat, invariably followed. Widespread reports of some of these episodes, in Rhode Island and Massachusetts especially, had a major impact. Yet four states do not make a trend, and the other nine state governments also had federal requisition quotas to pay. Did these governments try to compel tax collection?

Two models characterize the tax-in-specie collection operations of these governments. Maryland, Virginia, New Hampshire, New Jersey, and possibly Delaware fit the pressure-resistance-retreat model of the four key states. Connecticut, New York, Georgia, and North Carolina conform more closely to a relief-relaxation model in which the coercion of taxpayers plays no part. Reliefer-led majorities that controlled the lower houses of the state assemblies during the 1780s kept these governments from forcing collection. Yet from the standpoint of raising hard money for Congress, the net result was the same for both categories of states. Either because rural counterpressures compelled them to back down, or because Reliefer majorities kept them from forcing collection throughout the decade, sooner or later every state in the Confederation adopted a relaxed approach to tax collection.

Thus, by late 1786–early 1787 not one state government was pressing tax collection in specie by seizure-and-sale proceedings, and seven had authorized the payment of taxes in state paper money. This relaxation on the part of all the states explains why requisition payments in hard money to the U.S. treasury had by then dwindled to almost nothing. It also explains what Edmund Randolph meant when he stated that "the nerves of government seem unstrung, both in energy and moneys" and referred to the "increasing languor of our associated republics," and what the Board of Treasury meant by noting the "stagnation in the receipt of Taxes at present throughout every State in the Union."[1]

Maryland

Historians of Confederation Maryland have written extensively on Maryland tax policy yet have not interpreted the state's postwar history in terms of the political battle to collect taxes.[2] The following offers a framework of analysis. Maryland's postwar taxes were levied for both state and federal purposes. They consisted of direct property taxes on real estate, slaves, and personal property, and a 2 percent ad valorem state impost on imported foreign goods. Substantial amounts of the direct property tax were appropriated for Congress, but when payment flagged, the legislature voted that money be paid Congress out of revenues from the state impost. The legislature also funded the state's war debt by a consolidated "general and aggregate fund" (January 1785). This fund provided for future payment of the principal in 1790 but required annual interest payments be paid state creditors from money owed the state from purchased Loyalist estates and other obligations, including taxes due before January 1783 but still unpaid.[3]

In postwar rural Maryland too, a shortage of specie and slumping commodity prices severely constrained the payment of these taxes. Of the several postwar taxes that earmarked funds for both state and federal purposes, by the end of 1786 £197,320 had not been paid into the treasury.[4] Tax arrearages were concentrated in those counties north and west of the Chesapeake most remote from market, but everywhere taxes were unpaid. Because the state intendant of revenue, Daniel of St. Thomas Jenifer (1782–86), did not enforce the law strenuously, no major crackdown on delinquent officers occurred until after Jenifer's departure from office early in 1786.[5]

Backing a more forceful collection policy were a group of wealthy planter-lawyer senators headed by Daniel Carroll, Charles Carroll of Carrollton, Edward Lloyd IV, Thomas Johnson, and other Maryland notables. This elite group sought to finance Maryland's accumulated war debt, stabilize the currency, recover overdue debts owed the state by the purchasers of confiscated Loyalist estates, and collect taxes for the state and Congress. They dominated the senate because of high property qualifications for senators and a system of indirect election by propertied electors. The popular lower branch, however, was dominated by Samuel Chase, Charles Ridgeley, Thomas Stone, and William Paca with ties to small farmers and planters. These Reliefers led the fight to protect farmers and small planters from the law's severity. Because each group dominated a branch of the legislature, the battles that occurred in the mid-1780s looked like institutional battles between the senate and the house of delegates, but the basic controversy was over taxes.

Although skirmishes occurred before the 1785–86 session, the battle began in earnest when these senators neutralized the office of the intendant of revenue by refusing to reappoint Jenifer. Early in 1786 a special house committee published a report highly critical of Jenifer's administration. Among various allegations, the report criticized the "large outstanding balances due by the collectors of the taxes to this state [that] continue to be reported by the intendant, when he, by law, is empowered to take the most decisive measures to effect a speedy payment of the same, in order that the state might be in a situation to execute her compact with the public creditors and her engagements with the United States." The report concluded that the office of intendant was expensive and no longer necessary. Jenifer countered that "he has taken every step in his power to compel payment from such collectors, consistently with the indulgences granted by the general assembly; judgments have been obtained, and upon executions issued, no person would bid for the property exposed for sale."[6] Although the house majority voted that Jenifer did not "merit their censure or disapprobation," the senate rejected 2 to 8 a house bill that called for Jenifer's reappointment to the intendancy. With neither house able to carry any other nomination, this action had the effect of vacating the office.[7]

Thanks to parliamentary maneuvering by the senate, the legislature then laid the basis for forcing action against taxables. The belief that personal failing caused tax delinquency may be seen in the senate's support for a high tax rate and for accelerated debt actions. "Timely exertions," the senate explained, would enable every man to pay his taxes; such exertions "will probably relieve us from the continuance and increase of those high taxes." Similarly, the senate asserted that "the facility of procrastinating payments to a long and indefinite term, is one of the principal causes of the improvidence of debtors, and the multiplication of lawsuits. To this source may be traced the exorbitant importation of foreign luxuries, ruinous and gambling contracts, and the extravagance and dissipation of money."[8]

In March 1786 the house sent up the bill "relative to the arrearages of taxes due the state before the first day of January 1783," a relief bill that authorized any collector of any tax due before 1783 to defer payment until 1790. Collectors were to post a bond pledging entire payment by 1790 plus an annual 6 percent interest payment on all the taxes owed from the period the taxes were originally due; the bill contained no enforcement requirement. In the session's final days, however, the senate amended the bill with the provision that the treasurers of the eastern and western shores *must* sue the bonds of any tax collector who failed to pay the accumulated 6 percent interest on the whole amount of taxes from the original due date by 1 September of each year. Since this requirement translated into suits for substantial amounts of unpaid interest, tax collectors would have to squeeze the money from their neighbors if they, the collectors, were to avoid seizure-and-sale proceedings against their own property. Either in the haste to adjourn or because the house majority misunderstood the technical implications of the provision, the house accepted the amendment and the bill became law.[9]

The senate also maneuvered the house into appointing a new governor who would enforce tax collection more sternly than the outgoing governor William Paca. Shortly before the committee report on Jenifer's administration as intendant, the senate put forth for house selection two nominees as Paca's successor—Major General William Smallwood and Daniel of St. Thomas Jenifer. An obvious ploy to get the house to accept Smallwood, the maneuver succeeded because the house majority stood by Jenifer as intendant. Smallwood was a Revolutionary veteran and commander of the Maryland Line; the outgoing William Paca, an Annapolis politician, had treated collectors and purchasers of confiscated property with flexibility.[10]

Jenifer's departure as intendant of finance made it possible to put new pressure on the system. On the same day that the senate denied Jenifer his office, house leaders introduced a bill vesting the intendant's powers in the governor and council. Perhaps because the new law merely "requested" that the governor and council "diligently" superintend the collection of taxes and see to it that bonds of negligent collectors "be put in suit as the law directs," the same house minority that had criticized the intendant's lenient administration voted against the bill. Nevertheless, after house approval, the senate went along.[11]

The governor and council immediately began pressuring local tax officers. Whether this new approach resulted from a tacit agreement between Smallwood and senate backers is not clear, but the governor and council's purpose cannot be doubted. First, the governor's office sent circulars to county and local tax officials instructing them to do their duty as the law required.[12] Next, the treasurers of the eastern and western shores were ordered to file court suits against the bonds of all collectors of taxes levied after 1 January 1783 for taxes not yet paid. The governor took a stern line: when the western shore treasurer, Thomas Harwood, asked for more time to notify delinquent collectors before starting legal proceedings, Smallwood and the council bluntly lectured him on why postponement was an ill-advised indulgence: "If once practised it will always be expected but when its Known that the Laws will be enforced that the Bonds will be put in suit immedy on failure of payment the Collectors will take care to make their payments in time but shoud the practice of giving notice prevail the Taxes will be delay'd from coming into the Treasury and our Business as Superintending the collection of the Revenue unnecessarily encreas'd."[13]

Harwood later asked whether "it would be proper to suspend any proceedings against the old Collectors," observing that "from the best Information I have been able to procure the Property of the Collectors and their Securities unless it sells very high, will not amount to near their Balances, if a Sale is to take place." To force Harwood's hand, the Smallwood administration at the August 1786 session of the general court of the western shore filed a suit against his bond for the recovery of the total sum of uncollected taxes owed by collectors under his jurisdiction. Two months later, the administration raised the pressure further by instructing the state attorney general, Luther Martin, to proceed with the sale of such of Harwood's property as was now under court execution.[14]

Swift action followed. Both treasurers, Dickinson and Harwood, filed suits in the general courts of the eastern and western shore against the bonds of tax collectors in their districts who still owed money for uncollected taxes. Some 800 execution writs were issued by the state's superior court against the property of tax collectors and purchasers of confiscated estates who owed the government money. With their own property thus threatened, the collectors in turn increased pressure on delinquent taxpayers. Throughout rural Maryland that summer and fall of 1786 loomed the prospect of massive levy-and-sale actions against delinquent taxpayers.[15]

Thus threatened, small farmers and middling planters girded against distress sales. Their tactics were familiar—petitions, no-bid agreements, and threats of violence. Warning that the lack of cash meant that the only way taxes could be raised was by auctioning property, collector William McLaughlin of Baltimore County urged house delegate Samuel Chase to use his influence with the governor and council "to get an indulgence to the Collectors until sometime after Harvest, and thereby in a great measure alleviate the distresses of the people at large."[16] But Chase could do nothing. As the collectors began attaching property, farmers and small planters took matters into their own hands. Instructions to legislators were circulated demanding an issue of paper money, payable for taxes, that could be borrowed. No-bid agreements were organized. At auction sales, farmers tried to intimidate would-be buyers. These tactics moved Sheriff Henry Hunt of Calvert County to ask Governor Smallwood for advice. Did the Governor think distrained property could be moved to another county and there sold? The governor replied that he knew "of no Law that will justify the Sheriff in removing Property taken in execution to discharge the public Assessment, out of the county for sale," and that he could not "advise the doing it although the measure may be necessary to defeat the unwarrantable combinations among the People not to purchase."[17]

Threats of violence against collection officers were the most extreme tactic. Handbills posted in public places warned sheriffs and collectors not to attempt collection if they wished to stay healthy. In December 1786 Sheriff Archibald Job of Cecil County, writing Governor Smallwood, described these threats. The sheriff currently had some 330 execution writs against tax collectors and purchasers of confiscated estates recently issued by the eastern shore superior court for the recovery of interest and costs due on £21,000. Already he had served 50 executions against delinquent collectors and taxpayers for tax arrearages and other public debts totaling £28,500; several of these persons had already been committed to the Talbot jail. "I have no Desire to Exagarate, but this Enormous Sum [£28,500] the officers of this County are Endeavouring to Collect by Every means in their power." He went on to describe the consequences of handbills sent to Cecil County calling for paper money that notified the people that they were "at the mercy of sheriffs and Collectors which seemed to raise a cool carelessness toward the officers. Shortly after advertisements were set up in many parts of the county But no name prefixed to them mentioning Threats to the officers as I have heard for I have seen none of them." Since then, the sheriff wrote, "Officers have been told by some Persons that they would not suffer Destraint to be made of their Property, all this shews a growing Restlessness among the People, And this Large number of Executions haveing come to hand I am afraid will increase it."[18]

With rural violence apparently close at hand, the battle focused on control of the state's two-house legislature. In the elections held that summer for electors to elect one-third of the new state senate, Reliefers tried unsuccessfully to unseat individual senators who the previous session had defeated a paper money relief bill enacted by the house of delegates. At the same time, in three house elections to replace delegates who had resigned, Reliefers published and circulated handbills attacking the new senate majority: "It is apparent, That the most wealthy men in the State, (some of them of overgrown and enormous fortunes) constitute a decided majority in the new Senate; and it is well known that *two thirds* of them are avowed opponents to an emission of money." The same pamphlet urged the election of Samuel Chase and William Paca, who had pledged to work for paper money relief legislation. "Inseparable in their personal friendship, and generally concurring in opinion on great personal questions, they will strenuously endeavour to obtain the desires of the people, not only as to an emission of Paper Money on *loan*, but any other matter requisite for their happiness, ease or convenience."[19]

Spurred by Chase and Paca, who won seats, the house at its Annapolis session that November quickly voted a five-month stay on forced tax collection and a paper money relief loan bill that provided £250,000 payable for taxes to be issued on loans secured by land mortgages. Unanimously rejecting the paper money bill, the senate gave ground on requirements that tax collectors be sued by accepting a temporary stay on all pending court executions against delinquent taxpayers and collectors until the following May.[20]

Deeming this concession insufficient, house Reliefer leaders made a public appeal to "the People of Maryland," calling on voters to instruct the senate to accept the house-legislated paper money bill; they then adjourned for two months until the voters could be heard from. Senate leaders quickly responded with their own published appeal that outlined the case against a paper money emission and attacked the house majority for trying to force its hand by appealing to the people.[21]

The following April when the assembly reconvened, neither branch would retreat. Although attempts were made to reach agreement on a debtor installment bill, that measure failed when the house refused to accept a watered-down senate version. In turn, the senate rejected house proposals for paper money and further tax postponement.[22] With the controversy intensifying, the senate majority again postponed taxes. That summer, after another round of court executions against delinquent taxpayers and collectors had been issued, the governor and council ordered that auction sales against several collectors be suspended. With Smallwood and the council majority retreating from a hard-line policy, senate leaders agreed that the due date on all tax collections be postponed.[23]

Just as the governments of Massachusetts, Rhode Island, South Carolina, and Pennsylvania tried to squeeze money from rural taxpayers who had no specie, so did Maryland's government push farmers and planters to the limit. Shaken by the ensuing backlash, a divided Maryland government retreated from the brink and eased the pressure.

Virginia

Less forcefully than Maryland but with the same result, Virginia's government squeezed the common people when taxes were not paid. Between 1781 and 1787 the Virginia assembly levied several heavy taxes but also voted relief measures of several kinds.[24] A large proportion of Virginia's taxes could be paid in state paper or tobacco and hemp inspection notes, but the law also required that taxes earmarked for Congress be paid in specie. The assembly also tried to ease the burden by postponing due dates, allowing payments in farm produce, and even remitting half of the 1785 tax. A certificate tax that levied money to pay holders of the funded state debt allowed holders to discount their debt certificates by a simple bookkeeping transaction. As Gordon Denboer concludes: "The tax burden was relatively heavy [in Virginia], and consequently debtor and tax relief policies formed an important part of the milieu of the Confederation era."[25]

Yet a sizable number of the assembly opposed moderate reliefs as fiscally, morally, and politically unsound. Mary T. Armentrout notes that the assembly was divided into unstable blocs of those "favoring consistent collection of taxes, in money if possible, and those sponsoring relief of debtors from their obligations and protection of those in arrears to the state, with the latter faction generally victorious." Newspaper essays insisted that taxes in money were "indispensably necessary" for establishing public confidence in Virginia's government and making Congress financially solvent. James Madison, George Washington, and other Virginia notables believed that tax relief was incompatible with supporting Congress, confidence in the government's ability to protect property rights, and the people's industriousness and frugality. Madison's remedy for the outflow of money was "a vigorous and steady collection of taxes [that] would make the money necessary here and would therefore be means of keeping it here. In our situation it would have the salutary operation of a sumptuary law." Advocates of relief such as Patrick Henry were looked upon as harboring a desire to "court popularity."[26]

Although moderate relief policies usually prevailed, the Virginia assembly rejected the most radical form of tax relief—paper money. In November 1786 the house of delegates condemned paper money relief legislation by a large majority, 85 to 17. Anticipating a proposal for paper money later in the session, George Mason and James Madison seized the initiative, moved that paper money was "unjust, impolitic, [and] destructive of public and private confidence, and of that virtue which is the basis of republican government," and carried both the resolutions and an order for their publication. Such action, assembly member David Stuart believed, would convince the people of Virginia that they could not expect the government to relieve them from what Madison termed their own "luxurious propensity."[27]

That same December 1786 session the assembly took steps to force the collection system into coercive action. A special committee headed by notables Frank Corbin, Theodorick Bland, and Richard Bland Lee reported what Virginia had paid Congress and what it still owed. Citing figures ($550,889 paid Congress; $1,453,724 not yet paid), the committee recommended that the state certificate tax be reduced, that the state impost be appropriated entirely for Congress, and that measures be adopted "so as to force the regular and faithful collection of taxes," and "to compel the payment of the arrearages of the certificate tax on or before 1 December 1787." Although the report did not actually recommend a method, the assembly's "Act to enable the Solicitor more effectually to collect the Arrearages of the Taxes, and proceed against public Delinquents" armed the solicitor general with new power to prosecute the bonds of county sheriffs and collectors who had not settled their accounts and mandated new tax reporting and accounting procedures.[28]

Corbin described the new legislation in a letter: "We have passed several Laws, which will I think, tend to facilitate and to ensure the faithful collection of the Taxes. We have given the Solicitor full power to proceed in

the most summary way agt public Delinquents." But the solicitor was not
to be legally compelled to act; hence, as Corbin described them, the measures were "not quite so radical nor so extensive as might have been proposed—but perhaps more practicable and as proper as any which the perplexity and confusion of things would admit of."[29] "Too many men [were]
in the Legislature who either have been or expect to be sheriff," Corbin
explained, "to carry any point which strikes even distantly and obliquely
at them."[30]

The following spring the solicitor sent notices of legal action to the sheriffs of thirty-two counties, and Virginia's general court issued numerous
attachment warrants against sheriffs with delinquent accounts. The fact
that sheriffs' properties were posted for public auction, and a reference to
the "many judgments" "obtained on behalf of this commonwealth against
sheriffs, for taxes due prior to 1787," afford further evidence of increased
pressure.[31] Although some sheriffs escaped unscathed because of the lack
of buyers, others had their property sold at auction. That sheriffs moved
against taxables is indicated by a November 1787 petition from Accomack
County describing the "undoubted fact that many of the poor last year and
the beginning of this had their corn seized in the field before and after
gathering, and the hogs in the pen and those necessaries of life sold out of
the mouths of them, and their children, at a small value, such things would
bring distress on persons even in affluent circumstances."[32]

Pressure by sheriffs whose property was under attachment explains the
"inflammatory summonses" that were posted at several crossroads in Hen-
rico and Hanover counties the following March "addressed to the people,
and feeling their pulse on taxes and executions."[33] It also explains the violence that summer of 1787 in King William and New Kent counties when
vigilantes set fire to the prison and other county buildings including the
clerks' offices. By law, the clerk of court kept tax records; burning their
offices down blocked collection. In Henry County in southside Virginia,
as assembly member Jonathan Dawson reported: "the high Sheriff has not
yet given security for the collection of the taxes, and I was told it wou'd
be dangerous for any person to offer. Of course no collection goes on, and
the people appear happy in this expedient of evading payment."[34] In
Greenbriar, James McClurg reported, some 300 men had signed "an As-
sociation, to oppose the payment of the certificate Tax, & in genl. of all
debts; & it is apprehended there, that they will attempt forcibly to stop the
proceeding of the next court."[35]

Later that same year the Virginia assembly did another about-face on
tax policy. The pressure on taxables had spurred not only stonewalling but
demands for paper money. Blaming the burning of the New Kent court
house on Governor Edmund Randolph's failure to issue a stern proclamation, Corbin noted disgustedly that "petitions are going about, I un-

derstand, for Paper Money, for Installments, or to make Property, on valuation, a tender for Debt—How many shapes does Fraud assume?"[36] Although none of these radical relief measures passed, the assembly allowed delinquent taxpayers to pay back taxes in depreciated state securities, made the 1787 tax payable in tobacco notes, and enabled sheriffs under prosecution to exonerate themselves from any further prosecution of their bonds provided they paid one half of the arrearages owed by 1 April 1788 and the balance by 1 August 1788.[37]

Important questions remain about the politics of taxation in Virginia's party-free environment. The inability of Virginia's ruling elite class to take a consistently firm line on taxes is difficult to explain but may relate to its political vulnerability. James Madison explained that against his better judgment he had voted for making part of the 1786 tax payable in tobacco rather than specie in order to head off a more radical relief proposal: "The Specie part of the tax under collection is made payable in Tobo. This indulgence to the people as it is called & considered, was so warmly wished for out of doors, and so strenuously pressed within that it could not be rejected, without danger of exciting some worse project of a popular cast." Rhys Isaac has suggested that the rise of a popular evangelical Baptist movement in Virginia prompted some of Virginia's Anglican ruling class to vote the Statute of Religious Freedom in 1786 to remove that divisive issue from politics. The same kind of explanation might clarify why members of the Virginia political elite seemed to vacillate on taxes.[38] Perhaps the popular demand for tax relief prompted a strategy of voting halfway measures of tax relief even while waiting for an opportunity to force the common people to pay the taxes they owed. Yet when popular violence threatened, the elite backed down.

Virginia may be classified as another state where specie tax collection broke down after a pressure-resistance-retreat cycle put an end to the government's attempts to force collection.

Connecticut and New York

By contrast with the states previously examined, Confederation Connecticut and New York experienced no rural violence against taxation. Because Reliefers commanded majorities in the lower houses of both states, these governments did not force the collection of specie. And although both governments contributed to the federal treasury, both had lower houses that rejected proposals for specie taxes to comply with federal requisition quotas.

Between 1780 and 1788 the Connecticut legislature levied nineteen property-poll taxes for federal and state purposes. Supplementing a state impost and excise, these property-poll taxes were appropriated for congressional requisitions, interest on the state debt, and operating expenses. But because circulating cash was scarce and farmers could not borrow, tax arrearages mounted. By 1788 the arrearages on direct taxes levied for state purposes (1781–87) totaled £26,894; for federal purposes, £16,649. Early in the decade the government had contributed an impressive £59,939 (specie) to Congress, but by 1788 it owed £55,744 (specie).[39]

Because property-poll taxes were heavy, tax policy became a divisive political issue. In 1782 town meetings protested heavy taxes, and in fall 1783 a popular convention met at Middletown. At issue was the state legislature's approval of a Congress-sponsored proposal to commute Continental army officers' salaries from half pay for life to full pay for five years and to invest Congress with the 5 percent federal impost. Formed by delegates from the state's poorer country towns, the Middletown convention wanted the heavy tax burden lightened by having the legislature repudiate its approval of the proposal. Such a rejection (for an estimated $5 million in all) would enable the Connecticut government to increase its state impost and lower the tax rate on property and polls. The controversy polarized Connecticut politics into rich and poor; in the fall 1783 state elections, champions of the poorer farming towns captured a majority of the lower house of the assembly. Although a well-to-do elite controlled the council and the governorship, the popularly elected lower house had a decisive prorelief majority.[40]

The lower house's pro-relief leanings became clear as the decade advanced. In 1783 and 1784 Reliefer Erastus Wolcott proposed a bill that would require the government to accept various forms of state paper including securities, treasurer's orders, and bills of credit for all past and present taxes; the bill passed the lower house but was rejected by the council of assistants. In 1786 the lower house flatly rejected a bill that would raise new taxes for federal requisitions. Explaining the rejection, the lower house instructed Governor Samuel Huntington to inform the president of Congress that "the Situation of this State, labouring under Embarrasments by reason of arrea[ra]ges of former Taxes and other reasons, induces a Non Compliance with requisitions at this time." Similarly in 1787 the lower house rejected a new tax for Congress on the grounds that "the present burdens upon the people of the state are heavy . . . [and] this makes it peculiarly difficult for us to raise money for the federal treasury."[41]

These political controversies have been construed as representing a nationalist-versus-localist alignment. But so-called localists supported financial contributions to Congress as long as they did not place an excessive burden of specie taxes on the common people of Connecticut. Because the same men who rejected specie taxes for Congress in 1786 and 1787 argued that the common people were taxed too heavily, and because many supported federal measures when they did not require heavy taxes, it seems more correct to interpret their behavior as motivated by relief than by an ideology of localism per se.[42]

The taxes levied by the Connecticut government were heavy, but the legislature frequently voted reliefs. During the 1780s several kinds of state paper were made acceptable for taxes for state purposes. Due dates were frequently postponed and towns exempted from monies not yet paid. Most important, the collection system itself was flexibly administered. Town collectors either did not seize property or suspended distress-and-sale actions; sympathetic town collectors in turn were eased by county sheriffs who looked the other way.[43]

To force collection the law authorized the state treasurer to issue execution warrants against any collector who did not collect the quotaed amount. Transmitted to county sheriffs, these execution warrants required the sheriff to sell defaulting collectors' property. But when the state treasurer issued the required warrants, county sheriffs did not serve them. In 1783 Oliver Wolcott, Sr., described the process. In his hometown of Litchfield, he had sought money that the state owed his son by importuning county officers, but, he wrote his son, "I have not since I saw you been able to get one penny from the Sheriff or any Collector, the genius of the [Middletown] convention advised the People not to pay their Taxes, which they cordially embraced and thereupon they sent almost all the money out of the state and the Demon of Popularity and Timidity restrain the Collection of any part of what remains."[44]

Notables like Oliver Wolcott wanted the assembly to force local sheriffs and collectors to collect taxes by coercion.[45] In spring 1785 the assembly enacted a bill that required collectors to be imprisoned if they failed to collect; town selectmen were also made personally responsible for uncollected taxes and their property made subject to seizure and sale. But the bill had little effect; a house committee later that same year reported that tax returns were "as usual, deficient, imperfect or unseasonable," but the House postponed a proposal for "dooming certain disobedient Towns for not returning their Lists for the year."[46] With the house securely in Reliefer hands, nothing stronger could be done. Reliefer opposition to any great pressure on tax collection by the assembly prompted member of the council Benjamin Huntington to fault not the state tax laws but their execution, "owing to the unreasonable degree of Popularity in a certain house of Assembly who get their seats by their agreeable conduct among the Populace and many obtain their Election by Crying among the People and in the House The People cannot support the Enormous Burthen of Taxes and the Collectors must forbear. This forbearance has been too much encouraged and most enormous arrearages of Taxes have accumulated on many and especially such as had Emigration in design."[47]

In 1787 when the house rejected a proposal for new taxes for Congress a second time, Huntington described the action in pejorative terms. Deaf to the warnings of Congress's possible dissolution, Huntington noted, the ignorant politicians who controlled this popular body refused to vote Congress funds because it would mean new taxes. "Our men of public virtue are taking the advantage of the distress they see their neighbours in & preach up terror to the people at large—but this will not convince our legislature (who are truly the representatives of the People) that it is best to *levy* the necessary taxes for the continental treasury nor will a majority of ignoramus's ever conduct with wisdom or prudence; 'tis not expectable."[48]

Thwarted by Reliefer opposition in the lower house, the Connecticut elite could neither levy new taxes to support Congress in 1786 and 1787 nor force the government's local tax collection officers to collect unpaid back taxes by legal coercion.[49]

Like Connecticut's, New York's Confederation government did not take a hard line on uncollected taxes. The result was greater rural tranquillity and political stability than in the states previously examined. The key to the state's tax policies lay in domination of the assembly by a Reliefer majority. More numerous than the upper-class membership of the assembly, a "country party" of farmers, small-town lawyers, and small-time professionals controlled the assembly. This party had its origins in controversies around such class-specific revolutionary war issues as the confiscation of Loyalist estates, proscription of Loyalists, and tax policy. By 1781, it was becoming a political party that pursued power within the different branches of New York's government. Although the composition of the senate and the council of revision (which had a legislative veto) fluctuated, the country party held a stable majority in the house of representatives and kept its man, George Clinton, securely in the governor's chair.[50]

As Edward Countryman has suggested, country party leaders during the Revolution sought legitimacy for New York's fledgling government by policies that catered to majoritarian concerns. These included the actions against Loyalists and the creation of a system of localized assessment that calibrated taxes "according to the Estate, and other Circumstances and Abilities to pay Taxes, of each respective Person, collectively considered."[51] The Clinton party's postwar fiscal and monetary policies can be understood in these terms as well. The New York government had levied heavy taxes during the Revolution (1775–81) but 65 percent had not been collected.[52] When newly appointed federal receiver of taxes and state assembly member Alexander Hamilton in 1782 proposed that the tax system be entirely overhauled, Clinton forces killed the measure. Clinton and his country allies kept rural taxes light. Between April 1784 and April 1786 the New York legislature levied no new direct taxes on the people of New York—a fact that made the state seem a farmers' paradise.[53] To ease taxes further, just before the legislature voted a 1786 tax bill, it authorized an emission of paper bills, payable for taxes, to be printed and loaned on land mortgages.[54]

Rather than tax rural New Yorkers, the assembly raised more than half its budget by taxing the burgeoning volume of foreign imports into New York City. Because a large proportion of these imports were then trans-shipped out of the state and sold in Connecticut and New Jersey, consumers in these states had shouldered a substantial part of New York's tax burden. The policy of taxing imports purchased by out-of-staters is part of the basis for labeling the Clinton government "localist" as opposed to "cosmopolitan" or "nationalist." But if New York's lucrative state impost siphoned off money from her neighbors by taxing foreign imports that passed through New York City, the state taxed neither domestic goods imported from other states destined for reexport nor shipping owned by citizens of other states that landed goods at New York. Moreover, the Clinton administration made the largest proportionate financial contribution to the federal treasury of any of the thirteen states. Of the total sum Congress required of New York after 1781 ($965,788), New York paid $648,528, 67 percent of its quota. The label "local" obscures the fact that the country party provided funds for Congress by actions that would not distress their middling and poor constituents.[55] These actions explain why New York did not experience the rural disturbances other states did. Because New York's contributions to the federal treasury resulted from a state impost that taxed the consumer, not direct taxes that taxed the farmer, New York could raise specie for Congress without forcing farmers to reach into their empty pockets. Although the minority, sparked by Alexander Hamilton, sought to tighten up the tax system, the country party defeated the measure, consistently blocking reforms that would deprive local officers of broad discretion over assessment and collection operations.[56]

Because the Reliefer-controlled lower house of the assembly protected rural taxpayers, New York better fits the relief-relaxation model than the pressure-resistance-retreat model characteristic of states that took a harder line. Cognizant of the large tax arrearages from the Revolution, state assembly member Alexander Hamilton in 1782 drafted legislation that would eliminate local discretion and force collection. Having accepted appointment as federal receiver of taxes in New York from superintendent of finance Robert Morris, Hamilton wanted the New York assembly to meet its federal requisition quotas more reliably, promptly, and completely. At present, Hamilton believed, New York's popularly elected tax officials allowed taxpayers to escape payment too easily. Logrolling, partisanship, and flexible collection would undermine New York's ability to meet its federal quotas.

At the August 1782 meeting of the assembly at Poughkeepsie, Hamilton proposed that preset schedules of graduated rates on different kinds of real estate and personal property be established and that collectors and county treasurers post large personal bonds that would be forfeited if they failed to collect their quotas. Many legislators who favored the plan in principle, Hamilton reported, were misled by Abraham Yates, who "*assures* them [that the people] are too poor to pay taxes." The New York legislature killed the proposal.[57]

Thus the discretionary tax system that allowed local officials to ease the poor and tax the rich remained. The system's apparently selective, arbitrary operation drew many protests. The mother of wealthy notable Robert R. Livingston protested extra-heavy taxes on the family's upstate holdings to make up for sums not collected from the middling and poor farmers among their neighbors. The county treasurer of downstate Sussex County inquired whether reports were true that the state treasurer had allowed the upstate counties to build up large arrearages of uncollected taxes but had been "more strickd on the southern Districts to oblige them to pay then he has been to the northerd."[58] The flexible enforcement of the tax system and the assembly's refusal to vote new taxes betokened an apparent lack of energy and decision. As the Connecticut merchant-financier Jeremiah Wadsworth declared from New York City in February 1785: "This State seems at present to have as little vigor & decision as any one in the union."[59]

In March 1787, two months before he went to the federal convention at Philadelphia, Hamilton and others revived his plan for annual direct and impost taxes based on preset rate schedules and upgraded collection, in part to meet state needs, in part to support Congress. But when country party leaders attacked the measure, the house rejected the bill. Senator Philip Schuyler, the magnate-politician and Hamilton's father-in-law, described these proceedings: "The new system of taxation has been rejected by a small majority of three, altho in reallity there was a considerable majority for it but they were afraid to vote, or [were] mis-lead by those who embarrass all our affairs and for which they will I trust before long have reason to repent." He held out little hope for the federal government, which was "rapidly dissolving. It certainly cannot reach the end of the year under Its present form unsupported as It is by the States."[60]

New York's lower house majority favored light rural taxes and a heavy tax on foreign imports. Enacted into law, these policies meant greater rural quiet than in states that forced local tax officials to coerce rural taxpayers. Nor did New York's government launch a crackdown on unpaid taxes.

Although the state paid a high percentage of its federal requisition quota, payments still fell short of the full required amount.

New Jersey, Delaware, and New Hampshire

New Jersey, New Hampshire, and possibly Delaware conform to the pressure-resistance-retreat model. All three states had heavy debts and requisition quotas; all levied heavy property taxes. New Jersey and Delaware, moreover, were severely handicapped by having no major port of entry where imported foreign goods could be taxed by a state impost. Instead, they had to import foreign goods from nearby Philadelphia and New York, the closest major seaports; thus, instead of paying an impost to their own government, New Jersey and Delaware consumers paid taxes into the New York and Pennsylvania treasuries. Both these governments pressured taxpayers and retreated when protest flared. In New Jersey auction sales of taxpayers' property in January 1785 generated protest, violence, and petitions for paper money. Initially rejected by the council, a £100,000 paper money relief bill finally passed in May 1786, when Governor William Livingston abstained.[61]

In Delaware the state treasurer pressured local tax collectors, who pressured taxables, but whether protest occurred that forced the government to back down must await further research.[62] In New Hampshire the government's pressure on the tax system produced a popular movement for paper money that ended when farmers demonstrated in front of the Exeter meeting house where the legislature was sitting, 20–21 September 1786. Although the legislature refused paper money and the demonstrators were dispersed by units of militia, the government did not press the coercion of taxpayers further.[63]

Georgia and North Carolina

Georgia and North Carolina fit the New York–Connecticut relief-relaxation model of governments whose dominant Reliefer majorities kept taxes light and fended off attempts to force collection. Although Georgia raised more from its state impost than either New Jersey or Delaware, its government also levied direct taxes, and arrearages mounted. But Georgia's dominant rural legislative majority would not force payment by coercing tax auction sales. Georgia's finances were additionally burdened by Indian hostilities that forced the government into military preparations. Instead of levying new taxes, £50,000 in paper bills of credit were emitted.[64]

Similarly, the North Carolina legislature had a dominant rural majority that kept taxes light by issuing paper money when the state's large small-farmer class found specie taxes too burdensome. Guided by Reliefers Timothy Bloodworth, Thomas Person, and Willie Jones, the North Carolina legislature twice (1783, 1785) ordered that £100,000 legal tender currency payable for debts and taxes be emitted.[65] The elite minority, merchant-planter-lawyer notables Samuel Johnston, James Iredell, Archibald McLaine, William R. Davie, and others who wanted the state government to take a firmer line by collecting hard money, got nowhere.[66] The Reliefer-controlled North Carolina government used this currency to pay off most of its revolutionary war debt and also withdrew its revolutionary currency from circulation at a greatly depreciated rate; Congress received nothing from North Carolina until 1787–88, when the state government used its own paper to purchase and sell tobacco to New York merchants, which yielded $36,887 specie it then paid Congress (but $435,419 in unpaid requisitions remained). Nevertheless, like New York and Connecticut, Georgia and North Carolina remained quiet because neither government pushed taxpayers hard.[67]

★

Patterns of pressure-resistance-retreat were played out in the Confederation histories of several of the nine states of the Confederation outside the four key states. Both Taxers and Reliefers in every state government tried to support Congress but could not agree how this was to be done. The collection of direct specie taxes for both state and federal purposes became increasingly difficult after hard money became scarce. The well-to-do class, having access to capital and out of touch with small farmers, favored direct specie taxes and forced collection. Less affluent rural folk wanted the payments for Congress to be supported by the state impost; opposing tax crackdowns, they favored reliefs, including the postponement of due dates and paper money issued on loan. These policies were more or less operative in the four states where Reliefers controlled lower houses, but financial support for Congress, which varied greatly, depended on the productivity of the state impost. From the standpoint of the well-to-do classes, however, the apparent inability of even those states with the strongest and most stable constitutions to compel their citizens to pay taxes in specie (Massachusetts and Maryland) meant that effective taxation for Congress by the states could not be counted on. These governments seemed unable to require their citizens to pay specie taxes for Congress or their own debts and expenses.

THE CRITICAL PERIOD AND
REPUBLICAN SYNTHESIS
INTERPRETATIONS

⋆ 10 ⋆

THE CRITICAL PERIOD:
A FISCAL BREAKDOWN

HARD MONEY taxes for Congress failed to materialize in nine of the Confederation states because the middling and poorer rural yeomanry, burdened by the weight of taxation and by a cash-depleted economy, resisted collection rather than have their property sold at auction. The other four state governments escaped confrontation with the yeomanry by not attempting to force collection and by voting paper money and other relief measures. Rather than parochialism or indifference, the simple inability to collect these taxes explains why the states did not provide Congress with the hard money it asked for.

In addition to explaining why requisition payments to Congress broke down in late 1786 and early 1787, the foregoing chapters also provide a framework for understanding why the Framers chose to reconstitute the central government rather than merely strengthen Congress by amendment. The following assumptions formed the basis of their decision.

1. The basic cause of the people's not paying their taxes was more a personal lack of effort (extravagance and indolence) than it was the fault of the system (lack of credit, expensive transportation, scarcity of cash, and so on).
2. To make Americans pay taxes required a government able to make itself be taken seriously, which meant a government able to compel collection by physical force.
3. The individual state governments did not have sufficient power and stability to exert this force.
4. Simple amendment of Congress would not provide the requisite force. Only a fundamentally altered central government with strong enforcement powers, independence, and stability would have this capability.

Strong evidence that these assumptions formed the basis of the Framers' decision is furnished by John Jay, a major Federalist leader. Jay in 1786–87 was in New York City serving as Congress's secretary for foreign affairs; as such he knew the straitened condition of Congress's finances. Yet

Jay favored reconstituting the central government rather than simple amendment. Judged by his numerous letters, Jay's position derived from the premise that the people had to be forced into paying taxes and that neither Congress nor the states could do so. In several letters written previous to and during the Constitutional Convention, Jay singled out "Relaxation in Govermt and Extravagance in Individuals" as the basic causes of Congress's bankruptcy. The "states in general pay little attention to Requisitions," Jay declared, not because of localism, but because "Our Governments want Energy," and because "too much has been expected from the virtue & good sense of the people." Accordingly, "the Treasury is empty tho' the Country abounds in Resources, and our people are far more unwilling than unable to pay Taxes. . . . Hence results Disappointmts to our Creditors, Disgrace to our Country, and I fear Disinclination in too many to any mode of Govt. that can easily & irresistably open their Purses." (For the full text of these letters, see appendix 3.)

Jay's letters identify the state governments' want of "Energy" as the central cause of Congress's insolvency. Other contemporary Federalist letters do not explicitly identify the breakdown of taxation in the states as such, but their use of terms similar to Jay's to describe the state governments—"relaxed," "debilitated," and "wanting energy"—and their use of language such as "the [several] present systems must go to the Devil" point to taxation as the probable referent (see appendix 3). Moreover, and most importantly, the breakdown of taxation has to be the referent: other possibilities either have to be ruled out or were part and parcel of taxation. It is also possible that certain other more localized and marginal events contributed to the sense of the Confederation system's breakdown that these letters reflect. But because the letters refer to *all* the states, and because these other episodes occur locally in only one or two states, taxation, common to all, is the more likely referent. (For further details on these localized episodes, see chapter 11.)

Finally, these letters either explicitly or implicitly call for much more radical changes in the central government than Congress's limited amendment. If the breakdown of taxing in specie was symptomatic of the people's extravagance and the government's weakness, it was also proof of basic weakness that only the radical reform of government at the center could remedy. "Our Govt is weak, languid, and inefficient" and cannot protect "the personal liberty & property of the subject," Christopher Gore of Massachusetts affirmed. "You of the federal convention must invent some plan to increase the circulation at the heart & thereby dispense heat & vigor to the extremities." Obadiah Bowen of Rhode Island declared that "the great debility of government" and the "present too general uneasiness amongst the majority of the people" cannot be corrected "without a thorough change." *Thorough* change is what John Jay meant when he wrote that "much is to be done, and the Patriots must have Perseverance as well as Patience." (For the full texts of these letters, see appendix 3).

According to the historian John Fiske, an across-the-board collapse of effective government at both federal and state levels drove the movement for the federal Constitution. This collapse so undermined law, order, prosperity, and unity in the United States that such a constitution became necessary for the nation's very survival. First, an impotent Congress could neither pay the war debt nor defend vital U.S. interests, including national independence. Second, the state governments waged commercial war against each others' trade and came close to civil war. Third, the state governments issued paper money, which allowed debtors to escape their creditors, caused financial chaos, and further crippled trade. Finally, riot and popular rebellion proliferated. Many parts of Fiske's Critical Period thesis have been challenged.[1] Yet because the image of the Confederation's generalized breakdown still dominates both the scholarly historiography of the Constitution and the popular literature surrounding the recent Bicentennial, it is important to clarify what this breakdown was and what it was not.

Congress's Failures in Defense, Finance, and Diplomacy

The Critical Period interpretation puts strong emphasis on Congress's inability to deal effectively with the array of problems relating to national defense, the federal debt, and U.S. diplomacy. These include Congress's inability to: (1) counter Great Britain's retention of the northern border posts and Spain's closure of the port of New Orleans; (2) protect the nation's borders against western Indians; (3) protect U.S. shipping and sailors in the Mediterranean against hostage-taking by Barbary states; (4) pay the scheduled interest and principal due foreign and domestic creditors; (5) raise troops to protect the Springfield arsenal during Shays's Rebellion; (6) counter restrictions on U.S. commerce with Britain's West Indies and other possessions and with Britain; (7) enable British creditors to bring legal proceedings against U.S. debtors without obstruction by state legislatures. Approaching crisis proportions, these problems, Critical Period historians maintain, tested the ability of the new republic to maintain its independence, thus making the 1780s a truly "critical period."[2]

As many contemporaries argued (the Antifederalists especially), the logical remedy to such problems was to invest the current Continental Congress with specific powers tailored to their individual solution. With two exceptions (British restrictions on U.S. commerce and legal proceedings by British creditors), each of the above issues could have been solved—or at least addressed—by investing Congress with the independent power to raise money by the 5 percent federal impost. But while this minimalist reform was preferred by Antifederalists and regarded by Federalists as preferable to no reform at all, the Framers carried out the far more sweeping program of an entirely reconstituted central government with legislative, executive, and judicial branches and powers. Thus Congress's finance-specific inability to deal with these defense, financial, and foreign policy problems does not in itself explain reconstitution.

The same holds true for British commercial discrimination against U.S. commerce. In July 1783 the British government closed its West Indies possessions to U.S. merchant vessels, thus denying the U.S. merchant fleet these highly lucrative prewar markets. Direct shipment of U.S. fish, meat, and other products on British vessels to the West Indies was also prohibited, and U.S. ships were prohibited from trade with Nova Scotia and New Brunswick. Discriminatory restrictions on U.S. exports to the British home islands were enacted. Yet during the 1780s Congress asked the states to approve an amendment to the Articles of Confederation that would invest Congress with the power to discriminate by a federal tariff against goods from nations not having commercial treaties with the United States; and in August 1786 a "Grand Committee" of Congress recommended that Congress be invested with the full power to regulate commerce with foreign nations including laying prohibitions and imposts, giving Congress a bargaining chip for negotiating British removal of these restrictions.[3] But the former proposal, which most of the states approved, had stalled; the latter, pending the movement for the Constitution, was postponed.

Although the 1783 Anglo-American peace treaty contained the general provision that no obstacle to debt recovery be placed in the way of the recovery of pre-war debts by British creditors in America, Virginia and North Carolina (and other states) enacted legislation that temporarily stayed British creditors from starting court suits against pre-war debtors. These stays were designed to prevent further drain of specie and to protect debtors from ruinous seizure-and-sale proceedings.[4] When the U.S. minister to Great Britain, John Adams, protested the retention of the northern border posts as violations of the 1783 treaty, British officials countered by pointing to these legislative stays as a previous violation. (The Virginia response was that the British had committed the first violation by not returning slaves carried off during the war.) As one solution to the growing legal snarl, the same "Grand Committee" proposed that Congress be empowered to establish a federal court with appellate jurisdiction to hear appeals from state courts in cases involving the interpretation of any U.S. treaty made with any foreign power.[5]

Each of these aforenamed problems could have been addressed (if not necessarily solved) by vesting Congress with limited powers to raise revenue and with the other specific powers or mechanisms discussed. The Framers chose the more ambitious and arduous path of complete reconstitution because by late 1786–early 1787 they believed that investing Congress with the 5 percent federal impost would not cure the weakness in the Confederation system as a whole that the breakdown of taxation by the states for Congress had (as they judged) laid bare. Investing the Continental Congress with a 5 percent federal impost was better than no reform at all. But such empowerment did not address the fact that *neither* Congress *nor* the state governments had power and stability enough to make the people of the United States pay taxes in hard money. Federalists believed that in attempting to raise hard money for Congress, the state governments (in the pressure-resistance-retreat cycles previously examined) had displayed a fatal structural weakness and instability. Even with the power to raise a 5 percent federal impost, the central government would require structures and powers equipping it to collect taxes by compulsion if necessary and to do so with greater independence, firmness, and forcefulness than any of the individual state governments could do. This was the crucial lesson of the failure by even the strongest and most stable state governments (Massachusetts and Maryland) to make their own citizens pay hard money taxes during the previous years.

John Jay's correspondence is again helpful. At least six months before the Constitutional Convention gathered in Philadelphia, Jay had made up his mind that Congress's simple amendment would not cure the weakness of the Confederation system. "Our Governments both particular and general are either too impotent or so very gently administered as neither to give much Terror to evil Doers, nor much Support and Encouragemt. to those who do well."[6] Prospects for a cure by the simple addition of the proposed federal impost promised "Little."[7] Citing the breakdown in the state requisition system as reflecting the lack of "energy" in "our Governments" and the want of "virtue & good sense" in the people, Jay reasoned that only a central government having independent legislative, executive, and judicial branches with strong powers and lengthy tenures would be forceful, independent, and stable enough to meet the necessary criterion of a "Govt. that can easily & irresistibly open [the people's] Purses."[8] And money, Jay repeatedly emphasized from his post as Confederation secretary for foreign affairs, was the basis of "National security & Respectability." He wrote Jefferson, "Much remains to be done and much to be attempted, but without a competent Govt. and adequate Funds, no national affairs can be well managed."[9]

The unsolved defense, financial, and foreign policy difficulties of the Confederation era pointed up and dramatized the need for a central government able to raise money and thus conduct a strong foreign policy, finance the federal debt, and defend the nation. But they do not tell us why the Federalists pursued the central government's reconstitution, rather than simple amendment (5 percent federal impost). For this, the history of the trial-and-failure attempts of the Confederation state governments to collect hard money taxes for Congress holds the best answer.

Interstate Commercial Warfare

Still another alleged manifestation of Critical Period breakdown is interstate "commercial warfare." In his chapter "Drifting towards Anarchy," Fiske describes the states as taxing each others' trade and cites this practice as another important example of the breakdown of cooperation and national unity among and within the states. Since the Articles of Confederation did not empower Congress to regulate interstate and foreign commerce or prohibit the individual state governments from taxing imports, the state governments could constitutionally impose discriminatory tariffs on each others' imported manufactures and agricultural products and tax each others' ships docking in their ports. Similarly, the states could increase their revenues by taxing foreign imports destined for reexport to purchasers in neighboring states. These opportunities, Fiske claims, were seized by the states, which engaged in a series of commercial bouts that came perilously close to open warfare. Events moved so far, Fiske asserts, that they "show us a glimpse of the untold dangers and horrors from which the adoption of our Federal Constitution has so thoroughly freed us that we can only with some effort realize how narrowly we have escaped them."[10]

This Critical Period reading of the states as warring commercially on each others' goods and ships does not stand scrutiny. Initially, a few states taxed imported products and goods grown or manufactured in other states; and some states also taxed the vessels of other states. By the time the Confederation era ended, however, all such taxes had been removed. The exceptions to this picture of interstate cooperation are the cases of New York and Pennsylvania. Both governments required that all imported *foreign* goods brought into their jurisdictions and reexported to neighboring states pay the state impost duty. Because a substantial reexport of imported foreign goods occurred via New York and Philadelphia merchants into the abutting states of Delaware, Connecticut, and New Jersey, New York and Pennsylvania siphoned off a considerable amount of cash from their neighbors.

But by the time of the Constitutional Convention the states were deescalating rather than escalating the exactions on each other's goods and shipping. This is the conclusion of William F. Zornow's several individual state studies of tariff and tonnage policies, which demonstrate that, by the time the Constitution was framed, every one of these governments had exempted from all duties agricultural goods and manufactures brought into their jurisdictions grown or made within any of their sister states. Similarly, all the states either exempted from any duty such ships as belonged to the citizens of other states or levied duties that were the same as those levied on their own citizens. New York State's stance is especially revealing. The administration of the allegedly local-minded governor George Clinton taxed imported foreign goods but explicitly exempted all U.S.-manufactured and agricultural goods imported into New York. Clinton's administration also exempted from the payment of import duties foreign goods destined for reexport on previous consignment. Similarly, New York levied discriminatory tonnage fees against foreign ships but not against ships owned by Americans from other states. As Zornow writes: "The era is one of cooperation as far as the state [of New York] is concerned. American goods moved freely across the border and there was a tendency to accord equal privileges to and to charge equal fees against all [U.S.] merchants whose ships entered the harbors of the state."[11]

By 1787 the other twelve states, like New York, had established tariff systems that allowed U.S.-made and U.S.-grown goods to enter duty free. (Simultaneously, these states taxed imports of foreign make and origin and placed higher duties on British goods and ships). These states also levied tonnage duties on U.S. ships no higher than those their own ship-owning citizens had to pay (foreign ships paid more). Most of these steps were taken in the early or mid-1780s, but Virginia seems to have been an exception. Virginia's across-the-board ad valorem impost levied duties not only on foreign goods but on U.S.-made goods and foreign imports until October 1786, when the state government exempted payment of goods brought into Virginia on U.S. ships "directly from the state in which they were originally produced or grown." By March 1788 the legislature had extended this exemption still further, excusing from any levy all produce or manufactures produced in any of the United States—a turnabout that Zornow describes as a virtual free trade: "By 1789 Virginia, like her sister states, was admitting American produce duty free."[12] Similarly, in 1783 Virginia placed tonnage duties on all ships entering Virginia ports but exempted ships owned by Virginia and Maryland. In 1786, however, the legislature reversed this policy, imposing higher tonnage duties on English vessels that entered Virginia's ports, but placing Virginians and shipowners from other states on an equal lower-rate basis.[13]

Foreign importations from abroad are a different story, however. All the state governments levied impost duties on imported foreign productions, earmarking the income for state debt funding or for Congressional requisitions. Attempting to pressure the British government to remove its restrictions on U.S. vessels trading with the British West Indies, the state governments imposed higher differential duties on both imported British manufactured goods and British ships entering U.S. ports. New York and Pennsylvania, however, capitalized on their strategic position and siphoned cash off from the other states. Foreign importations into New York and Pennsylvania reexported by New York and Philadelphia merchants to other states were taxed at the port of entry; thus taxed, the goods acquired an add-on cost that had to be absorbed by buyers in New Jersey, Connecticut, and Delaware. The sums involved were quite substantial. John Kaminski estimates that the money from these add-on imposts cost New Jersey buyers alone £40,000 annually.[14] Yet both states specifically exempted from the impost any foreign goods landed but bound *by consignment* to any merchant in a neighboring state.

While the New York and Pennsylvania state imposts on foreign goods re-exported to New Jersey, Connecticut, and Delaware thus drained cash from those states, this policy must be placed in a context in which the state governments created a virtual common market for each others' manufactured and agricultural goods by the time the Constitutional Convention met in Philadelphia. This can hardly have been what Federalists meant by the general "relaxation" of the state governments.

Paper Money

Despite the efforts of E. James Ferguson, James R. Morrill, John P. Kaminski, and others who have written important works on the paper money programs of the Confederation era, the sinister aura of financial quackery and dishonesty still hangs over the various paper money emissions of the Critical Period.[15] Following closely the Federalist party line, Critical Period historians have depicted this paper money as an unwise and harmful capitulation to the demands of spendthrift and dishonest debtors. It injured private creditors, disrupted interstate and foreign trade, frightened investment, and further damaged the country's already shaky credit standing abroad. The state governments nevertheless weakly capitulated to these dishonest demands. Thus the several state paper money issues of the 1780s provide yet another evidence of the general breakdown of honorable, effective government.

Ferguson's book demonstrates, however, that the paper money loan office emission was a well-tested method that eighteenth-century colonial governments had used to reflate prices and provide credit to farmers. Much previous colonial experience had seen paper money banks fulfill these credit and commercial purposes successfully. Kaminski's dissertation shows that the paper money loan banks of the 1780s performed a similar function by providing the yeomanry of the states with credit and by helping to reflate prices. Why were these paper money issues of the 1780s so bitterly opposed by Federalists?

Like their eighteenth-century English and European counterparts, the well-to-do elites of the Confederation era believed that gold and silver specie coin formed the most stable, reliable monetary medium available to governments and the international community for their dealings and transactions. Disillusioned by the depreciated paper money currencies of the Revolution era, most of the elite had come to regard gold and silver coin as far more stable and reliable than state paper money, whatever the perceived utility of the latter before the war. Gold and silver had intrinsic value that made them much less variable than paper money. Gold and silver coin commanded the confidence of business people the world over who wanted their loans and contracts paid in stable money. Because of its stable value, gold and silver coin—or paper fully backed by gold and silver coin—was the money used by the most honorable European governments to pay creditors, armies, and civil officers. Gold and silver coin commanded general acceptance at relatively stable, standardized rates everywhere in Europe and the United States regardless of what particular governments did or did not do.[16] Because coin was required to pay the interest and principal to its Dutch and French creditors, and because it hoped to build a credit standing equal to the most honorable European governments, Congress insisted that the states pay specie for requisition payments and refused to accept payments by the states in their own paper.

Chastened by the revolutionary war experience with paper money finance, the U.S. elites of the Confederation era deeply mistrusted state paper money. During the Revolution Congress had issued huge amounts of paper money that depreciated ("not worth a Continental"), and the states had used currency to finance their Revolution budgets with the same result. Much of this depreciation was attributed to the state governments' failure to carry out the hard and unpopular measures necessary to sustain the value of paper money—namely taxation. When the state governments did not tax citizens sufficiently during the Revolution, and when the collection of taxes levied by the Confederation state governments faltered, the view that the elected state governments were too weak to assure a stable paper medium gained further credibility within business and financial circles.[17]

Thus, despite its utility during the colonial era, the elites and their business and financial associates regarded the issuing of paper currency by state legislatures as commercially, morally, and politically pernicious. It was commercially pernicious because it produced hoarding, frightened credit, and defeated the very economic recovery it was supposed to promote. Soon after the Constitutionalists took control of the Pennsylvania government and began printing and loaning paper money (1785), the Pennsylvania

Republican Sharp Delany reported how doing so had stimulated hoarding: "Paper & Tender Laws has shut up all hard money—& almost banishes confidence between Man & Man." Thomas Paine, newly established as a pamphleteer against Pennsylvania's state paper money, wrote that it would be impossible to restore credit or borrow at fair rates of interest as long as paper was not "publicly reprobated and extirpated."[18]

Paper money loans were seen as morally pernicious because they encouraged the very indolence and profusion in the lower classes believed to be responsible for tax and debt defaults in the first place. Instead of encouraging industriousness and saving—the real antidotes to debt—paper money did the reverse. A favorite metaphor was to compare paper money to alcohol: "Like dram-drinking, it relieves for the moment by a deceitful sensation, but gradually diminishes the natural heat, and leaves the body worse than it found it." Rhode Island's James M. Varnum described that state's recent issue of paper money as an instance of the legislature's "debauching the minds of the common people." The same message of paper money as a demoralizing snare and delusion was conveyed by depicting its petitioners as lazy, extravagant ne'er-do-wells: "Jeronymous No Tax, Amos Spendthrift, John Sharper, Jo Lawless, Jeromiah Putoff, Jerolomen Feartoil, Hezekiah Dolittle" were the imaginary signees of a paper money petition presented to New Jersey's legislature.[19]

And since there seemed no sound case to be made for issuing paper money, Federalists branded the advocates of paper money as demagogues whose concern was not for the well-being of the common people but for their own popularity and reelection: "Justice! Whither art thou fled? Honour! Truth! Virtue! Where have ye taken up your abode? That any legislature should ever be made the dupes of such unconscionable, prevaricating, double-minded insidious petitioners! That any legislature should for *their* relief, pass acts necessarily tending to annihilate all publick faith, and all private credit! Ah! The passion for ensuring elections per sas & nefas."[20]

Yet these same elite groups recognized that because gold and silver coin were scarce, some kind of supplementary paper medium was necessary to supply the credit and currency needs of a growing commercial community. Next to specie coin, the most reliable, stable monetary medium was not government-issued paper but private bank paper loaned to selected borrowers by privately managed merchant banks. In 1781 Robert Morris, the newly appointed superintendent of finance, orchestrated the first such bank—the Bank of North America—the prototype model for Alexander Hamilton's later chartered First Bank of the United States. "There is no reason why paper should not pass equivalently with Silver," Morris wrote, "if it be issued on proper funds, and with proper precautions, so that the demand for it be great." But, he continued, any paper money to be issued "must be a Bank paper, because the general promises of Government having been violated, men cannot be prevailed to confide in them."[21] In 1786 the Rev. John Witherspoon, scholar-president of the College of New Jersey, argued for private banks as more reliable sources of paper money than state legislatures. Witherspoon acknowledged that a crucial emergency might require a state-issued emission of paper money; if so, the paper should be in limited quantity, subject to strict interest, mortgage, and repayment requirements, and payable only for taxes, not private debts.[22]

During the 1780s, seven Confederation state governments legislated paper money issues. Pennsylvania, New York, New Jersey, South Carolina, North Carolina, and Rhode Island set up state land banks that loaned the paper on land mortgages and required repayment over time at fixed interest rates. Georgia printed bills of credit to meet the emergency caused by the escalating Creek Indian War, earmarking the money to pay for supplying the troops raised for service against the Creeks. Massachusetts, Maryland, Delaware, New Hampshire, Connecticut, and Virginia rejected paper money legislation.[23]

As the case studies in this book demonstrate, the paper money legislation of the 1780s was primarily a response to the rising opposition of distressed farmers and rural artisans threatened by ruinous tax sales. In Pennsylvania and Rhode Island paper money banks were voted by Reliefer legislative majorities; South Carolina's paper money bank was legislated by the state's upper-class establishment. In each instance paper money was part and parcel of a "relaxation" by the government after pressure on taxpayers to collect their taxes backfired. On the other hand, the Massachusetts general court repeatedly rejected proposals for paper money and ordered a crackdown on unpaid taxes until Shays's Rebellion forced it to back off.

Once issued, the several state paper issues fluctuated greatly in real value. The strongest was New York's (1786), which held its value in relation to specie well. The worst was Rhode Island's (1786), which plunged to 20 percent of its specie value. The key to these differences was business community support. Although opposed to the paper money relief program backed by Governor George Clinton, New York City's Chamber of Commerce pledged support for the paper money once it became law. Similarly in South Carolina, the elite-sponsored paper money bill commanded support among Carolina's business community, and the paper held its value. The paper issued by Pennsylvania and New Jersey also held its value, dropping by some 10–15 percent discount at most. By contrast, when the Providence and Newport business communities refused to accept the new paper in any transaction, Rhode Island's paper plummeted by 80 percent. Similarly in North Carolina and Georgia, lack of support by the business community caused the paper issued by those two state legislatures to depreciate materially.[24]

Five of the seven states that issued paper money made their currencies legal tender and as such payable not only for past and present taxes but for private debts as well. This may also be interpreted as prompted by the tax crackdowns that generated pressures for debt relief. In South Carolina, Rhode Island, and Massachusetts, the pressures on delinquent taxpayers forced them to sue their own debtors for unpaid private debts. And when rumors of impending paper money legislation frightened the merchant community, merchants and monied men stepped up court actions to pressure their debtors into payment. Thus the tax crackdowns were the cause of private creditor actions that, in turn, generated pleas by rural citizens for legal tender currency that would enable them to save their property from sheriff's auction sales. Reliefers like the Rhode Island relief party, New Jersey's Abraham Clark, and others espoused the cause of delinquent private debtors as well as that of delinquent public taxpayers to defuse rural discontent and head off further protests and riots.

The work of Ferguson, Morrill, and Kaminski has effectively discredited the Critical Period interpretation of the issuance of paper money as a dishonest ploy to escape just debts. Yet as perceived by the Federalists, the paper money issues of the 1780s had just such meaning. More importantly, they signaled the state governments' inability to stand up firmly to their own citizens and force them to pay taxes in specie. Guided by their own class conditioning and remote from the daily grind of the dirt farmer, the Federalists could not grasp that these were relief and order-restoring measures, not dishonest, demoralizing political charlatanism.

Anarchy and Disunion

Drawing on contemporary Federalist warnings of "anarchy," Critical Period historians point to Shays's Rebellion and other outbreaks as evidence of spreading mass anarchy. Similarly, they take as valid Federalist warnings of the Union's imminent breakup. Yet close reading indicates that in Federalist letters the terms *anarchy* and *disunion* had less catastrophic meanings than when they were used rather loosely in public rhetoric to drum up support for the Constitution.

The direst warnings of anarchy usually appeared either in the public rhetoric of Federalist leaders during the ratification battles immediately after the Constitutional Convention or in correspondence directed to persons they wanted to persuade to support the Constitution. ("Anarchy with its horrid train of miseries seem[s] ready to overwhelm this region marked by nature for happiness," wrote Henry Knox.)[25] Federalists did believe that anarchy would probably occur if the central government were not reconstituted, but a specific, localized kind of anarchy, not general mass disorder.[26] Similarly, disunion was a possible event that the demise of an insolvent Congress might produce at a future time. But the imminence of massive anarchy or immediate disunion became the standard Federalist party line once the Constitution issued from the Philadelphia convention and the ratification battles began.[27]

When Federalists wrote privately about anarchy, the image that often emerges is not a massive uprising or total breakdown of order but the use of violence by discontented groups ("factions") to force the state governments into some desired policy change. *Anarchy* in this sense suggests localized, issue-specific opposition directed at some unpopular, unwanted policy measure of the state governments. Henry Knox warned that continuation of the Confederation state-centered system would "precipitate us into the gulf of separate [state] anarchies." Knox's language suggests a continuing process of discrete, limited "mobbings" or risings to force changes in unwanted state laws, not a generalized massive breakdown of law throughout the United States. His point is that Congress's limited amendment would not lift the state-centered Confederation system out of its vulnerability to popular pressure, tumults, and civil disobedience.[28] When that most discrete Federalist James Madison, Jr., wrote his father of the anxiety among members of the convention over reports of tumults in some of the states, he drew a picture not of massive defiance of the law throughout the United States but of "the unruly temper of the people" in some states and the "unwise and wicked proceedings" of the governments of other states. Madison here contrasts those states that had already enacted "unwise and wicked" relief measures with those states that had not yet done so; in the latter the "unruly" people were trying to force their governments into the "unwise and wicked" relief measures of the former. When Colonel Francis Johnston endorsed the Constitution, he welcomed it as creating a government with the energy to deal with "still more Dangerous and factious Democracy"—meaning the phenomenon of popular resistance to laws that the common people ("the Democracy") found burdensome or did not like.[29]

Federalists also sometimes invoked "anarchy" as a warning of future probabilities, not a description of current realities. Federalist Christopher Gore called for reconstituted central government that would energize government throughout the Union. Without it, Gore predicted, "We shall descend to anarchy & disgrace"—meaning, I think, that the use of popular violence to force changes in state government policy would become endemic and pervasive. If *anarchy* in this sense meant forcing policy changes by popular resistance and defiance, would not "relaxation" by all the state governments put an end to this anarchy-as-mob-pressure? Knox at one point casts the issue between adopting the strong central "government of Laws" promised by the Constitution on the one hand, and continuing the current "misrule of anarchy *or* [italics mine] a government of convenience & caprice" on the other; he thus seems to expect either "anarchy" or "convenient" government but not both.[30] Federalists seem to have based their notions of future anarchy on extrapolation from their experience with the episodes of popular resistance to taxation in the states. Predictably, therefore, once a government retreated, the anarchy would end, just as it had in each of the states. But anarchy could certainly occur as many times as there were objectionable or unpopular policies or laws.

That observers at the time testified to the existence of peace and order in the states further suggests that by *anarchy* the Federalists meant limited popular risings against specific unpopular or unwanted policies, not a generalized breakdown of law and order. That the Antifederalists rejected the Federalist claim that anarchy existed or was imminent is no surprise. The Antifederalists had staked their policies on the premise that relief to the rural lower classes would restore peace, order, and quiet in the countryside. A former Pennsylvania Reliefer recalled, shortly after the Constitution was framed and ratified: "There was no Anarchy nor any considerable Degree of Licentiousness in Pennsylvania."[31] If anarchy or breakup of the union had been imminent in 1787, the Antifederalists would not have opposed the Constitution so strenuously. Nor would there have been the movement, which promised to delay ratification, for a second Constitutional Convention to propose amendments to the Constitution. Once Shays's Rebellion ended, even some Federalists portrayed the current situation as peaceful. In September 1786 member of Congress from Connecticut Stephen Mitchell worried that the court blockings in Massachusetts would spread to Connecticut. The present generation is "a set of inflammable & turbulent Beings" who, "when a little pressed with their necessities, [will be] prone to resort to the old Method of opposing force to Law." Yet in letters written in July and September 1787 to Connecticut's convention delegate William Samuel Johnson, Mitchell implicitly endorsed a revamped central government; he wondered only, as "tis a time of profound peace within & without," whether "subjects will at such a time be cautious how they give power to their Rulers. . . . No thots are entertained of any great alteration in the form or force of foederal Government by the people at large." He assured Johnson, "If you are able to devise such measures as this people in a time of profound peace within & without, will chearfully adopt, & yet have Energy in them, & give us respectability at home & abroad you will deserve great Credit."[32]

Alongside the specter of anarchy, the image of national breakup also hovers over Critical Period historiography. But in view of the efforts by the state governments to cooperate in interstate trade, cede western claims to Congress, and settle peacefully such controversies as that between Connecticut and Pennsylvania over Wyoming, it is difficult to see how disunion could have been the imminent prospect that the Federalists claimed. During the ratification debates the Federalists sounded the certainty of national disunion if the Constitution were not adopted, and Federalists often presented themselves as the "friends of order and union"—presumably implying that the Antifederalists were the friends of disorder and disunion. (*Publius* in the *Federalist* warns repeatedly that disunion would be the outcome if the Constitution were rejected.)[33] But Federalist private correspondence brings us back to the Congress's financial insolvency as the only conceivable basis on which a reasonable possibility of disunion could be projected. Without the money to pay current expenses, by early 1787 some delegates were talking seriously about an insolvent Congress dissolving itself and sending the delegates home. If Congress disbanded, then predictably the Union would dissolve—not immediately but eventually. Conceivably, coordination of policy by the state governments through informal communication could have kept the states together for a time. Sooner or later, however, Federalists extrapolated, without a Congress in which to thrash out disputes and coordinate policy, friction among the states would escalate and the Union would break up. Alternatively, intrigues by European powers would cause the states to form regional confederations for their own protection.[34] But these were hypothetical predictions of future possibilities, not reports of present realities. Once again, if it had been merely a question of keeping Congress financially afloat and thus maintaining a central forum for the Union, the Federalists could have simply invested Congress with an independent 5 percent impost rather than pursue reconstitution.

In sum, once the several traditional Critical Period interpretations of the Constitution are critically examined, the case for the breakdown of hard-money taxing in the states as the central impetus of the movement for reconstitution gains credibility. The breakdown of taxation is the only phenomenon that occurred in all the states, caused Congress's financial bankruptcy, was reflected in the several paper money issues enacted during the period, and was the basis for Federalist warnings of anarchy and disunion. It is also the only phenomenon that fully explains why the Federalists resorted to root-and-branch reconstitution rather than to limited amendment.

★ II ★

An Unvirtuous People:
The Federalists' View

MANY HISTORIANS consider Gordon Wood's *Creation of the American Republic 1776–1788* (1969) the most important book on the origins of the Constitution published in the past twenty-five years.[1] Wood, whose book is the centerpiece of the current "republican synthesis" of the revolutionary and early republican eras, holds that the Framers established the Constitution because they believed that the Republic under the Articles of Confederation would not be sustained by an unvirtuous American people.[2] The revolutionary generation assumed that public virtue, meaning a spirit of patriotic self-abnegation and disciplined austerity, was the requisite, all-important basis of a republic. By the time of the Constitutional Convention, the Framers had become convinced that communal self-abnegation and austerity were not part of the American character. Describing this conviction, Wood writes: "The American people apparently did not possess and were unwilling to acquire the moral and social character necessary to sustain republican governments"; "they were 'a Luxurious Voluptuous indolent expensive people without Economy or Industry.' "[3]

Public virtue thus defined was certainly a major concern of many on the eve of the Constitutional Convention. A writer in a Springfield, Massachusetts, paper in mid-1786 warned: "Still we are ruined, but how or by what? by our vanities and debaucheries which day and night prevail." A Philadelphia newspaper contributor lamented the decline of "that virtue, which is necessary to support a republic," and declared that "by recurring to the principles and integrity of public spirit, and the practice of *industry, sobriety, oeconomy, and fidelity in contracts*, and by acquiescing in laws necessary for the public good, the impending ruin may be averted and we become respectable and happy." A Charleston, South Carolina, newspaper writer urged: "Let honesty and industry be thy companions; and spend one penny per day *less* than thy *clear gains*, and then *hide-bound pockets* will soon begin to thrive." A Boston writer in late 1786 compared the people of Massachusetts with their virtuous Puritan forbears: "What a *falling off* there is at this day from the examples set us by our illustrious ancestors—

we may call our present character liberality, or christen it with what name we please, but its baneful effects best tell its inutility—we may talk of the rigid manners, and the puritannical usages of our progenitors, but far better would it be for us, if we copied their frugality, their honesty, and their *reverence for laws & rulers*, which it is known they possessed."[4]

Other kinds of evidence sound the theme of an unvirtuous people. John Quincy Adams's 1787 Harvard commencement oration, Royall Tyler's 1787 play *The Contrast*, and Noah Webster's 1787 public lectures may be read as commentaries on the declining state of Americans' public virtue defined as industriousness, frugality, and respect for law.[5] Leaders explicitly linked waning virtue with the possible overthrow of republican government. Connecticut's William Samuel Johnson (1785) affirmed that the state governments were in no immediate danger, but if current trends of luxury and dissipation continued they would be. "The greatest Danger in that regard that we are in seems to arise from that strong propensity we have to run into Luxury & dissipations of every kind. The fatal tendency of which to overturn our Constitutions our Countrymen do not seem to be sufficiently aware of." New Jersey's William Livingston (1787) found himself "more distressed by the posture of our public affairs, than I ever was by the most gloomy appearances during the late war. We do not exhibit the virtue that is necessary to support a republican government."[6] The circulation of nonconsumption covenants pledging signers not to purchase foreign goods is another symptom of the contemporary concern over the excesses of unvirtuous behavior.[7]

Wood attributes the Framers' belief that Americans were unvirtuous to the special interest politics of the Confederation state assemblies, and to the rise to power in these assemblies of the Federalists' social and political inferiors.[8] I believe that the calls for industriousness and frugality should be read, at least in part, as class-specific responses to popular demands for tax relief and to the popular obstruction and resistance that greeted the governments' tax crackdowns. The Federalists also saw the marks of an unvirtuous people in other contemporary events and phenomena that confirmed their sense of Americans as an unvirtuous people.

The Framers and Human Nature

An unspoken premise behind all the warnings and laments about declining virtue was the assumption that human morals and behavior could be changed for either the worse or the better. Otherwise, it would make no sense to call upon Americans to banish luxury and dissipation and strive to be industrious and frugal.[9] Until recently, however, historians have described the Framers as proponents of a Calvinist-Hobbesian view of human nature that ruled out any such possibility of improvement. According to this view, human beings were basically acquisitive, ambitious, prideful, selfish, envious, irrational, and incapable of amelioration; the only way to achieve a livable, orderly society was to keep them in check through the constant regulation and supervision of strong government and of other social mechanisms such as the church, education, and the family. This Hobbesian view has been aptly expressed by Richard Hofstadter, who concludes in his famous essay on the Framers that they "had no hope and they offered none for any ultimate organic change in the way men conduct themselves." Other historians hold that the Framers viewed humanity somewhat less pessimistically as individualistic, self-interested beings whose behavior was governed by their own self-interest, usually economic; the task of government thus became the accommodation of the sum of these interests through adjustment and compromise.[10]

Recent scholarship has suggested a third, more behaviorist Federalist view of human nature that is expressed in a body of eighteenth-century social science thought known as faculty psychology. Recently invoked in a brilliant rereading of *The Federalist* by Daniel Walker Howe, this view represented the best, most up-to-date theory of human nature of the day and was well known to such leading Federalists as Madison, Hamilton, and Jay. Faculty psychology identifies human nature as a complex amalgam of emotional and rational drives and powers. But it also assumes a human nature that can be developed and improved through externally applied training, education, and discipline.[11] The outgrowth of a tradition of philosophers and thinkers stretching back to Aristotle, perhaps its most influential eighteenth-century exponents were the well-known Scottish moral philosophers Thomas Reid (Glasgow University) and Francis Hutcheson (University of Edinburgh). Although each had his own classification and hierarchy of the different faculties, they shared a common notion that the human psyche consisted of the so-called animal faculties, such as passions, desires, and affections, and the so-called rational faculties, such as reason and conscience. Depending on a given person's background, training, and development, the animal and rational faculties could be at different stages of development and strength, each exercising a differential impact on behavior. In their primitive, untutored state, individuals were more subject to their animal than to their rational faculties. In their more educated and developed state, they could bring to bear reason and conscience.

Much as one develops a muscle through strengthening exercises, faculty psychology held that reason and conscience could be exercised, cultivated, and developed to the point where they could effectively control the animal passions. Thomas Reid's "Essays on the Active Powers of Man," first published in 1788, expounds on the various ways the faculties of reason and conscience could be developed through education, example, and discipline. Reid also assigns government an important role in the training process. In a telling passage, he terms the art of civil government "the medicine of the mind," the most useful part of which "is that which prevents crimes and bad habits, and trains men to virtue and good habits by proper education and discipline." Presumably, once one learns through one's rational faculty that it is in one's interest to obey the well-framed policies of government, one develops habits and attitudes that then take over and make future obedience automatic.[12]

In Confederation and Federalist America, several voices preached the gospel of faculty psychology. One was the Rev. John Witherspoon, Scottish president of the College of New Jersey and mentor of such U.S. Federalists as James Madison and H. H. Brackenridge. Witherspoon's *Lectures on Moral Philosophy*, delivered annually at the college until his death in 1794, sound a cautious message of improvability through the exercise and development of reason and conscience as well as of Christian piety and faith. Noah Webster, the Connecticut Federalist, championed a broad program of moral and behavioral schooling and training that he expounded in public lectures and magazine essays. In the view of one biographer, Webster's theories of behavioral conditioning, advanced during the 1780s, mark him as an early "pragmatic behaviorist." And, as Howe has argued, faculty psychology guided the hand of James Madison, Alexander Hamilton, and John Jay when they wrote *The Federalist*.[13]

Many, perhaps most, of the major Federalists were self-consciously engaged in furthering what Henry May has called the "moderate eighteenth-century Enlightenment." They shared an assumption that human life and the natural world operated according to regularities and laws and that through empirical investigation and reason these regularities and laws could be discovered and put to the service of human improvement. Holding to the assumptions of faculty psychology, these Federalists extended the idea of improvability to human nature. But at the same time faculty psychology postulated that individuals' faculties must be trained, disciplined, regulated, and exercised if their rational rather than their animal faculties were to prevail. If reason and conscience were to rule the passions and appetites, individuals must be shaped by such conscience-strengthening, behavior-forming agendas as schools, family training, religious instruction, and government could carry out. This behaviorist view of human nature directed the various improvement projects sketched in chapter 4. And it informed the Federalists' reaction to the popular pressure for tax bailouts and paper money.

The Fruits of Relaxed Government:
A Decline in Public Virtue

Wood's concept of public virtue posits a self-abnegating patriotism that devotes itself to the collective common good over individual interest or personal preference. Challenging this view, Lance Banning has argued that the Framers accepted the play of individual self-interest as an inevitable part of politics but meant by *public virtue* a willingness to obey duly enacted law without requiring coercion. Both authors may be right. *Public virtue* is such a flexible word-concept that it could easily accommodate both patriotic self-abnegation and respect for law, depending on the context.[14]

Wood also emphasizes the many exhortations against luxury that appear in the press and pamphlet literature of the Confederation era. "Throughout all the secular and religious jeremiads of the eighties the key term was 'luxury,' that important social product and symptom of extreme selfishness and pleasure-seeking. Over and over men emphasized 'the destructive tendency of luxury,' so much so that it had become by 1788 'a beaten topic.' " Wood reads this as evidence of disenchantment with the special interest politics of the state assemblies. Since individualistic self-interestedness contradicted the republican ideal of communal self-abnegation, the condemnations of luxury represent laments over Americans' failure to live up to this ideal.[15]

But the condemnations of luxury can be read another way. If luxury means extravagance and indolence, its opposites are industriousness and frugality. From this perspective, condemning luxury was a way of urging Americans to greater industriousness and frugality. Industriousness and frugality, in turn, would boost exports and reduce imports and thus bring specie into the economy. Industriousness and frugality would also produce the wherewithal to pay taxes and debts. The causal link between hard work and saving and an increase in specie and the payment of taxes and private debts is explicit in a resolution by the Andover, Massachusetts, town meeting: "That, in their opinion, a deviation from the principles of industry and economy have been the great cause of the scarcity of specie, the delinquency in the payment of taxes, and in the discharge of private debts; which delinquency naturally tends to mar the reputation and destroy the energy of government."[16]

The Massachusetts lexicographer Noah Webster described the protests against taxes in central and western Massachusetts as the fruits of popular indolence and extravagance. Massachusetts farmers and husbandmen, Webster held, had squandered their money in taverns and grocery shops and now, finding themselves without cash, were clamoring against their taxes. As Webster remarked smugly: "It is fact, demonstrated by correct calculation, that the common people in this Country drink Rum & Tea sufficient every year to pay the interest of the public debts—articles of luxury which so far from doing them any good, injure their morals, impair ye health & shorten their lives."[17]

If luxury deprived the country of specie and incapacitated the people from paying their debts and taxes, it followed that the failure of the government to force the people to pay their taxes would encourage luxury still further. In December 1786 John Jay described the Confederation as experiencing "much Public and private Distress, & much public and private want of good faith," which he attributed to "Extravagance in Individuals" and "Relaxation in Govermt." In a follow-up letter to the same recipient two months later, Jay described how the states "pay little attention to Requisitions" and then explained why. "Our Governments want Energy, and there is Reason to fear that too much has been expected from the virtue & good sense of the People." Jay's attribution of both the Confederation's financial difficulties and the people's financial distress to popular "extravagance" and the relaxed government of the states, and his call for a reassessment of "the virtue & good sense of the People," are important indicators of how Federalists viewed the interplay of government policy and popular morals. "Virtue" is juxtaposed with its opposite, "extravagance," and by implication it is the latter, unchecked by the relaxed state governments, that is responsible for Congress's and the states' bankruptcy and the people's current financial distress.[18]

Many Federalists pointedly faulted the state governments for allowing their citizens to become luxurious. By not forcing the people to work and save and by indulging the people with tax bailouts, exemptions, and loans, the states rewarded people's lack of industry and extravagance. Interpreted in the language of faculty psychology, this meant that the lower animal faculties (the passions) were exercised and strengthened while the higher rational faculties (reason and conscience) were allowed to atrophy. Virginia notable Charles Lee ascribed what he took to be the current demoralization of the Virginia common people to the legislature, which had "pursued a system, it may be said ever since the beginnings of the commonwealth, tending to efface every principle of virtue and honesty from the minds of its citizens and this is particularly obvious in the laws respecting delinquent officers and delinquent individuals as to taxes." The enactment of laws made "to favor and relieve (as it is expressed) those who might have failed to pay what was rightly due the Commonwealth" has created "an opinon [that] now generally prevails among the delinquents that they will never be compelled to pay." Virginia Framer James McClurg's reference to "the continual depravation of Men's manners, under the corrupting Influence of our Legislature" captures the same idea. By suggesting that "Anarchy first & civil Convulsions afterwards" will occur unless a more "efficient" central government is established, McClurg is suggesting that this recurrent legislative corruption of the common people is taking the people of Virginia down a slippery slope of extravagance, indolence, and dishonesty into anarchy.[19]

In the rural pressures for paper money relief that first developed when the tax collection process threatened farmers with ruinous auction sales, the Federalists saw further evidence that Americans were becoming an unvirtuous people. They should shoulder their obligations as citizens and work and save, not count on paper money relief that might temporarily relieve their debts but could only deprave and demoralize them still further. Henry Knox viewed paper money as an addictive means by which the common people could escape taxation and indulge their aversion for labor. He could not, he told George Washington, predict whether the present "commotions" in Massachusetts against the government (Shays's Rebellion) would break out in other states of the Confederation, but whether they did or not would depend "a good deal on the habits of the States, and their compliance with paper money and other measures tending to avert taxation and industry." Thus, when the state governments enacted paper money relief measures or took other steps to relax taxation, the action became, for men like Knox, both a dishonest ploy to escape current obligations and an incentive to further habit-forming indolence and evasion.[20] In New York State, when the Reliefer Clinton party pushed through a paper money bill early in 1786, New York merchants regarded the measure not only as hurtful to commerce but as symptomatic of the depraved state of popular morals and of the government's capitulation to popular demands. The paper "is not, nor ever will be equal to gold and silver," Collin McGregor warned a colleague, and would "cut deep in profits" by requiring a premium to purchase bills of exchange. "I have been looking round, and really it does not appear to me to be a time to risk much in this Country; what from the very unstable situation of the Country, the depraved state of the people in general, and the relaxed principles of the whole, it frightens me."[21] Similarly, a Federalist visitor to Savannah, Georgia, where the Reliefer-dominated government had enacted a paper money bill to pay for the Creek Indian war, reported that "the Place is agreeable & pleasant enough were the government & manners fixed & principled."[22]

Less prevalent than the pressures for tax relief that occurred in every state were other, more marginal episodes that also produced Federalist disenchantment with the state governments and American morals. One of these episodes developed during the hardship years of the mid- and later 1780s, a movement in rural Massachusetts and Connecticut that attacked the legal profession for excessive fees and expensive court proceedings. Proposed reforms included a system of regulated state-paid lawyers, reduction in the number of lawyers, community approval of lawyers before qualifying them to plead in court, and reduction and regulation of lawyers' fees.[23] Shortly before he left for the Philadelphia convention in May 1787, the well-known Connecticut Anglican cleric, president-elect of Columbia College, and Federalist delegate, William Samuel Johnson, warned his son in the West Indies not to return to his hometown of Stratford to open a law practice because of this antilawyer agitation, observing pessimistically: "In general, throughout our States, in proportion as our Governments relax, & we grow licentious & embarrass'd in our affairs (which by the way seems everywhere encreasing) a Clamour is excited against the Lawyers & attempts are made to diminish their profits & injure the Profession. How this is to end I know not." Johnson concluded with the observation that a convention was soon to meet in Philadelphia "to endeavour to strengthen our federal Government & restore our affairs."[24]

Similarly confirming the Federalist assumption that relaxed government corrupted the people were popular demands for private debt relief. Pressured by popular forces burdened by heavy tax bills and private debts incurred in trying to meet these bills, all the state governments during the period legislated some form of tax relief; others went further and voted debt relief. The most common form of tax relief was to suspend or postpone the deadline when tax collectors were to seize and sell the property of delinquents. Debt relief measures included legal stays on court-directed debt actions, delayed debt payback schedules, and personal property tender legislation. Paper money banks were a more radical relief measure. Between 1781 and 1788, seven state governments legislated paper money payable for taxes in order to relieve distressed taxpayers and reflate their state economies. Five of the seven went further and made the paper money legal tender, payable for both taxes and private debts.[25]

None of this legislation even hinted at the repudiation of public or private debts. In fact, its purpose was to enable debtors to pay their debts at a fair value by affording them sufficient time and monetary means. Nevertheless, by the eve of the Constitution, many in the well-to-do class believed that it was only a matter of time before the popular classes would force their popularly elected legislatures to void all tax and debt obligations by outright repudiation or some other dishonest ploy.

The assumption that tax reliefs were corrupting the people's morals explains the fear that private debt repudiation was close at hand. Virginia's Charles Lee explicitly linked the Virginia assembly's tax policies with popular demoralization and predicted that without a central government "more powerful and independent of the people, the public debts and even private debts will in my opinion be extinguished by acts of the several Legislatures of the several States." Already the enactment of tax reliefs by the Virginia legislature had created "an opinon [that] now generally prevails

among the delinquents that they will never be compelled to pay." Repudiation of all debts would be next. "The temper of the people in general,
their habits, their interests all combine in producing such an event, and
against these, natural justice will make but a feint opposition."[26] Another
Virginia Federalist declared: "We are in a wretched condition [in Vir-
ginia] at present, no money to be got for any practice or old debts—Unless
a new Government forms some permanent System we shall all be ruined
by rascals and faithless debtors—paper money &c. if not controuled."[27]
Even limited concessions to relieve private debtors such as the South Carolina tender act (1785) suggested that members of the legislatures were
deliberately courting votes by enabling men to escape their just debts. In
South Carolina, one Federalist observed, "while men are madly accumulating enormous debts, their legislators are making provisions for their
nonpayment. The almost universal advantage which is taken of these iniquitous laws at once illustrates & confirms the maxim that a corrupt government necessarily bespeaks a corrupt people."[28]

Descent into Anarchy

Implicit in previous Federalist comment was the assumption that the interplay between relaxed government and an unvirtuous people would
eventually lead to anarchy. The more the state governments relaxed the
reins of government, the more the people's animal faculties would rule
their behavior. The more the passions ruled, the more the common people
would press their elected governments into further concessions, including
repudiation of public and private debts and other dishonest measures. As
this process spiralled downward, the people's moral restraints would further atrophy. Indolence and extravagance would then become licentiousness; licentiousness, lawlessness; and lawlessness, anarchy.

Early signs of deterioration were to be found in reports of an increase
in theft, forgery, arson, fraud, and murder during the mid- and latter
1780s. Savannah, Georgia (1787): "We have for Several Months past
been Surrounded with a Vast Number of Villains practising every kind of
Fraud, to relate the different practices that have come to light would fill
2 or 3 sheets of paper." Charleston, South Carolina (1788): "The town
at present, My Dear Brother is more infested with villains than ever it
was remembered to have been. Murders are very frequent but robberies
still more so." New York (1788): "Robberies & Burglaries are so frequent & the perpetrators so numerous, that we must have something like
Drum Head Courts Martial & send them from the Bar to Sheriff Willetts
Pigeon House." Boston, Massachusetts (1786): "If any comparison is made
between the expence of this office [attorney general's office] now & before

the War, it must be observed that Crimes of all Sorts and of the most dangerous kind have increased in the most alarming manner."[29]

Yet two studies of the incidence of crime during the Confederation era are too inconclusive to support any final generalization about an increase in crime. Nevertheless, as the above evidence indicates, government officials and observers believed crime was increasing. And the 1786 founding date of the Society of the Friends of Justice, formed by Wilmington, Delaware, notables to combat a rash of horse thefts, is also suggestive.[30]

These particular reports of increasing crime do not explicitly connect crime with the relaxed operations of any state government per se. But South Carolina Chief Justice Henry Pendleton, in a 1786 grand jury charge, did: "Crimes and misdemeanors are more prevalent than ever, . . . disorder and disobedience to law is gaining ground, and the terrors of punishment, which formerly awed the most refractory into submission and caution, [are] set at defiance by bad men." Pendleton also declared that our citizens are "insecure both in their persons and estates" and that our governments are "without authority to compel even our citizens to obey the law."[31]

Symptoms of another kind of lawlessness were to be found along the western frontiers of states that abutted on Native American lands. Because in these frontier regions formal law enforcement was weak or nonexistent, their inhabitants were considered to be especially turbulent and unruly. Eastern elites held that the aggression of land-hungry whites was responsible for the hostilities that occurred between Native Americans and whites along the Georgia, North Carolina, Virginia, and Ohio frontiers. In Georgia (1786) backcountry settlers clashed with Upper Creek warriors in the Oconee District, an area previously ceded by Lower Creek chiefs to Georgia in a treaty tainted by fraud and double-dealing. The Upper Creeks retaliated by raiding homesteads. After bitter political debate, the Georgia assembly authorized a military expedition (financed by £50,000 in paper money) to prepare an attack on the Creek towns.[32] Clarity in this complicated story now disappears, but the low-country elite believed that land speculators had incited the war and that Georgia's assembly was too weak to resist popular demands for an all-out attack on the Creeks. In Savannah on 4 July 1787 "a number of respectable citizens dined at the Coffee House" and toasted "Energy to Government, and a Federal Head" and "A Truce with Land Speculation and Indian Wars."[33] With the earlier aggression of Georgia's settlers in mind, the Savannah merchant Joseph Clay observed pointedly that "the back Inhabitants are too many of them of too lawless a disposition to preserve treaties but by compulsion, & less authority than that of the United States will never effect that." Angry low-country representatives boycotted the assembly in August 1787 to block it from authorizing hostilities.[34]

Similar frontier episodes occurred in western North Carolina, where John Sevier and his party broke with the state government, formed the state of Franklin, and proceeded to survey and sell off lands between the French Broad and the Tennessee which North Carolina authorities had guaranteed to the Cherokee (1785–88). When the Cherokee refused to leave, the Franklinites in 1786 marched into a Cherokee town, killed and wounded several Cherokees, and burned buildings and cornfields; the possibility that Cherokees would join the Creeks in an all-out attack on the western settlements loomed.[35] In Virginia's southwestern Washington County, lawlessness also seemed to reign when Arthur Campbell organized settlers into committees to resist tax collection; he then proceeded to work for secession and the county's incorporation into the state of Franklin.[36] On the Pennsylvania-Ohio border, hostilities flared despite the presence of Harmar's handful of U.S. troops. This violence prompted President Charles Nisbet of Carlisle College in Pennsylvania to express the hope that "those white Indians who are the Cause of it, were either sent away to their copper-coloured Brethren, or knocked on the Head, as they deserve. But this supposes a Government, which does not exist among us at present."[37] John Jay cited these Native American–white clashes as examples of aggression by lawless white settlers and the weakness of government. "The newspapers herewith sent will give you Information in Detail of Indian affairs but they will not tell you what however is the Fact that our People have committed several unprovoked acts of violence against [the Indians]—these acts ought to have excited the notice of Government and been punished in an exemplary manner."[38]

Intermittent violence in Pennsylvania's Wyoming Valley during 1787 and 1788 provided another example of how government weakness seemed to encourage lawlessness. The region had been the scene of clashes between rival Connecticut and Pennsylvania claimants to the same land. When the Pennsylvania assembly sent Timothy Pickering to adjudicate claims, he met with defiance, personal threats, and other violent obstruction. Pickering believed this violence stemmed from the inability of the weak Pennsylvania state government to restore order and from "the natural instability of the common people, but especially of that settlement, where during so many years they have lived in anarchy." Such conditions did not promise well for establishing law and order in Wyoming under the present state-centered system: "The dangerous insurrections in Massachusetts under Shays, will convince you how much mischief may be done by one desperate man & a few assistants in a united & well ordered government, as was that of Massachusetts; and that it must be infinitely easier for a similar character to raise a tumult in this county [Wyoming]."[39]

The most alarming symptoms of an unvirtuous people, however, were the risings by impecunious farmers and rural artisans against taxes, most visibly and dramatically in Shays's Rebellion, which began as a series of localized acts of civil disobedience and escalated when the hard-line Bowdoin administration issued proclamations and made arrests. To many notables, among them Connecticut's Oliver Wolcott, Jr., Shays's Rebellion represented the coming true of what they feared would happen in all the states if the presumed laxity of government was not reversed. "Genl Lincoln I trust will suppress the Rebellion in the countys of Hamshire and Worcester," Wolcott wrote, "But whether that will give permanent peace to the Massachusetts or whether the Union will not soon be invoulved in great Perplexity is in my judgment, very uncertain. Upon experience their will be found such radical Defects in our general System as will unless soon remedied produce unhappy convulsions."[40]

A similar premise prompted Virginia's Henry Lee, who believed it "unquestionably true that present appearances portend extensive national calamity—The contagion will spread and may reach Virginia," and for which he blamed the weakness of government: "The objects of the malcontents are alluring to the vulgar and the impotency of government is rather an encouragement to, than a restraint on, the licentious."[41]

Tobias Lear, George Washington's private secretary, in the months following Shays's Rebellion also anticipated outbreaks of anarchy in Virginia. In July 1787 when tax resisters set fire to the county clerk's office and the prison in King William County, Lear termed the event "a very serious & alarming affair" that might well involve far more people than Shays's Rebellion had. He agreed with Benjamin Lincoln, Jr., then in Massachusetts, that Virginia might soon have its own convulsions, and "that an insurrection [in Virginia] would be more dangerous than among you; 3/4 of the people have nothing to lose."[42] By the eve of the Constitution, upper class elites throughout the land believed that the presumed weakness and indulgence of the state governments had so accustomed the common people to ignore or break the law that the outbreaks of anarchy would further multiply.

Gordon Wood's *Creation of the American Republic* has correctly identified the major support for the Constitution as the states' elite upper classes and a major source of their motivation as a concern for a republic whose common people were unvirtuous. But the source of this concern was not, as Wood concluded, special interest politics within the states or the rise of socially unqualified men to positions of political power. Rather it was the inability of the popular classes to pay taxes in hard money levied by the state governments, and the demands of these classes, sometimes forced on the states by violence, that the states finance themselves and Congress by state-issued paper money. Other, more localized episodes of presumed moral decline reinforced this impression of an unvirtuous people.

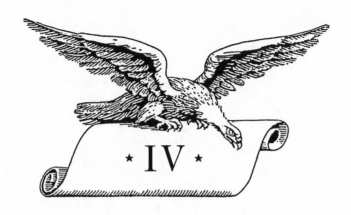

AN EMERGING

FEDERALIST AGENDA AND

ITS OPPONENTS

★ 12 ★

EARLY PROPOSALS
AND TRIAL BALLOONS

THE JOURNEY that took the Framers to the federal Constitution began long before the Constitutional Convention gathered in May 1787. The first retreats from forced tax collection occurred in the early 1780s; the earliest symptoms of disillusion with the power and stability of the state governments date from this early period as well. Conceivably, the disillusion with the state governments began sooner in states where the turnabouts first took place than in states where tax collection did not break down until later. On the other hand, because reports of these outbreaks against taxes were privately disseminated, disenchantment may have resulted as much from word-of-mouth reports from other states as from personal experience with any single government. Evidence indicates that advocacy of a stronger, self-executing central government correlates closely with the timing of the states' on-again, off-again taxing operations.

A Revamped Central Government

As early as November 1782 John Lowell, Boston notable and leader of the Massachusetts house of representatives, was pondering the subject of the "Continental constitution & general Taxes." Lowell's ideas went farther than simply equipping Congress with the power to tax. Lowell envisioned a centralized federal legislature and a single executive empowered to enforce its laws. Angry because the Massachusetts assembly had just refused a tax for the Continental officers' pay, Lowell explained that those responsible for the measure's defeat "were fully determined never to come into the Measure & that they, & thier Constitutents are opposed to [it] in every Shape." Taxes for complying with federal requisitions were unpopular with the voters, Lowell complained; but even if the most influential leaders of the state governments were honest, the state governments would not be able to carry and enforce their measures. On the other hand,

"If we were in any sense one Government with one Legislative & one Executive, there would be no difficulty in laying general Taxes."[1]

Such expressions in the early 1780s were infrequent. In 1783 a Rhode Island "Lover of Liberty" proposed a plan for the central government's reconstitution. The state assemblies should be replaced by a centralized two-house national legislature that would "have the sole power of giving and granting supplies, regulating laws, choosing all the civil officers for each State to execute their laws, and to collect taxes or duties; the Senate to be chosen yearly by the Congress, and the Congress to be chosen yearly by each state in the same manner as we now choose them." Significantly, the writer advocated not only vesting Congress with broad substantive powers but equipping the central government with the power and machinery by which Congress's powers would be enforced.[2]

In April 1783 Jonathan Jackson, Boston lawyer and close friend and political ally of John Lowell, outlined a scheme for establishing a powerful central government. Labeling his remarks "utopian animadversions," Jackson proposed a supreme national legislature to consist of two branches, each elected and each with a veto on the other; the existing states to be merged into one mass, with all inhabitants to be called "Columbians"; new legislative districts to be drawn with representation apportioned equally among them; each district to have "seperate legislatures for internal Police & for Reference & Deliberation on all great Matters where the Supreme ought to go to the People for their opinions"; and an executive "Statdholder" to be established but "limited as to do us no essential harm were he inclined & so endowed as to preserve the Balance of Power & do us possible Good."[3]

The timing of these early calls for the central government's radical revision roughly correlates with the dates of the states' first retreats from forced tax collection. In Pennsylvania a plea for the Confederation system's total reform was issued just after that government's tax collection efforts collapsed. In 1783 the Republican-controlled assembly launched its efforts to coerce tax collection; by midsummer 1784 tax collection had stalled, and the popular tide was running against the Republicans in favor of Constitutionalist Reliefers who took control of the assembly in the October 1784 elections. On 4 August 1784 an anonymous pamphleteer in Philadelphia proposed: "in my humble opinion, no reformation, or amendment can effectually answer any good purpose short of the abolishment of our state governments and the forming a constitution, whereby the whole nation can be united in one government." The essay centered on the weak, inconstant operation of the state governments under the state-centered Confederation system. When the American Revolution first began, Patriots had hoped that such "essential improvements in the science of government" could be accomplished in the framing of American governments that they would reach "such perfection as to excite the emulation of other nations." Instead, "we have suffered the most amazing weakness and absurdity to assume the place of energy, and consistency [and we have] rendered our political interests perplexed, exhibited a striking proof of the fallibility of human wisdom and inconstancy of human nature, and rendered our government a matter of wonder, both to the present and future ages."[4]

A year later Boston's "Observator" disparaged the present ineffective state-centered Confederation system and called for "an efficient national government." Citing the "innumerable evils" that "we experience every day" from the "sovereign and independent" state governments, and preferring that the state governments be done away with entirely, "Observator" acknowledged that "our prejudices are so many and so strong, that a sacrifice of this favorite Hobby Horse would be an event scarcely to be hoped for at this time."[5]

From mid-1786 to mid-May 1787 published pieces in favor of the central government's major reconstitution increased appreciably. This greater frequency correlates with the two most visible and dramatic episodes of the pressure-resistance-retreat sequence—Rhode Island's political "revolution" (April 1786) and Shays's Rebellion in Massachusetts (September 1786–April 1787).

In August 1786 an essay published in New York and republished in South Carolina explained the requisition system's failure. Convincing the state governments that Congress needed requisition money was not the problem, the writer seemed to be saying. Rather, the state governments did not have enough power to comply with these requisitions by taxes collected from their own citizens. And because the state governments could not effectively tax their citizens, the New Yorker went on, the central government ought to be equipped with the power to collect its own taxes. Indeed, the writer added, Congress ought to have the power not only to tax but to regulate commerce and to enforce these measures on the people of the United States.[6]

That same August 1786 another essayist writing in a Boston newspaper put forth ideas for reconstituting Congress into "a free, yet energetic government." Congress could neither raise money to pay its own expenses, nor levy troops to fight a war, nor enforce its own treaties, the writer noted: "In short, they may DECLARE everything, but can DO nothing." Nor did the popular governments of the states have vigor. Warning that anarchy and confusion would be the inevitable result of such governmental weakness, "Bostonian" urged that Congress be vested with not only effective legislative power but also executive and judicial power. Comparing the Confederation system with a "headless body, where the tremulous motion of the severed nerves, is the only sign of remaining life," the writer further warned that "if there be no coercion, a general decadence ensues, till the component parts separate by fermentation, and the whole dissolves into confusion."[7]

In September 1786 another Boston essayist published an even more explicit analysis of the Confederation system's defects. The writer of this article prefaced his recommendation that the central government be given new powers by analyzing the weak, unsteady governments of the individual states: "That a part of the political evils we are now groaning under, arise from the want of stability and energy in the measures of government, is a matter of universal complaint.—The frequent repugnancy of our laws, the remissness with which many of them are executed, the great inequality in the collection of taxes, the daring opposition to the measures of government, and a great variety of other circumstances, discover a most dangerous relaxation and want of energy and spirit,—evils that must be remedied, or the government languish into dissolution."[8]

That there was advocacy for the idea of a reconstituted central government prior to Shays's Rebellion is further demonstrated by the case of the wealthy Boston merchant Stephen Higginson, who wrote Henry Knox in November 1786 that the rebellion was preparing the public mind to accept a plan for a stronger, more energetic central government and should be used to further this goal: "The present moment is very favorable to the forming further & necessary arrangements, for increasing the dignity & energy of government. What has been done, must be used as a stock upon which the best Fruits are to be engrafted. The public mind is now in a fit state, & will shortly I think become more so, to come forward with a system competent to the great purposes of all civil arrangements, that of promoting & securing the happiness of society." Later that same November, Higginson cited the government's weak military response to the Shaysites as proof that state powers should be centralized. The assembly's "conduct the last session," Higginson argued, "will tend much to prepare the public mind, for transferring power from the individual Governments to the federal."[9]

In September 1787 the Connecticut notable Jeremiah Wadsworth also looked to Shays's Rebellion to dramatize the need for a stronger central government. The rebellion demonstrated the weak, unstable nature of the Massachusetts state government, and, worried that the newly published federal Constitution might be defeated in Connecticut, Wadsworth expressed a wish that the rebellion had continued longer. "There is a strong party forming against the Convention [in Connecticut] and much reason to fear the new Government will not go down—if the Massachusetts Rebellion had continued we might hope," he exclaimed.[10]

Another committed to reconstitution before Shays's Rebellion was John F. Mercer of Maryland, who in March 1786 conveyed to James Madison, Jr., his disenchantment with both Congress and the state governments: "Few circumstances could give me more pleasure than to see these Governments answer the ends that were expected, but my doubts go far beyond my hopes. The confederal Government was always an object of derision rather than anything else with me—its like a man's attempting to walk with both legs cut off—all our Executives are water mixed with water—wishy washy stuff." Mercer's solution was to consolidate the legislative, executive, and judicial branches and powers of the state governments into a single reconstituted central government: "If the whole Governments coud be amalgamated & made into a tolerable good one I confess it woud be very satisfactory to me."[11]

From Annapolis to Philadelphia

Pleas for a stronger central government also appeared in the public prints in the eight-month period between the Annapolis Convention (September 1786) and the convening of the federal Convention (May 1787).[12] Because few were published and because their prescriptions differ so markedly, however, these pleas do not seem to have been part of any organized Federalist effort to instruct the convention or to build up public pressure for a preconcerted program.

In January 1787 the Pennsylvania Federalist Benjamin Rush published a signed article that proposed the central government's substantial revision. Rush's plan would reconstitute Congress into a bicameral legislative body (Council of States; Assembly of States); would establish a president to be chosen annually by joint ballot of both houses who, with a privy council, would appoint federal executive officers; and would vest Congress with direct power to levy taxes, spend money, regulate commerce, make treaties, and declare war and peace. Compared to other plans Federalists were already privately discussing and circulating at the time, Rush's plan seems relatively conservative: it would not invest Congress with the power to raise armed forces or establish a judiciary, or make the executive anything more than Congress's agent for appointing executive officers.[13]

One other plan for root-and-branch revision published during this eight-month period appeared in a Philadelphia newspaper on 31 May 1787. Timing publication to coincide with the opening of the federal Convention, "Harrington" recommended that the central government be reconstituted along lines considerably more radical than those of Rush's plan. The article enumerated the defects of the state-centered Confederation system: "The present foederal constitution . . . has been found ineffectual to support public credit—to obtain alliances—to preserve treaties—to enforce taxes—to prevent hostilities with our neighbours, and insurrections among our citizens." Next the article cited "the present relaxed state of government in America" and proposed a centralized republic composed of an elected two- or three-house national legislature and an elected executive.[14]

Several other essays on the subject of how to strengthen the central government published during this same eight-month period advocated limited changes that would not basically alter the Confederation system's state-centered format. "A Word of Consolation," published by Matthew Carey's *American Museum* (March 1787), simply stated: "Congress must be invested with larger powers—powers to carry into effect their requisitions, and fully to regulate commerce." In May 1787 the *Museum* carried a more detailed plan for strengthening Congress's powers within the existing framework of the Confederation system. Obviously intended to influence the coming Constitutional Convention in the direction of the Confederation system's limited amendment, "Z" offered an agenda of specific but limited changes: Congress should have "the sole and exclusive power of regulating trade, of imposing port duties, of appointing officers to collect these duties, of erecting ports, and deciding, by their own authority, all questions which concern foreign trade and navigation upon the high seas."[15] "Z" was here staking out what subsequently would be the Antifederalist agenda.

Monarchy and Regional Republics

In addition to these early plans for reconstituting the central government, suggestions for monarchy and for dividing the United States into regional republics were also aired.

In spring 1786 Rhode Island's "revolution" had replaced the incumbent ruling establishment with a rural Relief party that had promptly stopped forced taxation and printed and loaned paper money payable for taxes and debts through a land bank. The controversy escalated when city merchants refused the new paper, closed their shops, and transferred ownership of their mortgages and state notes to persons in other states. Crowds then took to the streets and threatened physical force when persons refused the paper. Dismayed by these events, in July 1786 Peregrine Foster of Providence proposed that "if this is the way in which we are going on, I pray the Lord soon to raise up some good Monarch or even an Oliver Cromwell to establish a government, which shall be stable & put our National Credit [on firm footing?] & secure the Lives & Property of the People neither of which are in any tollerable measure occurg with us." Things had reached a sorry state when "carrying the Heads of those who will not render an implicit Obedience to the Law aforesaid on Polls through the Streets has been publicly talked of—How unhappy the People where the Laws are so unstable as Ours or rather where there is none at all."[16]

Others whose disenchantment with the apparent weakness of the state governments to protect life and property carried them towards monarchy included Benjamin Tupper, a Massachusetts state legislator. "I cannot give up the idea that Monarchy in our present situation is to become absolutely necessary to save the States from sinking into the lowest abbiss of Misery," Tupper wrote privately in 1786 or 1787.[17] In December 1786 an anonymous Connecticut man, who "was once as strong a republican as any man in America," now found a republic "almost the last kind of government I should choose. I should infinitely prefer a limited monarchy, for I would sooner be subject to the caprice of one man, than to the ignorance of a multitude. I believe men as individuals enjoy more security, more peace and real liberty, under a limited monarch, take Princes as they rise, than in republics, where people sometimes get furious and make laws destructive of all peace and liberty." By way of comparison, "some of the late laws of Rhode Island are greater stretches of tyranny than have been tolerated in the despotic governments of Europe, and life and property are less secure in Massachusetts, than in the Turkish dominions."[18]

It is not possible to say how many others espoused the idea of monarchy during the middle 1780s. James Madison worried at reports that "the late turbulent scenes in Massts. & infamous ones in Rhode Island, have done inexpressible injury to the republican character in that part of the U. States; and a propensity toward Monarchy is said to have been produced by it in some leading minds," as he wrote from New York in February 1787. In 1788 Hector St. John de Crèvecoeur described many New Englanders as so disillusioned with popular government "that they Sigh for Monarchy & that a very large number of persons in several Counties would like to return to English domination."[19] These hearsay reports are difficult to assess. At the very least, they suggest growing disillusion with the state governments.

Another proposal premised on such disillusion would combine the powers of several state governments into three or four energetic, stable regional republics. In March 1787 the New York gentleman-politician General Philip Schuyler privately confided his preference for a centralized northeastern republic to be called "Columbia." He had long doubted that the Continental Congress, based on state representation and requiring the cooperation of the states, could successfully govern the nation, he wrote fellow New Yorker Henry Van Schaack. Even if the Confederation were amended so that Congress could raise an income by a 5 percent impost, the central government must sooner or later prove unable to keep the states from quarreling. Both to obtain the most energetic republican government possible, and to obviate future quarrels between New York and the New

England states and New Jersey, Schuyler proposed a regional Republic of Columbia that would combine the states east of the Delaware River and north to the Canadian boundary.

Structurally, Columbia's government would consist of a three-year executive appointed by a two-house legislature; election of each legislative branch would be on a three-year rotational basis with one-third of its members elected annually. The powers of this republic, Schuyler contended, should be substantial: "all taxes and all Laws to be in the legislature of Columbia." Compared to an amended Confederation Congress, Schuyler added, the Republic of Columbia would be much more vigorous and forceful. "If a good Government was established, the states to the eastward of Delaware would have more force than If connected with the rest."

Schuyler was unsure whether it was possible to frame a strong, stable, centralized national republic patterned on the Republic of Columbia but extending over the entire Union. But whether regional or national, he believed, a more powerful, stable entity of centralized government was needed if the country was to be effectively defended and peace and order upheld. "I conceive if any foederal government is established with less Stability and power than this [Republic of Columbia], It will be inadequate, not only to oppose an enemy, but to prevent internal commotions, and if so, must sooner or later, give way, to perhaps a chance Government, which may be Despotism, arbitrary Monarchy, Aristocracy, or what is still worse an oligarchy."[20]

Whether Schuyler ever spoke out publicly for his plan of regional republics is not known, but other men did. On 15 February 1787 the Boston *Independent Chronicle* printed a call by an anonymous author for a nation of New-England: "Let then our General Assembly immediately recall their Delegates from that shadowy Meeting which still bears the name of Congress, as being a useless and expensive establishment. Send proposals for instituting a new Congress, as the Representative of the nation of New-England, and leave the rest of the Continent to pursue their own imbecile and disjointed plans."[21]

Member of Congress William Bingham of Pennsylvania, his colleague James Madison recorded, advocated the plan of separate, more vigorous confederacies. "Mr. Bingham alone avowed his wishes that the Confederacy might be divided into several distinct confederacies, its great extent & various interests, being incompatible with a single Government." Madison also reported that southern and middle-state members of Congress "seemed generally anxious for some republican organization of the System which wd. preserve the Union and give due energy to the Govermt. of it."[22] Commenting on the reported talk of monarchy, Madison declared that if forced to chose between monarchy or regional republics, most of the people in the United States would choose the latter plan. But either plan would be a devastating setback to the dream of the states as one nation organized and governed as a single republic.[23]

Constitutional Prescription

Root-and-branch reconstitution of the central government was not the officially announced agenda when the federal convention convened in Philadelphia in May 1787. In September 1786 the Annapolis Convention had been called to devise measures for empowering Congress to regulate foreign commerce. Instead, it had recommended that a second convention of the states be held to deal with the exigencies of the Union. But its published recommendation gave no hint that the entire revision of the central government might be contemplated. Nor, in the ensuing months, was there any official indication that the convention would do anything more substantial than recommend that the existing Congress be empowered to levy a 5 percent federal impost and retaliate commercially against foreign nations. Responding to Federalist initiatives, all the state legislatures except Rhode Island's passed resolutions that authorized and selected delegates for the upcoming convention. But the phrasing of these instruments did not specify that root-and-branch revision was to be the agenda. Rather, the usual formula was to empower the states' chosen delegates to discuss "such Alterations and farther Provisions as may be necessary to render the Foederal Constitution [Articles of Confederation] adequate to the Exigencies of the Union" and to report "such an Act for that purpose to the United States in Congress as when agreed to by them and duly confirmed by the several States will effectually provide for the same." Nothing was said about designing or establishing an entirely new system of central government.[24]

In fact, between the Annapolis Convention and the Philadelphia Convention, Federalists kept their hopes and plans for reconstitution to themselves so effectively that when the convention actually did decide in principle in favor of thorough revision in the very first week of sessions, Antifederalist delegates were taken by surprise. New York's Antifederalist delegates Robert Yates and John Lansing left the convention once it became clear that a majority intended the central government's reconstitution and that they could not defeat it. And once the convention was over, Antifederalists bitterly charged that the federal convention had illegally exceeded its official mandate.

In the months before the convention, Federalists had quietly discussed among themselves how to make the government of the United States more effective. To avoid stirring controversy, they said little publicly but confined themselves to private letter and face-to-face conversation. As surviving letters indicate, they agreed upon much. Thorough reconstitution of the central government was greatly preferred to simple amendment of the Articles. The convention should be persuaded to form a plan that would replace the existing Confederation system with an entirely new republican central government of a radically different format. Powers vested by the Confederation system in the individual state governments must be transferred to the central government, which must have separate structures for legislating, executing, and enforcing law.[25]

An early exposition of these ideas is to be found in the letters of Federalist Henry Knox of Massachusetts. In January 1787 Secretary of War Knox outlined to George Washington "a rude sketch" of ideas he hoped might be adopted by the coming convention as the basis for a "durable & efficient" government. As the secretary stated, this sketch included "ideas which have presented themselves from reflection, and the opinion of others." Knox's sketch outlined a tripartite structure of "General Government" consisting of federal legislative, executive, and judicial branches.

> Were it possible to effect, a general government of this kind it might be constituted of an assembly, or lower house, chosen for one two or three years, a senate chosen for five six or seven years, and the executive under the title of governor general chosen by the assembly and senate, for the term of seven years, but liable to an impeachment of the lower house, and triable by the Senate—a judiciary to be appointed by the Governor General during good behavior, but impeachable by the lower house and triable by the Senate. The laws passed by the general govermt to be obeyed by the local governments, and if necessary to be enforced by a body of armed men to be kept for the purposes which should be designated.[26]

In May 1787 Knox again repeated his ideas for a revamped central government with greatly enhanced powers and a new tripartite structure. Insisting that the state-centered Confederation's powers were too dispersed to be effective, that state legislatures and executives were too dependent on popularity to be vigorous and independent, and that the concentrated power and enhanced stability of a strong central government were greatly needed, Knox outlined a plan for a "strong *national republic*" that exactly duplicated his earlier proposal.[27]

Others also espoused these ideas, as Knox's January letter to Washington acknowledged, including members of Congress. In the already quoted confidential letter written February 1787 to Colonel Josiah Harmar, the Pennsylvania congress member William Irvine declared that the coming Philadelphia convention must either "revise and mend the Confederation—or frame an entire new government." The latter was to be preferred. "Under the present Government it is much to be feared—that insurgency—& Rebellion may pervade more States than Massachusetts," he warned. He was dropping the "forgoing hints," he said, "meerly to give you some general Ideas—of what is passing"; "you will therefore not I am persuaded make an improper use of them."[28]

Member of Congress William Pierce of Georgia also expressed a preference for reconstitution. Because Pierce would shortly attend the convention and sign the federal Constitution, his ideas are especially important. In two letters written in the spring of 1787 Pierce declared that the convention ought to make substantial changes in the central government in order to empower it to carry out its own directives. The first letter, written in April 1787, took the position that the central government ought to be invested with greater power and energy than it had under the present system, which was "very incompleat, and deficient in point of energy." Yet the states will "not make such a surrender of their sovereignty as may be found necessary to give the federal head compleat weight in the Union": "nothing will produce such a surrender but a sense of the greatest danger." In his second letter, written in May 1787 to Pennsylvania's George Turner, Pierce asserted that any effective reform must empower the central government to enforce its own laws promptly and effectively, with certain qualifications:

> The Convention is much talked of here, and various are the conjectures about the alterations that will probably take place in the foederal Government. You are, I find, for having matters *highly toned.*—I am for powers equal to a prompt and certain execution, but tempered with a proper respect for the liberties of the People.—I am for securing their happiness, not by the will of the few, but by the direction of the Law. . . .
>
> To depart from the general freedom of our Governments which act by giving laws, and attempt to step into a Monarchy which will at times be despotic, would plunge the States into a tumult infinitely worse than anarchy itself: torrents of blood would follow the confusion.[29]

That the central government ought to be made independent of the state governments and empowered to enforce its own laws was implicit in the letters of other budding Federalists before the convention. As early as November 1786 Stephen Higginson, the Boston Federalist merchant-politician, reported how opinion in Massachusetts was rallying behind the idea "of increasing the powers of Congress, not merely as to commercial objects, but generally." "By the next summer," Higginson predicted, "I expect we shall be prepared for any thing that is wise & fitting"— including a federal army and a single consolidated "general & efficient" government. Congress, Higginson advised, should get ready to capitalize on this sentiment, not only by preparing plans "to support a proper force in the field, but to consolidate the several Governments into one, general & efficient— but I am going too fast, adieu."[30] In July, 1787, while the convention was meeting behind closed doors, Samuel Breck, a Boston merchant and assembly leader, outlined a plan for a "National Government" that closely resembled Higginson's and Henry Knox's. Breck's plan called for the largest possible transfer of state power to the central government and a total restructuring of the central government from a single legislative body into a tripartite government with legislative, executive, and judicial branches (like the Massachusetts government): "I fully agree with you in the necessity of a National Government & hope that a System, in some measure resembling ours, will be adopted, which opperating upon the large scale must, in a relative view, reduce the powers of each state to that of our counties; such a Government in my humble opinion would extend its authority over all *these Petty States* & increase in the proportion as they are augmented by new ones; perhaps there never was a time more favorable for such a Revolution."[31]

Still other Federalists outlined ideas much like these. In a letter written in June 1787 Virginia's Edward Carrington advised James Madison, then attending the convention, that "a good republic," with centralized power and a tripartite structure, should be framed. He also advocated a congressional veto over state actions—an idea that Madison would strongly but unsuccessfully advocate. Although "Some Gentlemen think of a total surrender of the State Sovereignties," Carrington acknowledged, "I see not the necessity of that measure for giving us National Stability or consequence." Instead, Congress should have a veto over state laws and other state actions: "The negative [effect] of the federal Sovereignty [on state laws] will effectually prevent the existence of any licentious or inconsiderate Act." While he wanted the general government invested with an effective quantum of independent power over "the Trade the Revenues, and forces of the Union, and all things that involve any relationship to foreign powers," he held that the state governments ought to retain powers over their own internal local affairs. He urged that the federal government be given "also the revisal of all State Acts. Unless it possesses a compleat controul over the State Governments, the constant effort will be to resume the delegated powers. Nor do I see what inducement the federal Sovereignty can have to negative an innocent act of a State . . . but let the liability to encroachments be rather from the federal, than the State, Governments. In the first case we shall insensibly glide into a Monarchy, in the latter nothing but Anarchy can be the consequence."[32]

The idea that the state-centered Confederation system ought to be radically reconstituted thus was first put forth at least five years before the federal convention framed the Constitution. In 1786 and early 1787 when tax collection in rural Rhode Island, Massachusetts, and Maryland backfired, thorough reconstitution received a major boost, and by the time the federal convention met, many of the elite were ready to support a radically made-over central government.[33] Notwithstanding their official purpose—limited amendment of the Confederation system—most delegates believed this was an opportune time to establish a reconstituted central government with the power to tax as well as other powers, and with the ability to enforce its laws.

★ I3 ★

FRAMING AN ENDURING REPUBLIC

THE FRAMERS went to the Constitutional Convention which met at the State House in Philadelphia from late May to mid-September 1787, to create an energetic centralized republic that could require Americans to obey its laws. Historians have described the convention as a continuous bargaining session at which delegates from small and large states, slave and free states, commercial and farming states, advocates of a strong and weak presidency, and so forth disagreed, negotiated, and compromised until they framed an acceptable plan. Thus the Constitution was a "bundle of compromises"—a product of compromise "at every point."[1] But in Leonard Levy's words, "consensus, rather than compromise, was the most significant feature of the convention, outweighing in importance the various compromises that occupied most of the time of the delegates."[2]

This consensus was demonstrated by the Convention's speedy agreement to most of the basic principles of the Virginia Plan. Introduced by Virginia's Edmund Randolph on the convention's second working day, 28 May, much of the plan was accepted by 5 June, and most of the rest by the end of the second week. The Virginia Plan called for forming an entirely new three-branched central government invested with substantial independent powers. Three weeks after the convention began its deliberations, as Levy notes, the delegates reaffirmed their acceptance of the essential principles of the Virginia Plan by another round of votes. These actions confirmed the delegates' nearly universal desire for "a strong, independent national government that would operate directly on individuals without the involvement of the states." That three other of the Constitution's most essential provisions—the tax power, the necessary and proper clause, and the supremacy clause—were, in Levy's words, "casually and unanimously accepted without debate" is further evidence of consensus.[3]

Levy argues that this consensus resulted from the Framers' experience during the 1780s with the "unconstitutional" noncompliance of the uniformly localistic state governments.[4] By contrast, I hold that the Framers' experience with the inability of the state governments to collect taxes had educated them to the Confederation system's inadequacy and predisposed them to radical reconstruction. Because the changeable state governments had proved an undependable financial basis for the central government and because the states' "laxity" and "indulgence" in fiscal and monetary matters were believed responsible for Congress's insolvency as well as for commercial distress and the putative decline of "public virtue," the Framers came to Philadelphia ready to accept the proposition that they ought to design a more energetic central government independent of the state governments.[5]

Consensus: Centralized Powers

Reconstitution, as envisioned by the Framers and carried out at Philadelphia, required a major reconfiguring of the central government's powers and structure. Centralization of important legislative, executive, and judicial powers over fields of activity heretofore exclusively or primarily the province of the state governments (taxation, commerce, armed forces, and so on) was the first such reconfiguring. Creation of separate legislative, executive, and judicial branches to carry out and enforce these powers was the second.

The major powers vested in the legislative branch by the Constitution include the power to levy imposts, excises, and direct taxes; to coin money; to regulate commerce with foreign nations and among the several states; to raise armed forces; to declare war and peace; to make treaties; and to provide for the calling up of the state militias. From the delegates' standpoint, the most important power, at least initially, was the power to tax, as its lead-off place in the list testifies: "The Congress shall have Power To lay and collect Taxes, Duties, Imposts and Excises, to pay the Debts and provide for the common Defence and general Welfare of the United States" (Article I, Section 8). Although the convention did not agree to the final form of the federal taxing power until mid-August, that the national legislature should have a tax power of some kind was assumed from the beginning.[6] But important substantive issues had to be resolved first, among them: should representation in the two-house national legislature be based on state population or state equality? Should the direct taxes among the states be apportioned based on population including or excluding slaves? Should a federal power to tax exported goods be denied or included? Once these issues were settled, the tax clause was adopted.

Yet if, as I have argued, the breakdown of taxation by the state governments drove the movement for the Constitution, why did the convention invest the central government with substantive legislative powers over commerce, money, war and peace, armed forces, and so forth? Why not be content with the tax power?

The Framers came to Philadelphia believing that they must equip the

new government with every power that would conceivably serve or benefit
the nation both then and in the future. Late in June convention delegate
James Wilson rose and stated: "When we are laying the foundation of a
building, which is to last for ages, and in which millions are interested,
it ought to be well laid." Likewise James Madison affirmed: "The government we mean to erect is intended to last for ages."[7] The delegates' continued preoccupation with both important and peripheral powers and
structural mechanisms for the proposed new government attests to their
sense that the current convention ought to consider vesting the new government with every possible power and structure that would benefit the
government and nation as a whole. Most probably believed with Edmund
Randolph that this might be their last chance to do so. "He wd [not] as
far as depended on him leave any thing that seemed necessary, undone.
The present moment is favorable, and is probably the last that will offer."[8]

In addition to the tax power, the convention wrote into the Constitution
powers currently vested in the Congress under the Articles of Confederation concerning, among other subjects, treaty making, war and peace, post
office, army and navy, commerce with the Indian tribes, and western
lands. Additional powers that from experience the delegates believed Congress should have were "to regulate Commerce with foreign Nations, and
among the several States, and with the Indian Tribes"; "raise and support
Armies"; "provide and maintain a Navy"; "provide for calling forth the
Militia to execute the Laws of the Union, suppress Insurrections and repel
Invasions." Vested in an energetic, steady central government, these powers, like the power to tax, would be executed with more uniformity, stability, and energy than if left in the hands of the state governments.

Statements by Federalists who were not present at the convention help
buttress this point. In December 1787, before his own state had ratified
the Constitution, Nathan Strong of Connecticut responded to criticism that
the document had invested the central government with too much power.
Strong affirmed: "The more I hear and speculate the more I am convinced
that now is the time for the federal Government to assume every power
which it shall ever need to exercise, it can be done more easily att this than
in any future Moment." Similarly, Virginia's Edward Carrington advised
James Madison the previous June that unless the central government's
reform was thorough, the work would have to be done again: "The work
once well done will be done forever, but patched up in accommodation to
the whim of the day, it will soon require the hand of the cobbler again,
and in every unfortunate experiment, the materials are rendered the less
fit for that Monument of Civil liberty which we wish to erect." Therefore:
"Constitute [the new government] in such shape that, its first principles
being preserved, it will be a good republic. I wish to see that system have
a fair experiment." Henry Knox agreed: "The state governments should

be deprived of the power of injur[ing] themselves or the nation—the people have parted with power enough to form an excellent constitution: But it is incerpted and diffuse[d] among bodies which cannot use it to good purpose. It must be concentered in a national government, the power of which should be divided between a strong executive, a senate—and assembly."[9]

Consensus: A Three-Branch Structure

The central government's reconfiguration into the three functionally complementary legislative, executive, and judicial branches formed the second phase of reconstitution. Here the object was to create structures for enforcing the central government's legislative powers energetically and firmly. When first introduced, the Virginia Plan empowered the central government "to call forth the force of the Union" against a delinquent state—presumably to force the payment of federal requisitions. The idea was quickly dropped after George Mason "argued very cogently that punishment could not [in the nature of things be executed on] the States collectively, and therefore that such a Govt. was necessary as could directly operate on individuals, and would punish those only whose guilt required it." Madison on 31 May reiterated the idea: "The more he reflected on the use of force, the more he doubted the practicability, the justice and the efficacy of it when applied to the people collectively and not individually."[10] Hamilton, in notes for a speech, wrote that the convention had three options to pursue: division into regional republics linked by treaty, limited amendment of the Continental Congress, and a reconstituted central government with "decisive powers" over the whole. The "prevailing sentiment," Hamilton noted, was for "forming a new government to pervade the whole with decisive powers in short with complete sovereignty."[11]

The convention might have empowered the central government with "decisive powers" to pervade the whole simply by vesting the existing Continental Congress with the power to legislate, execute, and judge.[12] In August 1786 a "Bostonian" proposed just this, arguing that such powers could be combined in "that Body without endangering the liberty of the subject" because of the existing provisions in the Articles of Confederation that provided for delegates' recall by the states and for rotation in office.[13] But within a week after the presiding officer's gavel first fell, the convention had voted its acceptance of the Virginia Plan resolution stating that "a national Governt. ought to be established consisting of a supreme Legislative Executive & Judiciary."[14]

The Framers preferred a separation of powers format as safer, more efficient, and more stable and independent than if the three categories of powers were vested in a single branch. Moreover, by vesting legislative, executive, and judicial power in different branches, the scope and use of these powers could be more exactly defined by law, and the persons who wielded them could be more effectively watched, checked, and held accountable for their proper, lawful exercise. And by vesting different kinds of powers in different persons, mechanisms could be established for checking and restraining the possible abuse of power by the other branches. Pierce Butler of South Carolina endorsed the safety side of the separation of powers theory by owning that he had "opposed the grant of powers to Congs. heretofore, because the whole power was vested in one body. The proposed distribution of the powers into different bodies changed the case, and would induce him to go great lengths."[15]

The Framers also believed that such a distribution of powers would make for greater efficiency.[16] Because the powers required different kinds of operations, responsibilities, and skills, it followed that different powers would be more effectively managed by different persons than by the same persons. The sheer burden of legislating, executing, and judging would be too much for the same persons to discharge. Moreover, executing the law was a continuous operation while legislating was an intermittent one. Finally, separation of powers made for greater responsibility and therefore better performance; with powers allocated by function, praise and blame could be more exactly located and better performance thereby encouraged. Madison endorsed the efficiency rationale of the separation of powers position when he stated that "a Government without a proper Executive & Judiciary would be the mere trunk of a body without arms or legs to act or move."[17]

Several months before the convention met, John Jay affirmed both the efficiency and the safety rationales for a three-branch rather than for a one-branch structure. Declaring that the new government ought to be invested with "the more [powers], the better," Jay argued that Congress could not effectively carry out the three categories of power simultaneously. Congress had too many members and too many different interests to exert the executive power with vigor; nor could responsibility for constitutional violations or other misdoings be properly fixed among so many.

> In so large a Body secrecy and Dispatch will be too uncommon and foreign as well as local influence will frequently oppose & sometimes frustrate the wisest measures.
>
> The executive Business of Sovereignty depending on so many wills, and these wills moved by such a variety of contradictory motives and Enducements, will in general be but feebly done.
>
> Such a Sovereign however theoretically responsible, cannot be effectually so in its Departments and Officers without adequate Indicatories.

I therefore promise myself nothing very desirable from any change which does not divide the Sovereignty into its proper Departments. Let Congress legislate—let others execute—let others judge.[18]

Consensus: Stability, Independence, and Enforcement

Contemporary political theory dictated relatively long and, where possible, staggered terms of office for independence and stability in government. The new national government, Henry Knox argued, "ought to possess full and complete powers within itself, unconfined by any preconcurrence of any state or corporate body to deliberate, decree, and execute." But to assure stability and independence, tenure in some of its branches ought to be based on good behavior. "That in order to render it truly a government of Laws, and not of caprice, some of its branches should be arranged on the principle of good behavior, the purest and noblest incitement to proper actions." Both Alexander Hamilton and John Jay wanted central governments whose upper houses and executive held office for life or good behavior.[19]

But the majority of the convention's members either were personally committed to the principle of republican accountability through regular direct or indirect elections or knew that a government such as Hamilton proposed would never be ratified. Hamilton's plan for a governor-general and upper house appointed for life terms was politely listened to and got nowhere.

Instead, the Framers took a middle road between tenure for life and the annually elected state assemblies. Three of the four proposed institutions of national government would be indirectly chosen for relatively long terms: the senate for six-year staggered terms chosen by the state legislatures; the president for four years chosen by an electoral college; and the judiciary for life terms chosen by president and senate. Even the popularly elected house would have two-year terms, longer than many of the state legislators' terms. Thus at no time could the entire national government be turned out by an angry or discontented electorate. Moreover, this national government would be physically more remote from most of the electorate than were the state governments. Long staggered terms, limited direct election, and physical distance would insulate the new national government from the popular pressures the Framers regarded as causing weakness and instability in the state governments in the 1780s.

With the entire continent subject to its jurisdiction, this new central government would have greater enforcement power and resources than either a single state government or an amended Congress. Because the state governments, including that of Massachusetts, could not force "an unvirtuous people" to pay taxes, the Confederation requisition system had broken down. An amended Congress, without either the structures or powers to compel obedience to its laws, would not be effective either. But a central government, with executive and judicial branches constitutionally empowered to carry out and enforce the national laws by means of resources *drawn from the entire continental United States*, that is, by a militia raised at the government's directive and paid and equipped by taxes, would be more powerful than would a single state government or an amended Congress.

Contemporary newspaper essays, letters, and speeches that call for a reconstituted central government assume that such a government would have greater coercive power. Samuel Breck's statement that a national government would "extend its authority over *these Petty States* & increase in the proportion as they are augmented by new ones" suggests an awareness that the more the Union's population and wealth increased by the addition of new states, the more powerful the central government would become.[20] South Carolina Framer Charles Pinckney asserted that the central government framed by the Constitution had "the compleat direction of the common force and treasure of the empire" and thus was able "to collect its powers to a point" both to maintain the Union and enforce its laws effectively.[21] Federalists differed over whether the central government would require a standing force of federal military at the ready or whether the mere potential to raise such a force would be sufficient.[22] But no one doubted that the central government would now have greater means to make the people obey its laws.

Comparing the central government of the federal Constitution with the current state governments, Charles Lee welcomed the former as a "government more powerful and independent of the people."[23]

Consensus: An Executive to Execute the Laws

The history of the creation of the presidency also affords support for the thesis that creating an energetic central government was the Framers' overriding purpose for coming to Philadelphia. Within the first ten days of sessions, the convention had approved a Virginia Plan resolution that provided for the creation of "a national executive" invested with "general authority to execute the National Laws." In addition, the executive was to appoint officers "not otherwise provided for," and was to exercise the "Executive rights invested in Congress by the Confederation."[24] What these rights consisted of, however, the convention did not specify. James Madison revealed an uncharacteristic uncertainty by proposing that the executive be constitutionally charged only with the execution of national laws and appointment of executive officers, and that Congress be empowered to vest the executive with additional powers and functions "not Legislative nor Judiciary in their nature as may from time to time be delegated by the national Legislature." Yet the fact that the convention accepted the Virginia Plan's unambiguous "general authority to execute the National Laws" as well as to appoint officers indicates that from the convention's beginning the execution of laws was deemed the executive's most important function. Charles Thach, whose early work on the creation of the presidency is extremely valuable, concludes: "The original concept of the executive power held by the convention was that primarily of law enforcement."[25]

As Thach's book reflects, after this initial agreement the convention went on to develop the executive branch by increments. These included early agreement that the executive should consist of a single individual, not three from the existing Union's three principal regions as John Dickinson and George Mason advocated; and that it should have a qualified veto over legislation enacted by Congress to force reconsideration of hastily framed or unwise legislation. Thach also shows how the convention formed the executive by adding other duties and powers. Here the Committee on Detail, charged by the convention in late July to draft a constitution, played a crucial role. Drawing on Charles Pinckney's previously tabled draft plan, which in turn had extensively borrowed executive provisions from the New York State constitution, the committee crafted the executive branch not only with law enforcement, appointive, and veto powers, but with provisions that empowered it to receive ambassadors, command the armed forces and militia as "commander-in-chief," and make legislative recommendations and a state of the union report to Congress.[26] The title "president" was probably taken from the official title of the Confederation Congress's presiding officer. After adopting these recommendations, the convention completed the executive branch by investing the executive with a decisive role in treaty making and providing for the president's election by an electoral college.[27]

In a telling passage James M. Burns observes: "The American presidency was not designed to be the center of leadership in the new republic. If any branch of government was to serve as a positive and innovative force in a system of carefully intermingled powers, it was the legislative. Certainly the President was not expected to be either a legislative leader or a party leader. He was to be chief *executive* . . . but he was not to be the executive *leader*."[28] Neither did the Framers intend the president to be the chief architect and manager of foreign policy. As Leonard Levy observes: "The Framers intended the Senate to be the principal architect of foreign policy . . . They meant . . . that the President should be the Senate's agent and, in matters involving war powers, the agent of Congress, in the sense of being the branch of government empowered to carry out or conduct policies formulated by the legislative branch."[29] It was left to future occupants of the presidential office to claim legislative and foreign-policy primacy. The Framers wanted an energetic republic, and drew upon the models of executives of their colony-states; the presidency they created in 1787 had federal law enforcement as its most important role.

Conflict and Compromise: Small versus Large States

The famous controversy between representatives of large and small states also demonstrates the basic consensus of the convention over the fundamental principles involved in reconstitution. Contrary to the usual interpretation, which depicts the small-state delegates as oriented toward states' rights, many of these delegates preferred a stronger, reconstituted central government rather than an amended confederation, but they wanted protection against ruinous taxation by the large states who would control the government unless the small states were adequately represented.

Because a reconstituted central government empowered to tax could injure states with small tax bases and no public lands, small-state delegates rejected the Virginia Plan formula that would vest the large states, which had larger tax bases and substantial public lands, with dominant representation in both houses of Congress. The basis of this formula was a simple population count; according to the Virginia Plan, representation for each state in each house was to be in proportion to its population. The smaller states (New Hampshire, Connecticut, New Jersey, Delaware, North Carolina, and, presumably, Rhode Island) wanted a formula that would give each state equal representation. Small-state delegates' concerns centered on trade and taxation. As John Dickinson put it: "What will be the situation of the smaller [states], if in *both* branches, the Representation is in the proportion mentioned? They will [be] delivered up into the absolute power of the larger. [The larger states] may injure them in a Variety of Ways. . . . They may destroy their Trade and draw it wholly to themselves. They may tax to relieve themselves."[30]

Small-state delegates were mindful of how the larger states had previously ceded their public land claims to Congress but then had retained substantial portions, thus depriving the small states of their pooled benefit. Delaware and New Jersey delegates knew that Pennsylvania and New York had taxed foreign imports moving through Pennsylvania and New York into their states. Armed with a direct taxing power, a Congress dominated by the large states could overburden small states' constituents with heavy direct taxes even while exempting their own constituents from the same burden.[31]

By discounting federal impost revenues collected within their own boundaries, larger states with seaports could lighten their own direct tax burden but place a heavier burden of direct taxes on the smaller states. If the small states had parity or near parity in Congress, they could require that federal impost revenues collected in large states' ports be treated as a common national fund and used to lessen every state's direct tax burden. The small states also wanted some assurance that as yet unceded public lands would be treated as common national property, also lessening the tax burden of all the states.[32]

Prompted by these concerns, delegates from the smaller states of Delaware, New Jersey, and Connecticut pressed for equal state representation in at least one of the proposed Congress's two houses and opposed the Virginia Plan formula that provided for representation in both houses of the new Congress on the basis of population. Only after their motions to guarantee equal state representation were defeated did the small-state delegates put forth the New Jersey Plan as a substitute for the Virginia Plan.

With its more limited powers and equal state representation, William Paterson's New Jersey Plan was in fact a small-states plan, but it was not their preferred plan.[33] Indeed, the plan's introduction on 15 June was at once a calculated tactic to win support for the principle of state equality and a fallback alternative to the Virginia Plan. As Delaware delegate John Dickinson privately informed Madison, the New Jersey Plan resulted from the convention's recent rejection of the proposed "equality of suffrage" formula for the upper house during the debates over the Virginia Plan on 11 June. "Mr. Dick[i]nson said to Mr. Madison you see the consequence of pushing things too far. Some of the members from the small States wish for two branches in the General Legislature, and are friends to a good National Government; but we would sooner submit to a foreign power, than submit to be deprived of an equality of suffrage, in both branches of the legislature, and thereby be thrown under the domination of the large States."[34]

Dickinson's draft plan for a reconstituted central government, recently published and analyzed by James Hutson, also indicates the personal preference of a small-state delegate for a strong, independent three-branch central government—provided the small states had equality in at least one legislative branch. The plan called for a "General Legislature with two branches," the first house composed of members elected by the state legislatures at staggered intervals with "each state having an equal vote," and the second house of members elected by the people of the states and apportioned according to "the sums of Money collected in each state and actually paid into the common Treasury within the preceding 3 Years." This bicameral legislature was also to regulate interstate and foreign trade and commerce; to raise a revenue by taxes on imports and exports, by stamp taxes, and "by such other Modes of Taxation" as "the Prosperity of the Union" necessitated; and to "pass acts for enforcing an Observance of the Laws of Nations and an Obedience to their own Laws." Dickinson's plan also provided for a three-person executive and for a supreme federal judiciary. Significantly, the plan excepted from any future calculation of contributions to the federal treasury "the sums arising from Imposts" and further provided that no state no matter how large its population would ever have representation beyond a certain prescribed ratio as compared with the state contributing the least.[35]

Other small-state delegates preferred complete reconstitution, but only if the small states were granted equal representation. Delaware's George Read "was agst. patching up the old federal System: he hoped the idea wd. be dismissed. It would be like putting new cloth on an old garment. The confederation was founded on temporary principles. It cannot last: it cannot be amended. If we do not establish a good Govt. on new principles, we must either go to ruin, or have the work to do over again."[36]

New Jersey's David Brearley also affirmed support for major revisions that would give "energy and stability to the Federal Government"—but not if it meant putting the small states at the mercy of the more populous Massachusetts, Pennsylvania, and Virginia. Even New Jersey's William Paterson, who proposed the unit-rule New Jersey Plan on 15 June, personally preferred the Virginia Plan's more sweeping revision—provided the states were equally represented. In his first speech to the convention on 9 June Paterson called for the vesting of Congress with direct powers over commerce and taxation but directed his principal opposition to the *expediency* of a complete revision and declared that "the people are not ripe for any other" than "a federal [confederation] scheme." Paterson's notes for the same speech indicate that he *personally* preferred more fundamental changes in the nation's government, although he would not publicly say what those were. He was not there, his notes attest, "to sport Opinions of my own—not to say wt. is the best Govt. or what ought to be done—but what can be done—wt. can we do consistently with our powers; wt. can we do that will meet with the Approbation of the People—their Will must guide." Moreover, although the "democratic Spirit beats high," the evil was "not half wrong enough to have a good Govt."[37]

On 16 July the convention finally resolved the issue by agreeing to the formula that combined the principle of representation apportioned by population in the House of Representatives with representation based on state equality in the Senate. Thus the Great Compromise won for the small states what they had wanted all along.

No less than the large-state delegates, the small-state delegates wanted the Confederation system replaced by a reconstituted energetic central government. The lesson that the state governments were too weak and unstable to support both a central government and law and order guided their thinking also.

Conflict and Compromise: Protecting Slavery

The history of how the infamous protections for slavery were written into the Constitution also demonstrates the delegates' commitment to a reconstituted central government with strong powers. From the start, southern delegates were determined that any reconstituted central government must not pose a threat to slavery either now or in the future. Even before the convention began, South Carolina's Charles Pinckney was circulating a plan for a reconstituted central government that provided the six slave-owning southern states with added congressional representation that would enable them to block any hostile federal action by a northern state majority. Pinckney's plan contained a provision that apportioned representation in the lower house on the basis of the formula that counted all free persons and made every five slaves equivalent to three free persons. Because at the time the South harbored 700,000 black slaves, this would give the six slave-owning states a close parity with the seven northern states. (With slavery still legal in both New York and New Jersey, northern members of Congress from these states might possibly join the proslavery forces in any congressional face-off over slavery.)[38]

The proposal to count slaves in the apportionment of the South's representation was first made to the convention during the third week. The Virginia Plan had apportioned representation in both houses either by the amount each state contributed to the federal treasury or by a count of free persons only. On 11 June James Wilson of Pennsylvania, a state that had recently ended slavery, moved that the latter formula be amended to apportion representation in the lower house on the basis of the total count of all free persons (men, women, children, bound servants, and apprentices) *plus* "three-fifths of all other persons not comprehended in the foregoing description, except Indians, not paying taxes, in each State." Wilson's motion was immediately seconded by Charles Pinckney. Two weeks earlier, Pinckney had placed before the convention his own plan, which had been tabled in favor of the Virginia Plan. Wilson's motion easily carried, nine states to two, the Delaware and New Jersey delegations alone voting nay.[39]

Wilson's and Pinckney's collaboration point to concerted planning. Although no direct proof has come to light, delegates from the Deep South probably were insisting on some version of the Pinckney three-fifths formula. Otherwise Wilson's proposal makes no sense. Although Wilson may be criticized for making a proposal that only strengthened slavery and the South, he later as much as acknowledged this as the price that had to be paid for southern support for the Constitution.[40]

Delegates from the Deep South insisted that the slave-owning South must have special protection. Because the previous votes to accept the Virginia Plan had been made by the Committee of the Whole and were not binding, the convention had to tackle once again the makeup of the two proposed legislative branches. The matter was complicated by continued small-state demands for state equality in the upper house despite several previous votes for proportional representation in both houses and the New Jersey Plan's defeat on 19 June. Perhaps encouraged by the ease with which their first demand had carried, southern delegates pressed proposals that would replace the three-fifths formula, which actually left the slave-owning states inferior in the lower house by a proportion of 35 to 30, with an even more favorable allocation of representation. These proposals included basing representation on each state's quotaed contribution to the federal treasury (in the allocation of taxes slaves would be counted as either polls or property, so this measure would increase southern representation); adjusting the allocation of representation arbitrarily in order to give the South parity with the North; and counting slaves as equal to free people. Each time these Deep South delegates made clear they regarded parity as essential to the South's security; General Charles Cotesworth Pinckney, for example, "did not expect the S. States to be raised to a majority of the representatives, but wished them to have something like an equality."[41] Only when Deep South delegates could not garner support from delegates from the upper south and the north did they retreat to the original three-fifths formula.

This retreat was made palatable by a new provision that capitalized on a southern expectation of future shifts in the population balance towards the South.[42] Proposed by Hugh Williamson of North Carolina, this was the constitutional guarantee of a federal census and reapportionment of representation every ten years. Assuming that the Southeast and Southwest would grow in population at a faster rate than would the Northeast and Northwest, southern delegates seized on this proposal and coupled it with the three-fifths formula. But before the new combined provision could win the necessary northern votes, the objection by northern delegates that this would be an incentive to accelerate slave importations from abroad had to be dealt with. The solution was to add an offsetting disincentive, sometimes called the "dirty compromise," which made both apportionment of direct taxes and apportionment of representation dependent on a count of all free persons plus "three fifths of all other Persons." Provision was also made for an initial representation of 35 to 30. By making periodic censuses and reapportionments mandatory, the slave-owning South could hope to gain parity in the near future by its own natural population growth.[43]

Other provisions that protected the slave-owning South were extracted from a convention that yielded to southern pressure rather than lose the South's support for a reconstituted central government. As Paul Finkelman has demonstrated, the unamendable constitutional prohibition of any federal law against African slave importations before 1808 was engineered by delegates from the Deep South who made this new demand just as soon as their demand for representation had been met. Warned by South Carolina delegate Charles Pinckney that "some security to the Southern states against the emancipation of slaves, and taxes on exports" was indispensable, the convention's Committee on Detail (with two out of five southern members) reported out provisions against ending the slave trade and requiring a two-thirds vote on any federal navigation act. When northern delegates objected to the two-thirds vote requirement, the delegates from the Deep South agreed to drop it in return for northern support for the constitutional ban on any federal prohibition of slave importations before 1808. On the other hand, the clause prohibiting any state from emancipating a fugitive slave and requiring any runaway to be returned to his master on demand was a last-minute proposal by southern delegate Pierce Butler (and possibly Charles Pinckney) that easily passed a weary convention anxious to wrap up the nearly completed Constitution.[44]

Should northern convention delegates have refused concessions that helped consolidate slavery and that, according to later abolitionists and neo-abolitionist historians, made the Constitution "a covenant with death"? Much depends on what one thinks of the chances of obtaining Southern support for a Constitution that did not include these provisions. Judging by the frequency, tenacity, and stridency of the demands made by delegates from the Deep South, and judging by the depth of white southern anxiety about the security of slavery, the odds are great that without such protections the delegates of the Deep South would not have supported the Constitution.[45] A reconstituted central government was not the only option available to them in 1787. Either a patchwork amendment of the existing Confederation system or establishment of a southern republic loosely linked to the other states through the existing Congress was a possible alternative. Southern delegates wanted a reconstituted republic that would last for ages only if it posed no threat to slavery.

Consensus: Prohibitions on the States

Finally, the powers *denied* to the states reflect the Framers' desire to end once and for all the controversies over the tax-related economic reliefs that had been so central to the pressure-resistance-retreat patterns of the 1780s. These provisions in article 1, section 10 barred the states from coining money; emitting bills of credit; making anything but gold and silver coin a tender in payment of debts; passing any bill of attainder, ex post facto law, or law impairing the obligation of contract; or laying any imposts or duties on imports or exports. Added to other textual prohibitions on the states carried over from the Articles of Confederation, they show the Framers' desire to ensure the central government's supreme authority and to prevent state legislation that might lessen the value of money, injure business and commerce, damage creditors' rights, create friction among the states, or diminish property rights.[46] In fact, these were the key issues faced by the state governments in the Confederation era and represented the reliefs enacted by many of those states. Clearly the Framers wanted to put an end to what they saw as the capitulation of the states to popular pressure for relief.

Ironically, these measures did not go far enough for the man most widely celebrated by historians and biographers as the chief author and "father of the Constitution"—James Madison. As Charles Hobson has shown, Madison worked long and unsuccessfully at the convention for a more thorough, effective method of preventing the state governments from capitulating to demands by popular majorities that violated the central government's policies and authority and damaged property rights. Madison's proposal was designed to vest Congress with a preclusive veto on all state legislation, a power he believed would check the states' proclivities for measures that threatened the authority of the national government and discredited republican government. It was decisively voted down on 17 July, much to Madison's disappointment. Until he swallowed his qualms sometime shortly after the close of the convention, Madison believed that the defeat of the congressional veto had seriously, perhaps fatally, compromised the central government's effectiveness.[47]

A proposal analogous to Madison's was Alexander Hamilton's scheme for the federal appointment of state governors, who would have an executive veto on legislation in all the states. This proposal would have enabled the central government to control state legislation through the actions of its appointed executive representative in each state, much as governors had done in royal colonies. John Jay also proposed to Washington a federal appointment power of this kind, with the additional provision that the central government appoint high-ranking civil and military officers in all the states. The latter would have enabled the central government to supervise state militias and presumably ensure that no state resorted to secession, started a war, or entered into a foreign alliance.[48]

As opponents predicted, the congressional veto would have required Congress to scrutinize every piece of legislation enacted by the states, which would have been tedious, technically complex, and, given the quan-

tity of such legislation, impossible. The federal appointment of state governors would have required that the states accept veto-wielding governors
appointed by the central government at a time when several state governments did not even have the executive veto. Both schemes intruded into
established state powers and practices and would have fatally jeopardized
ratification. The practical and political liabilities inherent in each were
overwhelming.[49]

Rejecting Madison's congressional negative and never even considering
Hamilton's proposed federal appointment of state governors, the convention instead proscribed the states from undesirable actions by specific prohibitions, including a ban on coinage and paper money. Simultaneously,
the Framers approved the supremacy clause that made the Constitution,
treaties, and federal laws "the supreme law of the land" and that bound
state and federal judges to uphold this supremacy. State judges thus became
the "first line of defense" against the unconstitutional acts of the states, and
the Supreme Court implicitly became the "ultimate line of defense" once
the judiciary's jurisdiction had been defined in article 3 and in the subsequent Judiciary Act of 1789. "Together, the supremacy clause, the judiciary article, and the restrictions on the states constituted the judicial substitute for the legislative negative on state laws"[50] and for the federal power
to appoint state governors and militia officers.

Despite two hundred years of continuous history, the Constitution was
not the inevitable event that hindsight sometimes suggests. While any
other system is difficult to imagine, Congress's limited amendment and
the three or four regional republics were alternatives, had the Framers
failed to agree on a constitution. The Framers were ingenious, flexible,
and adept at compromise, qualities that helped greatly to resolve the several disputes that threatened the convention's success. But shared predispositions were more important. Without the Framers' preference for a
centralized republican government of three branches, the delegates would
not have reconciled such divisive issues as proportional-versus-equal representation and protections for slavery. Yet the very intensity of the battles
over these issues affords evidence of their common predispositions. Had
they not intended a government thus reconstituted and empowered, they
would not have demanded safeguards against the possible hurtful application of its powers against their states. Such a desire was the fruit of previous experience with the changeable state governments.

★ 14 ★

THE ANTIFEDERALISTS AND
THE RATIFICATION CAMPAIGN

CONTRARY to the implication of its "We the People" preamble, only some of the people wanted the federal Constitution to become the nation's frame of central government. Between the Constitution's publication by the convention in September 1787 and its ratification by the ninth requisite state—New Hampshire, in June 1788—the Antifederalists almost defeated the Constitution. In Massachusetts and Virginia, where the Antifederalists and Federalists were closely balanced, popularly elected state conventions approved the Constitution by narrow margins. In Pennsylvania ratification occurred because the Federalists acted before the Antifederalists could organize, in South Carolina because malapportioned election districts gave the Federalists additional voting strength, and in New York because some Antifederalists defected once they saw the prospect of exclusion from the Union after the requisite nine states had ratified. In other states where the Antifederalists were more numerous than the Federalists, pressure by the new George Washington administration tipped the scales towards ratification (North Carolina in December 1789 and Rhode Island in June 1790). Only in Delaware, New Jersey, and Georgia, the Union's three smallest states, did popularly elected conventions unanimously approve the Constitution. In short, the Federalists needed to bring to bear much energy, resourcefulness, and tactical skill to carry the federal Constitution. That they did so is a classic example of how a determined minority can decisively change the course of history.[1]

From the beginning, the Federalists realized that ratification of the Constitution would be an uphill struggle. In August 1787, while the convention was still meeting behind closed doors, the Pennsylvania Federalist Anthony Wayne predicted that "turbulent spirits" in every state would try their hardest to defeat any plan for a strong, stable central government. As Wayne graphically put it, "a serious & determined opposition" could be expected "from a Class of people in each state—whose Political existance depends upon Anearchy & Confusion—consequently, any regular & efficient sistem will not be relished by them."[2]

Ever since Charles A. Beard's *An Economic Interpretation of the Constitution*, historians have grappled with the question of the exact identity of the Antifederalists and why they opposed the document. Most studies begin with the assumption that any explanation of why the Federalists framed and ratified the federal Constitution must also explain why the Antifederalists opposed it. According to Beard, Federalists and Antifederalists represented different property interests that stood to gain and lose from adoption of the Constitution, the Federalists concerned with personalty property, the Antifederalists with realty property. In Merrill Jensen's view, Federalist elites mistrusted the common people and wanted a government able to control them, while Antifederalists had more trust in the common people and wanted a more "democratic" government that would allow the numerical majority a greater say in their own affairs. According to Stanley Elkins and Eric McKitrick, the Federalists were "young men of the Revolution" whose career experiences on the national stage led them to identify with the nation; the Antifederalists were older state-based politicians who naturally identified with their particular states. Recently, Van Beck Hall, Jackson T. Main, and Norman K. Risjord have explained the Federalist-Antifederalist dichotomy in terms of "cosmopolitans" and "localists": thus Antifederalists opposed the Constitution because of their parochial, localized life experiences and horizons; Federalist "cosmopolitans" had a broader vision that could not presumably be realized without a stronger central government than the Confederation provided.

Like these historians, I begin with the premise that any valid explanation of the Federalists' support for the central government's reconstitution must also explain the Antifederalists' opposition. Thus the state's on-again-off-again taxing operations that disillusioned the property-owning gentry must have in some way influenced the Antifederalists' opposition to the Constitution.

Long suspected by historians, correlations between Confederation-era legislative groupings and the Federalist-Antifederalist protagonists have been established through quantitative studies by Jackson T. Main, Owen S. Ireland, Van Beck Hall, and others. Although disagreeing over how to interpret their data, these historians agree that the same legislators who battled each other over fiscal, financial, and other political issues in the state legislatures of the Confederation *before* the Constitution were one and the same with the Constitution's Federalist advocates and Antifederalist opponents *after* the Constitution was framed.

In the most ambitious study to date of pre-Constitution and post-Constitution voting, Jackson T. Main reports data that demonstrate continuities between the proponents of firm taxing by the states and Federalists, and between Reliefers and Antifederalists. Although Main's interpretation, categories, and terminology differ from mine, his investigation of 425 delegates in the state ratifying conventions of 1787–88 shows strong correlations between delegates' votes in state legislatures on tax-related issues and their support for or opposition to the Constitution. Thus the localists (Main's appellation) who before the Constitution voted in favor of a long list of relief and other measures including lower taxes, postponement of tax collection, stay laws, paper money, and the like opposed the Constitution. The cosmopolitans (again Main's appellation) who earlier voted against these same relief measures supported the Constitution.[3]

Similar data from Owen S. Ireland's pioneering analysis of 500 legislative roll-call votes of 225 Republicans and Constitutionalists in Pennsylvania shows strong correlations between Republican assembly delegates and Pennsylvania Federalists, and between Constitutionalists and Pennsylvania Antifederalists. Although Ireland argues for ethnic-religious determinants as the basis of Pennsylvania Confederation politics, his voting data indicate that the state's Republican party loyalists (the mainstay of the firm line on tax collection before the Constitution) backed the Constitution. On the other hand, the Constitutionalists (the mainstay of tax reliefs before the Constitution) opposed the Constitution.[4]

Data reported in Van Beck Hall's study of pre-Constitution legislative voting in Confederation Massachusetts furnishes more evidence of these continuities. Based on the analysis of more than eighty roll-call votes between 1780 and 1791, Hall's study correlates persistent legislative support for the state's fiscal-monetary program and its heavy taxes with the Federalists of 1787; persistent opposition to that program correlates with the Antifederalists. "Although the turnover in membership discourages statistical analysis of the individual legislators," Hall reports, "the voting patterns of the towns [reflected in the votes of their elected representatives] are remarkably consistent throughout the period."[5]

These studies point to rural and urban Reliefers from the ranks of the middle and lower gentry as the backbone of the Antifederalist political coalition. As Reliefers they had carried the battle for rural tax and debt relief into the state legislatures when the forced collection of taxes had produced the first signs of rural resistance. As Antifederalists they would carry the battle against the Constitution into the elections for delegates to the ratifying conventions and onto the convention floors. In Pennsylvania they were the Constitutionalist party chieftains, including George Bryan, Rev. John Ewing, Dr. James Hutchinson, John Smiley, William Findley, and Charles Pettit. In South Carolina, they included Aedanus Burke, Thomas Sumter, and Rawlins Lowndes (but not Alexander Gillon). In Rhode Island they were John Collins, Jonathan J. Hazard, and other country party leaders. In Massachusetts they were Israel Hutchinson, William Fessenden, Amos Singletary, and other Reliefers. In Maryland they included Samuel Chase, Luther Martin, William Paca, and Charles

Ridgely; in Virginia, Patrick Henry and George Nicholas; in Connecticut, General James Wadsworth; in New York, the Clinton party with its rural and urban chieftains Abraham and Robert Yates, John Lamb, and Marinus Willett; in New Jersey, Abraham Clark; in Delaware, Thomas Rodney; in North Carolina, Timothy Bloodworth and Willie Jones; in Georgia, George Walton.

States' Rights Antifederalist Program

Historians of the Antifederalists correctly describe them as favoring the Confederation system's limited amendment, but not root-and-branch revision. While differing about Antifederalist motivation, Jackson T. Main, Alpheus T. Mason, and Robert Rutland hold that Antifederalists were prepared to invest Congress with a federal impost power and a federal power to pressure Great Britain by retaliatory commercial legislation but opposed reconstitution at the time the Constitution was drafted. Main concludes that "the typical Antifederalist" wanted to strengthen Congress by limited amendment. Mason holds that while "most Antifederalists" did not want the system changed, they did believe "that the central government under the Articles needed invigoration." Rutland maintains that many Antifederalists wanted the Confederation retained with Congress strengthened by a federal impost and a commercial power to retaliate.[6] Statements by Antifederalists in Pennsylvania, South Carolina, Rhode Island, and Massachusetts confirm these conclusions.

The Writer of this had confined his Views of Alterations to be made in the old Confederation to a mere Enlargement of the powers of Congress, particularly as to maritime affairs. He thinks the Experiment ought at least have been tried, whether we could not have succeeded under a Confederation of independent states, before we proceeded to consolidate all power in one general government. (A Pennsylvania Antifederalist, in 1788 or 1789)

Mr. [Rawlins] Lowndes expatiated some time on the nature of compacts— the sacred light in which they were held by all nations, and solemnly called on the house to consider whether it would not be better to add strength to the old confederation, instead of hastily adopting another; asking, whether a man could be looked on as wise, who, possessing a magnificent building, upon discovering a flaw, instead of repairing the injury should pull it down, and build another? (A South Carolina Antifederalist, fall, 1787)

The old Confederation, with proper amendments; May each State retain their sovereignty in the full extent of republican governments. (Rhode Island Antifederalist toasts, 4 July 1788)

Yesterday a select body of REAL FEDERALISTS examined the ship OLD CONFEDERATION, as she now lays up in Congress's dock-yard.—They report she is [of] sound Bottom, and strong built, and that no further repairs are wanting, than a thorough Calking; which might be done in a few weeks—provided the Owners would unite to set the workmen about the business:—They are wholly averse *to breaking her up*, as they think it a needless expense to put another on the stocks upon a *New Construction*, while they are in possession of One of *good seasoned Timber*, which might be compleated fitted to answer every purpose. (A Boston Antifederalist caucus, January 1788)[7]

Behind the Antifederalist program for adding limited powers to the existing Congress was the unspoken premise that the existing state-centered Confederation offered superior benefits and advantages for both the individual states and the nation as a whole. These advantages followed logically from the premise that the state governments had performed well enough to make their continued retention as the basic units of the nation's system of government desirable.

Rather than decode the long list of Antifederalist indictments of the Constitution (in Pennsylvania's ratifying convention, James Wilson counted 241 different Antifederalist objections),[8] we can think of the Antifederalist opposition as predicated not on specific objections but on the more fundamental grounds of preference for an amended state-centered Confederation. States' rights Antifederalists still believed that the Confederation could realize the essential objects of personal security, protection of property, prosperity, order, and union.

A major premise of the Antifederalists' case for the Confederation was the state governments' greater responsiveness to popular opinion and their greater ability to provide relief and protection from oppressive or abusive government. The state-centered Confederation, the Antifederalists argued, would thus elicit greater trust and voluntary compliance on the part of the common people than would a remote, removed, coercive central government. Building on the natural loyalty that their responsiveness would foster, the Confederation state governments would generate voluntary popular support for law and order and for the union as a whole. By contrast, a central government that was out of touch with the personal situations of the common people would have to resort to physical coercion more frequently to instill obedience.

Writing shortly after his state had ratified the Constitution, the Pennsylvania Antifederalist William Findley, a Constitutionalist loyalist and Reliefer leader, guardedly explained why the basic format of the Confederation system was superior. Skeptical of his Federalist correspondent's warnings about "the dangers that threaten us most," Findley did "not object to the construction of the new system but to the powers as they extend to internal objects, and [that] eventually leaves us no means of relief or protection in the state governments." He found the new system impractical because it failed to accommodate to "our extended situation and our thinness of settling, our proportioned scarcity of men for armys, and small resources for supporting them," and to the "independence of our habits and situation and consequent jealousys now much excited." "Our government must be a government of confidence, it must be a government supported by affection arising from an apprehension of mutual interest, and security, not of fear and apprehension."[9]

Samuel Chase, the prominent Maryland Reliefer and Antifederalist, based his objections to the proposed new central government on its unresponsiveness relative to the state governments. The Constitution, Chase made clear in a 1788 letter, would create a government that was out-of-touch with the common people and, therefore, more likely to be oppressive. Flatly dismissing the notion that a federal bill of rights would offer sufficient protection against future oppression by the new government, Chase declared that "some of the powers must be abridged, or public liberty will be endangered, and, in time destroyed." Rather than concentrate on the omission of a bill of rights, Chase considered the Constitution "radically defective in this essential; the bulk of the people can have nothing to say to it." Furthermore, "the government is *not* a government of the people. It is not a government of representation. The people do *not* choose the House of Representatives. A right of election is declared, but it cannot be exercised. It is a useless nugatory right. By no mode of choice, by the people at large, or in districts, can they choose representatives. The right is immediate and given to all the people, but it is impracticable to be exercised by them."[10]

The key to the states' rights Antifederalist position lies in a different interpretation of the pressure-resistance-retreat episodes that the Federalists regarded as proof that government in the United States needed to be strengthened at the center. Reliefers saw these episodes as demonstrating that the state governments were effectively responsive to the needs and problems of the common people. By a logical extension, Reliefers reasoned that this decentralized Confederation not only was better suited to a sprawling, disparate, and heterogeneous country than was a centralized, restructured, remote central government, but would prove a safer path to a more secure, prosperous, and unified America than would the federal Constitution. Different interpretations of the same phenomena impelled Reliefers to become Antifederalists and Taxers to become Federalists.

Limited Amendment Antifederalists

By contrast with the states' rights Antifederalists, limited amendment Antifederalists favored a reconstituted central government but wanted the Constitution amended before adoption. They objected to the absence of a bill of rights and other details of the plan rather than to the fundamental structure and powers of the plan itself. Having been prominent in the revolutionary war leadership, they felt a personal commitment to republican principles as they construed them; some were "Old Revolutionaries" who regarded it as their special obligation to defend and uphold these principles.[11] Limited amendment, in their view, would also make the Constitution more acceptable to the people.

The most active limited amendment Antifederalists were Elbridge Gerry of Massachusetts and Richard Henry Lee and George Mason of Virginia, each well connected, well educated, and wealthy. Gerry was a Harvard-educated Marblehead, Massachusetts, merchant who had recently married an heiress and retired to "Elmwood" in Cambridge, where he lived the life of a country gentleman. Lee, scion of one of Virginia's great families, owned "Chantilly," a tobacco and grain slave plantation on the upper Potomac River. Mason owned Gunston Hall, 5,000 or more acres in plantation land on the upper Potomac, over a hundred slaves, and vast tracts of wild lands; he was one of the wealthiest men in Virginia.[12]

Each of the three held convictions that could easily have been those of any mainline Federalist, such as the notion that better personal behavior would remedy the distress caused by heavy taxes and private debts. Shortly before the Constitutional Convention, Lee wrote that "those evils which happen independently of us, we must bear with manly firmness; and those that flow from our misconduct we have no right to complain of. Among the last is the pressure of private debt, which almost universally arises from idleness and extravagance; one or both. This will be corrected & remedied by industry & economy."[13]

Likewise, each man believed that the state-centered Confederation must be replaced by a forceful, energetic government at the center. Lee reported approvingly after a visit to Philadelphia during the summer of 1787 that the convention was preparing a plan of government "not unlike the B[ritish] Constitution, that is, an Executive with 2 branches composing a federal Legislature and possessing adequate Tone." He viewed "this departure from simple Democracy" as "indispensably necessary, if any government at all is to exist in N. America.—Indeed the minds of men have been so hurt by the injustice, folly, and wickedness of the State Legislatures; & State Executives—that people in general seem ready for any thing."[14]

Gerry, as a delegate to the convention, reported that most of the delegates like himself feared that "unless a system of Government is adopted by Compact, *Force* I expect will plant the Standard; for such an anarchy as now exists cannot last long. Gentlemen seem to be impressed with the necessity of establishing some efficient system, & I hope it will secure us against domestic as well as foreign invasion."[15] Mason, also a delegate, approvingly described to his son just before the convention how many of the delegates favored "a total alteration of the present foederal system."[16]

Yet when it came time to endorse the Constitution all three insisted upon amendment. As delegates, Mason and Gerry had been part of the majority that framed the Constitution's basic structure, but after unsuccessful attempts to persuade the convention to modify the plan, including the incorporation of a federal bill of rights, they refused to sign the final document.[17] Shortly after, both men publicly avowed their dissatisfaction with parts of the Constitution and called for its amendment. Mason held that the state ratifying conventions should alter and amend the Constitution as a precondition of ratification; his own list of mandatory amendments included a bill of rights, more extensive popular representation in the House of Representatives, and restrictions on the powers of the Senate.[18] Gerry publicly acknowledged that the Constitution "in many respects . . . has great merit" but, insisting that "proper amendments" (much like Mason's) were required, backed a second Constitutional Convention for this purpose.[19] Lee privately told Mason that the new Constitution, with proper amendments, would make "a fine system" but also pursued a strategy involving a second Constitutional Convention or, alternatively, state ratifying conventions that would require a bill of rights and other changes as preconditions of ratification.[20]

Motivating these limited amendment Antifederalists was a sense of obligation that they must act on their duty as the country's most reliable guardians of republican principles. Hence, when a flawed Constitution issued from the convention, the Old Revolutionaries insisted that it be amended even if to do so meant delay and possible defeat. Limited amendment Antifederalists thus defied the Federalist Framers with whose general agenda of reconstitution they agreed and insisted that the Constitution's several glaring defects be corrected prior to its adoption.[21]

Gerry and Lee had additional reasons for pressing the Constitution's amendment. Gerry wrote his wife that he found the daily reports of the states' rights Antifederalist opposition highly disquieting: "I am exceedingly distrest at the proceedings of the Convention being apprehensive, & almost sure they will if not altered materially lay the foundation of a civil war, this entre nous."[22]

On similar grounds, Lee warned Mason that although "this constitution has a great many excellent regulations in it and if it could be reasonably amended would be a fine system—As it is, I think 'tis past doubt, that if it should be established, either a tyranny will result from it, or it will be prevented by a civil war. I am clearly of opinion with you that it should be sent back with amendments reasonable and assent withheld until such amendments are admitted."[23]

Rural Voters

Anticipating (in the words of General Anthony Wayne of Pennsylvania) the "serious & determined opposition" of "a Class of people in each state—whose political existance depends upon Anearchy & Confusion," the Framers provided that the Constitution would take effect when only nine out of thirteen states had ratified. Once the Constitution had been approved by Congress for transmittal to the states for ratification, the battle between Federalists and Antifederalists for votes and delegates to the ratifying conventions began in earnest.

Numerous studies demonstrate that the Antifederalists' most consistent popular support came from the middling and poorer class of yeoman farmers and planters in every state except New Jersey, Delaware, and Georgia. As Alfred Young and others have shown, the estimated 14,000 New York Antifederalist voters were concentrated in the rural counties along the middle and upper Hudson, on Long Island, and in the northeastern counties, the very areas where middling and poor farmers were especially numerous and the landlord influence was weak or nonexistent. New York Antifederalists and Federalists alike described "the common people," "the yeomanry," and "the Country" as the Antifederalists' most consistent support. Robert Yates informed George Mason that it had been the "Spirit and Independency of the Yeomanry" in New York State that had produced the current Antifederalist majority at the ratifying convention.[24] The estimated 10,500 Federalist voters, on the other hand, centered in commercial areas in and around New York City and Albany and consisted of merchants, professionals, and artisans; the great landlords and their tenants and frontiersmen were also Federalist.[25]

Likewise in the Chesapeake states of Maryland, Virginia, and North Carolina, Antifederalist delegates came from those areas where middling yeoman planters and small farmers were numerically dominant. As Norman J. Risjord has shown, the northern counties of Maryland (Harford, Cecil, Baltimore), where farmers were poor, and southside and southwest Virginia, where small tobacco farmers had little or no cash and had been petitioning for paper money, were strongly Antifederalist. Antifederalist voters were also numerous among the small and middling farmers of the Virginia Piedmont. The counties where wealthy planters were politically dominant sent Federalist delegates to the ratifying convention, including the Northern neck and the lower tidewater; commercial centers like Richmond, Norfolk, and Alexandria were also predominantly Federalist. Sensing the potential of the Antifederalist appeal to the rural poor, Federalists warned that Antifederalist leaders like Patrick Henry would "poison and prejudice the lower orders of the people."[26]

Antifederalist strength centered in the rural counties of middle and western Pennsylvania. This rural opposition to the Constitution was deep and bitter: even after ratification by the state convention, Antifederalist petitions calling for the assembly and Congress to repudiate ratification garnered more than 6,000 signatures in Northampton, Dauphin, Bedford, Franklin, Cumberland, Westmoreland, and Northumberland counties. A rural Antifederalist publicly warned: "You may depend upon it, whatever you in the city may think of the business, we country people do not consider the new Constitution adopted by this state. We look upon all yet done to be the work of a junto in the city, etc. We shall be very apt to make some *experiments* in the spring."[27]

At the same time, the wealthier rural classes of planters, country gentry, and commercial farmers in these states supported the Constitution. The "patricians of the Hudson" (R. R. Livingston, Philip Schuyler, Stephen Van Rensselaer, Pierre Van Cortlandt, James Duane) were Federalist; not surprisingly New York Federalists were described by contemporaries as "the better sort," "the better kind of people," and "the well born."[28] The wealthy grain and tobacco planters of rural Maryland, Virginia, and North Carolina were Federalist,[29] as were most of the well-to-do commercial farmers of Pennsylvania and the New England states. In Pennsylvania, as contemporaries well understood, the more remote, poorer, country counties were Antifederalist; but divisions in the backcountry were reported between the "People of the Hills ag[ain]st those in the Valley"— an observation that probably reflected a division between poor and well-to-do.[30]

Quantitative studies provide further support for these generalizations. Using legislative roll-call votes and aggregate town tax apportionment data, Van Beck Hall correlates legislative voting patterns from the Confederation and Constitution eras in 342 Massachusetts towns. Hall shows that the Antifederalists derived their strongest support at the ratifying convention from delegates from the poorest, least commercial, most rural Massachusetts towns, the hill towns of Worcester, Hampshire, and Berkshire counties. The wealthiest, most commercial towns—Boston, Salem, Newburyport, Worcester, and Springfield—sent Federalist delegates. Small towns that had commercial farmers, merchants, artisans, and poor farmers in roughly equal numbers divided equally.[31] In Reliefer-Antifederalist Rhode Island, Ruth Herndon's unpublished dissertation correlates tax lists with poll lists for a 1788 referendum on the Constitution and shows that the minority of wealthy voters in the poorer country towns supported a ratifying convention while the poorer voters in the majority opposed.[32] Norman Risjord's comparison of voters listed in a 1789 election poll for Amherst County, Virginia, with tax lists shows poorer voters supporting the Antifederalist candidate for congress, James Monroe, and the wealthier voters supporting Federalist James Madison. "Those with fewer than five slaves (or less than £150 in land) cast more ballots for Monroe than Madison received altogether. Expressed differently, a poor man was twice as likely to vote for Monroe, while a wealthy man was twice as likely to vote for Madison."[33]

Much of the rural middle class and all of the rural lower class in every state but New Jersey, Delaware, and Georgia opposed the Constitution because they anticipated that their state governments would protect them against ruinous taxation more reliably than would the central government established by the Constitution. Most of them had been the chief beneficiaries of the relief policies enacted by the states during the 1780s. Heavily burdened by taxes in hard money and threatened by ruinous distress sales, they had escaped disaster when the state governments reversed themselves and voted tax postponements and paper money issues (Pennsylvania, South Carolina, Rhode Island, Massachusetts, Maryland, Virginia, New Jersey, Delaware, and New Hampshire). By the same token in states where Reliefers had been able to deflect tax crackdowns or where farmers had positively benefited from the relief-relaxation policies of incumbent administrations from the beginning, farmers looked to their state governments with appreciative eyes (New York, Connecticut, North Carolina, and Georgia). Indeed, this group of voters regarded these state relief programs as not only beneficial but their economic salvation, proof that their state governments *would* respond to farmers' pleas when ruin threatened.

Moreover, in the states where state imposts formed an important part of state finance, these same rural groups believed that the state governments could manage fiscal and monetary affairs without resorting to either heavy taxation or a reconstituted central government. Significantly, the Antifederalists in New York emphasized the argument that adoption of the Constitution would deprive New Yorkers of their lucrative state impost and would likely result in the yeomanry's being taxed as heavily as their Massachusetts and Connecticut neighbors.[34]

Because they had benefited personally, immediately, and concretely from state relief measures and because the comparative advantages of the Constitution seemed remote and risky, many middling and most poor farmers responded positively to Antifederalist arguments that the state-centered Confederation system was the safer, sounder system. Similarly they hearkened to Antifederalist warnings that the Constitution would create a government by the rich that might well strip them of their property and reduce them to ruin.[35]

By contrast, substantial and successful upper-class rural property holders and commercial farmers favored the Constitution over the Confederation system because it promised a more energetic, stable, efficient central government that could protect their property interests and provide a hospitable environment for the market-oriented commerce in which they were already involved. Accepting the premise that hard money was a more reliable medium than paper money and that the common people could have paid the hard money taxes levied on them, the well-to-do propertied groups of rural America believed that state relief legislation was corrupting the work and spending habits of the common people and was injuring business and commerce as well. Far from spurring the economy and reflating prices, paper money had had the opposite effect. Demonstrably, paper money had driven hard money out of circulation, frightened commercial and business credit, caused merchants and investors to invest profits abroad, disrupted commercial transactions, and enabled debtors to pay creditors in money worth less than its specie value. Thus, because the states' relief programs had been detrimental to their interests, an energetic stable central government able to tax and pay its debt obligations in hard money, invigorate men's productivity and effort, and assure a stable currency seemed to guarantee a revitalized commerce.

In three states these generalizations do not hold, however. Almost entirely rural, Delaware ratified the Constitution on 7 December 1787 by a vote of 30 to 0 and thus became "The First State"; New Jersey followed suit on 18 December by a vote of 38 to 0; and Georgia ratified on 31 December, 26 to 0. (In the meantime Pennsylvania, where the Federalists hurried ratification before the Antifederalists could organize effectively, ratified 46 to 23.) Obviously most if not all of rural Delaware, New Jersey, and Georgia favored ratification.

In fact, farmers in the three states supported the Constitution because it offered relief from heavy direct taxes that could be achieved in no other feasible way. By contrast with their sister states, Delaware and New Jersey had no means of raising money by an impost because they lacked seaports. Especially for the payment of federal requisitions but also to support their own finances, direct taxes were their only source of revenue. In addition both states were losing cash to Pennsylvania and New York as their citizens paid add-on prices for goods bought from Philadelphia and New York City merchants to compensate for the imposts collected by Pennsylvania and New York. Thus, short of outright repudiation, Delaware and New Jersey could not handle their finances without increasing the direct tax burden on their farming class. For the farmers of these states, the Constitution, with its federal impost power and its prohibition on any state impost, offered a way to lighten their tax burden which the state-centered Confederation system as currently organized could not provide. This was what Federalist William R. Davie had in mind when he predicted New Jersey's decisive adoption of the Constitution: "I have not yet heard what the N. Jersey Convention have done; however I think there is little Doubt, but they will adopt the Government proposed—as its consequences are so highly favorable to the non-importing states."[36]

States' rights Antifederalists in Delaware, New Jersey, and Georgia could not even rouse a token opposition. Two who might have been expected to organize opposition to the federal Constitution were Thomas Rodney of Delaware and Abraham Clark of New Jersey. Rodney, in 1787 Delaware house speaker and the sponsor of a pending £10,000 relief paper money bill, believed that the Constitution was too radical a departure from the state-centered Confederation which, suitably amended, he wanted to retain. Yet, as he later explained, he had not actively opposed the Constitution during the ratification campaign because "I thought it best to Improve the System that carried us thro' the war without altering from its principles; for I did not like to risk the Independence of America on so great a change as was proposed, but seeing that the greater number of wise men of America were for the change I did not oppose it, but hoped it would turn out for the best." Furthermore, "as I saw the people greatly oppressed I was in hopes it would afford relief."[37]

Rodney's reluctance openly to oppose the Constitution is to be explained by the overwhelming sentiment for adoption among Delaware farmers who anticipated thereby relief from taxes. Such tax relief was what a Delaware legislative committee desired when it expressed the hope in May 1787 that the Philadelphia convention "will in their superior wisdom alleviate the distresses of the United States as well as to put it in the power of this State, by the Legislative thereof to make their constituents happy, & not to be so grievously pressed." If, however, the convention should rise "without constituting some means for the General Relief of the distressed aforesd," the committee continued, a paper money relief measure should be adopted.[38]

Similarly the reluctance of Reliefer Abraham Clark of New Jersey actively to oppose the Constitution is to be explained by his realization that his constituents—the middling and poor farmers of New Jersey—favored the Constitution by an overwhelming majority. During the 1780s Clark had guided several relief measures through the New Jersey legislature, including the May 1786 £100,000 loan office paper money bill and a debtors' property-appraisement law.[39] When the Constitution was debated in New Jersey, as Richard McCormick notes, Clark did not actively oppose it but pursued a course that was "no worse than a neutral position"— so much so that "with their logical champion on the sidelines, the erstwhile paper-money host left the field in the complete possession of the forces of federalism."[40] The prospect that a federal impost would, as Federalist Lambert Cadwalader put it, generate "immense sums" that "will ease the farmer and landholder and make the burden light," was so appealing to New Jersey farmers that Clark kept quiet.[41]

In Georgia the anticipated expenses of the Creek Indian war prompted an overwhelming majority of small farmers and planters to favor the Constitution. Although Georgia's government had a small income from a state impost (£4,637), direct property taxes were badly in arrears and the only way to finance the war was to raise new taxes. Handicapped by an empty state treasury, Governor George Mathews labored to raise troops and supplies, using paper money issued the preceding year, and promising land bounties to volunteers. Everyone agreed that the state's resources were inadequate to the heavy burden of financing an all-out war against the Creeks in the west and defending the state against a possible future attack by the Spanish south of the Georgia-Florida border.[42] Because the Constitution promised a federal government that would take over the financial and logistical burdens of defending Georgia's western and southern borders, it was highly attractive to middling and poor Georgians.

Shortly after the Constitution's official ratification, the Pennsylvania notable General Anthony Wayne, owner of a confiscated Georgia plantation, launched a behind-the-scenes lobbying effort to be chosen Georgia's first federal senator. Pressing his candidacy by letters, Wayne promised that if the legislature chose him he would immediately set to work to shift the heavy financial burden of fighting the Creek war and protecting Georgia's southern and western borders off the backs of the people of Georgia and onto the new federal government: "I am therefore Induced at this alarming Crisis to offer myself a Candidate as a *Senator* of this State to Congress, in which character I will venture to pledge myself to relieve this State from the heavy specific & other taxes that we now experience, & of the burthen of the War, by making it an immediate Continental business, & establishing such posts as will put an effectual stop to the Indian Depredations & to *Spanish Protection* in future."[43]

Yet amidst the general rural support for the Constitution, a dissenting voice was briefly heard. Just before the state ratifying convention, a "Georgian" anonymously took the Philadelphia convention to task for having "thought fit to destroy such a useful fabric as the Articles of Confederation . . . and, on the ruins of that, raised a new structure rather favorable to aristocratical and destructive to democratical government." As no further Antifederalist newspaper publications appeared, this essay was probably a trial balloon to test whether popular sentiment could be mobilized against the Constitution.[44] It may have been written by or at the behest of the prominent Georgia Reliefer George Walton, a Burke County lawyer, popular politician, longtime champion of Georgia's small farmer class, and detested political enemy of the low-country elite establishment.[45]

Earlier Walton had signified a preference for the Confederation System by not attending the Philadelphia convention in the Georgia delegation despite his appointment by the assembly. Nor did Walton attend the state ratifying convention the following December, although elected a delegate.[46] Walton's uncharacteristic absence from these important events is best explained by the same calculations that constrained his Reliefer counterparts in New Jersey and Delaware from actively opposing the Constitution. Having championed tax reliefs that eased the burden of small farmers and planters, Walton believed the flexible state-centered Confederation system was more suited than the new Constitution to popular needs.[47] Yet his constituents preferred any reform at the center that would equip the central government to assume defense of Georgia's western and southern borders. After briefly testing the political waters and seeing the futility of opposing the Constitution in Georgia, Walton abstained from any further opposition.[48]

Urban Voters

In sharp contrast with most of the rural United States, the seaports and market towns overwhelmingly supported the Constitution, as the elections for Federalist and Antifederalist delegates to the state ratifying conventions document. In the Philadelphia election, Federalist candidates easily defeated Antifederalists by margins of 5 to 1, the highest vote total for a Federalist delegate being 1,215 and the highest for an Antifederalist 235. (Even former Reliefer-Antifederalist assembly leader Charles Pettit received only 150 votes.) In New York City the Federalist vote was 2,735 to 134 for the Antifederalists. The Federalists swept the elections in Portsmouth, Boston, New Haven, Baltimore, Alexandria, Norfolk, Wilmington, New Bern, Charleston, and Savannah as well. This almost universal urban support for the Constitution was reported by observers, among them Levi Hollingsworth, a Philadelphia merchant: "We are all Foederal here except a few place men and pensioners"; another stated, "You can have no idea of the Enthusi[a]stic Zeal that Prevails in this city, a Man hazard ill usuage & insult who dare's avow his disapprobation."[49]

Urban support for the Constitution included virtually all parts of the merchant communities of the seaport and market towns. Thomas Doerflinger's study of the Philadelphia merchant community shows that, driven by "a vigorous spirit of enterprise," large, middling, and small merchants and shopkeepers welcomed the Constitution as promising an environment more hospitable to business than the current changeable state governments.

During the Revolution many of the larger merchants had "lost thousands of pounds in book debts that were paid off in depreciated currency, and their commercial operations were deranged by violent fluctuations in the price level." Yet because a stable currency served as "a store of value and a unit of account," all merchants considered a stable currency indispensable to commerce.[50] The Constitution, with its prohibition on state paper money and its promise of a central government strong enough to tax in hard money without being forced by popular pressure to issue paper money as a relief to farmers, offered the promise of a more stable currency.

The backing for the Constitution by the numerous urban middling and small artisans and shopkeepers is more difficult to explain. Federalists and Antifederalists directed appeals to this group, which formed a sizable swing minority in seaports and market towns. In earlier political contests, artisans and shopkeepers had backed Reliefers, the core of the Antifederalist coalition. Now they enthusiastically welcomed the Constitution, voted for Federalist candidates to state ratifying conventions, and joined the Federalist gentry in celebrating the Constitution's ratification.[51]

The political odyssey of these groups in Philadelphia, New York, and Boston is among the more perplexing problems of the Confederation era. Whether they backed the first tax, monetary, and debt-funding programs that the states enacted early in the era is not known. But when rural resistance to hard money taxes flared, many cast their votes for the urban politicians who offered paper money relief programs to quiet the countryside and boost prices and prosperity. When the commercial recovery promised by Reliefers failed to materialize, when the paper money depreciated, when their own incomes suffered, and when taxation by the state governments for Congress collapsed, urban artisans and shopkeepers gravitated toward the Federalist fold. By 1787 they were ready for the promise of an energetic centralized government.

Investigations of the artisan-shopkeepers of Philadelphia by Ronald Baumann and of New York City by Alfred Young support these generalizations. In the early 1780s the Republicans captured all fourteen of Philadelphia's city and county seats; presumably artisan-shopkeepers' votes contributed to this success. But when rural protest against hard money taxes developed in late 1783 and early 1784, the Philadelphia Constitutionalist merchant Charles Pettit stood for a vacated seat in the assembly in a city by-election in spring 1784 and won. Pettit's candidacy promised new prosperity-restoring financial measures that ultimately materialized in the Constitutionalist funding–paper money relief program. Pettit's election *before* the Constitutionalist attack on Robert Morris's Bank of North America suggests that taxes and money played a key role in artisan-shopkeepers' voting for the Constitutionalists. That their support elected Pettit was further confirmed in October 1784 when urban Constitutionalists swept the city and county elections and gained a large majority in the assembly.[52]

The Constitutionalist relief program paid paper money as annual interest to state holders of the federal debt and made paper money payable for taxes available on loan to farmers. But newspaper essays published in 1785 and signed by "a Mechanic" complained that the vaunted Constitutionalist funding–paper money program did not benefit urban craftsman and shopkeepers and that the Constitutionalists had broken faith with Congress, the bank, and the laws of the state.[53] When the paper's value depreciated, artisans and shopkeepers resented being paid for goods and labor in paper that was worth less than specie and that both merchants and the Bank of North America rejected.[54] Partly because of growing artisan-shopkeeper disillusion with the Constitutionalist paper money program, in the October 1785 assembly elections Robert Morris, George Clymer, and Thomas Fitzsimons gained seats in the assembly from Philadelphia city; other Republican candidates were elected from Philadelphia county. The ensuing 1786 and 1787 elections saw these Republican election successes in Philadelphia city and county repeated.[55]

Concerned by the depreciation of paper money and its depressing effect on trade, artisans and shopkeepers in Philadelphia, New York, and Boston were receptive to Federalist arguments that the central government provided by the federal Constitution would encourage commerce by providing a stable medium of monetary exchange. Appealing to that sentiment, a Boston Federalist hoped Boston's artisans would "not blindly throw away their votes upon any man who does not EXPLICITLY and OPENLY" support the Constitution; their "hopes of business, employment, and adequate pay" depended on its adoption.[56] Requested by Boston Federalists to prod convention delegate Samuel Adams into voting to ratify the Constitution, Boston artisan-shopkeepers turned out en masse and unanimously voted resolutions of support for ratification. "THAT, it is our opinion, if [the] said constitution should be adopted by the United States of America, trade and navigation will revive and increase, employ and subsistence will be afforded to many of our townsmen, who are now suffering from want of the necessaries of life; that it will promote industry and morality; render us respectable as a nation; and procure us all the blessings to which we are entitled from the natural wealth of our country; our capacity for improvement, from our industry, our freedom and independence."[57]

In the elections for delegates to state ratifying conventions held in Boston, New York, Philadelphia, and Charleston, urban artisan-craftsmen and tradesmen joined merchants and professionals to elect Federalist delegates.[58] They also joined merchants in the Federalist celebration parades in Boston, New York, Philadelphia, Baltimore, and other smaller cities and towns to welcome ratification. These parades were designed to create an impression of approval by all classes, but the representatives of forty-four different crafts (cordwainers to plasterers) in the Philadelphia ratification parade on 4 July 1788 marched by choice. Displaying the Federalists' message of moral and commercial recovery was Federalist Richard Bache on horseback, attended by a trumpeter, the words "New Aera" in gold letters pendant from the herald's staff, with the following lines: "Peace o'er our land her olive wand extends / And white robed Innocence from Heaven descends / The crimes and frauds of Anarchy shall fail / Returning Justice lifts again her scale."[59]

Ratification

By contrast with the timely and unanimous approval of the Constitution by ratifying conventions in Delaware on 7 December 1787, New Jersey on 18 December 1787, and Georgia on 31 December 1787, ratification in eight of the other nine states took much longer to accomplish, and the margin was often much narrower. In Pennsylvania the Federalists forced boycotting Antifederalists to attend the state assembly to make a quorum, which enabled the former to vote an early ratifying convention and ratify the Constitution on 12 December 1787, but these strongarm tactics were not repeated.

In Connecticut the Federalists capitalized on larger than expected rural support and approved the Constitution on 9 January 1788, 128 to 40. (There rural votes may have favored the Constitution because the federal impost would help Connecticut—essentially a nonimporting state—ease direct taxes.) In Massachusetts, on the other hand, a closely divided convention met in Boston through late January and early February 1788; neither side seemed ascendent until the Federalists offered a series of recommended amendments which captured just enough votes to carry the Constitution on 6 February 1788, 187 to 168. New Hampshire's convention met in Exeter with rural Antifederalists in the majority; by voting several months' adjournment, proposing recommended amendments, and then invoking Maryland's 26 April 1788 and South Carolina's 23 May 1788 ratifications, the Federalists persuaded just enough delegates to switch sides and carried ratification on 21 June, 57 to 47. In June a closely divided Virginia convention met in Richmond, consumed three weeks in tense debate, and finally ratified 89 to 79 on 25 June. A set of recommended amendments sponsored by the Federalists together with the news that New Hampshire, the ninth state, had ratified helped tip the balance. The most dramatic shift was in New York where the Antifederalists had a clear convention majority. But the tactic of recommended amend-

ments, the previous ratification by nine states, the news of Virginia's ratification (sent by Madison by rider from Richmond), the influence of the
Federalist papers, and the threat of New York City's secession if the state
failed to ratify combined to persuade enough delegates to change their
votes and ratification narrowly carried on 26 July 1788, 30 to 27.

Both holdout North Carolina and Rhode Island, where Reliefer-Antifederalist forces were in the majority, also ratified but only after protracted
and bitter Antifederalist opposition—North Carolina on 21 November
1789, 194–77; Rhode Island on 29 May 1790, 34–32. The possibility
of losing the benefits of Hamiltonian state debt assumption and the threat
of federal tariff discrimination by the Washington administration eventually helped tip the balance in Rhode Island.

The Antifederalists were a loose coalition of states' rights Antifederalists
and limited amendment Antifederalists who opposed the Constitution for
different reasons. The former preferred the Confederation system because
they believed that the state governments were more attuned to popular
needs than the Constitution's centralized distant government would be.
The latter, members of the elite whose disillusion with the state governments paralleled that of the Federalists, wanted the Constitution amended
to make it safer and therefore more acceptable to the voters. Believing in
the necessity of reconstitution at the center, they could more easily be
pulled into Federalist ranks by assurances of amendments than could the
states' rights Antifederalists. The defection of limited amendment Antifederalists helps explain the Federalists' ability to capture enough votes at
the ratification conventions in the key states of Massachusetts, Virginia,
and New York to carry the Constitution despite their minority status.

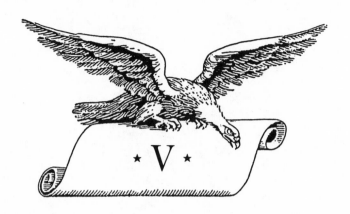

BEYOND RATIFICATION

⋆ 15 ⋆

THE PROMISE OF
AN ENERGETIC REPUBLIC

DESPITE widespread popular apathy and hostility and strong Antifederalist opposition, the Federalists carried the Constitution's ratification. Numerous studies have described how the Federalists overcame the Antifederalists' numerical advantage by superior organization, parliamentary skill, energy (the production, for example, of eighty-five *Federalist* papers), and, in the case of Pennsylvania's ratification, physical coercion. The simple fact that the Federalists had a Constitution they could get behind while the states rights' and limited amendment Antifederalists had no common plan also helps explain ratification when so much popular opinion was either hostile or uninterested.[1]

The Framers' Motivation

Deeming the state-centered Confederation system deficient in energy and stability, the Federalists framed a Constitution that would establish an energetic government that not only would be effective in its own right but would strengthen the state governments. Greater security of tenure through longer, staggered terms and different methods of election would enable the members of a bicameral Congress to retain office while enacting necessary laws that might be initially unpopular. A strong executive would enforce these laws, and an independent federal judiciary would try cases involving their infraction. With supreme jurisdiction over taxation, commerce, money, and armed forces, the central government could pay its operating expenses, finance the national debt, and direct and regulate the nation's commerce, money supply, foreign policy, and defense. Empowered to raise money and troops from the entire Union, the central government could overwhelm local resistance to its laws. At the same time, the states could no longer make anything but gold or silver legal tender; they could not issue paper currency, impair contracts, or tax imports. Through the influence of its steady, forceful execution of law, the central government would also encourage the state governments into steadier, more vigorous operation.

The question of the Framers' motivation in establishing the Constitution has long been debated by historians. Following Charles Beard some historians emphasize economic motives.[2] I argue that the Framers anticipated various benefits from the Constitution, including economic benefits. Certainly, the strong, steady central government established by the Constitution would enhance property of all kinds—investments in the public debt, commercial property, and real estate. It would establish a stable climate necessary for a prosperous commerce which the fear of paper money had greatly inhibited. The possibility that the state governments would sooner or later repudiate their public and private debts would also be dispelled. Some Framers had investments in state or federal debts which now would be secured. Some had mercantile businesses and law practices that would stand to gain if stable currency and economic prosperity returned.

Influential as these economic concerns were, the Framers' commitment to the revolutionary mission of building an enduring Republic was an equal if not more important motivation. At the beginning of the Revolution, each of the states had adopted new governments with republican constitutions. Disillusion with the English king and the imperatives of their own historical experience with elected assemblies had pushed the Revolutionary generation towards republicanism. The absence of any aristocratic class or eligible candidates for a monarchy and the need to make the Revolutionary movement as broad-based as possible had also worked in that direction.[3] Yet the choice was contrary to the weight of a received European tradition that depicted republican governments as weak, unstable, easily swayed systems that often ended in an anarchy of interclass or intergroup warfare, as had Rome and the English Commonwealth.[4] Unwilling to accept this bleak prognosis, the revolutionary leadership insisted that republican government promised a freer, more secure, more prosperous future than other "despotic" forms. But the breakdown of taxation and the "retreats" of the state governments into paper money and other relief measures began to raise fresh doubts. Could governments in which the popular majority had the final say guarantee property, protect personal security, and promote economic prosperity? In August 1786 George Washington had expressed this doubt when he asked whether the ability of republican government to protect society was indeed "ideal & fallacious."[5]

Concerned over the apparent inability of the state governments to protect property and security and promote economic prosperity, the Framers worried that unless the Confederation system was decisively reformed "the better sort of people"—people of property, education, and a large stake in society—would turn against republican government. Members of the business and propertied classes themselves, the Framers rightly sensed that support among the well-to-do was wearing thin. Influential men were talking openly of the superior merits of monarchy. The urban propertied classes held most of the nation's investment and commercial capital and commanded influence far in excess of their numbers. It was time to act before their disillusion grew any worse. A republican government must be designed that would be strong and stable enough to raise taxes to finance the public debt and pay for its own operations, protect creditors' rights, assure a stable currency, and provide for the nation's security. Otherwise, "the better kind of people" would soon be inclined to want to replace republican government with "a monarchical form of Government" that would guarantee order, prosperity, and security.[6]

Such concerns prompted important members of the Convention and their allies to believe, as did James Madison, that the present crisis in government was (in historian Charles Hobson's words) "foremost a crisis of republican government."[7] From New York, Virginia's Edward Carrington urged Madison to work for the framing of "a good Republic" and added, "I wish to see that system have a fair experiment."[8] Like Carrington, many of the Framers frequently expressed the sense that the future of the American Republic was at risk. Thus Madison told the convention that "as it was more than probable we were now digesting a plan which in its operation wd. decide forever the fate of Republican Govt we ought not only to provide every guard to liberty that its preservation cd. require, but be equally careful to supply the defects which our own experience had particularly pointed out." Gouverneur Morris of Pennsylvania declared that "he came here as a Representative of America; he flattered himself he came here in some degree as a Representative of the whole human race; for the whole human race will be affected by the proceedings of this Convention." Elbridge Gerry of Massachusetts expressed the same idea when he said that "something must be done, or we shall disappoint not only America but the whole world." Rufus King of Massachusetts stated that "his feelings were more harrowed & his fears more agitated for his Country than he could express, that he conceived this to be the last opportunity of providing for its liberty & happiness: that he could not therefore but repeat his amazement that when a just Governt. founded on a fair representation of the *people* of America was within our reach, we should renounce the blessing, from an attachment to the ideal freedom & importance of *States*."[9]

Citing a growing disillusion with the state governments, James Madison, Edmund Randolph, and Alexander Hamilton urged the Convention to frame a strong, stable Republic.

[James Madison] conceived it to be of great importance that a stable & firm Govt. organized in the republican form should be held out to the people. If this be not done, and the people be left to judge of this species of Govt. by ye operations of the defective systems under which they now live, it is much to be feared the time is not distant when, in universal disgust, they will renounce the blessing which they have purchased at so dear a rate, and be ready for any change that may be proposed to them.

Mr. [Edmund] Randolph was not scrupulous on the point of power. When the salvation of the Republic was at stake, it would be treason to our trust, not to propose what we found necessary. He painted in strong colours, the imbecility of the existing confederacy, & the danger of delaying a substantial reform. . . . A Nat'l Govt. alone, properly constituted, will answer the purpose; and he begged it to be considered that the present is the last moment for establishing one. After this select experiment, the people will yield to despair.

[Alexander Hamilton] concurred with Mr. Madison in thinking we were now to decide for ever the fate of Republican Government; and that if we did not give to that form due stability and wisdom, it would be disgraced & lost among ourselves, disgraced & lost to mankind for ever. He acknowledged himself not to think favorably of Republican Government; but addressed his remarks to those who did think favorably of it, in order to prevail on them to tone their Government as high as possible. He professed himself to be as zealous an advocate for liberty as any man whatever, and he trusted he should be as willing a martyr to it though he differed as to the form in which it was most eligible.[10]

The Framers set out to rebuild their Republic from the bottom up. They wanted to design a centralized Republic that would last for generations, perhaps for centuries. Accordingly, they transferred substantial powers from the state governments to the central government and vested these powers in three distinct branches; sharing certain powers, these branches also had separate powers of legislating, executing, and enforcing law directly on the people. The Framers also sought stability and independence by establishing a Senate with terms of office that would set men above the fate of sudden turnouts at the polls; an executive whose four-year term of office would promote independence and energy; and a federal judiciary whose good behavior terms would assure judicial independence. Above all, the new government would have the power to enforce compliance with its laws by its power to call forth and direct the combined money and manpower of all the United States.

During the period between publication and ratification, other Federalists responded to the Constitution's promise of a more effective Republic that would be energetic yet accountable to the people. Such descriptors as "energy," "efficiency," "vigor," "stability," and "firmness" abound not only in Federalists' public statements but in private correspondence as well. The existence of checks and balances was recognized, as well as officers' accountability through republican elections and impeachment.

> Every thing I hear, everything I know, convinces me, that unless we have as speedily as possible a Firm, Efficient, Federal Constitution established, all must go to Ruin, and Anarchy and Misrule, [and] blast every Hope that so Glorious a Revolution entitled us to Expect. (General Horatio Gates)

> I own I am sanguine upon every Point, and I am persuaded that the new Government while it secures our Liberties & Property by its Benignity, will be as all Governments ought to be a *Terror* to Evil Doers. (Peter Van Schaack)

> My opinion is, It is a Government full of Energy & calculated to promote the happiness of the people. By its wise Oeconomy and complete protection of personal Liberty and enjoyment of such property as may be acquired thro' honest Industry, every man is secured from the lawless & rapacious hands of uplifted royalty, of proud & headstrong Aristocracy, or still more Dangerous and factious Democracy. (Colonel Francis Johnston)

> I am informed that there is a decided majority in the [Pennsylvania] Council and Assembly, of Republicans & Federal men; which promises good to the Continent, to the State, & to the County of Lucerne [Wyoming Valley]; for the best good that can happen to all, is a vigorous, effective, yet safe republican government. (Timothy Pickering)

> I am much pleased with the proceedings of the foederal Convention. The Constitution, which they have proposed, and which, I hope, will be adopted by the United States, is very similar to the Constitution of Great Britain, and not very unlike the Constitution of [New York]; both of which, in my opinion, are admirably constructed for supporting the Government, with becoming Dignity, and while it vests the Authority with Powers adequate to govern with Energy, it at the same time is calculated to secure and preserve inviolate the Rights of the Citizens. (Abraham Bancker)[11]

The Many Benefits of an Energetic Republic

The Constitution, the Framers affirmed in the preamble, had been framed to "secure the Blessings of Liberty to ourselves and our Posterity," which meant establishing a Republic that would endure for ages. Yet an energetic Republic that would last for ages was not their only objective. Other objectives stated in the preamble included "to form a more perfect Union, establish Justice, insure domestic Tranquility, provide for the common defence, [and] promote the general Welfare." Plain logic led the Framers to extrapolate that this reconstituted central government would better carry out and secure these important objectives than would the existing state-centered Confederation.[12]

During the ratification struggle the Federalists publicly warned that unless the Constitution were adopted the Union would either dissolve into its original component units—the states—or have to be reorganized into regional republics.[13] Privately, however, Federalists held that these alternatives would occur only if the Constitution were *not* adopted *and* Congress were *not* invested with an independent financial power. If both the Constitution and Congress's amendment failed, a bankrupt Congress would have to disband: without the common forum of Congress, the states would go their own way, and the Union would be at an end.[14] Some Federalists also worried that even with Congress's amendment, proliferating popular lawlessness and defiance of government would produce the nation's breakup, but this phenomenon was by no means imminent or certain.[15]

Despite the exaggerated nature of their public warnings about imminent disunion, the Federalists' claim that the Constitution would "form a more perfect Union" was more than empty rhetoric. Returning to South Carolina from the Constitutional Convention, delegate Charles Pinckney explained how the proposed central government would better unite the nation and more effectively direct the nation's resources to common national objectives. Although Congress's limited amendment "might for a time avert the inconveniences of a dissolution, yet it was impossible that a government of that sort could long unite this growing and extensive country." Unlike the state-centered Confederation, an efficient central government would enforce federal law uniformly and vigorously throughout the nation and prevent local and private interests from impeding its operations. Equipped with the "compleat direction of the common force and treasure of the empire," the central government could effectively quell any localized resistance that might threaten the nation's integrity, and counter any foreign invasion which under the Confederation required time-consuming agreement and action by the states. Without "strong government" that "collects its powers to a point," Pinckney warned, "the spirit of disunion" would delay and weaken the government's ability to govern consistently or to respond to an invasion. "[This spirit] weakens the consistency of all public measures, so that no extensive scheme of thought can be carried into action, if its accomplishment demands any long continuance of time. It weakens not only the consistency, but the vigour and expedition of all public measures; so that while a divided people are contending about the means of security or defense, an united enemy may surprize and invade them."[16]

The Constitution, the preamble holds, would also "establish Justice," which in the context of 1787 meant in one sense the new government's ability to guarantee just compensation to the public creditors who held the central and state governments' depreciated debt obligations. Authorized to lay and collect imposts, excises, and direct taxes and able to collect them by its own action, this new central government would make fair and certain provision for payment of the interest and principal on the depreciated federal debt and thus ensure federal creditors the money owed them. In another sense, to "establish Justice" meant having a government able to finance itself by taxing in sound money and able to withstand local pressures for paper money finance. Sound money, in turn, would assure fairness in commercial and creditor transactions.

These readings of "establish Justice" were indicated by contemporary responses to the Constitution's publication. Predicting numerous benefits from the Constitution's adoption, Bishop James Madison affirmed: "I doubt not also, but under the new Constitution, national Faith, a great & important Object certainly, will be effectually restored." Conversely, if the Constitution were not established, Federalists feared that the popularity-dependent state governments would diminish the value of public and private debts by allowing payment in depreciated paper currency. Virginia's Charles Lee believed that "unless there be a quiet and peaceable transition from the present American government, into another more powerful and independent of the people, the public debts and even private debts will in my opinion be extinguished by acts of the several Legislatures of the several States."[17]

Invigoration of the state governments' tax and debt operations was also included in how Federalists interpreted *justice*. With a central government able to back them up with force, state courts and state sheriffs could vigorously collect taxes and enforce debt contracts. At the same time, the Constitution's prohibitions against the states making anything but gold and silver legal tender and impairing the validity of contract would prevent the state legislatures from indulging debtors by measures that (in the eyes of propertied Federalists) were tantamount to legalized robbery. In Bishop Madison's words, the new Constitution "will be the Means of giving Stability & Vigour to the State Govts., & prevent those frequent Vacillations from one iniquitous or absurd Scheme to another, wch. has destroyed all Confidence among Individuals." The Portsmouth, Virginia, Federalist merchant James Hunter predicted that ratification would make creditors' actions at law against delinquent debtors more certain to be decided in the creditors' favor by strengthening the courts' backbone: "Our Courts have lately been very remiss [in trying and deciding debt suits], [but] we look forward to the new Constitution for general Reform."[18]

To "insure domestic Tranquility" throughout the United States by an effective "government of laws" was another Federalist purpose.[19] Henry Knox declared that without the central government's thorough reform, "the democracy" would be fatally polluted by the "vile state governments"; the result would be either "the misrule of anarchy or a government of convenience & caprice."[20] Thomas Fitzsimons, a Pennsylvania delegate to the convention, identified the Constitution with the establishment of "order & Good Governmt in America."[21] Rhode Island's Theodore Foster hoped that "the Glorious new Constitution" would "come over us like a Mantle and Shield us from the Dire Evils of anarchy and the Triumphs of Despotic Licentiousness and Shayism."[22] Georgia merchant Joseph Clay predicted that "if the foederal head is once well established and supported, it will tend to support and bring about regularity and good Order in the individual States."[23]

Empowered to raise, finance, and deploy the nation's military forces, the new government would better "provide for the common defence" than would the Confederation. Dependent on the popularity-driven state governments, the Confederation Congress could not mobilize money and men for defense without the unlikely help of the states. If hostile forces occupied a remote border area or part of a state, the state governments not immediately threatened would be loath to risk popularity by raising and contributing money and soldiers to repel the invasion. Connecticut's delegate to the convention Roger Sherman predicted "deplorable circumstances" "if [the Constitution] should not be adopted. . . . Our credit as a nation is sinking. The resources of the country could not be drawn out to defend against a foreign invasion nor the forces of the Union to prevent a civil war."[24]

John Jay, Congress's current secretary for foreign affairs, privately declared while the convention was still in session that if a strong central government were not established, not only would "the Duration of the union . . . become problematical" but U.S. borders and territory would be exposed to raids or invasion by some hostile or predatory foreign nation. By contrast, a strong, well-constructed national government would command money and manpower from the entire United States and thus force foreign nations to respect it. He wrote to John Adams: "For my own part I am convinced that a national Govt. as strong as may be compatible with Liberty is necessary to give us national Security & Respectability."[25]

Affirming that every person "friendly to any stable, energetic government at all" believed the United States to be in a most "deplorable state," nearly incapable of "present defense," and exposed to "some fatal revolution in government," a Federalist delegate to the Maryland ratifying convention warned that if a foreign attack did occur at the present time, it could not be repelled. "Should any enemy from abroad invade any part of these United States, I demand, whether it be capable of repelling the danger by itself, or could reasonably expect assistance from the rest." Tempted by Congress's current bankruptcy and lack of power, Spain,

France, or Great Britain would launch raids on our coast or attempt to seize parts of the mainland. Such raids or invasion "may either be confined to plunder, or aim at partial or an entire conquest. . . . Although, Sir, I will not pretend to predict from what particular quarter an attack will come, I take it for granted, that without a great change in our political management, it soon must come."[26]

Joseph Clay of Georgia emphasized the securing of the nation's Indian frontiers as an important benefit of the new government's energy. Eying Georgia's sputtering border war with the Creeks, Clay held that under the new central government not only would the Creeks be effectively deterred, but unruly trespassing Georgians would be kept off Indian treaty lands by federal power: "Until Congress have the intire management of Indian Affairs, that business will never be well conducted nor amity preserved with the Indians—the back Inhabitants are too many of them of too lawless a disposition to preserve treaties but by compulsion, & less authority than that of the United States will [n]ever effect that."[27]

Including the catchall phrase "promote the general Welfare" in the preamble was probably done to cover benefits either too controversial to specify, too trivial to mention, or not yet discernible. As Bishop James Madison suggested after listing such benefits as the redemption of "national faith," invigoration of the state governments, and habit-forming obedience to law: "These & many other happy Effects, may reasonably be expected from a Govt so wisely conceived in it's general Plan, & wch. must possess Vigour & Energy suff[icien]t to execute the Measures adopted under it."[28]

Although the preamble does not talk about property, the favorable effect of the Constitution on property values was certainly on the Federalists' agenda. By establishing law and order, securing the public debt, and establishing a stable money supply, the new government would protect physical and paper property holdings against destruction by both lawless mobs and the legislation of popularity-conscious state legislatures. Once men of capital felt that property values were safe, they would loan money and expand commercial and manufacturing operations, which in turn would create new demand for the products of farm, forest, and ocean and would mean employment for mechanics, artisans, apprentices, and laborers. Savannah merchant Joseph Clay explicitly linked the security of property with economic stability and a rise in property values. "Under our new constitution we expect property will increase in value & security for it & every thing else valuable in Society will become certain."[29] When Samuel William Johnson, son of Connecticut convention delegate and Columbia College president William Samuel Johnson, weighed whether to return to Connecticut from British Bermuda where he had been practicing law, he regarded the prospects of establishing a law practice or managing the family property in Stratford as much more attractive if the Constitution were ratified: "The result of the Deliberations of the Convention opens new scenes and prospects to every Inhabitant of the United States; should the proposed Constitution be received we should again see energy in Government, and security to the Persons and Property of the Subjects. It might then possibly be in my power to form an eligible establishment on the Continent."[30]

In fact, Federalists anticipated substantial benefits from the Constitution for all kinds of property, including real estate. Samuel Johnson suggested that once the Constitution was ratified, "perhaps real property will soon encrease in value."[31] Georgia merchant Joseph Clay predicted in September 1788 that once peace was made with the Creeks and the new Constitution put into operation, there would be "such a change for the better, as greatly to enhance the price of all our lands." Accordingly, he recommended "the propriety of delaying the sale of the Lands" in upcountry Georgia "at this time."[32] When Federalist newspaper essays and ratification speeches predicted the rise of real estate values, they echoed Federalists' private views.[33] Such prosperity, indicated by the rise in land values, would spread down and out through the entire economy and bring material benefit to rich, middling, and poor.

Many Federalists, including W. S. Johnson's other son, predicted a generalized prosperity from ratification. At the Stratford town meeting that elected his father a delegate to the state ratifying convention, Robert C. Johnson urged the Constitution's adoption in these terms: "Energetic Govt., Peace, opulence & respectibility to America." Federalist parades, staged to celebrate ratification, also conveyed the message that the Constitution would mean prosperity for commerce, manufacturing, and agriculture. Philadelphia's 4 July 1788 parade, for example, included not only merchants but representatives from forty-four crafts and trades and from the Agricultural Society "with ploughs, &c."[34]

At the time the Constitutional Convention was addressing how to constitute the Senate, Pennsylvania delegate James Wilson had advanced the argument that with a stable, independent senate, the central government could do what the Confederation's central government had not been able to do—bring Great Britain to the bargaining table. Wilson did not rest his case on the power of a new central government to retaliate with discriminatory tariff duties in order to force more favorable treatment of U.S. maritime commerce. No commercial treaty with Great Britain had been possible up to now, Wilson contended, because the Confederation central government could not—and the weak, unreliable, popularity-driven state governments would not—enforce treaties with foreign nations on their own soil. Until the United States had a government that could enforce a treaty directly on Americans—including any treaty provision for the recovery by British creditors of their just debts in U.S. courts—no commercial treaty with Great Britain was possible. "The true reason why G. Britain has not yet listened to a commercial treaty with us has been, because she had no confidence in the stability or efficacy of our Government."[35]

In the same vein, the Pennsylvania Federalist merchant-manufacturer Miers Fisher, in a letter to an English correspondent, outlined the Constitution's major structural principles and then described the numerous benefits it would bring the United States and Pennsylvania once the new government was ratified and established. The great defect in the present Confederation, Fisher affirmed, was "the want of a Sovereign head with an energetic Frame of Government for the United States," but once "a stable effective Government" was in effect, he anticipated "before the Expiration of another year to see . . . the Foundation laid of a permanent Treaty with Great Britain."[36]

Republican Government and Human Nature

For many Federalists, the crisis of the Confederation that climaxed in Congress's bankruptcy in 1786–87 had put republican government at risk.[37] Madison made the point explicitly at the federal convention when he observed "that as it was more than probable we were now digesting a plan which in its operation wd. decide forever the fate of Republican Govt," and when he wrote privately that the convention's ability to devise an effective central government "must have a material influence on our destiny, and on that of the cause of republican liberty."[38]

Yet the Framers knew that even a more energetic Republic could not succeed if Americans would not obey its laws willingly and without coercion. The problem was doubly complicated by the perception that the vacillation, weakness, and indulgence of the Confederation state governments had "corrupted" the lower classes into fatal habits of indolence, profusion, disorder, and lawlessness. How could an energetic centralized Republic govern effectively if Americans were "an unvirtuous people"?

The answer is to be found in the behaviorist premises of "faculty psychology" previously described. Faculty psychology as espoused by the Federalists and later by the Whigs presumed that the upper classes were better able than the lower classes to check the "passions." But it also assumed that the lower classes *could* be trained, through upbringing, teaching, and habit, to do the same. Like the muscles of the body, the higher faculties of reason and conscience could be strengthened by exercise and discipline; hence the implicit Federalist-Whig assumption that the lower classes could be brought to order, discipline, productivity, saving, and reason. And hence their further belief that firmly exercised, habit-forming governmental restraints and encouragements (as well as the education, economic, and moral reform programs of their Enlightenment improvement societies) could reverse the degeneration of the lower orders and bring about their discipline, order, and prosperity. If the lower classes could be corrupted by bad government, so could they be improved by good government.[39]

Faculty psychology thus holds the key to the Federalists' hopes that an energetic Republic could be permanent despite their pessimism about the current fallen condition of popular morals and behavior. An energetic central government could train the common people to disciplined living and elicit their voluntary, noncoerced respect for law. By firm punishments and wise rewards, the so-called animal passions could be checked, and the rational passions of reason and conscience exercised. In John Jay's phrase, by being at once "a Terror to evil Doers" and a "Support and Encouragemt to those who do well,"[40] the new central government could coax forth, develop, and make a matter of habit the morals and behaviors necessary for law-abiding, productive citizenship.

Thus Bishop James Madison held that the new government's "Vigour & Energy" "will create the Habit of Obedience to the Laws, & give them that Energy wch is unquestionably essential to a free Govt."[41] The New York Federalist Ebenezer Hazard predicted that when ratification of the Constitution "takes place, we may hope for a Reformation of manners, & that wholesome Laws will restrain the Passions of [the] unprincipled & protect Reputation as well as Property."[42] In May 1788 the Philadelphia Federalist Benjamin Rush invoked a scriptural image when he predicted that adoption of the Constitution would bring Americans safely through "the present wilderness of anarchy and vice" into a promised land of "order, peace & happiness." Earlier Rush had held that the new government not only "establishes justice, ensures order, secures property, and protects from every species of violence" but "encourages virtue."[43] The expected moral and behavioral improvement the new central government would foster prompted the Boston editors of *Bickerstaff's Boston Alamanack, or, The Federal Calendar* to announce their 1788 edition with the caption: "For the Year of our REDEMPTION, 1788."[44] The hope that wise laws energetically enforced by the new central government would invigorate the entire body politic and restore it to health (meaning, I think, greater personal exertion, labor, and obedience to law) prompted South Carolina's Edward Rutledge to invoke a biological metaphor: "There must be a Centre of Union thro' which, & from which, the pure blood of the States must flow, or the Body in general will languish, & the Limbs fall to decay."[45]

Even the often cynical Gouverneur Morris, who chaired the convention committee that drafted the Constitution and who was the document's principal stylist, could anticipate beneficial behavioral changes once the new government was set in motion. Calling on George Washington to let himself become the first president, Morris cited the general's "cool steady Temper" as indispensable "to give a firm and manly Tone to the new Government." Then Morris likened Washington to the driver of a chariot and the people of the states to unruly horses. "The Exercise of Authority depends on personal Character; and the Whip and Reins by which an able Charioteer governs unruly steeds will only hurl the unskillful Presumer with more speedy & headlong Violence to the Earth. The Horses once trained may be managed by a Woman or a Child: not so when they first feel the bit."[46]

Federalists thus hoped that once the Constitution's central government took over from the popular state governments, Americans' morals and behavior would be greatly, and, Federalists hoped, permanently improved. Not only would this energetic central government set bounds to the passions and appetites by deterring the lawless, it would encourage reason to regulate behavior which, through exercise and repetition, would bring permanent habits that would make men productive, peaceful and happy. Wise, property-protecting legislation by the central government would appeal to reason and thus prompt citizens to honest, diligent, orderly, and lawful behavior; steady, vigorous, stable operation by the central government would then make these behaviors a matter of permanent and lasting habit.[47] Despite its paternalistic stance and its bourgeois economic morality, this Federalist behaviorism—this moral and social engineering—represents, like the Constitution itself, the Federalists' moderate Enlightenment belief in human improvement.

Such improvement, such self-discipline, would redeem the Republic and assure its permanence.

★ 16 ★

THE CONSTITUTION PREVAILS

THE PRECEDING chapters place the breakdown of taxation by the state governments at the center of the story of the Constitution's genesis. The retreats of the state governments into paper money and other relief measures convinced upper-class elites that the Confederation system could not protect property rights, assure a stable currency, finance Congress, or provide for national defense. Presuming republican government to be at risk, the Framers designed a national authority capable of paying its own expenses, stabilizing the currency, financing the domestic and foreign debt, regulating commerce, and raising adequate military and naval forces. Simultaneously, the states were forbidden to issue paper money, make anything but gold and silver legal tender, impair contracts, or tax imports. Thus, state taxation holds the key to the Framers' decision to reconstitute the Republic rather than amend the Articles of Confederation, when amendment would have been the simpler solution.

Analysis of the inability of the states to tax in specie and their retreats into tax reliefs also explains the Federalist-Antifederalist division over the Constitution. From the Federalist viewpoint, the state governments' previous enactment of tax and debt reliefs had been dishonest, demoralizing, and harmful to commercial interests. Hence Federalist elites supported the Constitution as promising a central government that could govern effectively, stand up to popular pressure, and if necessary use force to execute its laws. But states' rights Antifederalists wanted government in the United States kept decentralized and responsive. Invested with a federal impost, Congress could begin to raise revenue that would enable it to finance the federal debt, strengthen the nation's armed forces, and begin to solve the Confederation's diplomatic problems, while state governments retained the balance of power over direct taxation, currency, and the armed forces.

At the time of the Constitution's ratification, only half or fewer of the nation's voters had favored the Constitution, and many Antifederalists in every state had opposed its adoption.[1] Yet within two years after its ratification, the Constitution had won over most of its former opponents and gained substantial majority support within all classes.

Prosperity and the End of Antifederalism

Historians offer several explanations to account for the rapid demise of Antifederalism.[2] The Antifederalists' tactical decision to pursue their objectives by constitutional amendment helps explain the decline of their active opposition.[3] Madison's successful promotion of the Bill of Rights reconciled opposition moderates and blunted the Antifederalists' public case against the Constitution.[4] Once the Constitution became a fait accompli, Antifederalists embraced it as a settled standard against which they could detect expected abuses and violations; as such, they became "constitutional literalists."[5] A surge in agricultural prices and the Federalists' astute management of federal tax policy up to the whiskey excise reduced the salience of the tax issue and helped reconcile rural America.

The well-attended celebrations that greeted the Constitution's ratification in every major city including Boston, New York, Philadelphia, Baltimore, and Charleston bespeak the nearly unanimous support for the Constitution by commercial, urban America.[6] By restoring confidence in government's ability to protect money values and private credit, the federal Constitution provided a powerful impulse to commercial interchange and enterprise. At the same time, crop failures in Europe, the French Revolution, and the comparatively low price of U.S. produce on the world market produced a demand for U.S. food exports abroad that boosted prices and brought farmers prosperity.[7]

Without the confidence that the Constitution inspired, it seems unlikely that the credit and investment necessary to sustain this recovery would have materialized. Merchant letters show the pivotal importance of the Constitution in restoring business confidence. In April 1788 Philadelphia merchant Levi Hollingsworth recorded: "Great quantities of wheat are shipping off for Portugal and flour for Spain and I flatter myself that the Federal government taking place a new spring will be given to trade and agriculture."[8] Anticipating increased domestic demand from the revival of trade, U.S. merchants sent orders to English and Irish suppliers for fabrics, wearing apparel, and other dry goods; for some, these were the first such orders since the Revolution.[9] Trade was further encouraged by the revival of private credit. Early in 1787 the New York City wholesale firm of Hill & Ogden described credit sales to retailers and shopkeepers as "very nearly at an End," but by November 1788 they were offering shopkeepers six-months' credit.[10] Working together, exports brought bills of exchange and specie into the country and confidence encouraged merchants and monied men to open their purses to borrowers and new enterprise.[11] By May 1790 the Philadelphia merchant Clement Biddle was writing optimistically: "The great quantity of our produce exported, which was last year beyond anything ever known before or since the war in quantity besides the addition in price has also thrown a greater plenty of money into circulation."[12]

The Constitution's impact on the money markets of Europe was equally favorable. Formerly doubtful of the capacity of Congress or the states to keep their promises, European investors now scrambled to purchase U.S. public debt certificates. In 1789 alone, Dutch bankers sold five large blocks of the certificates in the Amsterdam market, and the vigorous competition of European and American investors pushed prices upwards toward par well before Alexander Hamilton unveiled his funding program.[13] The central government was able for the first time to borrow in the Amsterdam and Antwerp money markets successfully on favorable terms. These transactions brought additional quantities of capital in the form of bills and specie into the U.S. economy.[14] As early as January 1790 Georgia member of congress Abraham Baldwin noted that the Constitution and the new prosperity were closely linked in people's minds: "People say the times are good and praise the new government."[15]

One important result of the new prosperity was tax relief for farmers and landowners. As money and credit became abundant and farm prices rose, taxes became easier to pay. In Massachusetts, treasury records show, tax officials were able to reduce dramatically the huge backlog of unpaid back taxes from £497,474 on 1 October 1787 to £33,847 on 1 May 1790; by contrast with 1786, these collections proceeded without incident.[16] Similarly, New York's government reported the reduction of back taxes levied since 1785 but not yet paid.[17] This trend helped remove the tax issue from the stage of state politics. By 1790, studies of Massachusetts and Virginia indicate, the tax and debt issues of the mid-1780s were replaced by other issues and alignments.[18] Thus the Constitution brought tax relief to rural America.

Hamiltonian Finance and the Whiskey Rebellion

Hamiltonian fiscal and monetary measures also contributed to the prosperity that made the Constitution accepted. Yet the Federalists relied almost entirely on indirect federal impost revenues until the added costs of Hamiltonian funding required selected internal excises. Does this circumstance undermine the thesis that a central government strong and stable enough to tax was the Federalists' primary objective in framing the Constitution?

The Constitution had outlined a framework of centralized government, but much basic legislation by the First Federal Congress was required before the new government could function. Thus the First Congress, which began its sessions in Federal Hall, New York City, in April 1789, provided for the departments of state, treasury, war, and the attorney general, legislated a federal judiciary, and passed the first federal tax measure, the revenue act of 1789. "For the support of Government, for the discharging the Debts of the U.S. and the encouragement and protection of Manufactures," it taxed imported goods and foreign tonnage at waterside. Yet important financial issues remained to be resolved when Secretary of the Treasury Alexander Hamilton took office the following September.[19]

The next two years (1790–91) saw the Federalists enact Hamilton's measures for refinancing the federal domestic and foreign debt, assuming and financing the state debts, establishing a central bank, and fostering domestic manufactures. The funding-assumption act of August 1790 laid the groundwork for refinancing of federal carry-over debt obligations and for assuming responsibility for the payment of past and present public debts of the individual states. By assuming the state debts, the federal government increased its domestic and foreign debt obligations to more than $70 million—a sum that could not be serviced by available tax resources. Accordingly, Hamilton made domestic and foreign loans, bolstered by federal impost and excise taxes, the cornerstone of his program. New long-term federal certificates paying lower interest were offered in exchange for current federal and state debt certificates. The foreign debt was to be refinanced through loans in Amsterdam. A system for the gradual payoff of the federal debt was established, including a sinking fund.[20] Yet the market value of both federal and state debts had greatly depreciated during the tax-deficient 1780s, and much of the debt had been purchased by monied investors at one-fifth to one-tenth its value. The Federalist majority overrode objections that by funding these debts at full nominal value, the government was penalizing the original holders who had sold their certificates to speculators at far less than face value.

The other major Hamilton-inspired measure—the First Bank of the United States—was chartered by Congress in 1791. A semipublic bank financed by public and private capital, managed by private bankers, and authorized to issue bank notes as currency, it would increase the nation's stock of reliable money and would provide money on credit for the business community and for the new government. Subsequently, Hamilton proposed protective duties, bounties, and other encouragements for a broad range of manufacturing industries, but Congress enacted only those relating to munitions, metal, and other defense-related concerns.[21]

Federal funding at full face value and federal assumption of state debts was not the only way the federal and state debts could have been financed. As E. James Ferguson has observed, the federal debt alone could have been managed out of current income from the 1789 revenue act, leaving the states responsible for their own debts. The federal and state debts could also have been liquidated either by federal taxation payable in debt certificates or by the exchange of debt certificates for federally owned public lands. The government could also have discriminated between original holders and current holders by funding current holders at the highest market price commanded by their certificates and paying original holders the difference between the highest market value and the face value.[22]

Hamilton's choice was guided by his desire to consolidate support behind the new government within the financial and business community and to pave the way for establishing the federal government's power over internal taxation. The former was achieved by committing the new central government to the full payment of federal and state debts, a policy that Hamilton expected would bind both federal and state public debt holders to the central government by ties of economic interest and by the prosperity that came from creating new capital and enhancing confidence. The latter was advanced by the assumption of the state debts, which would "leave the States under as little necessity as possible of exercising the power of taxation."[23] Laying a federal claim to domestic taxation, Hamilton proposed not only increases in federal duties at waterside but new taxes on carriage wheels, lawyers' licenses, wine and spirits sales, and domestically distilled spirits.

But why not tax lands and other forms of property as the Confederation states had done, or polls, windows, and hearths as the Federalists would later do during the naval war with France (1798–1800)? Direct federal taxes of this kind, Hamilton and other Federalists believed, would evoke resistance and revolt such as had disrupted state tax collection during the mid-1780s. Not until money became more available and Americans became more disciplined and industrious would direct taxation be possible. At the Constitutional Convention during debate over federal export taxes, Gouverneur Morris had warned: "For a long time the people of America will not have money to pay direct taxes. Seize and sell their effects and you push them into Revolts."[24] In July 1788, well before the new government was organized, Hamilton predicted that the federal debt would be funded, but not by direct taxes: "The fund will be sought for in indirect taxation; as for a number of years, and except in time of war, direct taxes would be an impolitic measure." More than a year later, in a letter to James Madison, then at Montpelier, Hamilton again betrayed keen awareness of how explosive the tax issue was. Would Madison send him advice on fiscal measures, including debt funding and taxes, that would be the agenda at Congress's next session? His chief perplexity, Hamilton confessed, was what taxes would be politically acceptable: "The Question is very much What further taxes will be *least* unpopular."[25]

Madison offered no advice on the public debt except to urge its rapid liquidation. More surprising was Madison's recommendation that the debt be extinguished through a broad program of federal taxes including not only increased duties on imported spirits at waterside, but "an excise on home distilleries," "a stamp tax" on federal court proceedings, and "a land tax." The land tax, Madison argued, would be simple, certain, fair, and cheap to administer and would foreclose prior action by the states: "It may be well also for the General Govt. to espouse this object before a preoccupancy by the States becomes an impediment."[26]

Stephen Higginson, the wealthy Federalist Boston merchant, gave Hamilton different advice. Warning that public debt finance was a political mine field, Higginson held that funding must be handled "without hazarding the peace of Society, or endangering Government." In order to avoid heavy direct taxes, Higginson proposed funding the federal debt at a lower rate of interest than the existing debt, paying the principal over an extended period, and raising the money from imposts and excises only: "The Idea of a sinking fund to pay off the Debt, by slow degrees, will be very popular; & such a resort may, in the infancy of Our government, be essential to its safety." Indeed, he was certain that the debt could not be financed by direct federal taxes on property. "I have no Idea, that any thing can be drawn from the States by requisition, or direct taxes. Impost & Excises are the only Sources that can be relied upon; & those you must have exclusively to make the most of them."[27]

As they developed, Hamilton's financial policies paralleled Higginson's rather than Madison's ideas. And as his own letters suggest, Hamilton believed that money must be more available, the new government's authority more firmly settled, and the people have better habits of obedience and industriousness before the central government could safely levy direct taxes on property.[28]

The Whiskey Rebellion also illustrates the Federalists' cautious, incremental approach to taxes. In part, the whiskey excise seemed necessary because means had to be found to finance a federal debt enlarged by assumption of the state debts. Probably also Hamilton, an advocate of the central government's expanded powers, wanted to assert its direct tax power. Justifying the proposed excise tax on whiskey, Hamilton cited those who had recommended an early excise on the grounds that it was "well to lay hold of so valuable a resource of revenue before it was generally preoccupied by the State Governments," and that "the authority of the National Government should be visible in some branch of internal Revenue; lest a total non-exercise of it should beget an impression that it was never to be exercised & next that it ought not to be exercised."[29] Because the whiskey excise affected only a small proportion of the nation's rural population, falling mainly on backcountry small farmers who made whiskey and backcountry artisans and laborers who consumed it,[30] Hamilton thought it could be effectively enforced.

Enacted in 1791, the whiskey excise inspired anger among small backcountry distillers and consumers because continuing cash deficiencies made it difficult to pay, because the law favored wealthy distillers, and because the law indirectly put cash in the pockets of investors in the public debt, many of whom were wealthy easterners. Defiance quickly spread through western Pennsylvania, Maryland, Virginia, the Carolinas, and all of Kentucky; in western Pennsylvania, moreover, small distillers and landless consumers brutalized federal excise officers and burned and ransacked their dwellings. Hamilton then urged coercion, but President Washington, reluctant to coerce Americans of any class or condition, waited nearly two years before doing so. By mid-1794 defiance had become so flagrant in western Pennsylvania that the president felt obliged to use force. His decision was also guided by other challenges to the government's authority in Georgia and Kentucky, and by his need to strengthen the government's hand in the coming Jay negotiations with Great Britain over neutral rights and other issues.[31] Calling on the states for militia, Washington marched 12,900 troops into western Pennsylvania but found that the disorganized rebels had either fled or fallen into line. By his low-key proclamations, his patience, and his pardon of those convicted of breaking the law, the president effectively conveyed an image of moderation.[32] Many on the frontier remained disaffected, however. In the backcountry the Federalists' use of armed force "helped to create a constituency for the Jeffersonian-Republican challenge to their reign."[33]

Nevertheless, by building business confidence, credit, and new active capital, Hamilton's fiscal and monetary measures helped advance the country's prosperity and, along with prosperity, acceptance of the Constitution.[34] At the same time the Federalists' deliberate avoidance of direct taxation during the early 1790s furthered the central government's acceptance. Finally, Washington's moderate but decisive use of federal coercion against the whiskey rebels instilled confidence in the government among the middle and upper classes if not among the frontier rural poor.[35]

The Rise of the Republican Opposition Party

The rise of the Jeffersonian Republican party in opposition to the Federalist administrations of George Washington and John Adams reflects the commitment of national and state leaders to the new Constitution as well as the demise of the tax issue. Historians dispute the nature and origins of the first U.S. party system, but most would agree that the first political parties developed from the top down through the polarization that resulted from "the cumulative effect of several issues" on politics at the federal capital.[36] Many historians identify Hamilton's financial measures and early Federalist foreign policy as having a highly divisive effect on federal legislative and executive personnel during the early and mid-1790s.[37] These measures raised difficult issues of fairness, constitutionality, preferential treatment, morality, and the very independence, security, and future of the Republic. When the depredations of Great Britain and France on U.S. merchant ships and seamen that began in 1793 forced emergency policy decisions on the Washington administration, including ratification of the disappointing half-a-loaf Jay Treaty with Britain in 1796, the process took a crucial turn. Increasingly the issues began to be fought out publicly, and federal, state, and local elections were contested with party labels, tickets, rallies, resolutions, and other election paraphernalia.

The Republican party thus had its origin in issues of finance and foreign policy that differed markedly from those of the 1780s, when the central issue had been whether the heavy specie taxes levied by the states for themselves and Congress could be paid by the rural classes. With the generalized prosperity that began in 1789 and the federal government's assumption of state debts and use of the federal impost as the main means of finance, taxation, with the exception of the whiskey excise, became a nonissue. In the debate over the funding system, the paramount question was not taxation as such but whether the windfall profits that befell commercial investors and speculators from funding were fair, healthy, or safe in a republican order.

Indeed, the emergent Republican opposition party had as its central purpose the permanent securing of the new government. By providing a peaceful, legal channel through which opposition to Federalist domestic and foreign policies could be mobilized and brought to bear peacefully and constitutionally through elections, Jeffersonian Republicans used party as an alternative to political violence. The party builders Jefferson, Madison, and their colleagues were in fact opposed to parties and did not envision the Republican party as permanent; rather, they saw it as an emergency measure that would save the new republican central government from subversion by Federalist crypto-monarchists.[38] They assiduously urged moderation, patience, and legal methods on their followers as they guided their party operations.[39] The overwhelming support of so many former states' rights Antifederalists for the new Republican party also argues that these former adversaries of the federal Constitution had made their peace with the new central government and would work within the system. A return to the state-centered Confederation system was not on their agenda.

Coming to Terms with the Federalists

The rapid recovery of commerce, the augmentation of money in circulation, and the credit extended to commercial and rural borrowers demonstrated the Federalists' understanding of the close link between business confidence and economic prosperity. The nation's propertied and business classes had become deeply hostile to the changeable state governments after the latter voted relief measures. Alarmed by these paper money and other reliefs, these classes had hoarded specie coin, refused credit, and curtailed investments that would have helped economic recovery. But after ratification of the Constitution, commercial confidence returned, credit expanded, foreign investment increased, and domestic and foreign commerce flourished. Establishment of a central government able to enforce its own laws, resist demands for paper money, and assure a hospitable economic environment greatly boosted the confidence of the domestic and foreign business and investment communities. Because many Federalist Framers belonged to or had close ties with the business class themselves, they saw how the Constitution would generate business optimism that in turn would produce an overall prosperity.

On the other hand, the Federalists' understanding of the psychology of the rural citizenry was badly flawed. During the 1780s the same wealthy elites who became the driving force behind the Constitution had held an unvirtuous people to be personally culpable for the rural protests and violence that shook the state governments and produced paper money and other legislative reliefs. Removed from the realities of a slumping rural economy, they did not understand the burden that heavy state taxes and systemic adversity imposed on the nation's small farmers. As I have consistently argued, they believed that popular indolence and extravagance had caused taxation to break down. Because, in their view, the state governments were too weak and changeable to command respect and collect taxes, they espoused a stronger, more stable central government that could require obedience to the law.

Yet despite their misreading of this lower-class resistance, the Framers' response to the fiscal breakdown of the Confederation System was resourceful, farseeing, and principled. Through the Constitution, the Framers created a strong central government that addressed the fiscal and monetary problems of the 1780s more effectively than limited amendment of the Articles. Not only did this reconstituted central government prove a better guarantor of national union, national defense, and internal order than its predecessor, but the confidence it elicited helped spur an economic revival that saw the disruptive fiscal and monetary issues of the mid-eighties disappear. By remaking the Republic in order to redeem the Republic, the Framers established a structure of central government that amply realized the purposes of its creation.

Equally important was the Framers' fidelity to the major principles of the American Revolution. Despite disenchantment with the behavior of the popular classes, they remained faithful to the principles of republican elections, constitutionalism, restraints on power, and constitutional flexibility. Even as they framed a central government with greater energy, power, and independence, they built on a foundation of republican accountability. Nor did they neglect the restraints of a written constitution and of interior checks and balances or fail to provide for changes in the Constitution by amendment and interpretation. By framing an energetic, stable, centralized government and by incorporating restraints against abuse and mechanisms for change, the Framers created a Republic, firm but flexible, that would last for ages.

Appendixes

APPENDIX I

EARLY POSTWAR FISCAL MEASURES: MASSACHUSETTS, RHODE ISLAND, PENNSYLVANIA, AND SOUTH CAROLINA

Massachusetts

Numbers in brackets [ ] refer to the Evans number in the Early American Imprint Collection. The legislation may also be found in the *Acts and Laws of Massachusetts* and in the Early State Record Collection (Microform Reading Room, Library of Congress).

DIRECT TAXES (PROPERTY AND POLL)

1. 1780 Continental tax: £5,601,025 payable in Continental currency [16838]
2. April 1780 gold and silver tax: £72,000 payable in specie for interest on army notes and new state bills of credit [16839]
3. May 1781 specie tax: £207,862 payable in specie for "public charges" [17224]
4. October 1781 specie tax: £303,634 payable in specie for "public charges" [17225]
5. 1782 Continental Tax No. 1: £200,000 payable in beef, Morris's notes, or Bank of North America notes [44217]
6. 1782 Continental Tax No. 2: £200,000 payable in Morris's notes or Bank of North America notes [17597]
7. 1783 State Tax No. 3: £200,000 payable in any money for state purposes [19423]
8. 1784 State Tax No. 4: £140,000 payable in army notes [18585]
9. March 1786 State and Continental Tax No. 5: £300,439 payable one-third in specie, one-third in army notes, one-third in federal indents. The act appropriated £145,000 for the September 1785 congressional requisition; £25,786 for state government expenses; £29,000 for in-

terest on state consolidated notes; £100,000 for redeeming army notes; and £11,001 for salaries of members of the general court (*Massachusetts Acts and Laws* 1786, 368–91).

The general court thus earmarked sizable sums of tax monies for federal requisitions. In June 1782 the general court passed a resolve "for granting & paying to the hon. James Lovell Esqr Receiver of the Continental Taxes the sum of two hundred thousand pounds specie out of the public Treasury being the sum granted by the General Court to the United States" (Massachusetts House Journal, 1782, 139). In his message of 24 October 1785, Governor James Bowdoin said that the state had made "some payments" of money to Congress, but that it still owed the federal treasury $931,615.

INDIRECT TAXES (IMPOST AND EXCISE)
AND THE FUNDED DEBT

1. The Massachusetts government began funding the revolutionary debt in January 1781. At that time it pledged payment of the principal and interest on its wartime obligations and set up machinery for "liquidation" and "consolidation" by which debts were to be translated into their specie equivalent according to a depreciation table. Subsequent legislation offered holders of the debt new interest-bearing consolidated notes in exchange for their old debt securities. See *Massachusetts Acts and Laws*, 1781, 8–10, 63–64.

2. State imposts and excises were levied as early as 1781 to pay the annual interest on the state's public debt (see Act of 1 November 1781 "for the Purpose of paying the Interest on Government Securities"). In 1785 Governor Bowdoin estimated the state's funded debt at £1,468,554 and the annual interest on this debt at £88,112. Income from the excise-impost fund was £57,353 (June 1784–June 1785) and from a 1 percent auctioneer's tax £1,173. The balance was to be raised from direct taxes (see March 1786 tax act). The impost taxed imported wines, spirits, tobacco, sugar, tea, cocoa, snuff, and so forth at specified rates and placed a 5 percent duty on all other foreign imports. The domestic excise taxed the sale of wines, spirits, rum, snuff, and other luxury items and taxed domestic manufactures such as rum, snuff, clocks, loaf sugar, cider. No duties were to be collected on goods imported into the state for reexport to another state or abroad. A direct tax was also levied annually on taverns, innholders, and sellers of liquor, and a heavy annual tax was placed on coaches, chariots, and other riding vehicles. See *Massachusetts Acts and Laws*, 1782, 196–205.

3. A Stamp Act passed in March 1785 to supply further revenue. The

act taxed legal instruments, newspapers, almanacs, and business paper. The act of July 1785 repealed the tax on newspapers and almanacs but taxed newspaper advertisements and the commissions of officeholders (£12 for a sheriff's commission) (*Massachusetts Acts and Laws*, 275–79, 303–6).

Rhode Island

References in brackets [ ] are to Rhode Island *Session Laws*, year, session, and page numbers and to the state treasurer's book labeled "Taxes Ft-1 1779–1787," Rhode Island State Archives (TB). Consult Clifford K. Shipton and James E. Mooney, *National Index of American Imprints through 1800: The Short-title Evans* (Worcester, Mass.: The American Antiquarian Society, 1969), for Evans numbers in the Early American Imprints Collection.

DIRECT TAXES (POLL AND PROPERTY)

1. February 1780 Continental tax: £180,000 payable in old Continental bills [TB]
2. May 1780 Continental tax: £180,999 payable in old Continental bills [TB]
3. May 1780 state tax: £180,000 payable in old Continental bills [TB]
4. July 1780 state tax: £10,000 payable in specie or new emission bills [July 1780, p. 35]
5. July 1780 Continental tax: £400,000 payable in old Continental bills [July 1780, pp. 46–51]
6. November 1780 state tax: £1,000,000 payable in old Continental bills [TB]
7. November 1780 state tax: £16,000 payable in specie [TB]
8. May 1781 state tax: £20,000 payable in specie [May 1781, pp. 37-40]
9. May 1781 state tax: £6,000 payable in new emission money [TB]
10. January 1782 state tax: £12,000 payable in specie [January 1782, pp. 43–45]
11. January 1782 Continental tax: £6,000 payable in specie for Congress [January 1782, pp. 46–48]
12. February 1782 Continental tax: £6,000 payable in specie for Congress [TB]
13. June 1782 Continental tax: £12,000 payable in specie [June 1782, pp. 13–15]
14. June 1783 state and Continental tax: £20,000 payable in specie;

£8,640 earmarked for congressional requisition of September 1782 [June 1783, pp. 18–21]

15. June 1784 state and Continental tax: £20,000 payable in specie; £12,147 earmarked for congressional requisition of April 1784 [June 1784, pp. 34–36]

16. August 1785 state and Continental tax: £20,000 payable in specie [August 1785, pp. 15–17]; at its October session the assembly directed that the entire proceeds be used to pay the state's quota of the September 1785 requisition. The tax was made payable either in gold or silver or federal loan office indents and teaming certificates.

INDIRECT TAXES (IMPOST AND EXCISE) AND THE FUNDED DEBT

1. At its June 1782 session, the Rhode Island legislature began funding the state debt. A procedure was established for determining specie equivalents and offering interest-bearing 6 percent consolidated notes in exchange [June 1782, p. 20; October 1782, p. 4; November 1782, pp. 7–8]. Interest on the debt was to be paid with the money collected from state impost and excise taxes.

2. The state impost was considered one of the state's most dependable income-producing sources; to maximize its yield, the assembly in 1782 unanimously rejected the proposed 5 percent federal impost. At its February 1785 session the assembly reversed itself and approved legislation that granted Congress funds consisting of a 5 percent impost plus a direct tax of one dollar on adult polls, horses, and every 100 acres of land [February 1785, pp. 23–25].

The state impost began as an across-the-board 2 percent on all imported goods of foreign manufacture or growth; later, the rates were raised to 2.5 percent and on certain selected items as high as 25 percent [June 1783, pp. 26–31; June 1784, p. 17; June 1785, pp. 18–19]. Rhode Island provided that foreign goods imported from another state that had already paid a 2 percent duty were exempt from the impost. State excise taxes were also collected on the domestic sale of spirits [November 1780, p. 15].

Pennsylvania

References in brackets [ ] are to James T. Mitchell and Henry Flanders, compilers, *The Statutes at Large of Pennsylvania from 1682 to 1801* (Harrisburg, 1896–1915) and to Pennsylvania *Session Laws*, found in the Early American Imprints Collection and the Early State Records Collection

(Library of Congress). Consult Shipton and Mooney, *Short-Title Evans*, for Evans numbers in the Early American Imprint Collection.

DIRECT TAXES (PROPERTY AND POLL)

1. 1780–86 Continental taxes: In December 1780 the assembly provided for an annual tax of £93,640.10 for six years to retire depreciated Continental currency currently in the state ("A Supplement to an Act entitled 'An Act for Funding and Redeeming the Bills of Credit of the USA and for Providing Means to bring the Present War to a Happy Conclusion,'" 19 December 1780) [*Statutes at Large*, 10:238–43].

2. 1781 state tax: An act of 7 April 1781 provided for a tax of £80,000 payable in newly issued state bills of credit. The bills of credit, issued to finance state war expenditures and as a medium of commerce, totaled £500,000 in legal tender state paper. The money was to be redeemed in stages by the sale of state public lands and the £80,000 tax ("An Act for Emitting the Sum of £500,000 in Bills of Credit, for the Support of the Army and for Establishing a Fund for the Redemption thereof," 7 April 1781) [*Statutes at Large*, 10:301–8].

3. 1781 Continental tax: The act provided that £200,000 in specie taxes for Congress be levied but provided that persons who had taken the oath of loyalty to the state could pay up to one-half their tax bill in the new state bills of credit ("An Act to Raise Effective Supplies for 1781," 21 June 1781) [*Statutes at Large*, 10:326–36].

4. 1782 Continental tax: The act levied £420,297.15 in specie taxes for Congress ("An Act to Raise Effective Supplies for the Year 1782," 27 March 1782) [*Statutes at Large*, 10:385–400].

5. 1783 Continental tax: £225,000 payable in specie was levied. The act also provided for the printing and issue of $300,000 in state paper notes payable as one-year's interest to Pennsylvanians holding federal debt certificates. Any taxpayer could pay up to one-half his or her tax bill in these state notes ("An Act for Providing the Quota of the Federal Supplies for 1783, and for the Relief of the Citizens of this State who have become Creditors of the USA by loans of money or other modes of furnishing public supplies," 21 March 1783) [*Statutes at Large*, 11:81–91].

INDIRECT TAXES (IMPOST AND EXCISE) AND THE FUNDED DEBT

1. State imposts, state excises, and the proceeds from the sale of state land carried most of the state's other costs. The state impost taxed imported

wines, liquors, tea, coffee, and sugar at fixed rates, and levied a 2 percent (eventually 3.5 percent) ad valorem duty on all other imported
articles or raw materials of foreign origin. No duty was to be collected
on any goods produced or manufactured by any of the United States
[*Statutes at Large*, 10:252–58, 11:53–63, 263–65; *Session Laws*, October 1782]. In January 1783 the assembly enacted new taxes on billiard tables (£15), coaches (£7.10), chaises (£4), and covered wagons
(£3) and required further that prothonotaries pay out of their office
fees 5s7p for every writ issued [*Statutes at Large*, 11:65–68].

2. Limited debt funding: By contrast with most other states, no funding
system was established until the Constitutionalists took over the assembly in October 1784. Because speculators were buying up debt certificates from veterans at depreciated prices, state leaders probably
feared a political backlash from a funding system that political adversaries could use to tar them with special favoritism to speculators. The
limited funding law (1783) bypassed speculators and earmarked revenue from the state excise to pay the annual interest due on pay certificates held by soldiers and officers of the Pennsylvania Line if in the
possession of the original holder. Holders of interest-paying certificates purchased from their original soldier owners could not qualify
("An Act to Appropriate Certain Moneys Arising from the Excise
for the Payment of the Annual Interest due on the Unalienated Certificates therein mentioned," 21 March 1783 [*Statutes at Large*, 11:
100–101]). See also John Dickinson to Anthony Wayne, 1 January
1783, Wayne Ms, HSP; Wayne to Major Fishbourne, 5 November
1784, Wayne Ms, Clements.

Payment of the annual interest due on other state debts was made
from such monies as came into the state treasury from the state impost and was paid out on application by State Treasurer David Rittenhouse at the order of the Supreme Executive Council [*Statutes at
Large*, 10:252–58].

South Carolina

References within brackets [ ] refer to the Evans number in the Early
American Imprints Collection. The legislation may be found in the *Acts
and Ordinances of the General Assembly of the State of South Carolina, Passed
in the Years 1783, 1784, and 1785*, Early American Imprints Collection
and Early State Record Collection (Library of Congress).

DIRECT TAXES (PROPERTY AND SLAVES)

1. March 1783 state tax: £54,254 (estimated) payable entirely in specie "for the Use and Service" of the state [Evans 18190]. As the act itself specified (see the state budget figures printed as part of the text), £45,600 of this first state budget of £87,506 (52 percent) was earmarked for Congress. The figure £54,254 is an estimate and derives from my assumption that 62 percent of the total state budget had to come from direct taxes and 38 percent from the impost, sale of lands, tax on auction sales, and other income sources. The state impost was earmarked to help pay the £45,600 set aside for Congress but the balance (about £30,000) was to be paid from direct tax revenues (estimated annual impost revenue = £15,000).

2. March 1784 tax act: £79,105 (estimated) to be paid in specie or discounted by paper interest "indents" payable as one year's interest on interest-bearing state debt indents [18789]. By 1784, the state budget (again printed with the law's text) had increased to £127,589, largely owing to the increase in the state's public debt. The budget itemized interest on the state public debt at £72,892. Upon application of a holder of a consolidated state debt indent, the treasury commissioner was to pay out "interest indents" equal to a year's interest. Yet the law only allowed holders of debt notes to pay up to the equivalent of one year's interest in this paper as taxes. Thus non-holders had to pay in specie or purchase state debt certificates that would qualify them to pay interest indents for taxes. Correspondingly, the money earmarked for Congress in the 1784 state budget was reduced to £35,441, or 28 percent of the total.

3. March 1785 tax act: £71,125 (estimated) payable in specie or in special state interest indents [19250]. This law allowed payment in either specie or interest indents and placed no restriction on either the amount or the payer. The budget of 1785 provided for no requisition money for Congress. In 1785 a Ways and Means Committee report claimed that the state had overpaid the receiver of Continental taxes on previous federal requisitions, but this seems intended more to justify reallocating scarce tax revenues to state purposes than to be a genuine explanation.

   (Method: the amounts to be raised by direct taxes are estimates and depend on an assumption that 62 percent of each annual budget was to come from direct taxes, and 38 percent from the impost and other sources, the proportions indicated in the Second Report of Committee of Ways and Means, 15 February 1786, where estimated returns from the impost, slave duty, vendue duty, land sales, and other sources total £45,610 and estimated total income from direct taxes totals £75,600 [19253].)

INDIRECT TAXES
(IMPOST, AUCTION SALES, SLAVE IMPORTS, ETC.)

1. State impost: In March and August 1783 the assembly established the state's impost system. Specific duties were placed on imported wine, beer, rum and spirits, sugar, coffee, and tea; all other foreign imports were to pay a 2.5 percent ad valorem duty. In addition the law taxed imported slaves. Also, an annual tax was placed on billiard tables (£50), and a license fee on taverns, alehouses, and punch houses.

   To help finance requisition payments, the assembly in 1783 and 1784 appropriated the entire proceeds of income from the impost for federal requisitions. The August 1783 impost law stated that all impost revenue (except that from the duties on tavern licenses, billiard tables, and slaves) "shall be appropriated towards the payment of this state's quota of the Interest and Principal of the Debts contracted on the part of the United States for the support of the War." In 1786 the revenue from this duty was estimated at £15,000; the revenue from a new duty on slave imports was £10,000.

2. Other sources of income: The government also anticipated income from a 2.5 percent duty on auction sales, from the sale of confiscated Loyalist estates, from a tonnage duty, and from other sources (*Acts and Ordinances*, March 1783, 68, 73–74).

3. In 1783 procedures were established for liquidating and consolidating the state's revolutionary war debt. According to "An Ordinance for ascertaining and regulating the Office of Receiver, Auditor, and Accountant General, of the Public Accounts, and for other Purposes therein mentioned," all monetary claims against the state were to be evaluated by the auditor general. After converting the claim to specie terms, that officer was either to satisfy the demand with an outright payment or instruct the treasury commissioners to issue a 7 percent interest-bearing note to the claimant (*Acts and Ordinances*, March 1783, 32–34; a depreciation table is mentioned in House Journal, January 1784 session, pp. 5–6). In the 1784 budget, the annual interest on these notes is stated as £72,892; in the 1786 Ways and Means Committee report, the total debt is stated as £889,738 [19253].

   Apparently, the government anticipated paying the annual interest on consolidated notes from such monies as were received from direct taxes, sale of confiscated estates, and other sources. When these revenues failed to materialize, the government in 1784 and 1785 resorted to the expedient of paying state creditors with the special paper "interest indents" payable for taxes.

Appendix 2

Notables and Leaders of Philadelphia's Improvement Societies

Library Company of Philadelphia (1731)

This semisubscription library, founded by Benjamin Franklin and other artisans and merchants in 1731, was formed to make the new Enlightenment learning available to its subscribers and the general public. During the 1780s the library, housed in Carpenter's Hall, collected books, natural curiosities, and scientific equipment. Members (£10 membership; 10s per year) included Robert Morris, George Clymer, James Wilson, John Dickinson, Sharp Delany, Francis Hopkinson, Samuel Powell, Richard Peters, and Charles Thomson.

American Philosophical Society (1742)

Modeled on the Royal Society, this premier Enlightenment society explicitly affirmed the improvement ideal ("The cultivation of useful knowledge, and the advancement of the liberal arts and sciences in any Country, have the most direct tendency towards the improvement of agriculture, the enlargement of trade, the ease and comfort of life, the ornament of society, the encrease and happiness of mankind"). During the 1780s the politically neutral Benjamin Franklin was president; vice-presidents were a Republican (Samuel Vaughan) and a Constitutionalist (Rev. John Ewing). Thomas Jefferson was a member (1779). Although Constitutionalists like David Rittenhouse and Rev. John Ewing were members, the upper-class members numbered at least eleven, including Robert Morris (1786), George Clymer (1786), and William Bingham (1787). Other notables included John Dickinson (1768), Charles Thomson (1768), Benjamin Rush (1768), James Wilson (1768), Henry Hill (1771), Sharp Delany (1774), Samuel Vaughan (1784), and John

Vaughan (1784). The out-of-state elite membership included Thomas Bee (1781), Thomas Heywood (1781), and Charles C. Pinckney (1789) of S.C.; James Madison (1785) of Va.; Jeremy Belknap (1784) of N.H.; James Bowdoin (1787) and John Lowell (1787) of Mass.; and John Jay (1787) of N.Y.

Philadelphia Society for the Promotion of Agriculture (1786)

Modeled after English county agricultural societies, this society, the first of its kind in the United States, held regular meetings, published papers on agricultural subjects, offered prizes for new and better farming methods, and planned a model farm outside the city. The founding membership consisted entirely of the urban elite and included George Clymer, Robert Morris, James Wilson, Henry Hill, and Thomas Willing.

Philadelphia Dispensary (1786)

Established as a day clinic providing free medical service to the poor, the dispensary was funded by private subscription. In 1787, 719 charity patients were treated. Among its managers were notables Thomas Fitzsimons, Samuel Powell, Samuel Miles, and John Baker.

Society for Political Inquiries (1787)

Founded in February 1787 to hear and discuss papers relating to the "arduous and complicated Science of Government," the society included such notables as George Clymer, Robert Morris, James Wilson, Gouverneur Morris, William Bingham, Tench Coxe, Francis Hopkinson, William Bradford, Jr., and Thomas Miflin. Its president-elect was Benjamin Franklin, a political neutral, but George Clymer and William Bingham were vice-presidents. The first paper read before the society was Benjamin Rush's "Enquiry into the Effects of Public Punishments upon Criminals, and Upon Society." Drawing on eighteenth-century faculty psychology, Rush proposed that the current wheelbarrow law be replaced by a House of Repentance where criminals would be reformed by a habit-forming regime of solitude and silence combined with cleanliness, diet, and labor. Rush's informing idea was the power of habit.

Pennsylvania Society for the Encouragement of Manufactures and the Useful Arts (1787)

Founded in February 1787 to encourage machine-made manufacturing, the society offered prizes for papers and opened a model cloth factory. In late 1788 reports to the society, George Clymer and Tench Coxe proudly described the amount subscribed by private persons (£1327), the steps taken to set up a linen and cotton cloth-making factory (a manufacturing house, a carding engine, 4 spinning jennies, and 25 looms costing £453), and the distribution during the winter of 1787–88 of processed flax to 200–300 women to weave in their homes. The report also claimed a profit on the first year's production of 30 percent, but stressed that because the purpose "of the factory being partly to employ the poor," the manufacturing committee had been "less particular about wages than a person would be who should carry on the business as his private occupation." Philadelphia notables George Clymer, Samuel Powell, Samuel Miles, and Tench Coxe were among the society's major promoters and organizers.

Sources: Whitfield Bell, Jr., "Science and Humanity in Philadelphia 1715–1790," Ph.D. diss., University of Pennsylvania, 1947, 40–250; George Geib, "A History of Philadelphia 1776–1789," Ph.D. diss., Wisconsin, 1969, 220–43; List of Members of the American Philosophical Society held at Philadelphia for Promoting Useful Knowledge, microfilm 33439, Microform Reading Room, LC; *Laws and Regulations of the American Philosophical Society*, Evans #11959, Early American Imprints Collection; Library Company of Philadelphia, *Charter, Laws and Catalogue*, Evans #11820, EAIC; Michael Meranze, "The Penitential Ideal in Late Eighteenth-Century Philadelphia," *Pennsylvania Magazine of History and Biography* 108 (October 1984), 419–50; George Clymer and Tench Coxe, Report to the Society for the Encouragement of Manufactures and the Useful Arts, 1788, *American Museum* 4 (November 1788), 404–9; reports by Samuel Miles and Samuel Powell, *American Museum* 2 (October 1787), 360–62, 3 (February 1788), 179; Jacob E. Cooke, *Tench Coxe and the Early Republic* (Chapel Hill: University of North Carolina Press, 1978), 102–8.

APPENDIX 3

RELAXED GOVERNMENT: SELECTED QUOTATIONS FROM THE FEDERALIST CAMP

John Jay (New York)

"Our country is fertile, abounding in useful Productions, and those Productions in Demand and bearing a good Price, yet Relaxation in Govermt and Extravagance in Individuals, create much Public and private Distress, & much public and private want of good faith." (To Thomas Jefferson, 14 December 1786, Jay Ms, Rare Book and Manuscript Library, Columbia University)

"The states in general pay little attention to Requisitions, and I fear that our Debts foreign and domestic will not soon be provided for in a manner satisfactory to our Creditors. The Evils to be expected from such Delays are less difficult to be foreseen than obviated. Our Governments want Energy, and there is Reason to fear that too much has been expected from the virtue & good sense of the People." (To Thomas Jefferson, 9 February 1787, Jay Ms, Rare Book and Manuscript Library, Columbia University)

"But my Dear Sir we labour under one sad Evil, the Treasury is empty tho' the Country abounds in Resources, and our people are far more unwilling than unable to pay Taxes—Hence results Disappointmts to our Creditors, Disgrace to our Country, and I fear Disinclination in too many to any mode of Govt. that can easily & irrisistably open their Purses. Much is to be done, and the Patriots must have Perseverance as well as Patience." (To John Adams, 21 February 1787, Jay Ms, Rare Book and Manuscript Library, Columbia University)

Charles Lee (Virginia)

"Our Legislature has pursued a system, it may be said ever since the beginning of the commonwealth, tending to efface every principle of virtue and honesty from the minds of its citizens and this is particularly obvious in the laws respecting delinquent officers and delinquent individuals as to taxes. There has scarcely been a session of the General Assembly but some law has been made to favor and relieve (as it is expressed) those who might have failed to pay what was rightly due to the Commonwealth. By this sort of conduct an opinion now generally prevails among the delinquents that they will never be compelled to pay and though the act of the last assembly has most unjustly enabled such persons to pay up the arrearages in depretiated securities yet it is not expected that any considerable part of the arrearages will even yet be paid.

"What the result will be, of retaining your public securities, is a thing of great uncertainty upon which opinions are very different: Unless there be a quiet and peaceable transition from the present American government, into another more powerful and independent of the people, the public debts and even private debts will in my opinion be extinguished by acts of the several Legislatures of the several States. The temper of the people in general, their habits, their interests all combine in producing such an event, and against these, natural justice will make but a feint opposition. If the proposed constitution be agreed to, and the administration be mild, just and wise, if it be so conducted as to engage the affections of the people, the public securities will appretiate and in a few years perhaps, be of considerable value." (To George Washington, 11 April 1788, Washington Ms, LC)

James McClurg (Virginia; Constitutional Convention delegate)

"I hope that our representative, [John] Marshall, will be a powerful aid to [George] Mason in the next assembly. He has observ'd the continual depravation of Mens manners, under the corrupting Influence of our Legislature; & is convinced that nothing but the adoption of some efficient plan from the Convention can prevent Anarchy first, & civil Convulsions afterwards." (To James Madison, 5 August 1787, James Madison, *The Papers of James Madison*, ed. Robert A. Rutland [Chicago: University of Chicago Press, 1977], 10:135)

Tobias Lear (Virginia)

"Much, indeed everything, depends upon the doings of the Convention, tho' I fear every good which is expected will not come out of it. The reins of Government are extreemly relaxed throughout the Union, the minds of the people are much unsettled, & in my opinion, they must feel as sensibly as they have in some of your westn. [Massachusetts] c[oun]ties before they will be brought to submit to a regular, permanent & energetic government." (To Benjamin Lincoln, Jr., 4 June 1787, Massachusetts Historical Society)

Edward Rutledge (South Carolina)

"We have chosen Delegates to the Continental Convention. My Brother, Genl Pinckney, Major Butler, & C. Pinckney, with Mr. Laurens were nominated. They will all attend but the last. He is precluded by want of Health. Our domestic appointments do us credit. But yet our Government has been so amazingly relaxed, that it will be as difficult to restore it to vigor, as it would be to restore the discipline of a licentious Army. Time, Vigilance, Perseverance, & a readiness to embrace every opportunity which presents itself, to promote the return of virtue, will at last accomplish the Business." (To John Jay, 27 March 1787, Jay Ms, Rare Book and Manuscript Library, Columbia University)

Benjamin Lincoln (Massachusetts)

"That the present systems must go to the Devil is almost certain, & must the establishment of another be left to accident? If the plan which shall be proposed by the [Constitutional] Convention should be a good one—men of property and principle and all who wish for *government* must combine and carry it down. The several legislatures being the bodies to accept or reject, the whole artillery of the wealth & address of the good ones of the community must be levelled against them. The weakness of some must be managed—the vices of others turned to advantage—the virtues (& here & there a virtue is yet to be found among the worst of characters) must be cherished & improved—& God send us good deliverance." (To George Thatcher, 9 May 1787, Thatcher Ms, Boston Public Library)

Obadiah Bowen (Rhode Island)

"At present we are destitute of a Head, a Head we unfortunately never since our Independence have possessed, but are void of a Congress, which at this critical crisis is necessary, tho' they do not possess sufficient power, yet they are both better able and more capable of directing some of the affairs of the nation than the individual assemblies of the States—I fear that greater evils are impending, than is generally supposed. The great debility of government and the present too general uneasiness amongst the majority of the people, are circumstances that have too solid a foundation to be removed, without a thorough change." (To Enos Hitchcock, 20 November 1786, Enos Hitchcock Ms, Box 1, Rhode Island Historical Society)

Christopher Gore (Massachusetts)

"Our Govt is weak, languid, and inefficient to support the great objects of civil institutions the personal liberty & property of the subject—You of the federal convention must invent some plan to increase the circulation at the heart & thereby dispense heat & vigor to the extremities—if you do not we shall descend to anarchy & disgrace." (To Rufus King, 28 June 1787, King Ms, New-York Historical Society)

A NOTE ON SOURCES AND METHOD

The basic core of this study rests on the published and unpublished legislative and administrative tax records produced by the Confederation state governments. Most of the states' published and unpublished legislative records pertaining to tax policy are on microfilm in the Early State Records Microfilm Collection in the Microform Reading Room, Library of Congress, Washington, D.C. Consult William Sumner Jenkins, *A Guide to the Microfilm Collection of Early State Records* (Washington, D.C.: Library of Congress, 1950) for desired items and call numbers. Short-term interlibrary loans and purchase of individual films can be arranged through the Microform Reading Room. Published state legislative records can also be found on microcard in the Early American Imprints Collection, issued by Readex Corporation and held by numerous university libraries, but microcards are more difficult to use than microfilm. The identification numbers used in Charles Evan's *American Bibliography* are keyed to the Early American Imprints Collection and must be used to obtain desired items. For easy access to identification numbers, consult Clifford K. Shipton and James E. Mooney, *National Index of American Imprints Through 1800: The Short-Title Evans* (Worcester, Mass.: American Antiquarian Society, 1969). When footnoting these materials, I have not cited their location in the Early State Records and Early American Imprints Collections.

Most of the administrative records pertaining to tax collection at the state and local levels require a personal visit to state archival depositories. The holdings of the Massachusetts State Archives in Boston and of the Pennsylvania Historical and Museum Commission in Harrisburg are especially rich. The Rhode Island State Archives in Providence also has much material, including the state's treasurer's tax returns record book, the only such complete record of its kind I found. Comparable tax records for South Carolina in the South Carolina Department of Archives and History are less numerous. I have sampled similar tax records for some of the other nine states but have not investigated them as thoroughly as I have those of Pennsylvania, South Carolina, Rhode Island, and Massachusetts. Nevertheless, I believe that further research will confirm the patterns described for the other nine states in Chapter 9.

The following paragraphs identify the major collections used. As noted in my Introduction, Robert Becker's *Revolution, Reform, and the Politics of American Taxation, 1763–1783* (Baton Rouge: Louisiana State University Press, 1980) pioneered the study of Revolutionary- and Confederation-era state taxation. I did not become aware of Becker's study until after I had formed my own methods and conclusions.

For Pennsylvania, the most important sources include the published *Minutes* of the Pennsylvania assembly in both the Early State Records Collection and the Early American Imprints Collection; the published letters of county commissioners in Samuel Hazard's *Pennsylvania Archives*; the published minutes and letters of the Supreme Executive Council in *Pennsylvania Archives*; the unpublished minute books of the county commissioners in the Pennsylvania Historical and Museum Commission Archives in Harrisburg; and the unpublished letters of the Supreme Executive Council, also in the Pennsylvania Historical and Museum Commission Archives. Important manuscript collections include the George Bryan Ms in the Historical Society of Pennsylvania, the Anthony Wayne Ms in the Historical Society of Pennsylvania and additional Wayne materials in the William Clements Library, University of Michigan, and *The Papers of Robert Morris*. A number of excellent published and unpublished studies cited in chapter 5 provide necessary background but do not discuss taxation.

For South Carolina, the unpublished state legislative journals and the South Carolina *Acts and Ordinances* are indispensable. The South Carolina Department of Archives and History at Columbia has only a few tax records for the period; I could find no records of the state treasury commissioners. South Carolina newspapers and letters from South Carolina notables in the Nathanael Greene Ms, Clements Library, throw light on state politics. Important letters from Edward Rutledge to John Jay are in the Jay Ms, Manuscripts and Archives, Columbia University Library. Secondary works that provide background for Confederation South Carolina are cited in chapter 6.

Rhode Island sources for this study include the published Rhode Island legislative records and the *Session Laws*. The General Treasurer's Record Book in the Rhode Island State Archives provides a complete record of returns on each of the several state taxes passed during the Revolution and Confederation eras. The Dwight Foster Family collection in the American Antiquarian Society at Worcester and the Brown Family Papers in the John Carter Brown Library in Providence provide valuable insight into the 1786 election and the ensuing controversy over the 1786 paper money relief bill. Important published and unpublished studies on Confederation Rhode Island are cited in chapter 7.

Massachusetts records used in this study include the unpublished journals of the house and senate, the *Acts and Laws of Massachusetts*, and the legislature's *Resolves*. Local tax collection can be traced through the rich array of treasurer's records, including both lists and accounts of treasurer's execution warrants and packets of returned treasurer's execution warrants with descriptive notations by county sheriffs. The plethora of excellent published and unpublished works on Shays's Rebellion and its background is cited in chapter 8 with additional work cited below. This is the first study, however, to describe the legislative's 1786 crackdown on uncollected taxes, originally levied for Congress, that detonated Shays's Rebellion.

The longstanding historiographical controversies surrounding the origins of the Constitution are numerous and complex. I have tried to deal with major interpretive issues in my Introduction and in chapters 10, 11, and 14. A newer controversy surrounds issues of the character and culture of the states' middling and small farmers, especially those located in central and western Massachusetts at some distance from commercial markets. According to David Szatmary, John L. Brooke, and others, interior Massachusetts farmers were deeply involved in subsistence agriculture and valued household, family, and neighborhood more than markets and profit. On the other hand, Bettye H. Pruitt, Winifred B. Rothenberg, and others hold that, despite distance from markets, the middling and small farmers of interior Massachusetts in the late eighteenth century were market conscious. Christopher Clark takes a middle ground, describing these farmers as subsistence-surplus farmers. Resolution of these issues is not required in order to understand why middling and small farmers used physical force to prevent tax collectors and sheriffs from seizing and selling stock, produce, and lands for taxes at ruinously low prices. Whether more subsistence or more market in orientation, these farmers considered their stock, produce, and land fundamental to their own and their families' security, independence, and survival. For discussion of these issues and relevant works, see Allan Kulikof, "The Transition to Capitalism in Rural America," *William and Mary Quarterly* 46 (January 1989), 120–44; subsequent publications include John L. Brooke, *The Heart of the Commonwealth: Society and Political Culture in Worcester County, Massachusetts 1713–1861* (Cambridge: Cambridge University Press, 1989), and Christopher Clark, *The Roots of Rural Capitalism: Western Massachusetts, 1780–1860* (Ithaca, N.Y.: Cornell University Press, 1990).

ABBREVIATIONS

AAS	American Antiquarian Society, Worcester, Mass.
Clements	William L. Clements Library, Manuscripts Division, University of Michigan, Ann Arbor, Mich.
Columbia	Rare Book and Manuscript Library, Columbia University, New York, N.Y.
CHS	Connecticut Historical Society, Hartford, Conn.
CSL	Connecticut State Library, Hartford, Conn.
EAIC	Early American Imprints Collection
ESRC	Early State Records Microfilm Collection, Microform Reading Room, Library of Congress, Washington, D.C.
GaHS	Georgia Historical Society, Savannah, Ga.
HSP	Historical Society of Pennsylvania, Philadelphia
JCBL	John Carter Brown Library, Brown University, Providence, R.I.
LC	Manuscript Reading Room, Library of Congress, Washington, D.C.
LCP	Library Company of Philadelphia, Historical Society of Pennsylvania, Philadelphia, Pa.
MA	Massachusetts State Archives, Boston, Mass.
MHR	Maryland Hall of Records, Annapolis, Md.
MHS	Massachusetts Historical Society, Boston, Mass.
NA	National Archives, Washington, D.C.
Newberry	Newberry Library, Chicago, Ill.
NHS	Newport Historical Society, Newport, R.I.
NYHS	New-York Historical Society, New York, N.Y.
NYPL	New York Public Library, New York, N.Y.
PHMC	Pennsylvania Historical and Museum Commission, Harrisburg, Pa.
RISA	Rhode Island State Archives, Providence, R.I.
RIHS	Rhode Island Historical Society, Providence, R.I.
SCDAH	South Carolina Department of Archives and History, Columbia, S.C.
UNC	Southern Historical Collection, University of North Carolina, Chapel Hill, N.C.
VaU	Alderman Library, University of Virginia, Charlottesville, Va.

VSA   Virginia State Archives, Richmond, Va.
Yale   Manuscripts and Archives, Yale University Library, New
           Haven, Conn.

NOTES

PREFACE AND ACKNOWLEDGMENTS

1. James Madison to Edmund Pendleton, 24 February 1787, James Madison, *The Papers of James Madison*, ed. Robert A. Rutland (Chicago: University of Chicago Press, 1977), 9:294–95.

INTRODUCTION

1. Rev. Ebenezer Dibblee to Rev. Samuel Peters, Stamford, Conn., 16 November 1787, Archives of the Episcopal Church, Austin, Texas.

2. John Brewer, *The Sinews of Power: War, Money, and the English State, 1688–1783* (New York: Knopf, 1989).

3. Theodore Sedgwick to Caleb Strong, 6 August 1786, *American Historical Review* 4 (January 1899):328–30; James McClurg to James Madison, 5 August 1787, James Madison, *The Papers of James Madison*, ed. Robert A Rutland (Chicago: University of Chicago Press, 1977), 10:135 (hereafter *Madison Papers*); Horatio Gates to James Madison, 26 November 1787, *Madison Papers* 10:272–73.

4. Thomas C. Cochran, *New York in the Confederation: An Economic Study* (Philadelphia: University of Pennsylvania Press, 1932), esp. 55–56; Robert A. Becker, *Revolution, Reform, and the Politics of American Taxation, 1763–1783* (Baton Rouge: Louisiana State University Press, 1980).

5. Van Beck Hall, *Politics Without Parties: Massachusetts, 1780–1791* (Pittsburgh: University of Pittsburgh Press, 1972); Forrest McDonald and Ellen Shapiro McDonald, *Requiem: Variations on Eighteenth-Century Themes* (Lawrence: University Press of Kansas, 1988), 59–83.

6. Jackson T. Main, *Political Parties before the Constitution* (Chapel Hill: University of North Carolina Press, 1973); Hall, *Politics Without Parties*. In Massachusetts, cosmopolitans opposed a localist proposal to reallocate part of the Massachusetts state impost fund earmarked for payment of the interest on the state debt to help pay the state's federal requisition. House vote, 3 and 7 March 1786, Massachusetts House Journal, 1786 House, 464–65, 483. In New York, the administration of localist governor George Clinton made the greatest proportionate contribution to the Confederation treasury of any of the thirteen states (67% of its quota). The point is not that one group favored and the other opposed money for Congress, but that the two groups disagreed over how best to raise the money.

7. Gordon Wood, *The Creation of the American Republic, 1776–1787* (Chapel Hill: University of North Carolina Press, 1969), esp. 471–518.

8. James H. Hutson, "Notes and Documents: John Dickinson at the Federal Convention," *William and Mary Quarterly* 40 (April 1983): 257–82.

9. Merrill Jensen, *The Articles of Confederation: An Interpretation of the Social-Constitutional History of the American Revolution, 1774–1781* (Madison: University of Wisconsin Press, 1940), and *The New Nation: A History of the United States during the Confederation, 1781–1789* (New York: Knopf, 1950); E. James Ferguson, *The Power of the Purse: A History of American Public Finance, 1776–1790* (Chapel Hill: University of North Carolina Press, 1961).

10. Leonard Levy, *Essays on the Making of the Constitution* (New York: Oxford University Press, 1987), 2d ed., ix–xl.

11. Daniel W. Howe, "The Political Psychology of *The Federalist*," *William and Mary Quarterly* 44 (July 1987): 485–509.

12. Even Charles Beard, famous for attributing motives of class and pecuniary interest to the Framers, came to acknowledge that concern for the Republic was an important category of motivation. Howard K. Beale, *Charles E. Beard: An Appraisal* (Lexington: University Press of Kentucky, 1954), 90–92, 250.

13. Roger H. Brown, *The Republic in Peril: 1812* (New York: Columbia University Press, 1964).

14. Wood, *Creation of the American Republic*, and Charles Hobson, "The Negative on State Laws: James Madison, the Constitution, and the Crisis of Republican Government," *William and Mary Quarterly* 36 (April 1979): 215–35, stress the theme of the republican government in crisis. Neither, however, locates the source of this concern in the perceived weakness of the state governments.

15. William Irvine to Col. Josiah Harmar, 27 February 1787, Harmar Papers, Clements; George Read (6 June), Max Farrand, ed., *The Records of the Federal Convention of 1787*, rev. ed. (New Haven, Conn.: Yale University Press, 1966) 1:137 (hereafter Farrand *Records*).

16. Archibald Stuart to James Madison, 9 November 1787, *Madison Papers*, 10:245–46.

17. Both Main, *Political Parties before the Constitution*, and Hall, *Politics Without Parties*, demonstrate how centrally tax-related issues affected the politics of the Confederation state legislatures.

CHAPTER 1. AN INSOLVENT CONGRESS

1. Jack N. Rakove, *The Beginnings of National Politics: An Interpretive History of the Continental Congress* (New York: Knopf, 1979), 135–215, describes the drafting of the Articles of Confederation. A unicameral assembly, Congress was composed of delegations (2–7 members in each delegation) from each of the Confederation's thirteen states, with each delegation having one vote. Chosen by their state legislatures and limited to three years of eligibility in every six, delegates were often absent so that Congress, lacking a quorum, could not do business. Congress's executive affairs were managed by a superintendant of finance (Board of Treasury after 1785), a secretary of war, and a secretary for foreign affairs, each chosen by Congress and responsible to it. Congress first met in the exigency of coordinating resistance to England (1774) and soon evolved into a working cen-

tral government. The Articles of Confederation defined the allocation of powers and responsibilities between Congress and the states as they had been worked out in practice during the early part of the war.

2. Ferguson, *Power of the Purse*, 33–34.

3. *Ibid.*, 30–31, 129–30.

4. *Ibid.*, January 1787 figures show a 70% compliance with the federal requisition of October 1781 and only a 23% compliance with the three federal requisitions of April 1784, September 1785, and August 1786 (see table 2).

5. See discussion on the breakdown of the requisition system and table 2 in chap. 2.

6. Charles Thomson to John Dickinson, 25 December 1780, Box 1, folder 19, R. R. Logan Collection, John Dickinson Ms, HSP.

7. Clarence L. Ver Steeg, *Robert Morris: Revolutionary Financier* (Philadelphia: University of Pennsylvania Press, 1954), 97–105.

8. Morris to state governors [circular], 6 and 25 July 1781, Robert Morris, *The Papers of Robert Morris, 1781–1784*, ed. E. James Ferguson (Pittsburgh: University of Pittsburgh Press, 1973), 1:242, 380–83.

9. Ibid., 25 July 1781, 1:380–83, and 16 May 1782, 5:192.

10. Morris diary, 14 May 1781, and Morris to Washington, 15 June, 2 July 1781, Morris, *Papers*, 1:61–62, 153, 213–15.

11. Morris diary, 18 September 1781, Morris, *Papers*, 2:291–92; Morris to Governors of North Carolina, South Carolina, and Georgia, 19 December 1781, Morris, *Papers*, 3:411–16.

12. Morris to federal receivers of taxes, 15 May 1782, Morris, *Papers*, 5:183.

13. Morris to Hezekiah Merrill, receiver of taxes for Connecticut, 14 June 1782, *Providence* [R.I.] *Gazette and Country Journal*, 6 July 1782; Morris to William Whipple, 4 June 1782, Morris, *Papers*, 5:336.

14. Morris diary, 28 June 1782, Morris, *Papers*, 5:495; Morris to John Lloyd, Jr., 18 September 1781, Morris, *Papers*, 2:294.

15. Editor's note, Morris, *Papers*, 1:176, n. 2; Ferguson, *Power of the Purse*, 134. Morris also paid Thomas Paine, author of the famous revolutionary pamphlet *Common Sense*, $800 a year to write and publish newspaper essays "respecting the propriety, Necessity and Utility of Taxation." Morris diary, 18 September 1781, Morris, *Papers*, 2:290, 291–92, n. 9.

16. Ferguson, *Power of the Purse*, 129; Hamilton to George Washington, 8 April 1783, Alexander Hamilton, *The Papers of Alexander Hamilton*, ed. Harold C. Syrett (New York: Columbia University Press, 1962–), 3:320 (hereafter *Hamilton Papers*).

17. Lance Banning, "James Madison and the Nationalists, 1780–1783," *William and Mary Quarterly* (April 1983): 227–55. In 1781 not only Madison but Morris and Alexander Hamilton were thinking in terms of having the states fund the federal debt by permanent *state* taxes. Hamilton to Morris, 30 April 1781, Morris, *Papers*, 1:31–58. By 1782, however, both Morris and Hamilton were advocating investing Congress with independent revenues, not only an impost but a land tax, a house tax, and an excise to be collected by Congress-appointed collectors.

18. Frederick W. Marks III, *Independence on Trial: Foreign Affairs and the Making of the Constitution* (Baton Rouge: Louisiana State University Press, 1973), 6–15, 36. Harry M. Ward, *The Department of War: 1781–1795* (Pittsburgh: University of Pittsburgh Press, 1962), 19ff.

19. Arthur P. Whitaker, *The Spanish-American Frontier: 1783–1795* (Gloucester Mass.: Peter Smith, 1962); also, Marks, *Independence on Trial*, 21–35.

20. Ray W. Irwin, *The Diplomatic Relations of the United States with the Barbary Powers, 1776–1816* (New York: Russell and Russell, 1931), 1–53, quotation on p. 52. James A. Field, Jr., *America and the Mediterranean World, 1776–1882* (Princeton: Princeton University Press, 1969), 38. Harold Sprout and Margaret Sprout, *The Rise of American Naval Power: 1776–1918* (Princeton: Princeton University Press, 1944), 15–19.

21. Alan S. Brown, "The Role of the Army in Western Settlement: Josiah Harmar's Command, 1785–1790," *Pennsylvania Magazine of History and Biography* 93 (April 1969): 168, 173, 175; Reginald Horsman, *The Frontier in the Formative Years, 1783–1815* (New York: Holt, Rinehart, and Winston, 1970), 33–49.

22. The Georgia and Virginia stories await definitive treatment, but for some details on Georgia, see chap. 11.

23. Robert Russell La Follette, "The American Revolutionary Foreign Debt and Its Liquidation" (Ph.D. diss., George Washington University, 1931). Also, Ferguson, *Power of the Purse*, 221, 234–38.

24. E. James Ferguson, "State Assumption of the Federal Debt during the Revolution," *Mississippi Valley Historical Review* 38 (December, 1951): 403–24, and Ferguson, *Power of the Purse*, esp. 220–50.

25. Ferguson, *Power of the Purse*, 36–40.

26. Ibid., 223–24.

27. Ferguson, "Assumption of the Federal Debt," 421, n. 66; Hall, *Politics Without Parties*, 42, n. 44.

28. According to Ferguson, the total sum of the federal "public debt" thus assumed and funded by the state governments of Pennsylvania, New York, and Maryland amounted to $9,000,000. Ferguson, "State Assumption of the Federal Debt," 420.

29. In *Independence on Trial* Marks argues that the cited diplomatic failures of Congress, a function of its financial impoverishment, posed the issue of whether Congress could defend the new nation's territorial integrity and independence. Yet the diplomatic record *alone* does not explain why the Framers created the Constitution instead of vesting Congress with a 5% impost.

30. Leonard Levy, *Original Intent and the Framers' Constitution* (New York: Macmillan, 1988), 30–53.

CHAPTER 2. THE FAILED QUEST FOR A FEDERAL TAX POWER

1. "Grant of Power to Collect Import Duties," 3 February 1781, in *The Documentary History of the Ratification of the Constitution: Constitutional Documents and*

Records, 1776–1787, ed. Merrill Jensen (Madison: State Historical Society of Wisconsin, 1976), 1:140–41. *Journals of the Continental Congress*, ed. John C. Fitzpatrick (Washington: U.S. Government Printing Office, 1904–37), 19:110, 112–13 (hereafter Continental Congress *Journals*).

2. Jonathan Arnold to David Howell, 29 June 1782, Frederick Peck Collection, Box 7, RIHS.

3. Nicholas Brown to David Howell, 5 November 1782, Brown Ms, JCBL; John Brown to Nathanael Greene, 10 March 1784, Greene Ms, Clements Library; "From a Gentleman to the Southward to his Friend in this Town," *Providence Gazette*, 26 October 1782. Because Rhode Island had no western lands that could be used to finance its debts and landed states did have lands, Rhode Island leaders insisted that all western lands be ceded to Congress for the purpose of financing all federal and state debts before Rhode Island would vote a federal impost that would undercut the state's ability to raise money by a state impost. Cf. Irwin H. Polishook, *Rhode Island and the Union, 1774–1795* (Evanston, Ill.: Northwestern University Press, 1969).

4. "Grant of Temporary Power to Collect Import Duties and Request for Supplementary Funds," 18 April 1783, *Documentary History* 1:146–48; Continental Congress *Journals*, 34:188–91, 257–61; Rakove, *Beginnings of National Politics*, 337–42. See also Banning, "James Madison and the Nationalists," 227–55.

5. Richard H. Kohn, "The Inside Story of the Newburgh Conspiracy: America and the Coup d'État," *William and Mary Quarterly* 27 (April 1970):185–220.

6. Cochran, *New York in the Confederation*, 19–38, 136–50, 173–79. For Congress's reaction to these actions, see Continental Congress *Journals*, 30:439–45, 31:532–35, 558–61.

7. Continental Congress *Journals*, 30:439–45; 31:505–13, 532–35, 558–61, 881.

8. Ferguson, "Assumption of the Federal Debt," 414.

9. "Schedule of Requisitions on the Several States by the U.S. in Congress Assembled," 31 March 1787, Papers of the Continental Congress, 1771–1789, microcopy #M247, roll 154, item 141, Estimates of the Board of Treasury, 1781–1789, vol. 2, frame 123, NA. These figures overstate the amount of monies actually received by Congress.

10. General Requisition, 2 August 1786 ($431,920 for military, civil, Indian affairs, and contingencies; $1,721,229 principal and interest due on French, Dutch, and Spanish debt; $1,606,560 one year's interest due on domestic debt), Continental Congress *Journals*, 31:461–66.

11. Special Requisition and Loan, 21 October 1786, Continental Congress *Journals*, 31:893–96.

12. Board of Treasury to Congress, 7 February 1787, Continental Congress *Journals*, 33:33–34. William Ellery to Board of Treasury, 27 February, 5 March 1787, William Ellery's Loan Office & Custom House Letter Book, 1786–94, NHS (hereafter Ellery's Letter Book). "Can it be expected that monies should be loaned on the credit of a requisition when that requisition is not complied with?" For the period 1 January–31 March 1788 the monthly pay-

ments by the states increased slightly from $18,519 to $40,697 per month ($122,092 in all). Requisition Schedules of 31 December 1787 and 31 March 1788, Papers of the Continental Congress, 1774–1789, microcopy #M247, roll 154, item 141, Estimates of the Board of Treasury, vol. 2, no. 484, vol. 1, no. 75, NA.

13. Board of Treasury Report to Congress, 23 February 1788, Papers of the Continental Congress, Letters of the Board of Treasury, vol. 2, no. 481, NA.

14. William Ellery, Continental Loan Officer for Rhode Island to Board of Treasury, 8 January 1787, Ellery's Letter Book.

15. Board of Treasury to Congress, 12 February 1787, Continental Congress *Journals*, 32:33–34. La Follette, "American Revolutionary Foreign Debt," 46–47. In June 1787 U.S. agents negotiated a third Dutch loan of $400,000 to meet interest payments on the Dutch loan, but the U.S. defaulted temporarily on the principal and interest due its French and Spanish creditors.

16. Stephen M. Mitchell to Jeremiah Wadsworth, 24 January 1787, Wadsworth Ms, CHS.

17. Roger Alden to Colonel Jonathan Trumbull, New York, 23 March 1787, Jonathan Trumbull, Jr., Ms, CHS.

18. Madison to Edmund Pendleton, 24 February 1787, *Madison Papers*, 9:294–95.

19. Thus, as early as August 1786, some members of Congress were proposing substantial revisions. "Amendments to the Articles of Confederation Proposed by a Grand Committee of Congress," 7 August 1786, *Documentary History*, 1:163–68. Continental Congress *Journals*, 31:494–98.

20. Rakove, *Beginnings of National Politics*, 361–99; Mervin B. Whealy, "The Revolution is Not Over: The Annapolis Convention of 1786," *Maryland Historical Magazine* 81 (Fall 1986): 228–40.

21. Whealy, "Annapolis Convention," 228–32; Rakove, *Beginnings of National Politics*, 361–99.

22. "Proceedings and Report of the Commissioners at Annapolis, Maryland," 11–14 September 1786, *Documentary History*, 1:181–85.

23. Compare Whealy, "Annapolis Convention," with Rakove, *Beginnings of National Politics*.

24. William Irvine to Colonel Josiah Harmar, 27 February 1787, New York, Harmar Papers, Clements Library: "Some States have complied in part with the requisitions of Congress—some not at all, and others have flatly refused—there is therefore no alternative—to giving up all at once for lost—but that of attempting to revise and mend the Confederation—or frame an entire new Government—whether the proposed Convention will be able to effect either it is hard to say—but an attempt is necessary and the sooner it is made it will be sooner compleated." Madison, Notes on Debates, 21 February 1787, *Madison Papers*, 9:290–92.

25. Levy, *Making of the Constitution*, xxiv–xl. See also chap. 13 here.

26. The Framers went to Philadelphia with their options partially concealed. At minimum, they held that Congress should be modified by a limited 5 percent amendment; at maximum, they hoped to engineer the central government's radical

reconstitution. The first option they were willing to acknowledge publicly, but not the second.

27. Irvine to Harmar, 27 February 1787, Harmar Papers, Clements; George Read (6 June), Madison's Notes, Farrand *Records* 1:136–37.

CHAPTER 3. HEAVY STATE TAXATION

1. Levy, *Making of the Constitution*, xvii, xix: "The states flouted their constitutional obligations"; "The 1780s taught that excessive localism was incompatible with nationhood." Also Richard B. Morris, *The Forging of the Union, 1781–1789* (New York: Harper and Row, 1987), 245–47; George Brown Tindall, *America: A Narrative History* (New York: Norton, 1988), 262–66.

2. Edmund Pendleton to James Madison, Jr., 7 April 1787, *Madison Papers*, 17:515–17.

3. Edmund Randolph to Washington, 24 November, 6 December 1786, George Washington Ms, LC.

4. Jay to Thomas Jefferson, 14 December 1786, to John Adams, 21 February 1787, Jay Ms, Columbia. See also appendix 3.

5. W. S. Johnson to Hugh Williamson, New York, 31 March 1787, draft, written on reverse side of Williamson to Johnson, W. S. Johnson Ms, Susquehannah Lands, CHS.

6. Board of Treasury to Wilhem and Jan Willink and Nicholas and Jacob Van Staphorst, 20 February 1788 (copy by S. Morris), Letters of the Board of Treasury, 1785–1788, Papers of the Continental Congress, 1774–1789, microcopy #M247, roll 153, item 140, 2:483, NA (hereafter Treasury Letter).

7. Helpful discussions of pre- and post-Revolution taxation are Becker, *American Taxation*, and Edwin J. Perkins, *The Economy of Colonial America* (New York: Columbia University Press, 1988), 160–240.

8. Julian Gwyn, "British Government Spending and the North American Colonies 1740–1775," in *The British Atlantic Empire Before the American Revolution*, ed. Peter Marshall and Gwyn Williams (London: Cass, 1980).

9. Becker, *American Taxation*, 34, 70–71, 106–7, 190.

10. Perkins, *Economy of Colonial America*, 239–40 suggests a multiplier of 90 to find the value in 1985 dollars of sterling amounts. Assuming .23£ sterling/per dollar, the average tax per household in specie and paper ($17.49) totals $361.80 in 1985 dollars.

11. Robert A. Gross, *The Minutemen and their World* (New York: Hill and Wang, 1976), 68.

12. James H. Flannagan, Jr., "Trying Times: Economic Depression in New Hampshire, 1781–1789" (Ph.D. diss., Georgetown University, 1972), 200–210; and more generally, Curtis P. Nettels, *The Emergence of a National Economy 1775–1815* (New York: Holt, Rinehart and Winston, 1962), 45–88.

13. W. Robert Higgins, "A Financial History of the American Revolution in South Carolina" (Ph.D. diss., Duke University, 1969) usefully examines South Carolina's debt management policies but does not address the issue of how that government tried to raise money for Congress.

14. See Higgins, "Financial History," 220, 241.

15. For a general discussion, see Becker, *American Taxation*.

16. Brewer, *Sinews of Power*, 88–89.

17. Richard Henry Lee to James Madison, 26 November 1784, Lee Family Ms, reel 7, LC. Also Governor Benjamin Harrison to President of Congress, 21 January 1781, quoted in Mary Trevers Armentrout, "A Political Study of Virginia Finance, 1781–1789" (Ph.D. diss., University of Virginia, 1934), 57.

18. Gordon C. Bjork, "Stagnation and Growth in the American Economy, 1784–1792" (Ph.D. diss., University of Washington, 1963); Bjork, "The Weaning of the American Economy: Independence, Market Changes, and Economic Development," *Journal of Economic History* 24 (December 1964): 54–60; Nettels, *Emergence*, 45–88, emphasizes the scarcity of specie and the hardships of paying heavy taxes and private debts.

19. According to Julian Gwyn: "The £16.2 million spent between 1740 and 1775 by Britain to administer and defend her colonies went a very long way to balance the continent's deficit in commodity trade with the mother country. In a word, much of the government's spending in America was employed to pay for importing from Britain." Gwyn, "British Government Spending," 81.

20. The Virginia legislature unanimously agreed to the following resolution proposed by George Mason in 1787: "Resolved, That the present scarcity of circulating money has been, in a great measure, caused by the general fear and apprehension of paper currency; inducing men to lock up their gold and silver or remit it to Europe, and prefer receiving a very low interest for it there, to the risk of lending or letting it out here." Quoted in Armentrout, "Political Study of Virginia Finances," 131.

21. Winifred B. Rothenberg, "A Price Index for Rural Massachusetts, 1750–1855," *Journal of Economic History* 39 (December 1979): 975–1001.

22. Flannagan, "Trying Times," 200–210. Flannagan's survey shows that only 36 persons out of 950 left some cash as part of their assets.

Chapter 4. Taxers and Reliefers

1. Arthur Bryan termed the dominant leaders of South Carolina's assembly and the Charleston city government "the great people," "the great," and "the aristocracy." Arthur Bryan to George Bryan, 9 April 1788, Charleston, S.C., George Bryan Ms., HSP. Rhode Island's Welcome Arnold used the language "first gentlemen of Boston" for the principal members of the Boston merchant firm of Russell, Derby, Tracy, and Swan. Quoted in Frank S. Coyle, "Welcome Arnold (1745–1798): Providence Merchant: The Founding of an Enterprise" (Ph.D. diss., Brown University, 1972), 171.

2. Gary B. Nash, "The Transformation of Urban Politics, 1700–1765," *Journal of American History* 60 (December 1973): 605–32. John M. Murrin, "Political Development," in *Colonial British America: Essays in the New History of the Early Modern Era*, ed. Jack P. Greene and J. R. Pole (Baltimore: Johns Hopkins University Press, 1984), 441–47, discusses the extensive literature on pre-Revolution political elites.

3. Edward Countryman, "Consolidating Power in Revolutionary America: The Case of New York, 1775–1783," *Journal of Interdisciplinary History* 6 (Spring 1976): 645–77; Robert L. Brunhouse, *The Counter-Revolution in Pennsylvania: 1776–1790* (Harrisburg: Pennsylvania Historical and Museum Commission, 1971). Ronald Hoffman, *A Spirit of Dissension: Economics, Politics, and the Revolution in Maryland* (Baltimore: Johns Hopkins University Press, 1973), describes the rise of Samuel Chase, "the common people's champion."

4. Robert Morris described his behind-the-scenes role in getting the Pennsylvania assembly to levy specie taxes thus: "I am also pressing our assembly to Levy effective Taxes in hard money; there are stronger objections made to this than the other measure." Robert Morris to George Washington, 15 June 1781, Morris, *Papers*, 1:153.

5. Republican Society Address, [Philadelphia] *Pennsylvania Gazette and Weekly Advertiser*, 24 March 1779; Address of the Constitutional Society, signed by member Charles Willson Peale, [Philadelphia] *Pennsylvania Gazette and Weekly Advertiser*, 28 April 1779; Brunhouse, *Counter-Revolution in Pennsylvania*; Owen S. Ireland, "The Ratification of the Federal Constitution in Pennsylvania" (Ph.D. diss., University of Pittsburgh, 1966); Douglas M. Arnold, "Political Ideology and the Internal Revolution in Pennsylvania, 1776–1790" (Ph.D. diss., Princeton University, 1976); Anthony Wayne to John Hannum, 9 January 1786, Wayne Ms, HSP: "I arrived from Phila: last evening our friends Morris, Clymer, Fitzimons &Ca. are exceedingly anxious about the Chester Election & requested me to write you on the subject."

6. Richard Maxwell Brown, *The South Carolina Regulators* (Cambridge, Mass.: Harvard University Press, 1963); Robert M. Weir, "'The Harmony We Were Famous For': An Interpretation of Pre-Revolutionary South Carolina Politics," *William and Mary Quarterly* 26 (October 1969); Jerome J. Nadelhaft, "The Revolutionary Era in South Carolina, 1775–1788" (Ph.D. diss., University of Wisconsin, 1965). For a key letter that identifies the "great people" as holding sway in both the assembly and the city government, see Arthur Bryan to George Bryan, 9 April 1788, Charleston, S.C., Bryan Ms, HSP.

7. Polishook, *Rhode Island and the Union*; James B. Hedges, *The Browns of Providence Plantations: The Colonial Years* (Cambridge, Mass.: Harvard University Press, 1952); and Coyle, "Welcome Arnold."

8. For Massachusetts, David Sewall to John Lowell, September 1782, 28 January 1783, Lowell Ms, MHS; Governor James Bowdoin to Nathaniel Gorham, 24 June 1786, Bowdoin-Temple Ms, Winthrop Papers, MHS (hereafter Bowdoin-Temple Ms); Caleb Davis to John Lowell, 30 May 1782, Lowell Ms, MHS. On Hancock, William M. Fowler, Jr., *The Baron of Beacon Hill: A Biography of John Hancock* (Boston: Houghton Mifflin, 1979), esp. 241–59. On Bowdoin, Gordon E. Kershaw, *James Bowdoin: Patriot and Man of the Enlightenment* (Brunswick, Maine: Bowdoin College Museum of Art, 1976); John Lowell, *An Eulogy on the Honorable James Bowdoin, Esq., L.L.D., Late President of the American Academy of Arts and Sciences* (Boston, 1791). On the unstable lower house, Hall, *Politics Without Parties*, and the changeable voting as reported in the unpublished Massachusetts House Journal. In the crises of 1782 and 1786, house voting on tax measures was extremely volatile.

9. Thomas Doerflinger, *A Vigorous Spirit of Enterprise: Merchants and Economic Development in Revolutionary Philadelphia* (Chapel Hill: University of North Carolina Press, 1986), 30, 183, 213.

10. Journal of the Proceedings of the Charleston Library Society, 1783–88, Charleston Library Society. Mount Sion Society Petition to S.C. General Assembly, n.d. (from internal evidence ca. 1784), Petitions to S.C. Assembly, Assembly Papers, S.C. Department of Archives and History, Charleston. *An Address to the Public from the South-Carolina Society for the Promoting and Improving Agriculture and Other Rural Concerns*, n.d. (from internal evidence 1786 or 1787), Evans 19254, EAIC. *Letters and Observations on Agriculture, &c. addressed to, or made by, the South-Carolina Society for Promoting and Improving Agriculture* (Charleston, 1788); Samuel A. Lilly, "The Culture of Revolutionary Charleston" (Ph.D. diss., Miami University, 1972), 37–42.

11. Hedges, *The Browns of Providence Plantations*, 197–98; Walter C. Bronson, *The History of Brown University, 1764–1914* (Providence: Brown University, 1914), 81; Coyle, "Welcome Arnold," 9; Reuben A. Guild, *Life, Times, and Correspondence of James Manning and the Early History of Brown University* (Boston: Gould and Lincoln, 1864), 330–31; *Catalogue of the Library of the Providence Atheneum, to which are Prefixed the Charter, Constitution, and By-Laws and an Historical Sketch of the Institution* (Providence: Knowles, Anthony, 1853), xiv, note; Minute Book for the Providence Library, 1–11, Providence Atheneum; *At a Meeting of the School Committee of the Town of Providence . . . 16 January 1786, The Hon Jabez Bowen in the Chair*, Evans 19943 EAIC; *A Catalogue of the Redwood Library and Athenaeum in Newport, R.I., together with a Supplement, Addenda, and Index of Subjects and Titles* (Boston: J. Wilson, 1860).

12. Kershaw, *James Bowdoin*, 70, 89; Lowell, *Eulogy*; Bruce Winchester Stone, "The Role of the Learned Societies in the Growth of Scientific Boston 1780–1848" (Ph.D. diss., Boston University, 1974); *A List of the American Academy of Arts and Sciences* (Boston, 1785), MHS; *The Institution of the Humane Society of the Commonwealth of Massachusetts; with the Rules for Regulating Said Society, and the Methods of Treatment to be used with Persons apparently dead* (Boston, 1788). Samuel Phillips, Jr., was the principal founder of the Phillips Academy at Andover (1778); John Phillips, his brother, founded the Phillips Academy at Exeter (1781).

13. Countryman, "Consolidating Power in Revolutionary America."

14. James Bayard to James Hutchinson, 25 November 1785 ("Present my best regards to Messrs. Whitehill, Smiley, Finley & our other Friends in Assembly &c."), Hutchinson Ms, American Philosophical Society, Philadelphia; George Bryan to William Atlee, 23 June 1785, Bryan Ms, HSP.

15. John Armstrong to William Irvine, 16 August 1787, Irvine Ms, HSP reporting a conversation with "a sensible but rigid Constitutionalist": "He said Aristocracy was [the Republicans'] object, and that no wreck nor ruin would by some be regarded (if like Samson they themselves should even die with the Philistines) in order to get clear of the humiliating line of republicanism &c." Also Richard Alan Ryerson, "Republican Theory and Partisan Reality in Revolutionary Pennsylvania: Toward a New View of the Constitutionalist Party," in *The*

Sovereign States in an Age of Uncertainty, ed. Ronald Hoffman and Peter Albert (Charlottesville: University of Virginia Press, 1981), 123.

16. "Plebian," [Philadelphia] *Freeman's Journal*, 8 January 1783; Anti-Bank Petition, *Pennsylvania Packet*, 4 March 1785, quoted in Arnold, "Revolution in Pennsylvania," 220. For the attacks on Republican taxes, see "Jacob Thrift," "Plebian," and "Belasarius," *Freeman's Journal*, 24 September, 9 and 28 January 1783.

17. For Gillon's background and holdings, see *Gazette of the State of South Carolina*, 5 September 1784; for his urban properties and his country seat, see *Columbian Herald*, 4 September 1786. For Gillon's popular tactics, see Pauline Maier, "The Charleston Mob and the Evolution of Popular Politics in Revolutionary South Carolina, 1765–1784," *Perspectives in American History* 4 (1970), and the articles in the *Gazette of the State of South Carolina*, esp. 22 April, 6 May, 9 August, 9 September 1784. The officers of the South-Carolina Marine Society (Alexander Gillon, president) are listed in the *Charleston Morning Post*, 14 February 1786. On Aedanus Burke, see George C. Rogers, "Aedanus Burke, Nathanael Greene, Anthony Wayne, and the British Merchants of Charleston," *South Carolina Historical Magazine* 67 (April 1966): 75–83. On Rawlins Lowndes and Sumter, see [Charleston] *State Gazette of South Carolina*, 4 and 14 February 1788; also on Sumter, S.C. House Journal, 1787 House, 241–42.

18. List of Persons Present, April 3, E. Greenwich, Brown Family Business Papers, P-PG, JCBL. For the election itself, see Peregrine Foster to Dwight Foster, 24 April 1786, Dwight Foster Family Ms, AAS, (hereafter Foster Ms): "We have in Providence a Majority of 297 for the Old Prox but the Country have a large majority for the above" ticket headed by Collins.

19. Superior Court Justice David Sewall described Reliefers in the Bay State as "small Politicians" who make their careers by championing tax relief. David Sewall to George Thatcher, 16 October 1786, Chamberlain Collection, Boston Public Library. Printed in "The Thatcher Papers," *Historical Magazine* 6, second series (November 1869): 257–58. For Reliefer activism during Shays's Rebellion, see Nathaniel Gorham to Nathan Dane, 29 March 1787, Charles G. Slack Collection of Autographs, Marietta [Ohio] College Library; Lunenberg Circular Letter to Athol Selectmen, March 1787, *Worcester Magazine*, 4th week, March 1787, p. 638; Stoughton Town Meeting to Dorchester Selectmen, n.d., printed under hostile caption "Sedition," Boston *Independent Chronicle*, 15 February 1787.

20. These Reliefers are analyzed further in chap. 9.

21. On George Clinton, see Alfred F. Young, *The Democratic Republicans of New York: The Origins, 1763–1797* (Chapel Hill: University of North Carolina Press, 1967), 3–58. Seeing that "all the great opulent families [of New York] were united in one confederacy," his "politicks," he said, were "to keep a constant eye to the measures of this combination." Quoted in Young, p. 5. On the Clinton administration's contribution to the federal treasury, see table 1. Between 1786 and 1787, when many states made no payments to the federal treasury, New York paid $25,000 in requisitions quotaed before 1786.

22. Charles Pettit to Nathanael Greene, 23 March 1785, Greene Ms, Clements: "Our measures are so calculated that whenever Congress pronounce their

ability to proceed, we can take a wheel from our Carriage & annex it to theirs without impeding the Machine."

23. Robert Morris to Governor Jonathan Trumbull, 14 June 1782, Morris, *Papers*, 5: 407. Also Walter Stewart to Horatio Gates, 17 November 1782, Horatio Gates Ms, NYHS (microfilm).

24. William Bingham to Cadwalader Morris, 6 November 1782, Strettel Ms, HSP.

25. Anthony Wayne to General Jackson, 18 August 1787, Wayne Ms, HSP. The frequent references to Reliefers as "factious men," "turbulent men," "Catalines," and "popular demagogues," also express this idea. See James Mitchell Varnum to George Washington, 18 June 1787, in Wilkins Updike, *Memoirs of the Rhode Island Bar* (Boston: T. H. Webb, 1842), 300–302; Edward Rutledge to John Jay, 12 November 1786, Jay Ms, Columbia; Samuel Hodgdon to Timothy Pickering, 4 October 1787, Pickering Ms, MHS, reel 40, LC; Sharp Dulany to Anthony Wayne, 10 April 1788, Wayne Ms, Clements.

26. The federal requisition of 2 August 1786 asked the states for $431,920 for military and civil pay, Indian affairs, and contingencies; $1,721,239 for principal and interest due on the French, Dutch, and Spanish debt; and $1,606,560 for one year's interest due federal domestic creditors. The last was to be paid in the paper interest indents previously issued by Congress to its creditors.

27. At the time Rhode Island funded its state debt in 1782, debt holdings were widely dispersed with notables holding relatively small sums. Welcome Arnold, for example, in 1784 owned about $1,068 in state debt securities; by 1790 he had increased his holdings to $17,813. John Brown's totals rose from about $7,369 in 1784 to $26,943 in 1790. Polishook, *Rhode Island and the Union*, 116–18. In Pennsylvania the assembly voted to pay interest to soldier-veteran creditors of the state out of current revenues but to exclude second purchasers who bought soldiers' certificates at depreciated prices. "An Act to Appropriate Certain Moneys Arising from the Excise for the Payment of the Annual Interest due on the Unalienated Certificates therein mentioned," 21 March 1783, *The Statutes at Large of Pennsylvania from 1682 to 1801*, comp. James T. Mitchell and Henry Flanders (Harrisburg: C. M. Busch, State Printer, 1896–1919), 11:110–11. Also Anthony Wayne to Josiah Harmar, 3 January 1783, Wayne Ms, HSP.

28. Robert Morris was especially optimistic that hard money taxation would produce confidence and productivity. Morris to Jacques Necker, 15 June; to George Washington, 15 June 1781, Morris, *Papers*, 1:149–53. See the Rhode Island petition arguing that the prosperity of *both* commerce and agriculture required sound fiscal and monetary measures. Providence *United States Chronicle*, 9 March 1786. For the converse idea that failure to protect property rights and assure a stable currency only hurt commercial confidence, see Brown and Benson to Hewes and Anthony, 1 May 1786, Brown Ms, JCBL.

29. Alexander Hamilton to Robert Morris, 30 April 1781, Morris, *Papers*, 1:58; Robert Morris, Report to Congress, 29 July 1782, Continential Congress *Journals* 22:431; Morris to William Whipple, 4 June 1782, Morris, *Papers*, 5:336. How to convert the common people's apathy into energy and enterprise also preoccupied Europeans such as David Hume, Bernard de Mandeville, and

other eighteenth-century political economists. See Drew McCoy, *The Elusive Republic: Political Economy in Jeffersonian America* (Chapel Hill: University of North Carolina Press, 1980), 28–47.

30. Edmund S. Morgan, *American Slavery, American Freedom: The Ordeal of Colonial Virginia* (New York: Norton, 1975), 319–26; Gary B. Nash, "Poverty and Poor Relief in Pre-Revolutionary Philadelphia," *William and Mary Quarterly* 33 (January 1976): 16–30.

31. Willi Paul Adams, "Republicanism in Political Rhetoric Before 1776," *Political Science Quarterly* (September 1970): 397–421. Critics of republican government stressed its instability and inconstancy. "Like ill-constructed machines set in motion, [the republics of Greece and Rome] perished by their own instability and unwieldiness." "Civis," *Philadelphia Ledger*, 6 April 1776, quoted in Adams, ibid., 414.

32. Matthew Ridley to Gouverneur Morris, 24 March 1783, Paris, Bernhard Knollenberg Collection, Yale.

CHAPTER 5. PENNSYLVANIA

1. Brunhouse, *Counter-Revolution in Pennsylvania*; Ireland, "Constitution in Pennsylvania."

2. Lemuel Molovinsky, "Pennsylvania's Legislative Efforts to Finance the War for Independence: A Study of the Continuity of Colonial Finance, 1775–1783" (Ph.D. diss., Temple University, 1975).

3. Molovinsky holds that for most of the Revolution the Constitutionalists aimed to keep taxes "at a minimum and rely on paper money received from Congress." Molovinsky, "Pennsylvania's Finance," 100.

4. Morris to George Washington, 15 June 1781, Morris, *Papers*, 1:153. These were the so-called "effective supply" taxes of 1781, 1782, and 1783. See Appendix 1 and *Statutes at Large of Pennsylvania*, 10: 326–36, 385–400; 11:81–91.

5. Morris diary, 14 May 1781, Morris, *Papers*, 1:61–62; Morris to George Washington, 15 June 1781, Morris, *Papers*, 1:153; Morris to Philip Schuyler, 25 June 1781, Morris, *Papers*, 1:177–78. After he became federal finance superintendent, Morris again pressed Republican leaders of the Republican-controlled assembly to continue their tax measures. Morris, Diary, 17 September 1781, Morris, *Papers*, 2:285–86.

6. Morris complained bitterly about state politicians who, he said, either voted against taxes outright or, more usually, agreed to taxes but artfully took care "to provide no competent Means to compel a Collection." Morris to Continental Receivers of Taxes, 5 October 1782, Morris Ms, Huntington Library, San Marino, Calif.

7. "An Act to Raise Effective Supplies for the Year 1782," *Statutes at Large of Pennsylvania*, 10:385–400. Earlier Constitutionalist tax legislation did not provide for action by the Supreme Executive Council against county boards of commissioners.

8. Bucks County Commissioners Minute Book, 12 November 1781 (8

Months Tax Minute Book), 28 November and 21 November 1783 (Supply and Class Tax Minute Books), microfilm, PHMC.

9. Ibid., 1 and 5 February, 19 March 1782, (Supply Tax Minute Book), microfilm, PHMC.

10. Bucks County Commissioners Minute Book, 5 November 1784; York Commissioners Minute Book, 4 March 1783; Chester Commissioners Minute Book, 18, 19, 20, 21 November 1785; York County Minute Book, 3 September 1783, microfilm, PHMC.

11. Bucks County Commissioners Minute Books, 5 February, 12 March 1782 (Class Tax Minute Book); 17 December 1784 (1784–87 Minute Book), microfilm, PHMC.

12. Nash, "Poverty and Poor Relief."

13. Anthony Wayne Resolutions, introduced 1 December 1784, *Pennsylvania Assembly Minutes*, 1784–85, 1st sess., 42, 49–52, 72–74 (hereafter *Pennsylvania Minutes*). On Wayne's role as floor leader, see Charles Pettit to Nathanael Greene, 23 March 1785, Greene Ms, Clements: "Genl Wayne was the hero of the opposition in the House." Also, *Council of Censors Journal* [10 November 1783–25 September 1784] (Philadelphia, 1784), 2d sess., 175, 179, Evans #18093, EAIC.

14. Committee on Public Accounts Report, 10 January 1781, *Pennsylvania Minutes*, 1780–81, 1st sess., 357–59; Ways and Means Committee Report, 21 November 1781, *Pennsylvania Minutes*, 1781–82, 1st sess., 516–17; House Resolutions, February, August 1782, *Pennsylvania Minutes*, 1781–82, 2d and 3d sess., 588, 666; Committee Report and House Resolutions, 18 September 1782, Pennsylvania *Minutes*, 1781–82, 3d sess., 706.

15. Supreme Executive Council Circular to County Commissioners, 11 December 1781, Pennsylvania Revolutionary Governments, Record Group 27, microfilm, PHMC.

16. John Armstrong to County Commissioners, 20 May 1783, Pennsylvania Revolutionary Governments, Record Group 27, PHMC.

17. Jacob Smyser to John Dickinson, 5 August 1783, *Pennsylvania Archives Selected and Arranged from Original Documents in the Office of the Secretary of the Commonwealth . . . by Samuel Hazard Commencing 1783* (Philadelphia: J. Severns, 1854), 10:77 refers to "threatning" letters from the council of 20 May and 24 July 1783, (hereafter *Pennsylvania Archives*).

18. Dickinson to General Assembly, 18 August 1783, *Pennsylvania Minutes*, August 1783, 3d sess., 886–91.

19. House Resolution, 10 November 1783, *Pennsylvania Minutes*, 1783–84, 1st sess., 21.

20. *Council of Censors Journal*, 1st sess. 8, 19, 31, and passim. Anthony Wayne to William Irvine, 15 June 1784, Wayne Ms, Clements.

21. Report of Committees on Tax Collection and Execution of Laws, *Council of Censors Journal*, 2d sess., 147–54; Report of Committee on Observance of Constitutional Procedures and Duties, *Council of Censors Journal*, 2d sess., 110–23, 134–46, 154–55. As the second session of the Council of Censors ended, an angry Anthony Wayne reported:

Our body . . . have lost sight of the *Executive* & the manner in which taxes have been levied & collected—as matters of little moment—but they pursue the Legislative branch with unremitting ardour & avidity—since the decision upon the printed report in which [the assembly] are D——d as violators of the Constitution & *unfaithful* Guardians of the people. . . .

The whole of this business is an Electioneering trick intended to Inflame the minds of the People against the present [Republican Assembly] members who I believe will modify the test Laws & repeal the Colledge Bill. (Wayne to William Irvine, 4 September 1784, Wayne Ms, Clements).

22. Bucks Commissioners Minutes, 2 August 1783 (Supply Tax Minute Book), microfilm, PHMC. Bucks County Commissioners Minute Book, 8 August 1783 (Class Tax Minute Book), microfilm, PHMC.

23. Bucks County Commissioners Minute Book, 22 October 1783 (Supply Tax Minute Book), microfilm, PHMC. This entry notes that lands previously advertised for taxes were ordered sold "without any further notice." See entries of 7, 21, 28, 29 November 1783 for further evidence of the stepped-up pressure. See also entry marked "settled on 11 August 1784 with David Rittenhouse, Treasurer."

24. Bucks County Commissioners to SEC President, John Dickinson, 31 July 1783, *Pennsylvania Archives*, 10:75–76.

25. Jacob Smyser, York County Commissioner to Dickinson, 5 August 1783, *Pennsylvania Archives*, 10:77.

26. Cumberland Commissioners to Dickinson, 14 August 1783, *Pennsylvania Archives*, 10:80. Lancaster (16 August 1783), Northampton (25 August 1783), and Washington County (9 July 1783, misdated 1784) boards to Dickinson, *Pennsylvania Archives*, 10:82, 92, 587.

27. 62 York County Petitioners to General Assembly, 2 March 1784, General Assembly, Petitions and Miscellaneous Records, Record Group 7, PHMC; 53 Westmoreland Petitioners, read 12 August 1784, General Assembly, Petitions and Miscellaneous Records, Record Group 7, PHMC; 60 Lancaster County Petitioners to Supreme Executive Council, 27 May 1784, Pennsylvania Revolutionary Governments, Record Group 27, PHMC.

28. Cumberland County Commissioners to Dickinson, 14 August 1783, *Pennsylvania Archives*, 10:80; York Commissioners Minute Book, April 1784 term; Commissioner Ephraim Douglass to Dickinson, 11 July 1784, *Pennsylvania Archives*, 10:588.

29. Westmoreland Commissioners to Dickinson, 4 September 1783, *Pennsylvania Archives*, 10:98–99; Ephraim Douglass to Council Secretary John Armstrong, 29 May 1784, *Pennsylvania Archives*, 10:582–83.

30. Washington Commissioners to Secretary John Armstrong, 9 July 1784, *Pennsylvania Archives*, 10:587.

31. David Rittenhouse to SEC President Dickinson, 27 April 1784, *Pennsylvania Archives*, 10:241–42.

32. The partisan composition of the 1783 and 1784 assemblies by delegates'

name, party identity, and county is found in Ireland, "Constitution in Pennsylvania," 260–65, tables 13 and 14.

33. "Belisarius," "Jacob Thrift," and "Sorrow," [Philadelphia] *Freeman's Journal*, 21 August, 24 September 1783, 18 August 1784.

34. At its second session in 1784 the house appointed a special committee to investigate the robberies of tax collectors, and at its third session the house ordered that papers "relative to the obstructions to the collection of taxes in the county of *Westmoreland*, and those relative to the robberies in the county of Fayette" be referred to the Supreme Executive Council. *Pennsylvania Minutes*, 1783–84, 2d sess., 249–50, 3d sess., 276. In March 1784 thirteen rural Republican members bolted party ranks by voting for a relief proposal that would print and loan £50,000 in paper money payable for taxes only. *Pennsylvania Minutes*, 1783–1784, 2d sess., 243–46. The following August–September when the bill came up for a third reading, the amount was increased to £100,000. This time, however, Republican ranks held firm and the entire measure was tabled. *Pennsylvania Minutes*, 1783–84, 3d sess., 296. See the account in Ireland, "Constitution in Pennsylvania," 156–60.

35. Brunhouse, *Counter-Revolution in Pennsylvania*, 152–69, and Ireland, "Constitution in Pennsylvania," 152–66, hold that the test laws, the college, and the 1776 constitution were the issues used by the Constitutionalists to generate their landslide. In an April 1784 call for a loan office bill to make paper money available to farmers, a Constitutionalist writer attacked the Bank of North America: "I will venture to say, that unless our legislature pass an act for the opening [of] a loan office shortly, the landed interest must fall prey to the bank. This sink of our specie has its benefits confined almost totally within the atmosphere of the city; but a loan office would diffuse them to the remotest part of the state." "Philopatria," [Philadelphia] *Freeman's Journal*, 14 April 1784.

36. In March 1784 the Republicans tabled petitions for reinstatement of the college charter and repeal of the test laws pending the outcome of upcoming sessions of the Council of Censors. *Pennsylvania Minutes*, 1783–84, 3d sess., pp. 306, 310, 321. Yet in March–April 1784, after Sharp Delany, a member from Philadelphia, resigned his seat and the house ordered a special election, the Constitutionalist leader, Philadelphia merchant Charles Pettit, was elected to Delany's seat. Pettit would later engineer the Constitutionalists' funding paper money–tax relief program. *Pennsylvania Minutes*, 1783–84, 2d sess., 181, 202.

37. "An Act for furnishing the quota of this state towards paying the annual interest of the debts of the United States; and for funding and paying the interest of the public debts of this state"; "An act for erecting and opening a Loan-Office for the sum of fifty thousand pounds," Pennsylvania *Session Laws*, 1784–85, 2d sess. The Funding Act also pledged income from the state impost and future direct taxes for the payment of interest on this funded debt. Designed to relieve both federal and state creditors *and* farmers, the act explicitly provided that interest payments to federal creditors would end once Congress resumed payment. Charles Pettit to Nathanael Greene, 23 March 1785, Greene Ms, Clements. Compare Ferguson, *Power of the Purse*, 228–30. The £150,000 paper emission would enable Pennsylvania taxpayers to pay not only current taxes but "the arrearages

of taxes now due, with greater ease and facility." *Pennsylvania Minutes*, 1784–85, 1st sess., 44–50.

38. *Pennsylvania Minutes*, 1784–85, 1st sess., 49–51, 72–74.

39. Supreme Executive Council Circular to Tax Commissioners, 20 January 1785, Pennsylvania Revolutionary Governments, Record Group 27, microfilm, PHMC.

40. Minutes of the Supreme Executive Council, 5 July 1785, *Pennsylvania Archives*, 14:494; Attorney General William Bradford to John Dickinson, 20 July 1785, Pennsylvania Revolutionary Governments, Record Group 27, microfilm, PHMC.

41. Court Docket Book, September 1778–December 1786, Pennsylvania Supreme Court, Eastern District, Court of Oyer and Terminer, Record Group 33, 318, PHMC. On 22 May 1786 the Cumberland jury returned a ruling of ignoramus—the equivalent of dismissal. At that point the attorney general seems to have dropped the several other cases. In York the trial was formally put off until a later term. See Court Docket Book, 316.

42. York County Commissioners Minutes, 12 November 1785, 18 January 1786, microfilm, PHMC.

43. Ireland puts the new assembly alignment at 33 Republicans and 33 Constitutionalists. Ireland, "Constitution in Pennsylvania," 266–67, table 15.

44. Sharp Delany to Anthony Wayne, 11 July 1786, Wayne Ms., Clements: "Paper & Tender Laws has shut up all hard money—& almost banishes confidence between Man & Man—for however willing to trust between acquaintance & friends the dispositon & duty of Executors &c under law puts a stop to all money transactions."

45. Ronald M. Baumann, "The Democratic-Republicans of Philadelphia: The Origins, 1776–1797" (Ph.D. diss., Pennsylvania State University, 1970), 61–62.

46. "An Act to enforce the due collection and Payment of Taxes within this Commonwealth," 24 March 1786, Pennsylvania *Session Laws*, 1785–86, 1st sess.; Bucks County Commissioners Minutes, 22 April 1786, microfilm, PHMC.

47. *Pennsylvania Minutes*, 1785–86, 2d sess., 252–53. The Logan-Morris proposal garnered only 10 Republican votes out of some 30 Republicans in the assembly.

48. See Robert Morris's alternative Plan B for reorganizing the state's finances, proposed and voted down in December 1785. *Pennsylvania Minutes*, 1785–86, 1st sess., 122–29. Morris's proposal was defeated by a vote of 23 to 39; the few Republican nays found it politically too risky. In February 1788 Fitzsimons wrote his former Republican, now Federalist ally, William Irvine: "We can at any moment blow up their [Constitutionalist] funding system if we think proper." Fitzsimons to Irvine, 11 February 1788, Irvine Ms, HSP.

49. Thomas Fitzsimons to William Irvine, 30 January, 11 February 1788, Irvine Ms, HSP.

CHAPTER 6. SOUTH CAROLINA

1. For background, see Higgins, "Financial History," 49–50, 252, and Becker, *American Taxation*, 99–104, 206–10.

2. Governor John Mathews, Speech to House, 24 January 1783, South Carolina Assembly Journal, January–March 1783 sess., 26–31.

3. "An Act for Raising and Paying into the Public Treasury of this State the Tax therein mentioned for the Use and Service thereof"; "An Ordinance for ascertaining and regulating the Office of Receiver, Auditor, and Accountant General of the Public Accounts, and for other Purposes therein mentioned," *South Carolina Acts and Ordinances*, 1783 (hereafter *Acts and Ordinances*). "An Act to impose certain Duties on Goods to be imported into this State," passed in August 1783, ordered that the revenue from the impost "be appropriated solely to the payment of this states quota of the National Expenditures, as Congress shall from time to time assess, agreeable to the Confederation." Annual state budgets are appended to the yearly tax legislation.

4. Higgins, "Financial History," 247, n. 5, finds that although all paper interest indents were eventually recovered by taxation, "no specie was received during these years [1784–87] for the general tax." But the treasurers' accounts as reported by a house committee in the January–March session of 1786 show that specie *was* collected through August 1785. Because indents were payable for the 1784 and 1785 acts, and because specie only was required by the 1783 act, the specie thus recorded was for the 1783 tax. See Accounts of Treasury Commissioners, Committee on Treasury Commissioners, South Carolina Assembly Journal, January–March 1786 sess., 275–79 (hereafter Treasury Commisioners). Also see table 7.

5. "An Act for Raising and paying into the Public Treasury" for 1784 and 1785, *Acts and Ordinances*, January–March 1784, 1785 sess. The new 1784 ad valorem tax act was designed in committees chaired by notables John Mathews and Dr. David Ramsay. S.C. Assembly Journal, January–March 1784 sess., 5–6, 200–204. See also "A Steady and Open Republican" and "Democratic Gentle-Touch," [Charleston] *Gazette of the State of South Carolina*, 17, 26 July 1784.

6. Despite these reallocations, in 1784 alone the Carolina government made five payments of specie to Congress totaling £16,849. See Treasury Commissioners.

7. "An Act for raising and paying into the Public Treasury of the State the Tax therein mentioned for the Use and Service thereof," *Acts and Ordinances*, January–March 1783 sess.

8. Robert A. Becker, "Salus Populi Supreme Lex: Public Peace and South Carolina Debtor Relief Laws, 1783–1788," *South Carolina Historical Magazine* 80 (1979): 65–75.

9. For specie collections received at the central treasury, see "Treasury Commissioners." For the basis of the 62% figure, see appendix 1, South Carolina. For the thirteen districts that made no payment on either the 1784 or the 1785 tax, see House Ways and Means Committee Report, 20 February 1787, Leg-

islative Reports, South Carolina Department of Archives and History (SCDAH). Also Chester County Petition to Carolina Senate (227 signers), 29 August 1788, Petitions to the General Assembly, General Assembly Papers, SCDAH.

10. St. Bartholomew Collection Tax Return, John Croskey collector, closed 12 October 1787. Of the £922 in tax receipts he turned over to the central treasury, John Croskey reported that £68 had been extracted from "sundry Persons who made no Returns but Paid the Constable"—a 7% proportion. Of the £806 in tax receipts they turned over to the treasury, Bartholomew collectors John and William Saunders reported that £118 had been raised "by Execution"—a proportion of 15%. St. Bartholomew Collection Return, John and William Saunders Collectors, closed 24 December 1787, Treasury Commissioners Tax Returns, Box 1, SCDAH.

11. Higgins, "Financial History," 245–47. For specie received at the central treasury, see Treasury Commissioners. See table 8. In 1787 the House Ways and Means Committee reported that the state had paid Congress $72,212 in specie at various times during the past decade. South Carolina Ways and Means Committee Report, 20 February 1787, Legislative Reports, SCDAH. Only the 1783 and 1784 budgets made provision for any payment to Congress, however.

12. Edward Rutledge to Arthur Middleton, August 1782, "Correspondence of Hon. Arthur Middleton," *South Carolina Historical and Genealogical Magazine* 27 (January 1926): 21; David Ramsay to Benjamin Rush, 11 July 1783, Rush Ms, LCP. See also Ramsay to Rush, 6 August 1786, Rush Ms, LCP: "The morals of the people are so depreciated that legal honesty is all that is aimed at by most people"; "We have neither honesty nor knowledge enough for republican governments"; Judge Henry Pendleton, Charge to Georgetown Grand Jury, *Charleston Morning Post*, 13 December 1786. "Mentor," "The Way to Make MONEY plenty in every Man's Pocket," [Charleston] *South Carolina Gazette and General Advertiser*, 28 May–1 June 1785. Also "Of the Advantages of Oeconomy," ibid., 18 August 1785.

13. See, for example, "An Act for Raising Supplies for the Year 1785"; "An Act for Establishing County Courts and for Regulating the Proceedings therein," *Acts and Ordinances*, January–March 1785 session.

14. Treasurer's Notice, 12 August 1784, Treasury Office, [Charleston] *South Carolina Gazette and General Advertiser*, 10–12, 12–14, 14–17, 19–21 August 1784.

15. St. Philip's and St. Michael's parishes collectors' notice, [Charleston] *South Carolina Gazette and General Advertiser*, 26 July, 14–17 August 1784. See table 8 for receipts for May and June 1785.

16. S.C. Assembly Journal, January–March 1785 sess., 35–36, 154, 389, 406.

17. S.C. Senate Journal, January–March 1785 sess., 145, 153, 252; "An act for raising supplies for the Year 1785," *Acts and Ordinances*, January–March 1785 sess.

18. See Charleston tax collectors' advertisements in [Charleston] *South Carolina Gazette and Public Advertiser*, 16–20, 23–27, 27–30 April 1785.

19. 7 September 1785 entry, *The State Records of South Carolina: Journals of*

the Privy Council 1783–1789, ed. Adele S. Edwards (Columbia: University of South Carolina Press, 1971), 168.

20. See Treasury Commissioners.

21. David Ramsay to Benjamin Rush, 31 January 1784, Charleston, Ramsay Ms in Rush Ms, LCP describes how reports of a paper money relief measure caused men to hoard specie: "Though I firmly believe they will not carry this measure in the house now sitting yet the apprehension of it has locked up the gold & silver in a great measure in the desks of the provident." "Appius," *Charleston Morning Post and Daily Advertiser*, 16 February 1787, describes the increase in debt suits in 1785 as resulting from merchants' fears their debts would depreciate or not be recoverable. For debt suits and recovery sales in and around Charleston see *South Carolina Gazette and Public Advertiser*, 30 March–2 April, 20–23 April, 7–11 May 1785.

22. "An Act for Establishing County Courts and for Regulating the Proceedings therein," *Acts and Ordinances*, March 1785. In 1784 the assembly signaled its desire to encourage foreign capital into the state. At Edward Rutledge's instigation, the house enacted an ordinance "to encourage subjects of foreign states to lend money at Interest on Real Estates within this State." S.C. Assembly Journal, January–March 1784 sess., 348.

23. Entry for 22 June 1785, *Journals of the South Carolina Privy Council*, 166.

24. 72 Camden Petitioners, 5 October 1785, Petitions to S.C. Assembly, Assembly Papers, SCDAH.

25. Little River District Petitioners to General Assembly, 7 March 1785, General Assembly Petitions, SCDAH.

26. "A Backcountryman to the Inhabitants of Ninety-Six District," [Charleston] *Gazette of the State of South Carolina*, 7 October 1784.

27. For example, the assembly rejected a proposed sheriff's sale regulation bill. S.C. House Journal, January–March 1785 sess., 245.

28. Entry for 21 October 1785, *Journal of the South Carolina Privy Council*, 170.

29. District Eastward of the Wateree Collection Return, William Murrell Collector, Treasury Commissioners Tax Returns, Box 1, SCDAH. On 16 September 1785 Murrell swore on oath before justice of the quorum Daniel Huger that he had issued the execution warrants to the constable, and that his own property, worth only £20, would not begin to cover the full amount of his still uncollected quota.

30. Benjamin Hawkins to Governor Richard Carswell, Charleston, 26 September 1785, *State Records of North Carolina*, ed. Walter Clark (Goldsboro, N.C.: Nash Brothers, 1899), 17:524–25; Benjamin Hawkins to Arthur Lee, Charleston, 11 August 1785, Lee Family Ms, reel 7, LC.

31. See "Extract of a Letter from Charleston," 23 May 1785, [Charleston] *Columbian Centinel*, 30 September 1785; Nadelhaft, "Revolutionary Era in South Carolina," 235–36; Becker, "Salus Populi Supreme Lex," 65–75.

32. See Treasury Commissioners. Also, table 8.

33. A Planter, "Thoughts on the Necessity of Emitting a Paper Currency in

the State of South Carolina," [Charleston] *Columbian Herald*, 28 September 1785.

34. Governor William Moultrie's Message, 26 September 1785, South Carolina Assembly Journal, September–October 1785 sess., 4–6.

35. [William Hornby], "To the Public in General," *Gazette of the State of South Carolina*, 19 August 1784 and *passim*.

36. "To the Republican Whigs and all others of the same VIRTUOUS denomination in the several Districts and parishes of the Commonwealth of SOUTH CAROLINA," [Charleston] *South Carolina Gazette and General Advertiser*, 14–16 September 1784. Bids for backcountry support are noted in "A Backcountryman," [Charleston] *Gazette of the State of South Carolina*, 7 October 1784.

37. "Democratic Gentle-touch," *Gazette of the State of South Carolina*, 6 May 1784; "To the Public in General," [William Hornby], *Gazette of the State of South Carolina*, 19 August 1784. In the Library of Congress copy of the *Gazette*, the anonymous author of the "Democratic Gentle-touch" essays is identified in an eighteenth-century hand as Alexander Gillon, but Gillon's ally Hornby later admitted authorship. *Gazette of the State of South Carolina*, 12 August 1784.

38. See [Aedanus Burke], *Considerations on the Society or Order of Cincinnati . . . Proving that it Creates a Race of Hereditary Patricians* (Charleston, 1783); S.C. Assembly Journal, January–March 1785 sess., 413; [Boston] *Massachusetts Gazette*, 2 March 1787; and [Charleston] *Morning Post*, 9 February 1787; S.C. Assembly Journal, January–March 1787 sess., 241–42; S.C. Assembly Journal, January–March 1787 sess., 188–91.

39. Nathaniel Pendleton to Nathanael Greene, 10 July 1784, William Washington to Nathanael Greene, 8 July 1784, and Lewis Morris to Nathanael Greene, 17 July 1784, Greene Ms, Clements; "A True-Born American," *Gazette of the State of South Carolina*, 16 December 1784; *South Carolina Gazette and General Advertiser*, 11–14, 25–28 May 1785; Aedanus Burke's petition to the General Assembly, February 1786, [Charleston] *Morning Post*, 7 February 1787; S.C. Assembly Journal, January–March 1787 sess., 12; John Lloyd to nephew, 7 December 1784, John Lloyd Ms, Charleston Library Society.

40. S.C. Assembly Journal, September–October 1785 sess., 24–25. The committee that drafted the loan office bill was composed of Chief Justice Henry Pendleton, Dr. David Ramsay, and John Mathews.

41. "An Act to establish a Medium of Circulation by Way of Loan, and to Secure its Credit and Utility," *Acts and Ordinances*, October 1785 sess.

42. The sheriff's sale valuation bill was drafted by a committee consisting of Major Thomas Pinckney and Justice Pendleton. S.C. Assembly Journal, September–October 1785 sess., 18; "An Act for regulating Sales under execution, and for other purposes therein mentioned," *Acts and Ordinances*, October 1785 sess.

43. Judge Pendleton's Charge to Georgetown, Cheraws, and Camden Grand Juries, 11 December 1786, [Charleston] *Morning Post*, 13 December 1786. Pendleton's charge alludes to the indolence and extravagance of Carolina citizens and holds that the "indulgence and lenity" of the state government had accelerated this "fatal degeneracy." It also asserts that "the period is at hand, when the punc-

tual payment of the taxes and of the debts, or the uninterrupted recovery of them in the courts of justice must be enforced."

44. Justice Pendleton's charge to Georgetown, Cheraws, and Camden Grand Juries, 11 December 1786, [Charleston] *Morning Post*, 13 December 1786.

45. The assembly's politics have been described as a contest between two fairly stable cosmopolitan and localist coalitions. Carolina assembly politics is more usefully conceived as a series of shifting battles between patricians and the Gillon-led opposition with both competing for the large uncommitted majority in the low country, up-country, and backcountry. See "A Backcountryman to the Inhabitants of Ninety-Six," *Gazette of the State of South Carolina*, 7 October 1784, and Arthur Bryan to Bryan, 9 April 1788, Bryan Ms, HSP.

46. For the alleged role of speculators and rabble-rousers, see Benjamin Hawkins to Richard Carswell, 26 September 1785, *State Records of North Carolina*, 17:524–25, and "Appius," [Charleston] *Morning Post*, 15 February 1787.

47. S.C. Assembly Journal, January–March 1787 sess., 298–300, 331–33; Edward Rutledge to John Jay, 27 March 1787, Jay Ms, microfilm, Columbia.

48. S.C. Assembly Journal, January–March 1786 sess., 76, 138.

49. "An Act for Raising Supplies for the year 1786"; "An Act for Raising Supplies for 1787," *Acts and Ordinances*, 1786, 1787. S.C. Assembly Journal, January–March 1787 sess., 238–39; S.C. Assembly Journal, January–March 1787 sess., 96, 242. [Boston] *Massachusetts Gazette*, 20, 23, 27 March 1787.

50. "An Act to amend an Act entitled 'An Act to establish a Medium of Circulation by Way of Loans, and to secure its Credit and Utility,'" *Acts and Ordinances*, 1786.

51. Treasury Commissioners, 5, 16, 275–79.

52. S.C. Assembly Journal, January–March 1787 sess., 22–25.

CHAPTER 7. RHODE ISLAND

1. See appendix 1 for Rhode Island fiscal measures.

2. J. Arnold to David Howell, Providence, 29 June 1782, Frederick Peck Collection, Box 7, RIHS.

3. Becker, *American Taxation*, 140–42; Caleb Arnold to General Assembly, October 1783, Petitions to Rhode Island General Assembly, 1783, 20:82, Rhode Island State Archives, Providence (RISA).

4. Report of Ways and Means Committee, *Rhode Island Session Laws*, November 1782, 25, 29–30.

5. Peregrine Foster to Dwight Foster, 24 April 1786, Foster Ms, AAS; Mack E. Thompson, "The Ward-Hopkins Controversy and the American Revolution in Rhode Island: An Interpretation," *William and Mary Quarterly* 16 (July 1959): 363–75.

6. Becker, *American Taxation*, 134–45.

7. "An Act for Granting and Apportioning a Tax of £12,000 in gold or silver, on the Inhabitants of this State," *Session Laws*, January 1782 sess., 43–45; General Treasurer "To the Sheriff of the County of Newport, or to his Deputy. Greeting," 19 September 1786, Evans #44261, EAIC.

8. *Session Laws*, February 1782 sess., 29; August 1782 sess., 19–23; October 1782 sess., 14; November 1782 sess., 21.

9. General Treasurer's Record Book, green volume, "Taxes Ft-1 1779–1787," RISA, 67–81, 83–96, 98–111, 113–26 (hereafter Treasurer's Record Book).

10. List of General Treasurer's executions and amounts issued on 1783 State Tax, 14 June 1784, Treasurer's Record Book.

11. "Present State of the Taxes," Newport, 7 May 1785, Papers Relating to the Adoption of the Constitution of the United States, 105, RISA.

12. Jabez Bowen, "To the Freemen of the State of Rhode Island," 13 April 1786, Evans #19521, EAIC.

13. *Session Laws*, June 1784 sess., 34–36; Becker, *American Taxation*, 143.

14. *Session Laws*, June 1784 sess., 34–38.

15. *Session Laws*, January 1782 sess., 9; August 1782 sess., 23; October 1784 sess., 29; August 1785 sess., 13–15.

16. *Session Laws*, February 1783 sess., 26–35.

17. *Session Laws*, November 1782 sess., 26.

18. *Session Laws*, South Kingston: January 1782 sess., 9; August 1782 sess., 23; May 1784 sess., 19–20. Coventry: February 1784 sess., 9. Scituate: January 1782 sess., 11. Foster: February 1784 sess., 16–17.

19. *Session Laws*, November 1782 sess., 21; June 1783 sess., 31–32; August 1784 sess., 21; October 1784 sess., 13–14; October 1785 sess., 38.

20. Fleet Brown to R.I. General Assembly, 31 October 1785, Petitions to R.I. Assembly, 1785–86, 22:66, RISA.

21. William Arnold to General Assembly, February 1784, Petitions to R.I. Assembly, 1784–85, 21:10, RISA.

22. Reynolds Knowles to General Assembly, February 1786, Petitions to R.I. Assembly, 1785–86, 22:87, RISA.

23. Abel Barnes to General Assembly, October 1783, Petitions to R.I. Assembly, 1783, 20:84, RISA. The assembly granted Barnes's request for a stay of two months.

24. Richard Gardner to R.I. Assembly, May 1784, Petitions to R.I. Assembly, 1784–85, 21:20, RISA; *Session Laws*, February 1785 sess., 20; Memo, Treasurer's Record Book: "Memo Richard Gardner Collr for the Town of S. Kingston was sold to Mr. Channing & the Sheriff Brown has a deed of the same for £486.18 in behalf of the State."

25. In the same thirteen-month interval, the number of Rhode Island towns listed on the general treasurer's accounts with deficiencies on the same 1784 tax was reduced from twenty-seven (£14,164 on £20,000 still owed) to eight (£1,699 still owed). Treasurer's Record Book.

26. Glocester Town Meeting Records, 13 January 1783, quoted in Ruth Herndon, "Governing the Affairs of the Town: Continuity and Change in Rhode Island, 1750–1780" (Ph.D. diss., American University, 1992), 249; Caleb Arnold to General Assembly, October 1783, Petitions to R.I. General Assembly, 1783, 20:82, RISA; Timothy Jenne and others to Upper House, 5 March 1783, Petitions to R.I. General Assembly, 1783, 20:22.

27. For pleas for paper money in 1785, see Peregrine Foster to Dwight Foster,

17 March 1785, Dwight Foster Ms, MHS. For 1786, see Town Meeting Resolutions: for Glocester, 14 February 1786, 41; for Middletown, 25 February 1786, 60; for Coventry, 25 February 1786, 63; for Cranston, 18 February 1786, 41; for Warwick, 25 February 1786, 41; for Foster, 6 February 1786, 59; for Smithfield, 24 February 1786, 50; Papers Relating to the Adoption of the Constitution, RISA.

28. *Session Laws*, February 1786 sess., 25 (postponement); *United States Chronicle* (Providence), 9 March 1786 (rejection of paper money). This bill's rejection was not reported in the printed *Session Laws*; *Session Laws*, March 1786 sess., 7, 10, 14–19 (other reliefs).

29. Treasurer's Record Book. For reports of "anarchy" during this period, see James M. Varnum to George Washington, 18 June 1787, quoted in Updike, *Memoirs*, 300–302; "Spectator" to Moses Brown, n.d., identified in an eighteenth-century hand as "Spectator about paper money 1786," Moses Brown Ms, V, #1452, RIHS. Theodore Foster to Dwight Foster, 8 August 1788, Dwight Foster Ms, MHS.

30. "List of Persons Present 3 Apl. E. Greenwich," Brown Family Business Papers, P-PG, JCBL; "To Relieve the Distressed," April 1786 election prox, Rhode Island Election Proxes, RIHS; Irwin H. Polishook, "The Collins-Richardson Fracas of 1787: A Problem in State and Federal Relations during the Confederation Era," *Rhode Island History* (October 1963): 11.

31. "Spectator" to Moses Brown, n.d., Moses Brown Ms, V, #1452, RIHS.

32. Peregrine Foster to Dwight Foster, 24 April 1786, Foster Ms, AAS; Governor William Greene to Assembly, 11 May 1786, *United States Chronicle*, 11 May 1786. The new lower house had forty-six newcomers and twenty-four holdovers out of seventy members. *Session Laws*, May 1786 sess., 3–9.

33. Peregrine Foster to Dwight Foster, 24 April 1786, Foster Ms, AAS.

34. Brown and Benson to Hewes & Anthony, 1 May 1786, Brown Ms, JCBL.

35. For the entire poem, see Patrick C. T. Conley, "Rhode Island's Paper Money Issue and *Trevett v. Weeden* (1786)," *Rhode Island History* (Summer 1971): 108–9.

36. Governor William Greene's statement to Assembly, 3 May 1786, *United States Chronicle*, 11 May 1786.

37. Joseph Shaw to Nicholas Brown, 19 February 1786, Brown Ms, JCBL; "List of Persons Present, 3 Apl., E. Greenwich," Brown Family Business Papers, P-PG, JCBL.

38. Jabez Bowen, "To the Freemen of the State of Rhode Island," 13 April 1786, Evans #19521, EAIC.

39. Rufus Hopkins to Nicholas Brown, 18 April 1786, Brown Ms, JCBL.

40. *Session Laws*, May 1786 sess., 13–17. Rhode Island legislatures during the colonial period had several times voted government land banks when money was scarce and prices low. See John B. MacInnes, "Rhode Island Bills of Credit, 1710–1755" (Ph.D. diss., Brown University, 1952).

41. Debate as Reported in *United States Chronicle*, 11 May 1786.

42. "A Friend to the Public," *Newport Mercury*, 27 February 1786.

43. "Spectator" to Moses Brown, Moses Brown Ms, V, #1452, RIHS.

44. *Session Laws*, May 1786 sess., 13–17; *Session Laws*, June 1786 sess., 8–9.

45. Wilkins Updike, *A History of the Episcopal Church in Narragansett Rhode Island* (Boston: Merrymount, 1907), 2:72–73.

46. Samuel Ward to Welcome Arnold of Providence, Warwick, 12 May 1786, Morristown Collection, reel 62, LC (hereafter Morristown Collection).

47. Peregrine Foster to Dwight Foster, 11, 20 June 1786, Foster Ms, AAS.

48. Peregrine Foster to Dwight Foster, 11 July 1786, Foster Ms, AAS. By May 1789, the paper money had depreciated to 18 to 1. Nicholas Brown to Richard Henry Lee, 5 May 1789, Richard Henry Lee Ms, reel 7, LC.

49. Peregrine Foster to Dwight Foster, 20 June, 11 July 1786, Foster Ms, AAS.

50. *Session Laws*, June 1786 sess., 8–9.

51. William Ellery to Federal Treasury Commissioners, 1 August 1786, Ellery's Letter Book, NHS. Peregrine Foster to Dwight Foster, 11 July 1786, Foster Ms, AAS; Smithfield Town Meeting Proceedings, *Providence Gazette*, 31 July 1786; East Greenwich Town Meeting Proceedings, 22 August 1786, *Providence Gazette*, 26 August 1786.

52. Peregrine Foster to Dwight Foster, 11 July 1786, Foster Ms, AAS.

53. Treasurer's Record Book.

54. *Session Laws*, August 1786 sess., 3–4, 8.

55. William Ellery to the Board of Treasury, 4 June 1787, 22 September, 2, 10 October 1786, Ellery's Letter Book, NHS; Congress Resolution, 18 September 1786, Continental Congress *Journals* 31:664.

56. *Session Laws*, December 1786 sess., 22.

57. James M. Varnum to Washington, 18 June 1787, quoted in Updike, *Memoirs*, 300–302.

58. Peregrine Foster to Dwight Foster, 11 July 1786, Foster Ms, AAS.

CHAPTER 8. MASSACHUSETTS

1. Important works include Robert A. East, "The Massachusetts Conservatives in the Critical Period," in *The Era of the American Revolution*, ed. Richard B. Morris (New York: Columbia University Press, 1939); Robert J. Taylor, *Western Massachusetts in the Revolution* (Providence: Brown University Press, 1954); J. R. Pole, *Political Representation in England and the Origins of the American Republic* (Berkeley: University of California Press, 1966), 226–44; Hall, *Politics without Parties*; McDonald and McDonald, "Disturbances in Massachusetts"; and David P. Szatmary, *Shays' Rebellion: The Making of an Agrarian Insurrection* (Amherst: University of Massachusetts Press, 1980).

2. For the £200,000 the general court voted to pay James Lovell, see 1782 Mass. House and Senate journals, 139, 144: "A resolve for granting & paying to the hon., James Lovell Esqr Receiver of the Continental Taxes the sum of two hundred thousand pounds specie out of the public Treasury being the sum granted by the General Court to the United States, Read & passed."

3. "An Act laying certain Duties of Excise on certain articles therein men-

tioned, for the purpose of paying the interest on Government Securities," 8 November 1782; State Impost Act, 22 March 1783, *Acts and Laws of the Commonwealth of Massachusetts* (Boston, 1781, 1782, 1783); 1781: 94–100; 1782: 196–205; 1783: 242–43. By 1785, the funded state debt totaled £1,468,554 with an annual interest of £88,112. The impost-excise fund yielded annually £57,353 (June 1784–June 1785); another £1,173 came from a special tax on auctions. See Governor James Bowdoin's message to General Court, 20 October 1785, House Journal, 1785 House, 206–13.

4. The five direct taxes the general court passed between 1782 and 1786 all required these procedures. See, for example, "An Act for apportioning and assessing a tax of Two Hundred Thousand Pounds" (Tax No. 3), March 1783, Evans #19423, EAIC.

5. See, for example, ibid.

6. "An Act laying certain Duties of Excise on certain articles therein mentioned, for the purpose of paying the interest on Government Securities," 8 November 1782; State Impost Act, 22 March 1783, *Acts and Laws,* 1781: 94–100; 1782: 196–205; 1783: 242–43.

7. Massachusetts *Resolves,* 21 January–12 March 1784; 26 May–9 July 1784; 13 October–13 November 1784; 19 January–18 March 1785; 25 May–4 July 1785; Supplement; 19 October–1 December 1785.

8. Before a treasurer's writ was issued against him, Shaw had collected £3,581. On 1 February 1783 High Sheriff Joseph Henderson, after serving a treasurer's writ for the balance, noted, "I return this Exen satisfied." Treasurer Gardner's execution writ against Francis Shaw, 11 November 1782; Treasurer Ivers's execution writ against Samuel Holden, 14 May 1785. Holden was jailed for the unpaid sum of £90; on 22 May 1786 Sheriff Henderson noted that payment had been made in full. "1781 Tax Acts, Sheriffs' Returns," Box 2, Massachusetts Archives, Boston (MA).

9. State Treasurer Thomas Ivers to House of Representatives, 15 February 1786, Box 1, Sheriff's Accounts, Barnstable-Plymouth, MA.

10. The inability of Reliefer forces to sustain a majority can be seen by the defeat of a bill to reduce the state's consolidated debt from its stated to market value in order to release revenue from the impost-excise fund and permit direct property taxes to be lowered. Initially, the measure passed the house 78 to 72. After several days of debate and backstairs pressure, the majority collapsed, and the measure lost, 83 to 44. House Journal, 1785–86 sess., 464–68, 483. See also the account in the *Hampshire Herald* taken from the *Boston Magazine,* 25 April 1786.

11. "Resolve respecting State executions, with direction to the Secretary to publish the same in several papers," 6 July 1786, *Resolves,* June–July sess., 55–56.

12. Mass. House Journal, May 1781–May 1782, 1st sess., 83; Senate Journal, May 1781–May 1782, 1st sess., 41. The money was needed to pay and supply the Massachusetts line in Washington's army. The house directed that the treasurer "suspend payment of hard money [to public creditors] till the Gratuity to the Soldiers is completed." Mass. House Journal, May 1781–May 1782, 1st sess., 50.

13. Town collectors and constables felt the pressure keenly. See the petition of Barnstable's selectmen praying that Benjamin Goodspeed, the town's constable, "committed to jail on an execution from the treasurer for back taxes," be credited with a sum of money due from the treasury to the town and be released. Mass. House Journal, 1782–83, 1st sess., 21.

14. Mass. House Journal, 1782–83, 1st sess., 52, 55, 65; *Massachusetts Spy* (Worcester), 18 April 1782. Worcester's convention focused on "THE IMMENSE SUMS OF PUBLICK MONEY, which have for several years been assessed upon them" and how they had been "DISPOSED OF." Joseph Hawley to Ephraim Wright, Northampton, 16 April 1782, E. Francis Brown, ed., "Shays's Rebellion," *American Historical Review* 36 (July 1931): 776–78.

15. Robert A. Feer, "Shays's Rebellion" (Ph.D. diss., Harvard University, 1958), 141–61; Robert E. Moody, "Samuel Ely: Forerunner of Shays," *New England Quarterly* 5 (1932):105–34; [Worcester] *Massachusetts Spy*, 29 May 1782; *Salem Gazette*, 6, 27 June 1782.

16. Depositions of Andrew Squire (154 M.A. 369), James Woodward (154 M.A. 362), and others on the James Harris case, MA. *Massachusetts Gazette* (Springfield), 1 October 1782.

17. House Journal, May 1782–March 1783, 1st sess., 79, 96–101, 122, 132–41, 150–56.

18. Report of the committee "to repair to the County of Hampshire to enquire into the Grounds of Dissatisfaction there, correct Misinformations and remove groundless jealousies," 28 August 1782, 237 M.A. 377; Hampshire Convention Resolutions 7 August 1782, 237 M.A. 380, MA.

19. *Resolves*, 29 May–14 November 1782, 109–10; *Resolves*, 21 January–12 March 1784, 101, 143; *Resolves*, 19 January–18 March 1785, 42, 89. See also boxes labeled "Tax Acts, Sheriffs' Returns" for each year between 1781 and 1786, MA.

20. Sutton Town Meeting minutes, quoted in William A. Benedict and Hiram A. Tracy, *History of the Town of Sutton, Massachusetts from 1704 to 1876* (Worcester, Mass.: Sanford, 1878), 121.

21. "Irenicus," *Hampshire Herald*, 2 November 1784; also Feer, "Shays's Rebellion," 141–77.

22. In his opening message to the general court of 2 June 1786, Governor Bowdoin made an explicit plea for the collection of taxes for Congress. Noting the state's large "arrearages" of requisition payments due Congress and the "great importance of fully complying with those requisitions," he urged the legislature "to take vigorous measures for enforcing the collection of taxes laid for that purpose." Previously, on 24 October and 3 November 1785 and 3 February 1786, the governor had conveyed documents requesting that the states make good on their requisitions. Bowdoin to General Court, 2 June 1786, House Journal, 1786–87, 1st sess., 28–38.

23. House Journal, 1785–86, 2d sess., 282, 291, 325; 3d sess., 385–407, 481, 547.

24. "An Act for Enforcing the Speedy Payment of Rates and Taxes, and directing the Process against deficient Constables and Collectors," *Acts and Laws*,

March 1786 sess., 351–58. For John Choate's role, see House Journal, 1785–86, 2d sess., 282, 310.

25. Resolve respecting Collectors of Public Taxes, 24 March 1786, *Resolves*, March 1786 sess., 248; List of Balances on executions delivered to Sheriff Hyde, 10 February 1786, Berkshire County Folder, Box 1, "Sheriffs' Accounts, Barnstable-Plymouth Counties," MA.

26. *Resolves*, May–July 1786 sess., 120.

27. "Resolve respecting State executions, with direction to the Secretary to publish the same in several papers," 6 July 1786, *Resolves*, June–July sess., 55–56. The resolve appeared in the Boston *Independent Chronicle* on 20 June 1786. Also Richard Cranch to Joseph Cranch, Boston, 2 August 1786, Christopher P. Cranch Ms, MHS: "Col. Porter [Hampshire Sheriff] has executions against collectors to a large amount on the Continental Tax No 1 and on other taxes which must be paid very soon or else the High Sheriff himself will be answerable according to a late act for that purpose."

28. Governor James Bowdoin to Nathaniel Gorham, 24 June 1786, Bowdoin-Temple Ms, MHS.

29. Compare McDonald and McDonald, "Disturbances in Massachusetts."

30. Treasurer Thomas Ivers to Caleb Hyde, 16 March 1785 (Treasurer's Office, Boston), Berkshire File, "Sheriffs' Accounts Barnstable-Plymouth counties," Box 1, MA.

31. Sheriff Caleb Hyde to Treasurer Thomas Ivers, 21 February 1786 (Lenox), Berkshire File, "Sheriffs' Accounts Barnstable-Plymouth Counties," Box 1, MA. For the Treasurer's execution writs sent out on 15 June and 5 July 1786, see "1781 Tax Acts, Sheriffs' Returns," Box 2, MA.

32. See execution writs in "1781 Tax Acts, Sheriffs' Returns," Box 2, MA.

33. Greenwich Petition to General Court, 16 January 1786, Shays's Rebellion Ms, AAS; Bernardston Petition to General Court, 6 June 1786, House Doc. 2043, MA.

34. See treasurer's executions against Morse, Walker, and Caulkins in "1781 Tax Acts, Sheriffs' Returns," Box 2, MA.

35. See the treasurer's execution writs for these counties in "1781 Tax Acts, Sheriffs' Returns," Box 2, MA.

Hampshire County farmers were the first to stop a county court from sitting (on 29 August 1786), supplied the most volunteers for Shays's army, and furnished the rebellion's principal leaders—Daniel Shays of Pelham and Luke Day of West Springfield. By contrast, Berkshire County farmers furnished fewer volunteers and were less well organized. District of Maine farmers, although angry at the government and sympathetic with the Shaysite cause, did not participate in the rebellion. On these details, see Feer's Harvard dissertation, "Shays's Rebellion."

36. Greenwich Petition to General Court, 16 January 1786, Shays's Rebellion Ms, AAS.

37. Lunenberg Petition to General Court, 30 June 1786, Senate Doc. 620:2, MA.

38. Bernardston Petition to General Court, 6 June 1786, House Doc. 2043, MA.

39. Greenwich Petition to General Court, 16 January 1786, Shays's Rebellion Ms, AAS; Bernardston Petition to General Court, 6 June 1786, House Doc. 2043, MA.

40. Dartmouth Town Meeting Instructions to William Davis, 18 May 1786, [Boston] *Independent Chronicle*, 8 June 1786; Newbury Town Meeting Instructions, 15 May 1786, [Springfield] *Hampshire Herald*, 20 June 1786. See also West Springfield Town Meeting Instructions, 7 March 1786, ibid., 7 March 1786.

41. Bristol County Convention Petition, 27 June 1786, M.A. 620/3, MA; Hampshire Convention resolves, 25 August 1786, *Worcester Magazine*, last week August 1786, 294–95; Worcester Convention, 26 September 1786, *Worcester Magazine*, first week October 1786, 318, second week October 1786, 334–35.

42. "Z," 17 July 1786, [Boston] *Independent Chronicle*, 20 July 1786.

43. Joseph Cranch to Richard Cranch, 31 July 1786 (Springfield), Christopher P. Cranch Ms, MHS. Anonymous Letter to Governor James Bowdoin, identified as "Insurgent Letter 1787" and arranged chronologically in the Bowdoin Ms at the beginning of 1787, Bowdoin-Temple Ms. Internal evidence indicates this letter was written in mid-1786.

44. Treasurer's execution writs sent to Berkshire's Sheriff Hyde in 1781, 1782, 1783, 1784, and 1785 were returned to Boston with notations indicating their disposition. But the flurry of treasurer's executions sent out 5 July 1786 were returned fresh, unmarked, and with no notations. See treasurer execution writs addressed to Hyde in "1781 Tax Act, Sheriffs' Returns," Box 2, MA. Of the heavy £300,439 tax passed March 1786 and due in the treasurer's office the following January 1787, only a fraction was collected—some 18 percent. By October 1787 many towns in western Massachusetts had not collected one penny on this tax.

45. Militants' Petition to Hampshire Court of Common Pleas and Quarter Sessions (copy), 29 August 1786, 318 M.A. 4, MA. For the mass actions against the courts in Northampton, Worcester, and Concord, see the unsigned eyewitness accounts, 29 August, 5, 12 September 1786, 189 M.A. 5, 7, 13, MA. On the Great Barrington action, see Sheriff Hyde to Governor Bowdoin, 13 September 1786, 318 M.A. 17, MA. For the December closings, see Bowdoin Message to General Court, 3 February 1787, House Journal, February 1787 sess., 369–74; Minutes of Governor's Council respecting Insurgents, 22 November–7 December 1786, Bowdoin-Temple Ms, MHS.

46. According to one tabulation, the new actions in Middlesex County Court of Common Pleas numbered as follows: 1782: 793; 1783: 1426; 1784: 1483; 1785: 1066; 1786: 806; 1787: 140. Brock Jobe, "Debt in Concord after the Revolution" (unpublished graduate seminar paper, Boston University, 1974), 14. Professor Robert Gross kindly furnished me a copy of this paper. My own tabulation of court executions issued against debtors by the Middlesex County Court confirms these findings. The court issued some 752 execution warrants for debt in 1785, but only 549 in 1786. See filing cabinet labeled Inferior Court Executions 1785–87, basement vault, Middlesex County Court House, East Cambridge, Mass. Van Beck Hall's figures also confirm the downward trend.

Recognizances for debt per 1,000 polls fell for Bristol (16 to 9); for Middlesex (20 to 17); for Worcester (32 to 30), and for Hampshire (6 to 2). See Hall, *Politics without Parties*, 195, table 47.

Szatmary, *Shays' Rebellion*, emphasizes court actions against private debtors as the chief cause of Shays's Rebellion.

47. According to the McDonalds, in 1787 the combined load of overdue and current taxes per adult male in Worcester, Hampshire, and Berkshire was £10 (total £286,265); the per capita private debt burden they estimate at less than £2 per adult male (£55,000). See McDonald and McDonald, "Disturbances in Massachusetts," 69. The total arrearages on all taxes for the entire state as calculated by Treasurer Alexander Hodgdon in October 1787 was £497,474; arrearages for the taxes levied before 1782 was £60,907. See Treasurer's Report to House of Representatives, 25 October 1787, Microfilm D. 24, reel 3, Massachusetts, ESRC. (Doc. 2602, MA).

48. In 1774 Patriot groups outside Boston responded to the British government's Coercive Acts and other punitive measures that followed the Boston Tea Party by forcing the royal government's county courts to close. Farmers who organized the court stoppings may have drawn on this precedent.

49. David Sewall to George Thatcher, 16 October 1786, Chamberlain Collection, Boston Public Library; "Mr. Parson's Opinion concerning ye Conduct of a Sheriff in regard to Riots, August 1786," Bowdoin-Temple Ms. MHS.

50. Bowdoin's Proclamation, 2 September 1786, [Boston] *Independent Chronicle*, 7 September 1786. On the overlooked impact of Bowdoin's proclamation see Judge William Whiting to Attorney General Robert Treat Paine, 19 March 1787, Robert Treat Paine Ms, MHS.

51. "An Act to prevent Routs, Riots, and tumultuous Assemblies, and the Evil Consequences thereof," 28 October 1786; "An Act for Suspending the Privilege of habeas Corpus," 10 November 1786, *Acts and Laws*, fall 1786 sess., 502–4, 510. Minutes of Governor's Council Respecting Insurgents, 22 November–7 December 1786, Bowdoin-Temple Ms. MHS.

52. Silvanus Billings to Joshua Stokes, 2 December 1786, Court Files Suffolk, September 1787, #155325, p. 27, Suffolk County Court House Library.

53. General William Shepherd to Governor Bowdoin, 26 January 1787, 318 MA 120, MA.

54. See the account in Feer, "Shays's Rebellion," 350–414. According to General Shepherd's estimates, the organized insurgent forces, at their maximum, numbered about 2,000 men. On 4 January 1787 General Bowdoin ordered out some 4,400 armed state militia. Major Shepherd's Estimate of the Number of Rebels, Bowdoin-Temple Ms, MHS; Shepherd to Lincoln, 21 January 1787, Morristown Collection, reel 50; Bowdoin's General Orders, 4 January 1787, 189 M.A. 60, MA.

55. Trooper T. Thompson's Letter-Journal, 22 March–4 April 1787, 3 April 1787 entry, Morristown Collection, reel 55.

56. Resolve 121, 17 November 1786, *Resolves*, September–November 1786; Resolve 110, 7 July 1787, *Resolves*, May–July 1787. In fact, the general court formally extended the deadline for sheriffs to comply with the July 1786 order until 1 March 1787.

57. Resolve 100, November 1786, *Resolves*, September–November 1786.

58. "An Act, providing for the more easy Payment of the Specie Taxes, assessed previous to the Year 1784," *Acts and Laws*, fall 1786 sess., 504–8.

59. Resolve 29, 17 February 1787, *Resolves*, January–March 1787. The first treasurer's execution writs on Tax No. 5 were not issued until January 1788. See the writs in box labeled "Colonial Division Sheriffs' Returns 1784–1787," MA.

60. House Journal, fall 1786 sess., 250; Resolve 51, 26 February 1787, *Resolves*, January–March 1787, 204.

61. "An Act Appropriating the Revenue Arising from the Duties of Impost and Excise," 17 November 1786, *Acts and Laws*, September–November sess.; Theodore Sedgwick to Rufus King, 18 June 1787, King Ms, NYHS.

62. "An Act Providing for the Pay and Subsistence of the Militia employed by Government in suppressing the dangerous Rebellion," 6 February 1787, *Acts and Laws*, winter 1787 sess., 546–47; Resolve 68, 30 October 1786, *Resolves*, September–November 1786, 126.

63. "An Act, for Suspending the Laws for the Collection of private Debts, under Certain Limitations," 15 November 1786, *Acts and Laws*, September–November sess., 523–25; Resolve 99 (Berkshire), 104 (Plymouth), *Resolves*, fall 1786 sess., 144–45; *Resolve* 7 (Hampshire), *Resolves*, winter 1786–87 sess., 178.

64. The measure certainly had advocates. But perhaps recalling how badly a proposed paper money land bank had lost the previous June 1786 (19 to 99), advocates of the bill probably preferred to concentrate on other relief legislation that had a better chance of enactment.

65. "To the Free, Virtuous, and Independent Electors of Massachusetts," Bowdoin election handbill, 1787 election, Imprint Collection, MHS.

66. Hall, *Politics without Parties*, 235–46.

67. Resolve 110, 7 July 1787, *Resolves*, May–July 1787, 40–41; Resolve 43, *Resolves*, October–November 1787, 61; Governor Hancock to General Court, 2 June 1787, *Resolves*, May–July 1787, 7; Hall, *Politics without Parties*, 235–36, 251.

68. Sedgwick to Nathan Dane, 3 June 1787, Shays Ms, MHS; to Nathan Dane, 5 July 1787, Sedgwick Ms, MHS. In October 1787 Sedgwick wrote again from the Massachusetts house: "Tax No. 5 is postponed till the 2nd Wednesday in January & No. 4 till the first day of feby. I am confident this measure was injudicious, but I thought strenuous opposition under the present circumstances would be impolitic & therefore made few observations on the subject." Sedgwick to ?, 28 October 1787, Sedgwick Ms III, MHS.

CHAPTER 9. THE OTHER NINE STATES

1. Edmund Randolph to George Washington, 24 November, 6 December 1786, Washington Ms, LC; Treasury Letter.

2. Philip A. Crowl, *Maryland during and after the Revolution: A Political and Economic Study* (Baltimore: Johns Hopkins University Press, 1943); Edward C.

Papenfuse, "The Legislative Response to a Costly War: Fiscal Policy and Factional Politics in Maryland: 1777–1789," Ronald Hoffman and Peter J. Albert, *Sovereign States in an Age of Uncertainty* (Charlottesville: University of Virginia Press, 1981), 134–56.

3. "An Act to establish funds to secure the payment of the state debt within six years, and for the punctual payment of the interest thereon," *Maryland Laws*, 1784–85 sess.; "An Act relative to the arrearages of taxes due the state before the first day of January 1783," *Maryland Laws*, 1785–86 sess.; "A Supplement to an act entitled, An Act to impose duties on certain enumerated articles," *Maryland Laws*, 1784–85 sess.

4. House Committee Report on Finances, November 1786, *Votes and Proceedings of the House of Delegates of the State of Maryland*, November 1786 sess., 86–87.

5. "An Act to Appoint an Intendant of Revenue," *Maryland Laws*, November 1784–85 sess. Collection of the property tax was done by county and local commissioners, assessors, and collectors who were to be supervised and if necessary disciplined by the state intendant of revenue and the treasurers of the eastern and western shores. The treasurers were to put the bonds of a delinquent collector into suit, but the intendant could order a suit suspended or adjusted.

6. *House Votes and Proceedings*, December 1785–March 1786 sess., 69–70; *Votes and Proceedings of the Senate of the State of Maryland*, December 1785–March 1786 sess., 68. *Report of a House Committee to investigate the Conduct of the Intendant of Revenue and His Reply*, Evans #19771, EAIC.

7. *Senate Votes and Proceedings*, 1785–86 sess., 68.

8. Ibid., 49–52, 66.

9. Ibid., 70; "An Act relative to the arrearages of taxes due the state before the first day of January 1783," *Maryland Laws*, 1785–86 sess.

10. *Senate Votes and Proceedings*, 1785–86 sess., 2. Paca's flexibility may be seen from the published and unpublished letters and minutes of the governor and council during Paca's administration, the unpublished state records collection in the Hall of Records, and Crowl, "Maryland during and after the Revolution," 61. In July 1786 Baltimore County tax collector William McLaughlin protested that this was the first crackdown on collectors since he had exercised his office (six years). William McLaughlin to Samuel Chase, 8 July 1786, Maryland State Papers, Maryland Hall of Records, Annapolis (MHR).

11. *House Votes and Proceedings*, December 1785–March 1786 sess., 193 ("An Act to vest certain powers in the governor and council"). *Senate Journal*, December 1785–March 1786 sess., 84, 86–87.

12. Governor and Council to Tax Commissioners of Ann Arundel, Washington, Frederick, and St. Mary's Counties, 18 May 1786, Governor and Council Letterbook, MHR.

13. Governor Smallwood to Western Shore Treasurer Thomas Harwood, 18 May 1786, Maryland State Papers, MHR. Eastern Shore Treasurer Henry Dickinson was pressured also. See Henry Dickinson to Smallwood, 21 April 1786, Maryland State Papers, MHR.

14. Harwood to Smallwood, 24 August 1786, Maryland State Papers, MHR; Council to ?, 27 April 1786, Maryland State Papers, MHR; *State vs. Thomas*

Harwood, Vendo. Exps. August Term, General Court of the Western Shore Docket Book, 1786, MHR; James Brice to Luther Martin, 13 October 1786, Governor and Council Letterbook, MHR.

15. Mr. Wilmot to Governor William Smallwood, 26 March 1787, Maryland State Records, MHR; Samuel Groom Osborne, Collector of Harford County, to Governor Smallwood, 17 April 1787, Maryland State Papers, MHR; List of Balances due from the Collectors in the Several Counties for 1783 & 1784 & 1785, Maryland State Papers, MHR; "An Address of the House of Delegates of Maryland to their Constituents," 16 January 1787, *House Votes and Proceedings*, 1786–87 sess., 86.

16. Collector William McLaughlin to Samuel Chase, 8 July 1786, Maryland State Papers, MHS; Otho Williams to Dr. Philip Thomas, 22 July 1786, Otho Williams Ms, Maryland Historical Society; Sheriff Archibald Job of Cecil County to Governor Smallwood, 11 December 1786, Vertical File, Maryland Historical Society.

17. Governor William Smallwood to Sheriff-Collector Henry Hunt of Calvert County, 22 August 1786, Governor and Council Letterbook, 1780–87, MHR.

18. Sheriff Archibald Job of Cecil County to Governor William Smallwood, 11 December 1786, Vertical File, Maryland Historical Society: "You see by this account the critical situation I am in. If I neglect my Duty, Escapes, Defaults, &c are to ruin my securities and me; and I think it impossible for any man to Execute the office fully; therefore no man Ever wanted your Instruction more than I do at this time nor will more thankfully Receive it no Person knows the Contents of this Letter but myself." Also Samuel Osborn to Governor William Smallwood, 17 April 1787, Maryland State Papers, MHR.

19. A Friend to Paper Money [Samuel Chase?], *To the Voters of Anne-Arundel County*, 23 September 1786, Elk-Ridge, Evans #44980, EAIC.

20. *Senate Votes and Proceedings*, 1st sess., November 1786–January 1787, 17, 24, 32–33; "An Act to suspend for a time the collection of the public assessment imposed November session, 1785"; and "An Act for the Relief of the collectors of the tax for the years 1784 and 1785," *Laws of Maryland*, November 1786–January 1787 sess.

21. Melvin Yazawa, *Representative Government and the Revolution: The Maryland Constitutional Crisis of 1787* (Baltimore: Johns Hopkins University Press, 1975).

22. *Senate Votes and Proceedings*, April–May 1787 sess., 49–51.

23. "An Act for the Relief of the Collectors of the tax for 1783, 1784, 1785, 1786," *Laws of Maryland*, December 1787 sess. The new law suspended all legal proceedings against collectors and set a staggered series of new due dates for payment (1/3 by 20 March 1788; 1/3 by 20 June 1788; 1/3 by 20 August 1788).

24. For an interpretation that stresses the differences between Virginia and Massachusetts taxation, see H. James Henderson, "Taxation and Political Culture: Massachusetts and Virginia, 1760–1800," *William and Mary Quarterly*, (January 1990) 47:90–114. Richard Henry Lee described Virginia's taxes as "extremely heavy" while North Carolina and Georgia have "little or no tax." R. H. Lee to Madison, 26 November 1784, Lee Family Ms, reel 7, LC.

25. Gordon Ray Denboer, "The House of Delegates and the Evolution of Po-

litical Parties in Virginia, 1782–1792" (Ph.D. diss., University of Wisconsin, 1972), 4. Denboer's is an especially helpful study. See also Armentrout, "Political Study of Virginia Finance," 106.

26. Armentrout, "Political Study of Virginia Finance," 58; St. George Tucker to Theodorick Bland, May 1781, quoted in Armentrout, 61; see "Farmer" and "Landholder" in *Virginia Gazette or American Advertiser*, 18 May 1782, quoted in Armentrout, 61; David Stuart to George Washington, 16 November 1785, Washington Ms, LC; Madison to Jefferson, 18 March 1786, *Madison Papers*, 8:500–504.

27. House Statement against Paper Money, November 1786, quoted in Denboer, "House of Delegates," 74–77. Also, *Virginia House of Delegates Proceedings*, October 1786 sess. (1 November 1786), 15. Madison, Notes for a Speech Opposing Paper Money, ca. 1 November 1786, *Madison Papers*, 9:158–60; Madison to Jefferson, 18 March 1786, *Madison Papers*, 8:500–504; David Stuart to George Washington, 8 November 1786, Washington Ms., LC.

28. Report of the Select Committee to consider the System of Finance, 2 December 1786, *Virginia House of Delegates Proceedings*, 1786–87 sess., 71–82; "An Act to enable the Solicitor more effectually to collect the Arrearages of the Taxes, and proceed against public Delinquents" enabled the solicitor to pursue action against sheriffs in the General Court four times a year instead of two. "An Act to Amend the Act entitled an Act for Ascertaining certain Taxes and Duties and for establishing a Public Revenue" tightened up accounting procedures, required that local tax accounts be furnished the solicitor, and made these accounts admissible evidence in court. *Virginia Assembly Acts*, 1786–January 1787 sess.

29. Report of Legislative Committee, 2 December 1786, *Virginia House of Delegates Proceedings*, 1786–87 sess., 71–82; Frank Corbin to Richard Henry Lee, 20 January 1787, Lee Family Ms, reel 7, LC.

30. Frank Corbin to Richard Henry Lee, 20 January 1787, Lee Family Ms, reel 7, LC.

31. Solicitor General L. Wood to Sheriff of Greenbriar and other Counties, 1 May 1787, Solicitors' Office Notices, General Court Records, Box 153, Virginia State Archives (VSA); Section 1, "An Act to encourage the Speedy Payment of Arrearages of Taxes into the Public Treasury," *Virginia Assembly Acts*, October 1787 sess. The Solicitor also demanded copies of sheriffs' bonds as a necessary preliminary to legal action. The squeeze was already on in King William County and elsewhere as numerous general court judgments against sheriffs for unsettled accounts indicate: 24 April 1787 (£560 1785 tax); 26 April 1787 (£2,312 1786 tax); 26 April 1787 (£1,532 1785 tax); 15 June 1787 (£50 1784 tax); 15 June 1787 (£1,297 1784 tax). Judgments on Commonwealth cases for the General Court, 1784–95, statement 10, Box 148, General Court Records, VSA. The sale of sheriffs' property was often stymied by the lack of purchasers. But in Campbell County, 10 out of 30 slaves were sold for £129. See Solicitor's Book, 3 June 1788, VSA.

32. Accomack County Petition to the General Assembly, 16 November 1787, VSA, Oversize Box 1.

33. Edmund Randolph to James Madison, 7 March 1787, *Madison Papers*, 9:303.

34. Jonathan Dawson to James Madison, 12 June 1787, *Madison Papers*, 10:47.

35. James McClurg to Madison, 22 August 1787, *Madison Papers*, 10:155.

36. Frank Corbin to Arthur Lee, 8 August 1787, Lee Family Ms, reel 7, LC.

37. "An Act to Encourage the Speedy Payment of Arrearages of Taxes into the Public Treasury," *Virginia Assembly Acts*, October 1787 sess.; Armentrout, "Political Study of Virginia Finance," 130–31.

38. Madison to Jefferson, 4 December 1786, *Madison Papers*, 9:191; Rhys Isaac, *The Transformation of Virginia: 1740–1790* (Chapel Hill: University of North Carolina Press, 1982), 293.

39. State Comptroller Oliver Wolcott Jr.'s Reports to Connecticut Assembly, 7 October 1788 and 14 May 1789, esp. accounts 30 and 31. Connecticut Comptroller's Records, Microfilm, ESRC.

40. Harvey Milton Wachtell, "The Conflict between Localism and Nationalism in Connecticut, 1783–1788" (Ph.D. diss., University of Wisconsin, 1971), esp. 71–79.

41. Wachtell, "Localism and Nationalism in Connecticut," 90–145; House Resolutions 1786, 1787, quoted in Wachtell, 226–31.

42. Localism-nationalism categories form the basis of Wachtell's useful dissertation, "Localism and Nationalism in Connecticut."

43. Wachtell, "Localism and Nationalism in Connecticut," 227–29.

44. Oliver Wolcott, Sr., to Oliver Wolcott, Jr., 28 December 1783, vol. 4, no. 18, Wolcott Ms, CHS.

45. Wolcott, Sr., to Wolcott, Jr., 18 February 1787, and other equally explicit letters, Wolcott Ms., CHS.

46. Connecticut House Journal, 4 November 1785, 52; Wachtell, "Localism and Nationalism in Connecticut," 220.

47. Benjamin Huntington to William Ellery, 30 January 1786, Ellery Ms, NHS.

48. Ibid., 16 July 1786, Ellery Ms, NHS.

49. In addition to Wachtell's dissertation previously cited, see Gaspar Saladino, "The Economic Revolution in Late Eighteenth-Century Connecticut" (Ph.D. diss., University of Wisconsin, 1964).

50. Joseph Gardners to George Bryan, 19 March 1785, Bryan Ms, HSP: "The country party in the New York Assembly are a majority and generally carry their measures in opposition to their *Senate* and their *council of revision* as they are called." Recent scholarship supports this assessment.

51. Countryman, "Consolidating Power in Revolutionary America," 648, 672; Edward Countryman, "Legislative Government in Revolutionary New York, 1777–1788" (Ph.D. diss., Cornell University, 1971), 208–16.

52. Cochran, *New York in the Confederation*, 52–56.

53. Connecticut merchant Peter Colt noted that farmers in Connecticut were selling out and moving to New York and Vermont "where the taxes are said to be one-tenth what they are here." Wachtell, "Localism and Nationalism in Connecticut," 218.

54. "An Act for Emitting £200,000 in Bills of Credit for the Purposes therein

Mentioned," 18 April 1786. The bills were payable for taxes and duties but were not legal tender except in cases involving actual law suits for debt. The "Act for Raising [£50,000] Money by Tax" was passed on 29 April 1786. See *New York Acts and Laws*.

55. See table 1. According to Cochran, the state impost generated revenue that paid more than half the state's budget. Before the state impost became lucrative, payments to Congress were considerably less. See Cochran, *New York in the Confederation*, 132–34, 151. In 1781 the assembly approved the 5 percent federal impost without conditions. In 1786 the assembly again approved the measure, this time requiring that the new New York paper bills, guaranteed by the state as equivalent to gold and silver, be payable for the federal impost, and that the federal impost be collected by New York state officers.

56. The foregoing generalizations rely heavily on: Edward Countryman, *A People in Revolution: The American Revolution and Political Society in New York, 1760–1790* (Baltimore: Johns Hopkins University Press, 1981), "Consolidating Power in Revolutionary America," and "Legislative Government"; Young, *Democratic Republicans of New York*; and Cochran, *New York in the Confederation*.

57. Alexander Hamilton to Robert Morris, 13 August 1782, *Hamilton Papers*, 3:132–44: "Here we find the general disease which infects all our constitutions, an excess of popularity. There is no *order* that has a will of its own. The inquiry constantly is what will *please* not what will *benefit* the people. In such a government there can be nothing but temporary expedient, fickleness & folly."

58. Margaret Beekman Livingston to R. R. Livingston, 30 December 1779, quoted in George Dangerfield, *Chancellor Robert R. Livingston of New York, 1746–1843* (New York: Harcourt Brace & Co., 1960), 116; Judge Jacob Strong to John Smith, 20 February 1788, Morristown Collection, reel 54, LC.

59. Jeremiah Wadsworth, 23 February 1785, Wadsworth Ms., photostats, CSL. Also Thomas Tillotson to R. R. Livingston, 15 December 1782, R. R. Livingston Ms, NYHS: "Never was there such an universal languor & neglect of Laws in any State or Nation as at present exists in this."

60. Philip J. Schuyler to Stephen Van Rensselaer, 11 March 1787, Personal Miscellany, LC; Philip Schuyler to Henry Van Schaack, 13 March 1787, Van Schaack Ms, Ayer Collection, Newberry. The house rejected the proposed tax reform bill on 9 March 1787, 23 to 28. Journal of the Assembly of the State of New York, January–April 1787 sess., 88, ESRC. For Hamilton's drafts of the proposed tax bill, see "An Act for Raising Yearly Taxes within this State," *Hamilton Papers*, 4:40–50.

61. "Diary or Memorandum Book kept by Joseph Lewis of Morristown 1 November 1783 to 26 November 1795," *Proceedings of the New Jersey Historical Society* 59 (January 1942): 58–66; Richard P. McCormick, *Experiment in Independence: New Jersey in the Critical Period, 1781–1789* (New Brunswick, N. J.: Rutgers University Press, 1950), 170–202.

62. "Votes and Proceedings of the House of Assembly," 26 January 1787, *Delaware Courant and Wilmington Advertiser*, 2 June 1787; State Treasurer Joshua Clayton to John Dickinson, 10 December 1788, R. R. Logan Collection, John Dickinson, 1784–89, Miscellaneous D-16-5 section 2, HSP: "I have done

everything in my power by threats and solicitations to induce the Collectors to bring forward the Taxes, but hitherto without effect"; *Delaware Courant and Wilmington Advertiser*, 14 July 1787.

63. Flannagan, "Trying Times," 214–316, esp. 296.

64. Kenneth Coleman, *The American Revolution in Georgia: 1763–1789* (Athens: University of Georgia Press, 1958), 201–8; George Handley to George McIntosh, 5 June 1786, Gratz Collection, HSP; State Chief Justice Henry Osborne's charge to the Burke County Grand Jury, 20 March 1787, [Savannah] *Georgia State Gazette*, 7 April 1787; Osborne's Charge to the Chatham County Grand Jury, October Term, [Savannah] *Gazette of the State of Georgia*, 18 October 1787.

65. James R. Morrill, *The Practice and Politics of Fiat Finance: North Carolina in the Confederation, 1783–1789* (Chapel Hill: University of North Carolina Press, 1969). Samuel Johnston's description of the North Carolina assembly as dominated by these leaders is pertinent: "But the Opposition of a few Bad men had more weight with the weak majority than Arguments Supported by reason and Justice." Quoted in Sheldon Fred Koesy, "Continuity and Change in North Carolina, 1775–1789" (Ph.D. diss., Duke University, 1963), 173.

66. Koesy, "Continuity and Change," 187–203.

67. Morrill, *Fiat Finance*, and Koesy, "Continuity and Change," support these generalizations.

CHAPTER 10. THE CRITICAL PERIOD: A FISCAL BREAKDOWN

1. John Fiske, *The Critical Period of American History: 1783–1789* (Boston: Houghton Mifflin, 1888). Fiske's harshest critic has been the late Merrill Jensen. Jensen, *New Nation*, esp. the Preface. For discussion of this literature, see Richard B. Morris, "The Confederation Period and the American Historian," *William and Mary Quarterly* 13 (April 1956): 140–56.

2. Marks, *Independence on Trial*, emphasizes the "critical" nature of the unsolved foreign policy problems of the 1780s.

3. Report of Grand Committee on Amendments to the Confederation, 7 August 1786, Continental Congress *Journals* 31:494–98.

4. Armentrout, "Political Study of Virginia Finance," 145 ff; Morrill, *Fiat Finance*, 62ff.

5. Report of Grand Committee, 7 August 1786, *Journals*, 31:497. Marks, *Independence on Trial*, 10–15.

6. Jay to Thomas Jefferson, 14 December 1786, and Jay to John Adams, 4 July 1787, Jay Ms, Columbia.

7. Jay to Jefferson, 9 February 1787, Jay Ms, Columbia: "The struggles for and agt. the Impost remain, but promise Little."

8. For Jay's comments on "Relaxation in Govermt and Extravagance in Individuals," see appendix 3. Jay to John Adams, New York, 21 February 1787, Jay Ms, Columbia. On 7 January 1787 Jay outlined in great detail his preferred plan for a three-branch government, proposing, among other things, a governor general "limited in Prerogative and Duration" and a two-house Congress with the

upper house "appointed for Life." Jay to Washington, 7 January 1787 (draft), Jay Ms, Columbia.

9. Jay to Jefferson, 25 November 1788, Jay Ms, Columbia. Earlier Jay had written: "For my own part I am convinced that a national Govt. as strong as may be compatible with Liberty is necessary to give us national Security & Respectability." Jay to John Adams, 4 July 1787, Jay Ms, Columbia.

10. Fiske, *Critical Period*, 153–54.

11. William F. Zornow, "New York Tariff Policies, 1775–1789," *New York History* 37 (January 1956): 40–63.

12. William F. Zornow, "The Tariff Policies of Virginia, 1775–1789," *Virginia Magazine of History and Biography* 62 (July 1954): 306–18, esp. 312–13; Zornow, "North Carolina Tariff Policies," *North Carolina Historical Review* 32 (April 1955); Zornow, "Massachusetts Tariff Policies, 1775–1789," *Essex Institute Historical Collections* 90 (April 1954): 194–215; Zornow, "Georgia Tariff Policies, 1775–1789," *Georgia Historical Quarterly* 38 (March 1954): 1–10; Zornow, "New Hampshire Tariff Policies, 1775–1789," *Social Studies* 45 (November 1954): 252–56.

13. Zornow, "Tariff Policies of Virginia," 306–18, esp. 312–13.

14. John P. Kaminski, "Paper Politics: The Northern State Loan Offices during the Confederation, 1783–1790" (Ph.D. diss., University of Wisconsin, 1972), 97.

15. Ferguson, *Power of the Purse*, 3–24; Morrill, *Fiat Finance*; Kaminski, "Paper Politics."

16. "Primitive Whig" [Governor Edward Livingston], *New Jersey Gazette*, January 1786, quoted in Kaminski, "Paper Politics," 104; David Ricardo, *Works and Correspondence*, quoted in John Kenneth Galbraith, *Money: Whence it Came, Where It Went* (New York: Bantam, 1975), 46.

17. Kaminski, "Paper Politics," 105.

18. Sharp Delany to Anthony Wayne, 11 July 1786, Wayne Ms, Clements; Thomas Paine, *Dissertation on Government, the Affairs of the Bank, and Paper Money*, 1786, quoted in Kaminski, "Paper Politics," 64, 69–70. The mere rumor of paper money could frighten monied men into hoarding specie. See David Ramsey to Benjamin Rush, 31 January 1784, Rush Ms, LCP.

19. Paine, *Dissertation on Paper Money*, 1786, quoted in Kaminski, "Paper Politics," 69; James M. Varnum to George Washington, 18 June 1787, quoted in Updike, *Memoirs*, 300–302; "Primitive Whig" [Governor Edward Livingston] in *New Jersey Gazette*, 16, 23 January 1786, quoted in Kaminski, "Paper Politics," 103–4.

20. "Primitive Whig" [Governor Edward Livingston] in *New Jersey Gazette*, 16, 23 January 1786, quoted in Kaminski, "Paper Politics," 103–4.

21. Robert Morris to Nathanael Greene, 19 December 1781, Robert Morris Ms (transcripts), Huntington Library.

22. [John Witherspoon], *Essay on Money as a Medium of Commerce with Remarks on the Advantages and Disadvantages of Paper admitted into General Circulation by a Citizen of the United States* (Philadelphia, 1786), 38, 47–53.

23. See Kaminski, "Paper Politics," 1–24.

24. On the northern state governments, see ibid. On North Carolina, see Morrill, *Fiat Finance*, 83–88.

25. Knox to Mercy Warren, 30 May 1787, Knox Ms, MHS, Knox microfilm, reel 20, frame 87, LC.

26. William S. Johnson to Samuel Johnson, 12 April 1787, Johnson Ms, CHS.

27. In Connecticut, as William Johnson's son Robert C. Johnson described, the Federalists framed the issue of the Constitution's ratification as between order and anarchy, freedom and tyranny: "If [the Constitution is] not accepted Amer. will in all probability be a scene of [a]narchy & confusion—if adopted it will be some time before peace & serenity prevail—I will sacrifice my Life in defense of it—I will wade up to my knees in blood before it shall be established—Energetic Govt. Peace opulence & respectability to America—Slavery & oppression, arbitrary aristocracy, Despotism preferable is the language." Robert C. Johnson to Samuel William Johnson, 3 December 1787, John Lawrence Ms, CSL.

28. Knox to Mercy Warren, 30 May 1787, New York, Knox Ms., MHS, Knox microfilm, reel 20, frame 87, LC; Knox, Notes for a Speech on the Constitution, Knox Ms, MHS, Knox microfilm, reel 20, frame 176, LC: "The principle of our governments is favorable to faction, faction and commotion are near neighbours, and most commonly fall prey to tyranny."

29. James Madison, Jr., to James Madison, Sr., 27 May 1787, Philadelphia, *Madison Papers*, 10:10–11; Francis Johnston to Josiah Harmar, Philadelphia, 9 October 1787, Harmar Ms, Clements.

30. Christopher Gore to Rufus King, 28 June 1787, King Ms, NYHS; Henry Knox to ? [draft], Knox Ms, MHS, Knox microfilm, reel 21, frame 125, LC.

31. Unsigned Document, AntiFederalist statement about Conditions in U.S. at time of Constitution and the Reasons for its Adoption, Bryan Ms, HSP, misdated and misfiled chronologically under 1786.

32. Stephen Mitchell to William Samuel Johnson, 14 September 1786, 26 July, 18 September 1787, vol. 2, Johnson Ms, CHS.

33. Federalists often framed the only choice as between the Constitution or disunion. This tactic—the fallacy of limited options—cast the issue starkly. On 8 April 1788 Virginia Federalist Edward Carrington informed Madison that a Mr. Ronald was standing as a delegate to the state convention from Powhatan County and that Ronald was safely Federalist—he had pronounced the Constitution "a great and good work, which, if adopted would give happiness & prosperity to America, and that should it be rejected a disunion must ensue to the utter ruin of the whole." Carrington to Madison, 8 April 1788, *Madison Papers*, 11:15–16.

34. Archibald Stuart to John Breckinridge, 21 October 1787, Breckinridge Ms, LC.: "Our present situation is alarming a total suspension of all payments to Congress will take place here till all ye states pay up, a Dissolution is ye Consequence . . . ye Constitution is our only hope, our all is at stake & if the measure is Delayed one year till our Enemies begin to intrigue or ye States lose their accommodating spirit and become obstinate & pertinacious in their respective interests, we are for ever undone." Also Stuart to John Breckinridge, 6 November

1787, Breckinridge Ms, VaU. John Brown to James Breckinridge, 28 January 1788, New York, Breckinridge Ms, LC: "The hope of [the Constitution's] succeeding is the only Prop which at present supports the Federal Government— If it was finally rejected I fear we should immediately experience the dire effects of Anarchy & the total dissolution of our Confederacy—But we will not yet despair there is still hope." Two months later John Brown wrote again: "I really dread the Consequences of [the Federal Constitution's] rejection—It has already damn'd the present Govt. in the estimation of the world, it cannot it will not drag on much longer, & should the new be rejected God only knows what will be the event." John Brown to James Breckinridge, 17 March 1788, Breckinridge Ms, VaU.

CHAPTER 11.
AN UNVIRTUOUS PEOPLE: THE FEDERALISTS' VIEW

1. Wood, *Creation of the American Republic*. After twenty years Wood's book is still considered the central work in the canon. See "The Creation of the American Republic, 1776–1787: A Symposium of Views and Reviews," *William and Mary Quarterly* 44 (July 1987): 549–611.

2. Robert Shallope usefully summarizes the "republican synthesis" in "Republicanism and Early American Historiography," *William and Mary Quarterly* 39 (April 1982): 334–56.

3. Wood, *Creation of the American Republic*, "Vices of the System," 393–429, esp. 415, 424, Wood is quoting Sylvius, "Letter III." See also Wood's chapter on "Republicanism," 46–90. McCoy, *The Elusive Republic*, emphasizes the preoccupation with "virtue" by the later Federalists and the Jeffersonian Republicans.

4. [Springfield] *Hampshire Herald*, 6 June 1786; [Philadelphia] *Independent Gazetteer*, 2, 9 January 1787; [Charleston] *South Carolina Gazette and General Advertiser*, 28 May–1 June 1785; [Boston] *Independent Chronicle*, 7 September 1786; also [Philadelphia] *Pennsylvania Packet and Daily Advertiser*, 1, 6 January 1787; *Newport Mercury*, 26 June, 31 July 1786. On 11 January 1787 the Philadelphia *Independent Gazetteer* reprinted from a Connecticut paper an essay that began "Reform—Oeconomise."

5. John Quincy Adams, Oration at Harvard Commencement, 18 July 1787, *Columbian Magazine* 2 (September 1787): 625–28; [Noah Webster], Remarks on Manners, Government, Law, and the Domestic Debt of America, [Philadelphia] *Pennsylvania Packet and Daily Advertiser*, 17 January, 15, 17, 19, 21 February 1787.

6. William Samuel Johnson to Benjamin Gales, New York, 2 February 1785, Johnson Ms, CHS; William Livingston to Elijah Clarke, 17 February 1787, quoted in Theodore Sedgwick, Jr., *A Memoir of the Life of William Livingston* (New York: J. S. Harper, 1833), 402–3.

7. See the Non-Consumption Agreement signed by 60 Members of the General Court, including James Bowdoin, Samuel Breck, Caleb Davis, and others, c. 1786–87, Bowdoin-Temple Ms, MHS.

8. Wood, *Creation of the American Republic*, 403–29, esp. 418–19, and 471–518 ("The Worthy against the Licentious").

9. Wood holds that the Framers did not believe the American people were susceptible of moral and behavioral improvement. See ibid., 475: "If [the Federalists] could not, as they thought, really reform the character of American society, then they would somehow have to influence the operation of the society and moderate the effects of its viciousness."

10. Richard Hofstadter, "The Founding Fathers: An Age of Realism," in *The American Political Tradition and the Men Who Made It* (New York: Vintage, 1948), 16; Daniel Walker Howe, "The Political Psychology of *The Federalist*," *William and Mary Quarterly* 44 (July 1987): 486–87.

11. Howe, "Political Psychology of *The Federalist*"; also Daniel W. Howe, *The Political Culture of the American Whigs* (Chicago: University of Chicago Press, 1979), chap. 2.

12. Thomas Reid, "Essays on the Active Powers of Man," in *The Works of Thomas Reid*, ed. William Hamilton, 7th ed. (Edinburgh: Maclachlan and Stewart, 1863). Reid concludes this passage by affirming: "The end of government is to make the society happy, which can only be done by making it good and virtuous." Elsewhere Reid says that the moral and rational faculties, like the earth itself, are "rude and barren by nature, but capable of a high degree of culture," and "that this culture [a person] must receive from parents, from instructors, from those with whom he lives in society, joined with his own industry," 530.

13. John Witherspoon, *Lectures on Moral Philosophy* (Princeton: Princeton University Press, 1912), 10, 18, 21, 24; Roger Jerome Fechner, "The Moral Philosophy of John Witherspoon and the Scottish-American Enlightenment" (Ph.D. diss., University of Iowa, 1974), esp. 101, 172–94; Garry R. Coll, "Noah Webster: Journalist, 1783–1803" (Ph.D. diss., Southern Illinois University, 1971), 26; Howe, "Political Psychology of *The Federalist*."

14. Lance Banning, "Some Second Thoughts on Virtue and the Course of Revolutionary Thinking," in *Conceptual Change and the Constitution*, ed. Terence Ball and J. G. A. Pocock (Lawrence: University Press of Kansas, 1988), 194–212.

15. Wood, *Creation of the American Republic*, 418.

16. Resolutions of Andover Town Meeting, printed in *Worcester Magazine*, reprinted in [Philadelphia] *Pennsylvania Packet and Daily Advertiser*, 21 February 1787.

17. Webster to Timothy Pickering, 10 August 1786, Pickering Ms, MHS, reel 19, LC.

18. Jay to Jefferson, 14 December 1786, 9 February 1787, Jay Ms, Columbia. See appendix 3 for full texts.

19. Charles Lee to Washington, 11 April 1788, Washington Ms, LC; James McClurg to Madison, 5 August 1787, *Madison Papers*, 10:135.

20. Henry Knox to George Washington, 17 December 1786, Washington Ms, LC.

21. Collin McGregor to Business Associate, 6 March 1787, Collin McGregor Letterbook, NYPL.

22. Rev. Penuel Bowen to Henry Hill, 18 October 1786, Bowen-Cooke Ms (typed copies), South Carolina Historical Society.

23. Maxfield Bloomfield, *American Lawyers in a Changing Society, 1776–1876* (Cambridge, Mass.: Harvard University Press, 1976), 40–56; "Honestus" [Benjamin Austin], [Boston] *Independent Chronicle,* 9, 23, 30 March 1786.

24. William S. Johnson to Samuel Johnson, 12 April 1787, New York, Johnson Ms, CHS.

25. See Kaminski, "Paper Politics."

26. Charles Lee to Washington, 11 April 1788, Washington Ms, LC.

27. Charles Mortimer to John Mortimer, 1 September 1787, Commonplace Book of Mary A. Fauntleroy (copy), Minor Family Ms, Virginia Historical Society, Richmond.

28. Joseph W. Barnwell, ed., "Diary of Timothy Ford," *South Carolina Historical and Genealogical Magazine* 13 (July, October 1912), 200–201.

29. Philip Hearn to Matthew Carey, 28 October 1787, Matthew Carey Ms, Edward Carey Gardiner Collection, HSP; see also Joseph Habersham to Isabella Habersham, 5 October 1787, U. B. Phillips Collection, Yale; Edward Rutledge, Jr., to John Rutledge, Jr., Charleston, 8 April 1788, John Rutledge Ms, UNC; N.Y. City Register Richard Varick to James Duane, 31 December 1788, Duane Ms, reel 3, NYHS; Attorney General Robert Treat Paine to Massachusetts House of Representatives, October 1786, Robert Treat Paine Ms, MHS.

30. In 1786 a group of Wilmington, Delaware, citizens founded the Society of the Friends of Justice to cope with horse stealings. See George H. Gipson, "Stop, Thief! Constitution and Minutes of the Friends to Justice, 1786–1794," *Delaware History* 9 (October 1964): 91–110. Henry B. Dawson, "The Motley Letter," *Historical Magazine* 9, 2d ser. (March 1871): 157–201, reports crime statistics from the city and county of New York over a five-year period (1784–89) which actually show a slight decline. Karin Wulf, "Crime in Pennsylvania, 1780–1789: A Case Study" (graduate seminar paper, American University, 1987), reports statistics from three Pennsylvania courts which show no discernible trend either up or down.

31. Hon. Judge Henry Pendleton, Charge to Grand Juries of Georgetown, Cheraws, and Camden Districts, Charleston, 11 December 1786, *Charleston Morning Post,* 13 December 1786.

32. Randolph C. Downes, "Creek-American Relations, 1782–1790," *Georgia Historical Quarterly* 21 (June 1937): 142–81. See also the Abraham Baldwin and Joseph Habersham Papers, U. B. Phillips Collection, Yale, and the James Habersham Papers, LC.

33. [Savannah] *Gazette of the State of Georgia,* 5 July 1787.

34. Joseph Clay to J. Wright Stanley, 20 August 1788, Joseph Clay Letterbook, GaHS; Abraham Baldwin to Joel Barlow, 20 July 1787, Baldwin Ms, Yale, and Baldwin to Nicholas Gilman, 20 December 1787, Charles G. Slack Collection, Dawes Memorial Library, Marietta College, Marietta, Ohio; James Habersham to brother, 22 October 1787, Habersham Ms, LC.

35. Col. Joseph Martin to Governor of Virginia, 26 March 1785; Gov. John Sevier to Gov. Patrick Henry, 19 July 1785; Joseph Martin to Henry, 14 August 1786, to Edmund Randolph, 16 March 1787, *Calendar of Virginia State Papers and Other Manuscripts from January 1, 1785, to July 2, 1789, Preserved*

in the Capitol at Richmond (Richmond: James E. Goode, 1884), 18, 42–43, 164, 256.

36. Arthur Campbell to Governor Patrick Henry, 26 July 1785; James Montgomery, William Edmiston, and Arthur Bowen to Governor Patrick Henry, 27 July 1785, *Calendar of Virginia State Papers*, 44, 45.

37. Charles Nisbet to Alexander Addison, 7 December 1787, Addison Ms, Special Collections, Darlington Memorial Library, University of Pittsburgh.

38. Jay to John Adams, 1 November 1786, Jay Ms, Columbia; to Thomas Jefferson, 3 December 1787, Jay Ms, Columbia.

39. Timothy Pickering to George Clymer, November 1787, to John Pickering, 4 August 1788, Pickering Ms, reel 35, MHS.

40. Oliver Wolcott, Sr., to Oliver Wolcott, Jr., 4 December 1786, 4 February 1787, Wolcott Ms, vol. 4, nos. 57 and 61, CHS.

41. Henry Lee to Madison, 27 October 1786, *Madison Papers*, 9:145.

42. Tobias Lear to Benjamin Lincoln, 30 July 1787, Benjamin Lincoln Ms, reel 8, MHS.

CHAPTER 12. EARLY PROPOSALS AND TRIAL BALLOONS

1. John Lowell to General Benjamin Lincoln, 20 November 1782, Miscellaneous Ms, MHS.

2. "A Lover of Liberty," *Providence Gazette and Country Journal*, 25 January 1783.

3. Jonathan Jackson to Benjamin Lincoln, 19 April 1783, J. S. H. Fogg Collection, Maine Historical Society.

4. [Anon.], *The Political Establishments of the United States of America: In A Candid Review of their Deficiencies* [1784], Evans #18735 EAIC; Edmund S. Morgan, ed., "The Political Establishments of the United States," *William and Mary Quarterly* 23 (April 1966): 286–308.

5. "Observator," [Boston] *American Herald*, 12 September 1785.

6. New York, August 24, 1786, printed in [Charleston] *State Gazette of South Carolina*, 14 September 1786.

7. "A Bostonian," [Boston] *Independent Chronicle*, 3, 10 August 1786.

8. "For the Independent Chronicle," [Boston] *Independent Chronicle*, 7 September 1786.

9. Stephen Higginson to Henry Knox, 12, 25 November 1786, Knox Ms, MHS, Knox microfilm, LC. These letters were first published in East, "Massachusetts Conservatives," 383–84.

10. Jeremiah Wadsworth to Henry Knox, 23 September 1787, Knox Ms, MHS, Knox microfilm, LC.

11. John F. Mercer to Madison, 28 March 1786, *Madison Papers*, 8:511–12. In 1787–88 Mercer was an Antifederalist, but not of the states' rights variety. John F. Mercer, Fragment of an Address on the Constitution, Annapolis, 20 December 1788, Mercer Ms, Virginia Historical Society, Richmond.

12. First put forth during 1786, the Annapolis Convention proposal had been a strategic maneuver to give congressional proponents of the 5 percent federal

impost a different forum from which to launch their impost proposal and other limited amendments. Rakove, *Beginnings of National Politics*, 361–80.

13. Benjamin Rush, "Address to the People of the United States," [Philadelphia] *American Museum*, January 1787.

14. "Harrington," "To the Freemen of the United States," [Philadelphia] *Pennsylvania Gazette*, 30 May 1787. Matthew Carey, editor of the *American Museum*, also reprinted in April 1787 the essay by "A Bostonian" from the August 1786 Boston *Independent Chronicle*.

15. "A Word of Consolation for America," and "Present Situation of Our Affairs," [Philadelphia] *American Museum*, March 1787; "Z," "On the Philadelphia Convention," [Philadelphia] *American Museum*, May 1787.

16. Peregrine Foster to Dwight Foster, 11 July 1786, Foster Ms, AAS.

17. Statement by Benjamin Tupper, quoted in Louise Burnham Dunbar, *A Study of "Monarchical" Tendencies in the United States from 1776 to 1801* (Urbana: University of Illinois, 1972), 73.

18. "A writer in a late Connecticut paper," quoted in [Philadelphia] *Pennsylvania Gazette*, 6 December 1786.

19. Madison to Edmund Pendleton, 24 February 1787, *Madison Papers*, 9:294–95. Statement by Hector St. John Crevecoeur, quoted in Dunbar, *Monarchical Tendencies*, 73–83.

20. Philip Schuyler to Henry Van Schaack, 13 March 1787, Van Schaack Ms, Ayer Collection, Newberry Library.

21. "A Correspondent," [Boston] *Independent Chronicle and Universal Advertiser*, 15 February 1787.

22. Madison, Notes on Debates, 21 February 1787, *Madison Papers*, 9:290–91.

23. Madison to Pendleton, 24 February 1787, ibid., 9:294–95.

24. Virginia Legislative Resolutions, 16 October 1786, *The Records of the Federal Convention of 1787*, ed. Max Farrand (New Haven: Yale University Press, 1966), 3:559–60. For other legislative resolutions, most of which follow closely Virginia's wording, see ibid., 563–86.

25. For evidence of Federalists concerting action before the convention, see Nicholas Brown to William Ellery, 8 February 1787, Brown Ms, JCBL. Also East, "Massachusetts Conservatives," 387–89.

26. Henry Knox to George Washington, 14 January 1787, Washington Ms, LC.

27. Henry Knox to Mercy Warren, 30 May 1787, Knox Ms, MHS, Knox microfilm, reel 20, frame 87, LC.

28. William Irvine to Col. Josiah Harmar, New York, 27 February 1787, Harmar Ms, Clements.

29. William Pierce to St. George Tucker, 14 April 1787, Tucker-Coleman Ms, Swem Library, College of William and Mary; William Pierce to George Turner, 19 May 1787, photostat in Charles E. Jackson Collection, CSL.

30. Stephen Higginson to Henry Knox, 25 November 1786, Knox Ms, MHS, Knox microfilm, reel 19, frame 58, LC.

31. Samuel Breck to Henry Knox, 14 July 1787, ibid., reel 20, frame 131.

32. Edward Carrington to James Madison, 13 June 1787, *Madison Papers*, 10:52–53.

33. For a different view, see Rakove, *Beginnings of National Politics*, 377–96. Rakove describes James Madison as the "catalytic agent" whose agenda-setting Virginia Plan was decisive in determining the convention's decision to rebuild the central government. But the plan was only one of several for the central government's thorough reconstitution that had jelled by the time the convention assembled.

CHAPTER 13. FRAMING AN ENDURING REPUBLIC

1. Max Farrand, *The Framing of the Constitution of the United States* (New Haven: Yale University Press, 1913), esp. 201, 203.

2. Levy, *Making of the Constitution*, xxxi.

3. Ibid., xxviii, xxix.

4. Cf. ibid., xvii, xix: "The states flouted their constitutional obligations." "The 1780s taught that excessive localism was incompatible with nationhood."

5. The texts of the Charles Pinckney, Alexander Hamilton, New Jersey, and John Dickinson plans also reflect a consensus on fundamental principles. Farrand, *Records*, 3:593–630; Farrand, *Records*, 1:20–23; James H. Hutson, "Notes and Documents: John Dickinson at the Federal Constitutional Convention," *William and Mary Quarterly* 40 (April 1983): 256–82. Although the New Jersey Plan retained Congress's unicameral body and unit-rule format, its provision for substantial new powers and separate executive and judicial branches puts it in the category of a halfway reconstitution rather than of simple amendment of the existing system.

6. The wording on the tax power was finally agreed to on 16 August. Farrand, *Records*, 2:304–9. Most of the Framers agreed that the new central government would initially have to tax imports and not levy direct taxes. Defending a proposed federal tax on exports, Gouverneur Morris declared: "Taxes on exports are a necessary source of revenue. For a long time the people of America will not have money to pay direct taxes. Seize and sell their effects and you push them into Revolts." Morris (16 August), ibid., 2:307.

7. Wilson (25 June), Yates's Notes; Madison (26 June), Yates's Notes; ibid., 1:413, 431. Madison recorded his own words as follows: "In framing a system which we wish to last for ages, we shd. not lose sight of the changes which ages will produce." Ibid., 422.

8. Randolph (16 June), Madison's Notes. Ibid., 255.

9. Nathan Strong to Oliver Wolcott, Jr., 3 December 1787, Wolcott, Jr., Ms, vol. 11, CHS; Edward Carrington to James Madison, 13 June 1787, *Madison Papers*, 10:52–53; Henry Knox to Mercy Warren, 30 May 1787, Knox Ms., MHS, Knox film, reel 20, frame 87, LC.

10. Mason (30 May), Madison's Notes; Madison (31 May), Madison's Notes, Farrand, *Records*, 1:34, 54.

11. Hamilton's Notes for a Speech, 18 June, ibid., 305.

12. The typology that classified the activity of all government as legislative,

executive, and judicial in nature began with the seventeenth-century English Commonwealth writers, but did not achieve broad acceptance until the second half of the eighteenth century. See W. B. Gwyn, *The Meaning of the Separation of Powers: An Analysis of the Doctrine from Its Origin to the Adoption of the United States Constitution* (New Orleans: Tulane University, 1965), 9:5, 101.

13. "A Bostonian," [Boston] *Independent Chronicle*, 3 August 1786.

14. 30 May, Madison's Notes, Farrand, *Records*, 1:35.

15. Butler (30 May), ibid., 34.

16. Louis Fisher, "The Efficiency Side of Separated Powers," *Journal of American Studies* 15 (August 1971): 113–31. Through the writings of Harrington, Sidney, Neville, Locke, Bolingbroke, and Montesquieu, both the "safety" and "efficiency" dimensions of the separation-of-powers doctrine were known to the Framers. See also W. B. Gwyn, "Separation of Powers."

17. Madison (5 June), Madison's Notes, Farrand, *Records*, 1:124.

18. Jay to Washington, 7 January 1787, Jay Ms, Columbia.

19. Henry Knox, Paper on the Constitutional Convention and a New Government, undated, Knox Ms, MHS, Knox film, reel 20, frame 176, LC; Hamilton, Notes for a Speech, 18 June 1787, Farrand, *Records*, 1:308–10; Jay to Washington, 7 January 1787, Jay Ms, Columbia.

20. Samuel Breck to Henry Knox, 14 July 1787, Knox Ms., MHS, Knox film, reel 20, frame 131, LC.

21. Charles Pinckney's Speech, 16 January 1788, *Debates which arose in the House of Representatives of South Carolina on the Constitution Framed for the United States by a Convention of Delegates Assembled at Philadelphia* (Charleston, 1788), 3–9, Evans #21470, EAIC.

22. *Debates in the House*, 33.

23. Charles Lee to George Washington, 11 April 1788, Washington Ms, LC.

24. Charles Thach, *The Creation of the Presidency 1775–1789: A Study in Constitutional History* (Baltimore: Johns Hopkins Press, 1923, 1960), 76–104, 119; Levy, *Original Intent*, 30–53.

25. Thach, *Creation of the Presidency*, esp. 76–104, 119.

26. The committee borrowed almost verbatim from Charles Pinckney's plan. Pinckney, in turn, had liberally copied relevant passages from the 1777 New York State constitution. Ibid., 108–13.

27. Eventually, after prolonged debate over the issue of how the executive should be chosen, the Committee on Unfinished Business fashioned the compromise provision that provided for an electoral college with each state choosing electors equal to their combined house and senate representation, but with the exact method of choosing state electors (legislative or popular election) left to state discretion.

28. James M. Burns, *Leadership* (New York: Harper and Row, 1978), 385.

29. Levy, *Original Intent*, 30, 45.

30. Dickinson, Notes for a Speech, 29 June (?) 1787, quoted in Hutson, "Notes and Documents," 272.

Small-state delegates also warned that a large state-controlled central government might use its power to partition and annex small states' home territory. See George Read to John Dickinson, 21 May 1787, Read Ms, LC.

31. Small-state delegates were perhaps remembering how states with claims to western lands had held back substantial portions even as they ceded their claims to Congress. Larry R. Gerlach, "Firmness and Prudence: Connecticut, the Continental Congress, and the National Domain, 1776–1786," *Connecticut Historical Society Bulletin* 31 (July 1966): 65–75.

32. For Delaware delegate George Read's desire that both public land sales and revenue from any future federal impost be applied "to the credit of the whole Union" as opposed to the credit of the states where collected, see George Read to Dickinson [copy], 6 January 1787 (?), R. R. Logan Collection, Dickinson Ms, D-16-5 section 2, HSP. See also Read to Dickinson, 4 January 1787, George Read Ms, Richard Rodney Collection, Book B, Delaware Historical Society; Jacob Broom to Thomas Collins, 23 May 1787, Society Collection, HSP.

33. See Levy, *Making of the Constitution*, xxvi: Paterson's Plan "was a small states plan rather than a states' rights one, for it too had a strong nationalist orientation."

34. Notation by Madison (15 June), Madison's Notes, Farrand, *Records*, 1:242.

35. Hutson, "Notes and Documents," 257–82.

36. Read (6 June), Madison's Notes, Farrand, *Records*, 1:136–37.

37. David Brearley Speech, 9 June 1787; William Paterson Speech, 9 June 1787; Notes for the Same Speech, Farrand, *Records*, 1:176–80, 185–88.

38. Pinckney introduced his plan on 29 May. Farrand, *Records*, 1:23, 3:595–609. The formula of five slaves equal three whites had been adopted by Congress in 1783 as the basis of allocating financial requisitions on the states.

39. Proceedings 11 June, ibid., 1:193, 201. According to Madison's and Yates's notes, only Elbridge Gerry of Massachusetts publicly objected to the proposal. For Charles Pinckney's original plan, see ibid., 3:605. Wilson must have been very familiar with Pinckney's Plan; chairing the Committee on Detail, he later drew heavily on it in drafting the powers and functions of the presidency.

40. Early in July, acknowledging contradictions and anomalies in the three-fifths formula, Wilson nevertheless defended it: "These were difficulties however which he thought must be overruled by the necessity of compromise." Wilson (11 July), Madison's Notes, ibid., 1:587.

41. General Pinckney (10 July), Butler and Pinckney (11 July), ibid., 567, 580–81, 596.

42. Williamson (11 July), ibid., 579.

43. George Mason of Virginia predicted that the South and Southwest would grow faster and outnumber the North and West before long. Mason (July 11), ibid., 586.

44. The best secondary accounts are Staughton Lynd, "The Compromise of 1787," in *Class Conflict, Slavery, and the United States Constitution: Ten Essays*, ed. Lynd (Indianapolis: Bobbs-Merrill, 1967), and Paul Finkelman, "Making a Covenant with Death," in *Beyond Confederation: Origins of the Constitution and American National Identity*, ed. Richard Beeman, Stephen Botein, and Edward C. Carter II (Chapel Hill: University of North Carolina Press, 1987), 188–225.

45. Compare Finkelman, "Making a Covenant with Death."

46. "No State shall enter into any Treaty, Alliance, or Confederation; grant Letters of Marque and Reprisal; coin Money; emit Bills of Credit; make any Thing but gold and silver Coin a Tender in Payment of Debts; pass any Bill of Attainder, ex post facto Law, or Law impairing the Obligation of Contracts." Article 1, section 10.

47. Hobson, "Negative on State Laws," 215–35; Farrand, *Records*, 2:28.

48. Hamilton proposed that the federally-appointed governors have a veto on all state laws contrary to the Constitution or federal law. Hamilton (18 June), Madison's Notes, ibid., 1:293. Jay's proposal is made in Jay to Washington, 7 January 1787, Jay Ms, Columbia.

49. On 17 July Gouverneur Morris stated he "was more & more opposed to the negative. The proposal of it would disgust all the States. A law that ought to be negatived will be set aside in the Judicary departmt. and if that security should fail; may be repeald by a Nationl. law." Morris (17 July), ibid., 2:28.

50. Hobson, "Negative on State Laws," 228–29.

CHAPTER 14.
THE ANTIFEDERALISTS AND THE RATIFICATION CAMPAIGN

1. Charles W. Roll, Jr., "We, Some of the People: Apportionment in the Thirteen State Conventions Ratifying the Constitution," *Journal of American History* 56 (June 1969): 21–40; Robert A. Rutland, *The Ordeal of the Constitution: The Antifederalists and the Ratification Struggle of 1787–1788* (Norman: University of Oklahoma Press, 1966).

2. Anthony Wayne to General James Jackson, 18 August 1787, Philadelphia, Wayne Ms, HSP.

3. Main, *Political Parties before the Constitution*. See esp. 359 and tables 12.1 (323–25), 12.6 (336–38), and 12.10 (348–50).

4. Ireland, "Constitution in Pennsylvania," 25, 213. See also table 18, appendix 1, 274–76.

5. Hall, *Politics Without Parties*, passim, xiv.

6. Jackson T. Main, *The Antifederalists: Critics of the Constitution, 1781–1788* (Chapel Hill: University of North Carolina Press, 1966), 179–81; Alpheus T. Mason, *The States Rights Debate: Antifederalism and the Constitution* (Englewood Cliffs, N. J.: Prentice-Hall, 1964), 15; Rutland, *Ordeal of the Constitution*, 39–40.

7. Statement of a Pennsylvania Antifederalist on the Constitution (George or Samuel Bryan?), misdated 1786, George Bryan Ms, HSP; Speech by Rawlins Lowndes, 17 January 1788, *Debates in the South Carolina House*, 27; Report of Federalist and Antifederalist 4 July 1788 celebrations, *Providence Gazette and Country Journal*, 12 July 1788; [Boston] *American Herald*, 28 January 1788.

8. Statement by James Wilson, *The Documentary History of the Ratification of the Constitution: Ratification of the Constitution by the States: Pennsylvania*, ed. Merrill Jensen (Madison: State Historical Society of Wisconsin, 1976) 2: 464, n. 4, 502–3 (hereafter *Documentary History*).

9. William Findley to General William Irvine, 12 March 1788, Irvine Ms, HSP.

10. Chase to General John Lamb, 13 June 1788, Lamb Ms, LC (transcripts from NYHS Lamb Ms). By ruling out the practical influence of the people in the election of representatives to the House of Representatives, Chase must have had in mind the notion that large election districts would disadvantage all but the most prominent wealthy candidates.

11. See Pauline Maier, *The Old Revolutionaries: Political Lives in the Age of Samuel Adams* (New York: Vintage, 1980).

12. George Billias, *Elbridge Gerry: Founding Father and Republican Statesman* (New York: McGraw Hill, 1976); Richard Henry Lee, *The Letters of Richard Henry Lee*, ed. James C. Ballagh, 2 vols. (New York: Macmillan, 1911); Pamela C. Copeland and Richard K. McMaster, *The Five George Masons: Patriots and Planters of Virginia and Maryland* (Charlottesville: University of Virginia Press, 1975). Gerry's personal security holdings may not have made him the "largest holder of public securities in the Convention," as has been held, but the holdings he did have in 1787 were substantial, totaling an estimated nominal value of $24,508. Billias, *Gerry*, 130–32.

13. R. H. Lee to Richard Lee, 13 September 1787, Lee, *Letters*, 2: 436.

14. R. H. Lee to Arthur Lee, New York, 14 July 1787, Lee Family Papers, microfilm, reel 7, LC.; also, R. H. Lee to ?, 27 August 1787, Roberts Collection, Haverford College Library.

15. Elbridge Gerry to James Monroe, 11 June 1787, Philadelphia, Monroe Ms, LC. Also Billias, *Gerry*, 156, 166.

16. George Mason to George Mason, Jr., Philadelphia, 1 June 1787, Mason Ms (microfilm), LC.

17. Billias, *Gerry*, 156, 166; Gerry to wife, 21, 26, 29 August, 1 September 1787, Collection of Elsie O. and Philip D. Sang (originals formerly on deposit in Morris Library, Southern Illinois University at Carbondale, copies in my possession). George Mason, Notes for a Speech on a Three-Man Executive, 4 June 1787, Mason Ms (microfilm), LC; Mason to Washington, 7 October 1787, Washington Ms, LC; Mason, "Objections to the Constitution of Government framed by the Convention," 1787, Mason Ms (microfilm), LC.

18. Mason's attempts to get the Constitution amended first by a second constitutional convention and then by the new Congress are described in *Documentary History: Commentaries*, 13:346–51; ibid., 14:147–58. Also Mason to Samuel Griffin, 8 September 1789, Mason Ms (microfilm), LC.

19. Elbridge Gerry, Objections to the Federal Constitution, New York, 18 October 1787, *Documentary History: Commentaries*, 13:546–50; Gerry to wife, 28 July 1788, Gerry Ms, MHS.

20. *Documentary History: Commentaries*, 14:364–72; for Lee's proposed amendments, see R. H. Lee to George Mason, 1 October 1787, Mason Ms (microfilm), LC. Lee tried to devise a strategy that reduced the risk of losing the Constitution altogether. Lee to George Mason, 7 May 1788, Lee, *Letters*, 2:366–69.

21. According to Billias, *Gerry*, 138, Gerry's guiding purpose as a statesman was to protect republican principles. For Mason's consciousness of him-

self as a custodian of republican principles, see Mason to George Mason, Jr., Philadelphia, 1 June 1787, Mason Ms (microfilm), LC. For Richard Henry Lee, see Lee to Washington, 11 October 1787, Lee Ms (microfilm), reel 7, LC.

22. Gerry to wife, 26 August 1787, Collection of Elsie O. and Philip D. Sang (original formerly on deposit in Morris Library, Southern Illinois University at Carbondale, copy in my possession).

23. R. H. Lee to George Mason, 1 October 1787, Mason Ms, (microfilm), LC.

24. Young, *Democratic Republicans of New York*, 92–94. Melancton Smith to Abraham Yates, 28 January 1788, Henry Oothoudt to John McKesson, 3 April 1788, James Hughes to John Lamb, 16 June 1788, Robert Yates to George Mason, 21 June 1788, quoted in ibid., 94, 103; Colin McGregor to ?, 4 March 1788, Colin McGregor Letterbook, NYPL. Young also notes that most of the Antifederalist convention delegates "had begun life in respectable families of the middling sort and at least three very likely were sons of tenant farmers." Young, *Democratic Republicans of New York*, 52.

25. Young, *Democratic Republicans of New York*, 83–105. The numerical estimates are Young's.

26. Norman K. Risjord, *Chesapeake Politics, 1781–1800* (New York: Columbia University Press, 1978), 10, 42, 46, 50, 57, 63, 286, 301, 329. James Duncanson to James Maury, 20 December 1787, March 1788, quoted in Risjord, 302.

27. *Documentary History: Pennsylvania*, 2:709–10; *Independent Gazetteer*, 3 March 1788, printed in ibid., 725; John Montgomery to William Irvine, 9 January 1788, Carlisle, Irvine Ms, HSP.

28. Melancton Smith to Abraham Yates, 28 January 1788, Henry Oothoudt to John McKesson, 3 April 1788, James Hughes to John Lamb, 16 June 1788, quoted in Young, *Democratic Republicans of New York*, 103.

29. Risjord, *Chesapeake Politics*, 23–27, 42, 57, 63, 312.

30. J. Duncan to William Irvine, 3 October 1787, quoted in Brunhouse, *Counter-Revolution in Pennsylvania*, 205.

31. Hall, *Politics Without Parties*, 286–93. Hall, 287, also notes that towns with larger than average arrearages of back taxes opposed the Constitution and those with less than average arrearages supported it.

32. Herndon, "Governing the Affairs of the Town," 97–121.

33. Risjord, *Chesapeake Politics*, 327–28. Using multivariate analysis in a study of 316 Virginia and 167 Maryland Federalists and Antifederalists, Risjord, 307–17, finds "a definite relationship" between a man's wealth and his position on the Constitution.

34. John Williams to Washington County Friends, January 1788, quoted in Linda G. De Pauw, *The Eleventh Pillar: New York and the Federal Constitution* (Ithaca, N.Y.: Cornell University Press, 1966), 174. In his "Conjectures about the New Constitution," Alexander Hamilton predicted "the disinclination of the people to taxes and of course to strong government." Quoted in Young, *Democratic Republicans of New York*, 58.

35. For example, see Benjamin Gales's speech against the Constitution, *Doc-*

umentary History: Delaware, New Jersey, Georgia, Connecticut, 3:423, 443; also Young, *Democratic Republicans of New York*, 105.

36. William R. Davie to James Iredell, 22 January 1788, Davie Letters, Iredell Ms, Duke University Library.

37. Thomas Rodney to John Adams, 20 November 1791, to Alexander Hamilton, 10 February 179?, Thomas Rodney Ms, Delaware Historical Society. Thomas Rodney's "Essay on the New Constitution," which he apparently never published, is also in the Thomas Rodney Ms, Delaware Historical Society.

38. The Committee on Petitions from the Inhabitants of Sussex County, Legislative Papers: Resolutions & Reports 1787: May–June, Public Archives Commission, Dover.

39. Richard McCormick describes Abraham Clark as "a professional politician, who was usually to be found on the side of 'popular measures' in the best traditions of his craft." See McCormick, *Experiment in Independence*, 198–99.

40. McCormick, *Experiment in Independence*, 276–78; Clark to Thomas Sinnickson, 23 July 1788, Conarroe Collection, HSP.

41. Lambert Cadwalader to George Mitchell, 8 October 1787, *Documentary History: Delaware, New Jersey, Georgia, Connecticut*, 3:51, 135–38, 152–53. "Marcus," widely published, also promised relief to the tax-burdened landowner and farmer once the Constitution was established.

42. The Georgia–Creek Indian war is discussed in Coleman, *American Revolution in Georgia*, and Downes, "Creek-American Relations," 142–81. For the alarm of Georgia's Governor George Mathews over the government's lack of resources and the low country delegates' boycott of the assembly, see Letter Books: Governors 1786–1789 Georgia, ESRC, esp. 16 October 1787.

43. Anthony Wayne to Asia Emanuel, 15 December 1788, Wayne Ms, HSP.

44. "A Georgian," *Gazette of the State of Georgia*, 15 November 1787, printed in *Documentary History: Delaware, New Jersey, Georgia, Connecticut*, 3:236–47; also, 247–48, 251. Compare John P. Kaminski, "Controversy Amid Consensus: The Adoption of the Federal Constitution in Georgia," *Georgia Historical Quarterly* 58 (Summer 1974): 244–61.

45. The Chatham Grand Jury Presentment, 4 March 1783, *Gazette of the State of Georgia*, 13 March 1783, refers to George Walton's "crimes of the blackest nature."

46. Reports of Elections of Convention Delegates: Convention Roster and Attendance Record, *Documentary History: Delaware, New Jersey, Georgia, Connecticut*, 3:266, 270.

47. Examples of Walton's "popular" stance on issues abound. Walton, Address to Wilkes County Grand Jury, November Term 1783, *Gazette of the State of Georgia*, 20 November 1783; Journal of the Georgia House of Assembly, July–August 1786 sess., 462–63, 470–80, 508 (votes on bill to issue £50,000 of legal tender paper money).

48. Georgia's support for the Constitution was described by a "Georgia Backwoodsman" as unanimous: "All men saw no alternative." [Savannah] *The Gazette of the State of Georgia*, 12 June 1788.

49. Baumann, "Democratic-Republicans of Philadelphia," 91; Young, *Democratic Republicans of New York*, 89–90; Levi Hollingsworth to ?, 18 October

1787, to Enoch Story, 23 October 1787; Swift to Griffiths, 18 October 1787, quoted in Baumann, "Democratic-Republicans of Philadelphia," 90.

50. Doerflinger, *Vigorous Spirit of Enterprise*, 201, 257.

51. Urban artisan-tradesmen's support for the Constitution is demonstrated in Baumann, "Democratic-Republicans of Philadelphia," 61–62, 90–99; Young, *Democratic Republicans of New York*, viii, 100–101; and *Documentary History: Commentaries*, 3:292–95. Baumann estimates that one-third of Philadelphia's electorate were artisans and tradespeople.

52. For the yearly rosters of assemblymen, see tables 8–16 in Ireland, "Federal Constitution in Pennsylvania," 246–70.

53. Kaminski, "Paper Politics," 53, provides evidence of Philadelphia artisan-tradesmen's disenchantment with the Constitutionalist relief program. Also, Baumann, "Democratic-Republicans in Philadelphia," 61–62.

54. By April 1786 both Philadelphia merchants and the Bank of North America were refusing the state paper money and accepting only specie. See William Allison to James McHenry, 27 April 1786, McHenry Ms, LC.

55. Ireland, "Federal Constitution in Pennsylvania," tables 14–16 on 263–70. By 1786, as Alfred Young notes, New York's artisan-mechanics had "deserted the Clintonians" and allied with the New York City merchant class. Young, *Democratic Republicans of New York*, 100–102. Like their Philadelphia counterparts, New York's artisan-shopkeepers turned against the Clinton paper money program because of its failure to restore prosperity.

56. "An Elector," *Massachusetts Gazette*, 20 November 1787, *Documentary History: Commentaries*, 3:289.

57. Resolutions of the Artisans of the Town of Boston, 7 January 1788, *Documentary History: Commentaries*, 3:292–93. The resolutions were drafted by printer Benjamin Russell and silversmith Paul Revere.

58. Baumann, "Democratic-Republicans of Philadelphia," 90–99; Young, *Democratic Republicans of New York*, 100–101.

59. Handbill titled "Order of Procession in honor of the Establishment of the Constitution of the United States, 4 July 1788," Wallace Ms, 1:185, HSP. Also, report of procession in Baltimore, Maryland, 6 May 1788, printed in the *Providence* [Rhode Island] *Gazette and Country Journal*, 24 May 1788.

CHAPTER 15. THE PROMISE OF AN ENERGETIC REPUBLIC

1. The Federalists' drive and energy are the starting point for the major interpretation of Federalist motivation by Stanley M. Elkins and Eric McKitrick, in "The Founding Fathers: Young Men of the Revolution," *Political Science Quarterly* 76 (June 1961): 181–216.

2. The classic statement is still Charles Beard, *An Economic Interpretation of the Constitution of the United States* (New York: Macmillan, 1913). See also Forrest McDonald, *We the People: The Economic Origins of the Constitution* (Chicago: University of Chicago Press, 1958). Excellent discussion and samples of interpretations are found in Levy, *Making of the Constitution*.

3. Pauline Maier, "The Beginnings of American Republicanism, 1765–

1776," and Jack P. Greene, "The Preconditions for American Republicanism: A Comment," in *The Development of a Revolutionary Mentality* (Washington, D.C.: Library of Congress, 1972). 99–124.

4. Adams, "Republicanism in Political Rhetoric," 397–421; Douglass G. Adair, " 'Experience Must be Our Only Guide': History, Democratic Theory, and the United States Constitution," in *The Reinterpretation of Early American History: Essays in Honor of John E. Pomfret*, ed. Ray Allen Billington (New York: Norton, 1968), 129–48. At the Constitutional Convention, Madison alluded to this tradition when he stated: "What we wished was to give to the Govt. that stability which was every where called for, and which the enemies of the Republican form alleged to be inconsistent with its nature." Madison, 12 June 1787, Farrand, *Records*, 1:218.

5. George Washington to John Jay, 1 August 1786, George Washington, *The Writings of George Washington*, ed. John C. Fitzpatrick (Washington, D.C.: U.S. Government Printing Office, 1938), 28:501–4.

6. John Jay to Washington, 27 June 1786, Washington Ms, LC.; Washington to John Jay, 1 August 1786, Washington, *Writings*, 28:501–4.

7. Hobson, "Negative on State Laws," 217.

8. Edward Carrington to James Madison, 13 June 1787, *Madison Papers*, 10:52–53.

9. Madison, 26 June 1787, Farrand, *Records*, 1:423; Gouverneur Morris, 5 July 1787, ibid., 529; Elbridge Gerry, 2 July 1787, ibid., 515; Rufus King, 30 June, ibid., 489–90.

10. Madison, 12 June 1787, ibid., 219; Randolph, 16 June 1787, ibid., 255–56; Hamilton, 26 June 1787, ibid., 424.

11. General Horatio Gates to James Madison, 26 November 1787, *Madison Papers*, 10:272–73; Peter Van Schaack to Henry Van Schaack, n.d. (from internal evidence sometime in 1788), Van Schaack Ms, Newberry Library; Col. Francis Johnston to Brig. Genl Josiah Harmar, 9 October 1787 [Philadelphia], Harmar Ms., Clements; Pickering to wife, 27 October 1787 [Philadelphia], Pickering Ms, MHS, reel 1–2, LC; Abraham Bancker to Evert Bancker [Staten Island, N.Y.], 23 September 1787, Bancker Ms, NYHS.

12. Such extrapolation directed the Federalists' reasoning in *The Federalist* and other expository justifications of the Constitution. Once the premise was laid down that this was to be a more stable, energetic central government than the Confederation, an almost infinite number of benefits could be logically predicted.

13. Even before the Constitution was published, Federalist writers were exaggerating the dire consequences of Congress's dissolution. See, for example, [Philadelphia] *Pennsylvania Packet*, 15 September 1787. See also Edward Carrington to James Madison, 8 April 1788, *Madison Papers*, 11:15–16.

14. Archibald Stuart to John Breckinridge, 21 October, 6 November 1787, Breckinridge Ms, LC.

15. John Brown to James Breckinridge, 28 January 1788, New York, ibid.; John Brown to James Breckinridge, 17 March 1788, Breckinridge Ms, VaU.

16. Charles Pinckney's Speech, 16 January 1788, *Debates in the South Carolina House*, 3–9. Pinckney acknowledged that at certain times the aroused "public spirit" of the entire Union could enable it to act as one. But since most of the

time this spirit was absent ("it will only prevail in moments of enthusiasm"), "the national union must ever be destroyed by selfish views and private interest."

17. Reverend James Madison to James Madison, Jr., c. 1 October 1787, *Madison Papers*, 10:183–85; Charles Lee to George Washington, 11 April 1788, Washington Ms, LC.

18. Bishop Madison to James Madison, Jr., c. 1 October 1787, *Madison Papers*, 10:183–85; James Hunter to Jonathan Mason, 6 October 1787 [Portsmouth], Hunter Ms, VaU.

19. Knox to unidentified recipient, draft, undated, Knox Ms, MHS, reel 21, frame 125, microfilm, LC.

20. Knox to Rufus King, 15 July 1787, ibid., reel 20, frame 132; Knox to unidentified recipient, draft, undated, ibid., reel 21, frame 125.

21. Thomas Fitzsimons to Noah Webster, 15 September 1787, Noah Webster Ms, NYPL.

22. Theodore Foster to Dwight Foster, 8 August 1788, Dwight Foster Ms, MHS.

23. Joseph Clay to John Galt, 24 August 1787, Clay Letterbook, GaHS. Samuel Hopkins to Moses Brown, 22 October 1787, Moses Brown Ms, vol. 6, folder 15, RIHS.

24. Roger Sherman to William Floyd, n.d., *Documentary History: Delaware, New Jersey, Georgia, Connecticut*, 3:353.

25. John Jay to John Adams, 4 July 1787, Jay Ms, Columbia.

26. "Private Citizen," Undelivered Speech to the Maryland Convention, *Maryland Journal and Baltimore Advertiser*, 25 July 1788.

27. Joseph Clay to J. Wright Stanley, 20 August 1788, Clay Letterbook, GaHS; Joseph Clay to James Jackson, 20 June 1788, ibid.; Joseph Clay to John Pierce, 17 October 1787, ibid.

28. Reverend James Madison to James Madison, Jr., c. 1 October 1787, *Madison Papers*, 10:183–84.

29. Joseph Clay to ?, 30 September 1788, Clay Letterbook, GaHS.

30. Samuel W. Johnson to William S. Johnson, 24 October 1787, Bermuda, Johnson Ms, CHS.

31. Ibid., 21 February 1788.

32. Joseph Clay to James Thompson, 20 June 1788, Clay Letterbook, GaHS.

33. As early as 15 September 1787, a Philadelphia Federalist essayist sketched the prospect of a rise in land values "should the foederal government be adopted." By 1789, his mock letter from interior Cumberland County predicted, real estate in the neighbourhood of Carlisle which sold for £5/acre would have doubled in value to sell at £10/acre. [Philadelphia] *Pennsylvania Packet*, 15 September 1787.

34. Robert C. Johnson to Samuel William Johnson, 3 December 1787, John Lawrence Ms, CSL; "Order of Procession in honor of the establishment of the CONSTITUTION OF THE UNITED STATES," 4 July 1788, 1:185, Wallace Ms, HSP.

35. Wilson, 26 June 1787, Farrand, *Records*, 1:426.

36. Miers Fisher to Robert Barclay, 20 October 1787, Public Record Office Series, Foreign Office Series 4, 5:657, copy in LC.

37. See again, Hobson, "Negative on State Laws."

38. Madison, Speech, 26 June 1787, Farrand, *Records*, 1:423; Madison to William Short, 6 June 1787, *Madison Papers*, 10:31; Archibald Stuart to Madison, 9 November 1787, Madison Ms, LC.

39. On faculty psychology, again see Howe, *Political Culture of the Whigs*, chap. 2, and "Political Psychology of *The Federalist*," 485–509.

40. Jay to John Adams, 4 July 1787, Jay Ms, Columbia.

41. Bishop James Madison to James Madison, 1787, *Madison Papers*, 10:183–85.

42. Ebenezer Hazard to Matthew Carey, 14 April 1788, Hazard Ms, Lea & Febiger Collection, HSP.

43. Benjamin Rush to Jeremy Belknap, 28 February 1788, 6 May 1788, "Belknap Papers," *Collections of the Massachusetts Historical Society* (Boston, 1891), 6th ser., 4:397–98.

44. *Bickerstaff's Boston Alamanck, or The Federal Calendar, For the Year of our REDEMPTION, 1788, Being Bissextile, or Leap Year, and Twelfth of Independency*, Evans #20879, EAIC.

45. Edward Rutledge to ?, 5 May 1788, Morgan Library, New York City.

46. Gouverneur Morris to George Washington, 30 October 1787, Washington Ms, LC.

47. See Theodore Foster to Dwight Foster, 22 January 1790, Dwight Foster Ms, MHS; Theodore Foster to William Channing, 24 May 1790, Channing-Ellery Ms, vol. 4, RIHS.

CHAPTER 16. THE CONSTITUTION PREVAILS

1. Roll, "We, Some of the People," 21–40.

2. The demise of Antifederalism has recently been disputed. See Richard E. Ellis, "The Persistence of Antifederalism after 1789," in *Beyond Confederation: Origins of the Constitution and American National Identity*, ed. Richard Beeman, Stephen Botein, and Edward Carter II (Chapel Hill: University of North Carolina Press, 1987), 295–314. Most if not all the states rights' Antifederalists accepted the Constitution once they saw there was no turning back without unacceptable risk and difficulty.

3. Steven R. Boyd, *The Politics of Opposition: Antifederalists and the Acceptance of the Constitution* (Millwood, N. J.: KTO, 1979), 139–64.

4. Levy, *Making of the Constitution*, 284–89.

5. Lance Banning, "Republican Ideology and the Triumph of the Constitution," in Banning, *After the Constitution: Party Conflict in the New Republic* (Belmont, Calif.: Wadsworth, 1989), 233–53.

6. Doerflinger, *Vigorous Spirit of Enterprise*, 263–80; Young, *Democratic Republicans of New York*, 69–105.

7. John J. McCusker and Russell R. Menard, *The Economy of British America, 1607–1789* (Chapel Hill: University of North Carolina Press, 1985), 63,

369–70; Stuart Bruchey, *The Roots of American Economic Growth 1607–1861: An Essay in Social Causation* (New York: Harper, 1968), 96–112; Anne Bezancon, *Prices and Inflation during the American Revolution: Pennsylvania, 1770–1790* (Philadelphia: University of Pennsylvania Press, 1951), 108 and passim.

8. Levi Hollingsworth to Mark Pragers, 21 April 1788, quoted in Bezancon, *Prices and Inflation*, 104. In July 1788 London merchants Bourdieu, Chollet, and Bourdieu made the connection between the establishment of the Constitution, the revival of credit, and the restoration of commerce. "When [the Constitution] is once properly established, America will rise again, & regain her Credit, & the Trade depending on it." Bourdieu, Chollet, and Bourdieu to Nicholas Low, London, 6 August 1788, Nicholas Low Ms., LC.

9. Benjamin Fuller to Doyle and Row, Dublin merchants, 15 November, 1 December 1787, quoted in Bezancon, *Prices and Inflation*, 307.

10. Hill & Ogden to Daniel Crommelin & Sons, 10 April 1787, to Peter R. Livingston, 3 November 1788, New York, Lewis Ogden Letterbook, NYPL.

11. James Cox to John Cox, Grenada, 8 January 1790, quoted in Bezancon, *Prices and Inflation*, 108. On 1 April 1790 the ship *Amsterdam Packer* brought dollars to Philadelphia: "Instead of European vessels entering our ports loaded, and returning with the specie of our country, we now find them coming to us for lading, and bringing specie to pay for it." *Gazette of the United States*, 10 April 1790, quoted in Broadus Mitchell, *Alexander Hamilton: The National Adventure, 1788–1804* (New York: Macmillan, 1962), 2:562, n. 56.

12. Clement Biddle to Richard Smith, 23 May 1790, quoted in Bezancon, *Prices and Inflation*, 123.

13. James C. Riley, "Foreign Credit and Fiscal Stability: Dutch Investment in the United States, 1781–1794," *Journal of American History* 65 (December 1978): 675, 677.

14. Riley, "Foreign Credit and Fiscal Stability," 668, 677. By 1796, Riley states, the new U.S. government had "acquired and retained an image of credit worthiness that was stronger than that held by France in the 1780s and, by the early 1790s, equivalent to that held by European states accepted by Dutch investors as the most secure risks."

15. Abraham Baldwin to Joel Barlow, 16 January 1790, Abraham Baldwin Misc. Ms, Yale. Also Benjamin Lincoln to ?, 5 January 1791, quoted in Mitchell, *Hamilton*, 562, n. 60; Richard Bland Lee, 1794 speech, quoted in Michael Kammen, *A Machine that Would Go of Itself: The Constitution in American Culture* (New York: Random House, 1987), 15.

16. Reports of Massachusetts State Treasurer Alexander Hodgdon, 1 October 1787, March 1788, 1 January 1789, and 1 May 1790, Massachusetts House documents 2606, 2292, 3218, 3374, MA; also D.24 Massachusetts, reel 3, ESRC. On 25 January 1790 Treasurer Alexander Hodgdon reported such "a very great alteration in No 6 Tax, by payments received from Collectors and Sheriffs" from 1 to 15 January 1790 that he was "happy to say the payments on that Tax from that time to the present have materially altered this statement of that Tax." Treasurer's Report, 25 January 1790, M.A. Document 3363; also D.24, reel 3, ESRC. Also, Hall, *Politics Without Parties*, 321.

17. Report of the New York State treasurer on arrears of taxes, extract, 15

March 1790, [New York] *Daily Advertiser*, 16 March 1790. Also cited in Mitchell, *Hamilton*, 562, n. 56. The report shows the almost complete payment of the £100,000 tax levied 6 May 1784 and a low arrearage total of £12,619 on three taxes enacted since 1 January 1785.

18. Hall, *Politics Without Parties*, 321–50, and Risjord, *Chesapeake Politics*, 342–82.

19. Kenneth R. Bowling, *Birth of a Nation: The First Federal Congress* (Madison, Wis.: Madison House, 1989); Margaret C. S. Christman, *The First Federal Congress: 1789–1791* (Washington, D.C.: Smithsonian Institution Press, 1989), 126.

20. New Dutch loans played a crucial role in the Hamilton program. By borrowing in Amsterdam and Antwerp, Hamilton was able to pay off debts owed the French and Spanish governments, reduce interest payments, and begin redemption of the domestic debt. See Riley, "Foreign Credit and Fiscal Stability."

21. Mitchell, *Hamilton*, 14–153.

22. Ferguson, *Power of the Purse*, 289–343.

23. Alexander Hamilton, Report Relative to a Provision for the Support of Public Credit, 9 January 1790, *Hamilton Papers*, 6:65–168.

24. Gouverneur Morris, 16 August 1787, Madison's Notes, Farrand, *Records*, 2:307.

25. Hamilton to Nathaniel Chipman, 22 July 1788, to James Madison, 12 October 1789, *Hamilton Papers*, 5:186, 439. Italics in original.

26. James Madison to Hamilton, 19 November 1789, *Madison Papers*, 12:449–51.

27. Stephen Higginson to Hamilton, 11 November 1789, *Hamilton Papers*, 5:507–11.

28. On this point, Hamilton's well known letter to Edward Carrington seems relevant: "On the whole, the only enemy which Republicanism has to fear in this Country is the Spirit of faction and anarchy." Hamilton to Carrington, 26 May 1792, ibid., 11:426–45.

29. Hamilton, Objections and Answers respecting the Administration of the Government, enclosed in Hamilton to Washington, 18 August 1792, ibid., 12:236–37.

30. Thomas Slaughter, *The Whiskey Rebellion: Frontier Epilogue to the American Revolution* (New York: Oxford University Press, 1986), 168.

31. Ibid., 190–204; Richard Buel, Review of Thomas Slaughter's *Whiskey Rebellion*, *American Historical Review* 92 (December 1987): 1272.

32. Richard H. Kohn, "The Washington Administration's Decision to Crush the Whiskey Rebellion," *Journal of American History* 59 (1972): 567–84.

33. Slaughter, *Whiskey Rebellion*, 226.

34. Bruchey, *Roots of American Economic Growth*, 108–13; Doerflinger, *Vigorous Spirit of Enterprise*, 280.

35. Slaughter, *Whiskey Rebellion*, 223–24.

36. John F. Hoadley, "The Emergence of Political Parties in Congress, 1789–1803," *American Political Science Review* 74 (September 1980): 776.

37. Joseph Charles, *The Origins of the American Party System: Three Essays* (New York: Harper, 1961); Noble Cunningham, *The Jeffersonian Republicans:*

The Formation of Party Organization, 1789–1801 (Chapel Hill: University of North Carolina Press, 1957); Richard Hofstadter, *The Idea of a Party System: The Rise of Legitimate Opposition in the United States, 1780–1840* (Berkeley: University of California Press, 1970); Richard Buel, Jr., *Securing the Revolution: Ideology in American Politics, 1789–1815* (Ithaca, N.Y.: Cornell University Press, 1972); Lance Banning, *The Jeffersonian Persuasion: Evolution of a Party Ideology* (Ithaca, N.Y.: Cornell University Press, 1978); M. L. Heale, *The Making of American Politics* (London: Longmans, 1977); and Hoadley, "Emergence of Political Parties in Congress." A helpful compendium of these and other writings on early parties is Banning, *After the Constitution: Party Conflict in the New Republic*.

38. Heale, *Making of American Politics*, 66–68.

39. See especially Richard Hofstadter, *Idea of a Party System*, esp. vii–xiii, 1–39, 74–121.

INDEX

Accomack County (Va.), 130
Adams, John, 144, 240
Adams, John Quincy, 157
Adams, Samuel, 105, 216
Alden, Roger, 27
Algiers, 18
American Academy of Arts and Sciences, 43
American Museum, 176
American Philosophical Society, 42, 255–56
anarchy, 182; and antifederalists, 154; and "Critical Period" interpretation, 152–54; and Federalists, 152–54, 164–67
Annapolis Convention, 28–31, 175, 179
Antifederalists: and anarchy, 154; and Constitution, 179, 204–5, 218, 234; demise of, 234–41, 323n.2; interpretations of, 4, 20–21, 132–33, 135, 143–67, 185, 200–203; popular support for, 208–11, 215–16, 318nn.24, 31, 33; program of, 4, 31, 143, 144, 176, 203–4, 206–8, 218
Armentrout, Mary T., 128
Armstrong, John, 59
Army, U.S., 18–19, 23, 26, 27–28
Arnold, Caleb, 87, 88, 90
Arnold, James, 46
Arnold, Dr. Jonathan, 83
Arnold, Welcome, 42, 43, 86, 94
Articles of Confederation, 11, 179. *See also* Antifederalists; Congress, Confederation; Constitutional Convention; "Critical Period" interpretation; impost, federal; reconstitution
artisans: and Constitution, 214, 215, 216, 217, 320n.51; and Reliefer program, 55, 66, 215, 216, 320nn.53, 55
Austin, Benjamin, Jr., 119–20

Bache, Richard, 217
Baker, John, 256
Baldwin, Abraham, 236
Baldwin, Laommi, 100, 106
Baltimore, Md., 216–17, 235

Bancker, Abraham, 225
Bank of North America, 45, 53, 64, 66, 150, 320n.54
Bank of the United States, 150, 237
Banning, Lance, 17
Barbary states, 18
Barclay, Thomas, 18
Barnes, Abel, 88
Baumann, Ronald, 215
Beard, Charles A., 201, 222, 270n.12
Becker, Robert A., 4, 84
Bee, Thomas, 42, 43, 45, 78–79, 256
Belknap, Rev. Jeremy, 43, 256
Benson, George, 92
Berkshire County (Mass.), 103–4, 111–12, 114–16, 119, 296n.35
Bernardston, Mass., 111, 112
Bickerstaff's Boston Alamanack, 232
Biddle, Clement, 236
Bill of Rights, 207, 235
Bingham, William, 43, 178, 255, 256
Blake, Edward, 73
Bland, Theodorick, 129
Bloodworth, Timothy, 46, 138, 203
Bocquet, Peter, 73
Boston, Mass., 108, 114, 116; artisans of, 215, 216–17, 235; crime in, 164
Bowdoin, Gov. James, 42–43, 109, 256; and relief measures, 117–19, 120; and Shays's Rebellion, 115–16; and tax collection, 108, 109, 295n.33; threatened, 114
Bowen, Jabez, 42–43, 85, 86, 91, 92
Bowen, Obadiah, 142, 261
Boylston, Mass., 116
Brackenridge, Hugh Henry, 159
Bradford, William, 42, 43
Bradford, William, Jr., 66, 256
Brearley, David, 194
Breck, Samuel, 43, 182, 190
Brown, Fleet, 87
Brown, John, 42, 43, 91–92
Brown, Joseph, 43
Brown, Moses, 43, 93
Brown, Nicholas, 42, 43, 86, 92